Old North State COOKIN'

Recipes Include Nutritional Analysis and Dietary Exchanges.

TELEPHONE PIONEERS OF AMERICA

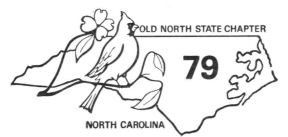

OLD NORTH STATE CHAPTER

79

NORTH CAROLINA

STATEMENT OF PURPOSE

* To promote and participate in activities that respond to community needs and problems;

* To provide a means of friendly association for eligible telecommunications employees and those retired;

* To foster among them a continuing fellowship and a spirit of mutual helpfulness;

* To contribute to the progress of the Association and promote the happiness, well-being and usefulness of the membership;

* To exemplify and perpetuate those principles which have come to be regarded as the ideals and traditions of the industry.

This cookbook is a collection of our favorite recipes which are not necessarily original recipes.

Published by Favorite Recipes® Press
P.O. Box 305142
Nashville, Tennessee 37230

ISBN: 0-87197-305-7
Library of Congress Number: 91-16599

Manufactured in the United States of America
First Printing: 1991 20,000 copies

TABLE OF CONTENTS

EXPRESSION OF APPRECIATION

I would like to take this space to thank and gratefully acknowledge all the people who contributed in so many ways to make this cookbook a success.

I especially want to thank the Life Members (retired employees). They "answered the call of need," when I asked for help.

I would like to thank Russ Tagert, Chapter Administrator, for his support and assistance.

A special thanks to Thelma Wilson, Chapter Administrator Assistant, and to Peggy Kiger for being my right arms.

And to Mabe Brown for the beautiful cover design.

And to the committee for all their help.

Jewel Smith
Cookbook Chairperson

COMMITTEE MEMBERS

Jewel Smith
Cookbook Chairperson

Old North State Chapter 79 Committee Members

Harriet Albright—Burlington Council
Aleene Cockerham—Winston Life Member Club
Etta Flup—Twin City Life Member Club
Caron Hairston—Greensboro Council
John Kelly—Burlington Council
Peggy Kiger—Twin City Council
Betty McPherson—Burlington Life Member Club
Carolyn Pulley—Burlington Council
Bill Radisch—Greensboro Life Member Club
B. J. Showerman—Greensboro Council
Russ Tagert—Old North State Chapter 79
Thelma Wilson—Old North State Chapter 79

A History of the Old North State Chapter 79

On November 2, 1911, 439 Long-service employees of the telephone industry met in Boston. They met to recognize the contributions of the people who had pioneered the telephone from its invention to an industry which by then had linked two-thirds of the United States with long distance spoken communication. This first meeting was such a success that, before leaving Boston, those assembled decided to charter themselves into an association called the Telephone Pioneers of America.

The purpose, stated in the original charter, was to promote fellowship and loyalty between the long-service employees of the telephone industry by an annual assembly of those eligible. In 1920, the number of people who could qualify as long-service employees had become several thousand in the U.S. and Canada. By this time a number of those who had met in 1911 had already retired. At the annual assembly in 1920, the stated purpose of the Telephone Pioneers of America was enlarged to include fellowship for telephone people, both active and retired.

At this same assembly, the organization elected to become localized with chapters in every state. The Telephone Pioneers were changed to year-round operation with friendly association between active and retired employees as its objective. In 1958, the Telephone Pioneers of America added to the stated purposes of the organization what had been a fact for years, the dedication of its members to worthwhile community service projects. By this time, the Association had created councils subordinate to the chapters and clubs within the councils.

A number of long-service employees moved to North Carolina in the late 1940's to start the Western Electric plants in Winston-Salem and Burlington. These people were invited to join Chapter 35, which is the Pioneer chapter of telephone people in North Carolina. In 1950, enough Western Electric and Bell System employees had achieved sufficient service to comprise a separate council of Chapter 35. Within 10 years, the council had grown to almost 2,000 members and petitioned the Association to become a chapter of its own.

A contest held by the N.C. Works Council resulted in the selection of the name Old North State, and the Association designated it as the 79th Chapter on July 1, 1970. It is now one of the largest in the Association, and is a consistent leader in the number of those eligible who choose to become members. We are over 9,000 members strong this year.

The Association of Telephone Pioneers with over 800,000 members, is the largest volunteer organization attached to a single industry in the world; almost 400,000 of those retired have lifetime membership. One would suppose that the work of the civic organization attached to an industry would ebb and flow with business conditions. Such has not been the case with Old North State Chapter 79. In good times and bad, the activities of its members especially in the area of community service, has always remained at a high level. This may have been the result of its leadership, but it is more likely that its members extend the industry dedication into their lives.

During the relatively brief existence of Old North State, numerous honors have come her way—local, state, regional, and national. Among them have been several in the national "People Who Care" awards:

1982—1st Place for "The American Children's Home"
1984—1st Place for Environment "E" Award
1984—2nd Place for "Community Health Fair"
1986—1st Place in Miss Liberty, Fund Raising
1987—2nd Place for "Pioneer 75 Super Saturday"
1989—Presidential Award & Citation for "A Place To Be Free"
1990—1st Place for "A Place To Be Free"
1990—Chapter of the Year

Old North State Chapter 79 members give more than 500,000 volunteer hours each year and their Community Service expenditures annually exceed $100,000.

A PLACE TO BE FREE

FREEDOM is a most precious and priceless commodity . . .
Freedom is the miracle found at Camp Carefree . . .

Carefree is a beautiful place for special children stricken with chronic conditions such as Leukemia, Hodgkins, Spina Bifida, Cystic Fibrosis, and Diabetes. Here the emphasis is on wellness rather than illness. Carefree is NOT just a day camp . . . it's the ONLY resident camp of its kind in North Carolina. Children come on referral from a broad spectrum of the Pediatric Community including the clinics at Duke and the University of North Carolina.

Come with us . . . imagine . . . you're a child . . . yearning for freedom but trapped in a body imprisioned by cancer.

Beginning in early summer such youngsters from 6 to 16 spend a glorious week in a lifestyle they have never dreamed . . . much less experienced . . . and FREE. Every day each child . . . whether walking or in a wheelchair . . . partipates in eight activities . . . swimming, canoeing, horseback riding, etc.

How did Carefree happen? Four years ago these children were almost forgotten. A cry for help went out and Pioneers met with others also concerned. Our efforts mushroomed into a fun and therapeutic facility.

Then, during the next three years 1,500 Pioneers cared enough to spend over 15,000 hours raising money and in building three duplex dormitories, a medical infirmary, a 40 x 60 foot recreation building...these with a value well over $400,000.

Add to this 40 truckloads of environmental cleanup; nature trail with 20 foot bridge; over 500 feet of wheelchair ramps and boardwalks; landscaping, and hundreds of shrubs and trees along with other incidentals.

Are we through? NOPE . . .

Lots of things will be done this year too . . . We'll paint the 6,000 foot main lodge and build more ramps; there'll be food, cooking, nursing, mowing 14 acres, laughing, hugging, playing, baiting kids' hooks, and more.

During the 1990 summer camping season, over 1,000 children will descend into the loving arms of volunteer counselors, and relationships will blossom and grow . . . BUT . . . there is a tough and difficult part . . . the tug-at-your-heart scenario of leaving and tears each Saturday.

Alas, a week of unforgettable experiences must end. A part of that ending is a delightful campfire ceremony . . . and songfest . . . and roasting of marshmallows.

The fire begins with the sharing of one small flame...when all candles are lit each little one adds his light to the fire. One night at this point in the ceremony, one little fellow with no hair and in a wheelchair *said it all*! He said . . . "Since we're having such a good time . . . why are we all crying?"

Camp Carefree will enable thousands of children from future generations to find some of that very elusive freedom . . . FREEDOM? YOU BET IT IS!

We're proud of our Carefree activities. President Bush is also proud of us! On November 17, 1989, in White House ceremonies, we received a prestigious Presidential Award for A Place To Be Free. Under the Presidents' Citation Program For Private Sector Initiatives this was one of the only 29 awards granted out of 517 projects evaluated nationwide. We are indeed proud!

In conclusion, we wish each of you could have the enriching experience of spending just one day with us at *A PLACE TO BE FREE*.

NUTRITIONAL GUIDELINES

The editors have attempted to present these family recipes in a form that allows approximate nutritional values to be computed. Persons with dietary or health problems or whose diets require close monitoring should not rely solely on the nutritional information provided. They should consult their physicians or a registered dietitian for specific information.

Abbreviations for Nutritional Analysis

Cal — Calories	Dietary Fiber — Fiber	Sod — Sodium
Prot — Protein	T Fat — Total Fat	gr — gram
Carbo — Carbohydrates	Chol — Cholesterol	mg — milligrams

Nutritional information for these recipes is computed from information derived from many sources, including materials supplied by the United States Department of Agriculture, computer databanks and journals in which the information is assumed to be in the public domain. However, many specialty items, new products and processed foods may not be available from these sources or may vary from the average values used in these analyses. More information on new and/or specific products may be obtained by reading the nutrient labels. Unless otherwise specified, the nutritional analysis of these recipes is based on all measurements being level.

- **Artificial sweeteners** vary in use and strength so should be used "to taste," using the recipe ingredients as a guideline.
- **Artificial sweeteners** using aspertame (NutraSweet and Equal) should not be used as a sweetener in recipes involving prolonged heating which reduces the sweet taste. For further information on the use of these sweeteners, refer to package information.
- **Alcoholic ingredients** have been analyzed for the basic ingredients, although cooking causes the evaporation of alcohol thus decreasing caloric content.
- **Buttermilk, sour cream** and **yogurt** are the types available commercially.
- **Cake mixes** which are prepared using package directions include 3 eggs and ½ cup oil.
- **Chicken**, cooked for boning and chopping, has been roasted; this method yields the lowest caloric values.
- **Cottage cheese** is cream-style with 4.2% creaming mixture. Dry-curd cottage cheese has no creaming mixture.
- **Eggs** are all large.
- **Flour** is unsifted all-purpose flour.
- **Garnishes**, serving suggestions and other optional additions and variations are not included in the analysis.
- **Margarine** and **butter** are regular, not whipped or presoftened.
- **Milk** is whole milk, 3.5% butterfat. Lowfat milk is 1% butterfat. Evaporated milk is whole milk with 60% of the water removed.
- **Oil** is any type of vegetable cooking oil. Shortening is hydrogenated vegetable shortening.
- **Salt** and other ingredients to taste as noted in the ingredients have not been included in the nutritional analysis.
- If a choice of ingredients has been given, the nutritional analysis reflects the first option.

APPETIZERS
and BEVERAGES

HOT CHEESE DIP

Yield:
36 servings
Utensil:
8x12 baking dish
Approx Per
Serving:
Cal 144
Prot 3 g
Carbo 1 g
Fiber <1 g
T Fat 14 g
Chol 19 mg
Sod 190 mg

Dietary
Exchanges:
Milk 0
Vegetable 0
Fruit 0
Bread/Starch 0
Meat 1/2; Fat 3

8 ounces shredded mozzarella cheese
8 ounces shredded sharp Cheddar cheese
2 cups mayonnaise
1 onion, chopped
1 4-ounce can chopped green chilies
1 1/2 ounces sliced pepperoni
1/2 cup sliced black olives

Combine mozzarella cheese, Cheddar cheese, mayonnaise, onion and chilies in bowl. Spoon into shallow 8x12-inch baking dish. Top with pepperoni and olives. Bake at 325 degrees for 25 minutes. Serve with tortilla chips or fresh vegetables.

Clarissa Brame, Graham

CLAM DIP

Yield:
30 servings
Utensil:
bowl
Approx Per
Serving:
Cal 30
Prot 1 g
Carbo <1 g
Fiber <1 g
T Fat 3 g
Chol 12 mg
Sod 26 mg

Dietary
Exchanges:
Milk 0
Vegetable 0
Fruit 0
Bread/Starch 0
Meat 0; Fat 1/2

8 ounces cream cheese, softened
1 teaspoon lemon juice
2 tablespoons minced onion
1/2 teaspoon Worcestershire sauce
1 6-ounce can minced clams

Combine cream cheese, lemon juice, onion and Worcestershire sauce in bowl; mix well. Drain clams, reserving juice. Rinse clams under cold water. Add to cream cheese mixture. Strain reserved clam juice. Stir into cream cheese mixture.

Maire S. Snodderly, Greensboro

CRAB DIP

Yield:
24 servings
Utensil:
bowl
Approx Per
Serving:
Cal 41
Prot 2 g
Carbo <1 g
Fiber <1 g
T Fat 3 g
Chol 17 mg
Sod 77 mg

Dietary
Exchanges:
Milk 0
Vegetable 0
Fruit 0
Bread/Starch 0
Meat 0; Fat 1

1 6-ounce can crab
   meat
8 ounces cream cheese,
   softened
2 teaspoons minced
   onion
1 tablespoon milk
1 teaspoon creamed
   horseradish
1/4 teaspoon salt
1 teaspoon
   Worcestershire sauce
1 teaspoon lemon juice

Combine crab meat, cream cheese, onion, milk, horseradish, salt, Worcestershire sauce and lemon juice in bowl. Blend until smooth. Garnish with sliced almonds.

Sharon M. Fanelli, Gibsonville

DILLWEED DIP

Yield:
64 servings
Utensil:
bowl
Approx Per
Serving:
Cal 65
Prot <1 g
Carbo 1 g
Fiber <1 g
T Fat 7 g
Chol 7 mg
Sod 227 mg

Dietary
Exchanges:
Milk 0
Vegetable 0
Fruit 0
Bread/Starch 0
Meat 0; Fat 1 1/2

2 cups mayonnaise
2 cups sour cream
2 tablespoons dillweed
2 tablespoons minced
   onion
2 tablespoons parsley
   flakes
2 tablespoons (or less)
   seasoned salt

Combine mayonnaise, sour cream, dillweed, onion, parsley flakes and seasoned salt in medium bowl; mix well. Refrigerate to enhance flavor. Spoon into serving bowl.

Betty Sutton, Burlington

Ham Dip

Yield:
48 servings
Utensil:
bowl
**Approx Per
Serving:**
Cal 37
Prot 1 g
Carbo <1 g
Fiber 0 g
T Fat 4 g
Chol 7 mg
Sod 48 mg

**Dietary
Exchanges:**
Milk 0
Vegetable 0
Fruit 0
Bread/Starch 0
Meat 0; Fat 1

8 ounces cream cheese, softened
1 2¼-ounce can deviled ham
2 tablespoons chopped pimento
½ cup mayonnaise
1 teaspoon onion flakes
1 tablespoon Worcestershire sauce

Combine cream cheese, deviled ham, pimento, mayonnaise, onion flakes and Worcestershire sauce in mixer bowl; mix well. Refrigerate, covered, until ready to serve. Spoon into serving bowl.

Joyce Smith, Winston-Salem

Hot Virginia Dip

Yield:
68 servings
Utensil:
baking dish
**Approx Per
Serving:**
Cal 46
Prot 1 g
Carbo 1 g
Fiber <1 g
T Fat 4 g
Chol 28 mg
Sod 110 mg

**Dietary
Exchanges:**
Milk 0
Vegetable 0
Fruit 0
Bread/Starch 0
Meat 0; Fat 1

1 cup chopped pecans
2 teaspoons margarine
16 ounces cream cheese, softened
5 ounces dried beef, chopped
¼ cup milk
½ teaspoon garlic salt
1 cup sour cream
4 teaspoons minced onion

Place pecans and margarine in small glass dish. Microwave on Medium for 2 minutes. Combine cream cheese, dried beef, milk, garlic salt, sour cream and onion in bowl; mix well. Spoon into 1½-quart baking dish. Top with pecans. Bake at 350 degrees for 30 minutes or until bubbly.

Dot Fesperman, Winston-Salem

LAYERED BEAN DIP

Yield:
140 servings
Utensil:
bowl
Approx Per Serving:
Cal 26
Prot 1 g
Carbo 2 g
Fiber <1 g
T Fat 2 g
Chol 2 mg
Sod 93 mg

Dietary Exchanges:
Milk 0
Vegetable 0
Fruit 0
Bread/Starch 0
Meat 0; Fat 1/2

2 16-ounce cans refried beans
1 4-ounce can chopped green chilies, drained
1 envelope taco seasoning mix
2 ripe avocados, chopped
2 tablespoons lemon juice
1 16-ounce jar taco sauce
1½ cups sour cream
1½ cups shredded Cheddar cheese
¼ cup black olives, sliced

Combine refried beans, chilies and taco seasoning mix in bowl; mix well. Combine avocados, lemon juice and ½ cup taco sauce in food processor container. Process with steel blade until smooth. Layer bean mixture and avocado mixture on 12-inch platter. Cover with sour cream. Top with shredded cheese, remaining taco sauce and sliced olives. May add lettuce and chopped tomatoes. Serve with tortilla chips.

Norma Hall, Mebane

MEXICAN DIP

Yield:
56 servings
Utensil:
bowl
Approx Per Serving:
Cal 19
Prot <1 g
Carbo 1 g
Fiber <1 g
T Fat 2 g
Chol 0 mg
Sod 30 mg

Dietary Exchanges:
Milk 0
Vegetable 0
Fruit 0
Bread/Starch 0
Meat 0; Fat 1/2

3 tomatoes, chopped
2 2-ounce cans sliced black olives
2 4-ounce cans chopped green chilies
6 tablespoons oil
3 tablespoons vinegar
1 tablespoon garlic powder
4 green onions, chopped

Combine tomatoes, black olives, chilies, oil, vinegar, garlic powder and green onions in bowl; mix well. Marinate, covered, in refrigerator for several hours. Serve with tortilla chips or assorted fresh vegetables.

Ruby Hicks

SHRIMP DIP

1 envelope unflavored
  gelatin
1/4 cup cold water
1 10-ounce can
  tomato soup
8 ounces cream cheese,
  softened
1 cup mayonnaise

1/2 cup finely chopped
  onion
1 cup finely chopped
  celery
1 pound cooked
  peeled shrimp,
  coarsely chopped

Soften gelatin in cold water. Combine tomato soup
and cream cheese in saucepan. Cook over medium
heat, stirring constantly until smooth. Stir in
gelatin. Cool to room temperature. Add mayonnaise, onion, celery and chopped shrimp; mix well.
Pour into greased 9-inch ring mold. Refrigerate for
8 to 24 hours. Unmold onto serving tray. Garnish
with parsley. Serve with round butter crackers.

Mavis Peterson, Elon College

SHRIMP AND CRAB MEAT DIP

8 ounces cream cheese,
  softened
1/2 cup milk
3/4 cup shrimp cocktail
  sauce
1 6-ounce can
  shrimp, drained

1 6-ounce can crab
  meat, drained
1 tablespoon
  Parmesan cheese
1/8 teaspoon onion salt
1/8 teaspoon garlic salt

Whip cream cheese and milk together in bowl until
smooth. Spread on flat serving plate. Chill for 1
hour. Cover with cocktail sauce. Top with shrimp
and crab meat. Sprinkle on Parmesan cheese, onion
salt and garlic salt. Serve chilled with crackers.

Kelli Topping Bailey

CREAMY SPINACH DIP

Yield:
96 servings
Utensil:
serving bowl
Approx Per
Serving:
Cal 25
Prot <1 g
Carbo 1 g
Fiber <1 g
T Fat 2 g
Chol 2 mg
Sod 35 mg

Dietary
Exchanges:
Milk 0
Vegetable 0
Fruit 0
Bread/Starch 0
Meat 0; Fat ¹/₂

1 cup sour cream
1 cup mayonnaise
¹/₂ teaspoon celery salt
¹/₂ teaspoon dillweed
¹/₄ teaspoon onion salt
3 cups frozen chopped
  spinach, thawed,
  drained

¹/₄ cup chopped green
  onions
1 8-ounce can water
  chestnuts, drained,
  chopped
3 tablespoons chopped
  red bell pepper

Combine sour cream, mayonnaise, celery salt, dillweed and onion salt in bowl; mix well. Stir in spinach, green onions, water chestnuts and red pepper. Refrigerate, covered, to blend flavors. Serve with vegetables, crackers or bread.

Dot Fesperman, Winston-Salem

HOT SPINACH DIP

Yield:
28 servings
Utensil:
saucepan
Approx Per
Serving:
Cal 52
Prot 2 g
Carbo 2 g
Fiber 1 g
T Fat 4 g
Chol 12 mg
Sod 238 mg

Dietary
Exchanges:
Milk 0
Vegetable 0
Fruit 0
Bread/Starch 0
Meat 0; Fat 1

2 10-ounce packages
  frozen chopped
  spinach
¹/₄ cup melted butter
2 tablespoons chopped
  onion
3 tablespoons flour
¹/₂ cup evaporated milk
¹/₂ teaspoon pepper

³/₄ teaspoon celery salt
³/₄ teaspoon garlic salt
1 tablespoon
  Worcestershire sauce
¹/₈ teaspoon red pepper
1 6-ounce package
  jalapeño cheese,
  softened

Cook spinach using package directions. Drain well, reserving ¹/₂ cup liquid. Combine butter, onion and flour in saucepan. Cook over medium heat for 1 minute, stirring constantly. Stir in reserved spinach liquid and evaporated milk gradually. Cook until slightly thickened, stirring constantly. Add pepper, celery salt, garlic salt, Worcestershire sauce, red pepper and cheese; mix well. Serve hot with crackers.

O. Sue Barnhardt, Mooresville

BEEFY CHEESE BALL

Yield:
50 servings
Utensil:
bowl
Approx Per
Serving:
Cal 56
Prot 3 g
Carbo 1 g
Fiber <1 g
T Fat 5 g
Chol 53 mg
Sod 235 mg

Dietary
Exchanges:
Milk 0
Vegetable 0
Fruit 0
Bread/Starch 0
Meat 0; Fat 1

1 envelope ranch salad dressing mix
16 ounces cream cheese, softened
3/4 cup shredded sharp Cheddar cheese
1 small onion, chopped
1 large jar dried beef, chopped
1/2 green bell pepper, chopped
1 teaspoon Worcestershire sauce
1/2 cup chopped pecans

Combine dressing mix, cream cheese, Cheddar cheese, onion, dried beef, green pepper and Worcestershire sauce in bowl; mix well. Shape into ball; roll in pecans. Chill, tightly wrapped, for 24 hours for enhanced flavor.

Phil and Glendore Epperson, Winston-Salem

PINEAPPLE-PECAN CHEESE BALL

Yield:
60 servings
Utensil:
bowl
Approx Per
Serving:
Cal 53
Prot 1 g
Carbo 1 g
Fiber <1 g
T Fat 5 g
Chol 8 mg
Sod 121 mg

Dietary
Exchanges:
Milk 0
Vegetable 0
Fruit 0
Bread/Starch 0
Meat 0; Fat 1½

16 ounces cream cheese, softened
1/4 cup minced green bell pepper
2 tablespoons grated onion
1 8-ounce can crushed pineapple, drained
1 tablespoon seasoned salt
2 cups chopped pecans

Combine cream cheese, green pepper, onion, pineapple, seasoned salt and 1 cup chopped pecans in bowl; mix well. Shape into ball; roll in remaining 1 cup pecans. Chill, tightly wrapped, in refrigerator.

Dot Fesperman, Winston-Salem

Three-Cheese Ball

Yield:
46 servings
Utensil:
bowl
Approx Per
Serving:
Cal 56
Prot 2 g
Carbo 1 g
Fiber <1 g
T Fat 5 g
Chol 13 mg
Sod 87 mg

Dietary
Exchanges:
Milk 0
Vegetable 0
Fruit 0
Bread/Starch 0
Meat ½; Fat 1

8 ounces shredded sharp Cheddar cheese
8 ounces cream cheese, softened
4 ounces bleu cheese
⅓ cup minced garlic
2 tablespoons milk
2 tablespoons Worcestershire sauce
½ cup chopped pecans

Place Cheddar cheese, cream cheese and bleu cheese in bowl. Let stand until room temperature. Add garlic, milk and Worcestershire sauce; mix well. Shape into ball. Chill, tightly wrapped, for 2 hours. Roll in pecans. Let stand at room temperature for 15 minutes before serving.

Angela White, Greensboro

Tuna Ball

Yield:
28 servings
Utensil:
bowl
Approx Per
Serving:
Cal 37
Prot 2 g
Carbo <1 g
Fiber <1 g
T Fat 3 g
Chol 11 mg
Sod 48 mg

Dietary
Exchanges:
Milk 0
Vegetable 0
Fruit 0
Bread/Starch 0
Meat 0; Fat ½

8 ounces cream cheese, softened
1 6-ounce can tuna, drained
1 tablespoon prepared horseradish
1 tablespoon lemon juice
1 tablespoon parsley

Combine cream cheese, tuna, horseradish and lemon juice in bowl; mix well. Shape into ball; sprinkle with parsley. Chill until serving time.

Carol Sawyer, Whitsett

Cashew Pimento "Cheese" Spread

Yield:
24 servings
Utensil:
blender
Approx Per
Serving:
Cal 35
Prot 1 g
Carbo 2 g
Fiber <1 g
T Fat 3 g
Chol 0 mg
Sod 42 mg

Dietary
Exchanges:
Milk 0
Vegetable 0
Fruit 0
Bread/Starch 0
Meat ½; Fat ½

1 cup raw cashews
½ teaspoon salt
½ teaspoon onion
  powder
⅛ teaspoon garlic
  powder
1 4-ounce jar pimentos
Juice of 1 lemon

Combine cashews, salt, onion powder, garlic powder, pimentos and lemon juice in blender container. Process at high speed until blended to desired consistency. Purchase cashews at health food store.

Kathleen Yax, Mebane

Chili-Bacon Cheese Spread

Yield:
30 servings
Utensil:
bowl
Approx Per
Serving:
Cal 59
Prot 2 g
Carbo 8 g
Fiber 1 g
T Fat 2 g
Chol 4 mg
Sod 149 mg

Dietary
Exchanges:
Milk 0
Vegetable 0
Fruit 0
Bread/Starch ½
Meat 0; Fat ½

1 cup shredded sharp
  Cheddar cheese
2 tablespoons chili
  sauce
2 slices crisp-fried
  bacon, crumbled
1 tablespoon minced
  onion
1 tablespoon minced
  green bell pepper
1 loaf party rye bread

Combine Cheddar cheese, chili sauce, crumbled bacon, onion and green pepper in bowl; mix well. Spread on slices of party rye bread. Arrange on broiler pan. Broil until cheese melts.

Mary Jane Daleiden, Greensboro

VICKI'S CRAB MEAT SPREAD

Yield:
24 servings
Utensil:
bowl
Approx Per
Serving:
Cal 58
Prot 2 g
Carbo <1 g
Fiber <1 g
T Fat 5 g
Chol 23 mg
Sod 105 mg

Dietary
Exchanges:
Milk 0
Vegetable 0
Fruit 0
Bread/Starch 0
Meat 1½; Fat 0

8 ounces cream cheese, softened
¼ cup melted butter
1 tablespoon lemon juice
1 6-ounce can crab meat, rinsed, drained, shredded
2 tablespoons milk
¼ teaspoon garlic salt
Whites of 3 green onions, minced
Tops of 3 green onions, sliced

Beat cream cheese in bowl. Add butter, lemon juice, crab meat, milk, garlic salt and onions, stirring well after each addition. Chill, covered, to enhance flavor. Let stand at room temperature for 1 hour before serving. Serve with potato chips or crackers.

Vicki Strickland, Greensboro

SHRIMP SPREAD

Yield:
16 servings
Utensil:
bowl
Approx Per
Serving:
Cal 79
Prot 3 g
Carbo 4 g
Fiber <1 g
T Fat 6 g
Chol 16 mg
Sod 162 mg

Dietary
Exchanges:
Milk 0
Vegetable 0
Fruit 0
Bread/Starch ½
Meat 1; Fat 1½

8 ounces shredded sharp Cheddar cheese
2 4-ounce cans shrimp
1 small onion, chopped
1 cup mayonnaise
1 teaspoon Worcestershire sauce
⅛ teaspoon salt
1 package English muffins

Combine cheese, shrimp, onion, mayonnaise, Worcestershire sauce and salt in bowl; mix well. Spread on English muffin halves. Arrange on broiler pan. Broil until cheese melts and bread is hot. Cut into fourths.

Nancy Garner, Burlington

TUNA SPREAD

1 6-ounce can tuna, drained
6 medium carrots, shredded
1/2 cup chopped celery
1 small onion, chopped
2 cups potato sticks
1 cup mayonnaise
3 tablespoons Thousand Island salad dressing

Combine tuna, carrots, celery, onion and potato sticks in bowl; stir to mix. Add mayonnaise and salad dressing; mix well. Serve with crackers.

Earline Goin, Hamptonville

CHEESE PUFF CRACKERS

1 egg white
1/2 cup shredded Cheddar cheese
1/2 cup mayonnaise
24 round butter crackers

Beat egg white at high speed in mixer bowl until stiff peaks form. Fold in grated Cheddar cheese and mayonnaise gently. Spread mixture on crackers. Arrange on baking sheet. Broil until lightly toasted and puffed.

Jessie Grandinetti

SEASONED OYSTER CRACKERS

3/4 cup canola oil
1/4 cup sesame oil
2 12-ounce packages
   oyster crackers

1 1/2 teaspoons
   Cavender's Greek
   seasoning

Blend canola oil and sesame oil in 9x13-inch baking pan. Add oyster crackers. Stir gently to coat crackers on both sides. Sprinkle with seasoning. Bake in preheated 225-degree oven for 10 minutes; stir. Bake for 10 minutes longer or until golden brown. Remove to paper towels to drain. Let stand until cool. Serve with cocktails or soup. Store in airtight container in refrigerator or freeze.

Nutritional information does not include Cavender's Greek seasoning.

Nancy Garner, Burlington

FRIED CHEESE STICKS

1 8-ounce package
   sliced mozzarella
   cheese
1/4 cup flour

1 egg, beaten
1/4 cup bread crumbs
1/2 cup oil for frying

Cut cheese slices in half; roll into strips. Coat with flour. Dip in egg. Roll in bread crumbs. Fry in hot oil in skillet for 1 minute; turn. Fry for 1 minute longer or until golden brown. Drain well. Arrange on serving dish.

Juanita Stone, Graham

CHEESE STRAWS

Yield:
180 servings
Utensil:
baking sheet
Approx Per
Serving:
Cal 50
Prot 1 g
Carbo 2 g
Fiber <1 g
T Fat 4 g
Chol 8 mg
Sod 47 mg

Dietary
Exchanges:
Milk 0
Vegetable 0
Fruit 0
Bread/Starch 0
Meat 0; Fat 1

2 cups butter, softened
1 pound sharp
   Cheddar cheese,
   shredded
1 teaspoon red pepper
1 teaspoon salt
4 cups flour
3 cups pecan halves

Combine butter and Cheddar cheese in bowl. Add red pepper, salt and flour, stirring well. Spoon mixture into cookie press. Squeeze by teaspoonfuls onto non-stick baking sheet. Top with pecan halves. Bake at 375 degrees for 12 minutes.

Floyd E. Page, Burlington

CHICKEN APPETIZERS

Yield:
32 servings
Utensil:
baking sheet
Approx Per
Serving:
Cal 158
Prot 10 g
Carbo 3 g
Fiber 0 g
T Fat 11 g
Chol 39 mg
Sod 190 mg

Dietary
Exchanges:
Milk 0
Vegetable 0
Bread/Starch 0
Meat 1½
Fat 1½

32 chicken wings
2/3 cup melted butter
1/2 teaspoon garlic
   powder
1 teaspoon salt
1½ cups bread crumbs
1/2 cup grated
   Parmesan cheese

Disjoint wings, discarding tips. Rinse; pat dry. Mix butter, garlic powder and salt in small bowl. Combine bread crumbs and Parmesan cheese in medium bowl; stir well. Dip chicken wings into butter. Coat with crumb mixture. Arrange on 10x15-inch baking sheet. Bake at 400 degrees for 25 to 30 minutes or until done. May substitute boneless chicken breast halves for chicken wings and serve as main dish.

Barbara A. Stewart, Graham

CHICKEN NUGGETS

Yield:
16 servings
Utensil:
baking sheet
Approx Per
Serving:
Cal 105
Prot 8 g
Carbo 2 g
Fiber 0 g
T Fat 7 g
Chol 19 mg
Sod 257 mg

Dietary
Exchanges:
Milk 0
Vegetable 0
Fruit 0
Bread/Starch 0
Meat 1; Fat 1½

4 whole chicken
  breasts, boned,
  skinned
½ cup bread crumbs
¼ cup Parmesan
  cheese

¼ teaspoon thyme
2 teaspoons Accent
1 teaspoon salt
½ cup melted
  margarine

Rinse chicken breasts; pat dry. Cut into 1-inch nuggets. Combine bread crumbs, Parmesan cheese, thyme, Accent and salt in medium bowl; mix well. Add melted margarine, stirring well. Roll chicken nuggets in mixture to coat. Arrange 1 layer at a time on foil-lined baking sheet. Bake at 400 degrees for 10 minutes or until golden brown. May substitute tenderloin for chicken breasts.

Grace Moody, Burlington

DELICIOUS CHICKEN WINGS

Yield:
30 to 40 servings
Utensil:
baking pan
Approx Per
Serving:
Cal 175
Prot 10 g
Carbo 19 g
Fiber <1 g
T Fat 7 g
Chol 28 mg
Sod 447 mg

Dietary
Exchanges:
Milk 0
Vegetable 0
Fruit 0
Bread/Starch 0
Meat 1½; Fat ½

30 to 40 chicken wings
1 cup soy sauce
1 32-ounce jar apricot
  jam
6 tablespoons sugar
5 tablespoons lemon
  juice

2½ teaspoons ginger
1¼ teaspoons
  cinnamon
1¼ teaspoons nutmeg
¾ teaspoon allspice
1⅛ teaspoons thyme
⅛ teaspoon garlic salt

Disjoint wings, discarding tips. Rinse; pat dry. Combine soy sauce, jam, sugar, lemon juice, ginger, cinnamon, nutmeg, allspice, thyme and garlic salt in bowl; mix well. Arrange chicken wings in 9x12-inch baking pan. Brush with sauce. Bake at 350 degrees for 2 hours or until tender, basting frequently with sauce. Serve hot or cold. May substitute peach or pineapple jam for apricot jam.

Ellen M. Mercier, Greensboro

CRAB MEAT MUFFINS

6 English muffins
1 7-ounce can crab meat, drained, flaked
1 5-ounce jar Old English cheese spread, softened
1 1/2 teaspoons mayonnaise
1/2 cup butter, softened
1/2 teaspoon (scant) garlic salt
1/8 teaspoon Tabasco sauce
1/8 teaspoon dried parsley
1/8 teaspoon paprika

Split muffins into halves. Cut each half into quarters. Combine crab meat, cheese, mayonnaise, butter, garlic salt, Tabasco sauce, parsley and paprika in bowl; mix well. Spread on muffin quarters. Arrange on baking sheet. Freeze for 30 minutes. Broil for 10 to 12 minutes, or until bubbly and golden brown.

Nancy McGinnis, Greensboro

HAM-CHEESE ROLLS

24 party rolls
8 ounces thinly sliced ham
8 ounces Swiss cheese, sliced
1 cup butter
2 tablespoons Worcestershire sauce
2 tablespoons prepared mustard
1/4 cup packed brown sugar
2 tablespoons poppy seed

Slice rolls in half horizontally. Place bottom piece in baking pan. Top with ham and cheese. Melt butter in saucepan. Add Worcestershire sauce, mustard, brown sugar and poppy seed; mix well. Bring to a boil, stirring frequently. Pour over prepared rolls. Replace top. Let stand for 2 hours. Bake at 350 degrees for 12 minutes or until cheese is melted and ham is heated through.

Jewel Smith, Clemmons

BEEF-BACON BALLS

1 pound ground beef
1 onion, minced
1/2 green bell pepper,
  finely chopped
1 1/4 cups bread crumbs
2 eggs, beaten
1 cup canned
  tomatoes, drained,
  chopped
1 teaspoon prepared
  mustard
1 teaspoon
  Worcestershire sauce
Salt and pepper to
  taste
8 to 10 slices bacon,
  cut in half

Combine ground beef, onion, green pepper, bread crumbs, eggs, tomatoes, mustard, Worcestershire sauce, salt and pepper in large bowl; stir well. Shape into meatballs, using 1/4 cup mixture for each. Wrap with bacon. Arrange in 9x13-inch baking pan. Bacon should not touch pan. Bake at 350 degrees for 45 minutes; drain. Place on serving dish.

Mary Jane Daleiden, Greensboro

PARTY MEATBALLS

1 pound ground beef
1/4 pound sausage
1/4 cup bread crumbs
1 teaspoon
  Worcestershire sauce
1/2 teaspoon garlic salt
1/8 teaspoon pepper
1/4 cup half and half
1 egg, beaten
1/2 cup grated
  Parmesan cheese
1 10-ounce jar grape
  jelly
1 10-ounce bottle of
  chili sauce

Combine ground beef, sausage, bread crumbs, Worcestershire sauce, garlic salt, pepper, half and half, egg and Parmesan cheese in large bowl; mix well. Shape into 1-inch balls. Brown on all sides in skillet; drain. Refrigerate, covered, overnight. Mix grape jelly and chili sauce together in 2-quart slow cooker. Heat until jelly melts, stirring occasionally. Add meatballs. Cook on Low for 2 to 3 hours, or until bubbly. Serve with toothpicks.

Barbara Westmoreland, Pfafftown

COCKTAIL WEINERS

Yield:
48 servings
Utensil:
2-quart saucepan
Approx Per Serving:
Cal 82
Prot 2 g
Carbo 5 g
Fiber <1 g
T Fat 6 g
Chol 10 mg
Sod 276 mg

Dietary Exchanges:
Milk 0
Vegetable 0
Fruit 0
Bread/Starch 0
Meat 1/2; Fat 1

1 10-ounce jar apple jelly
3/4 cup prepared mustard
1/4 cup catsup
1 48-count package cocktail weiners

Combine apple jelly, mustard and catsup in saucepan. Heat until jelly melts; stir well. Add weiners. Cook over low heat for about 2 hours or until sauce is of desired consistency.

Gaylene Fogleman, Graham

HANKY PANKY

Yield:
30 servings
Utensil:
skillet
Approx Per Serving:
Cal 129
Prot 9 g
Carbo 4 g
Fiber <1 g
T Fat 8 g
Chol 31 mg
Sod 371 mg

Dietary Exchanges:
Milk 0
Vegetable 0
Fruit 0
Bread/Starch 0
Meat 1; Fat 1

1 pound sausage
1 pound ground beef
16 ounces Velveeta cheese, chopped
1 teaspoon oregano
1 teaspoon garlic powder
1 8-ounce loaf party rye bread

Brown sausage and ground beef in skillet, stirring until crumbly; drain. Add cheese, stirring until melted. Add oregano and garlic powder; mix well. Spread on rye bread. Bake at 375 degrees for 15 to 20 minutes or until bubbly. May be frozen before baking.

Antoinette Cerrito, Greensboro

COVERED OLIVES

Yield:
50 servings
Utensil:
baking sheet
Approx Per Serving:
Cal 48
Prot 2 g
Carbo 2 g
Fiber <1 g
T Fat 4 g
Chol 5 mg
Sod 108 mg

Dietary Exchanges:
Milk 0
Vegetable 0
Fruit 0
Bread/Starch 0
Meat 0; Fat 1

1 cup flour
1 teaspoon salt
1/2 cup margarine, softened

2 cups shredded sharp Cheddar cheese
50 green olives

Combine flour and salt in medium bowl. Cut in margarine until crumbly. Add Cheddar cheese; stir well. Cover each olive with mixture. Place on baking sheet. Bake at 450 degrees for 12 minutes or at 350 degrees for 15 minutes.

Teresa M. Crispino, High Point

PICKLED MUSHROOMS

Yield:
24 servings
Utensil:
saucepan
Approx Per Serving:
Cal 33
Prot <1 g
Carbo 2 g
Fiber <1 g
T Fat 3 g
Chol 0 mg
Sod 85 mg

Dietary Exchanges:
Milk 0
Vegetable 0
Fruit 0
Bread/Starch 0
Meat 0; Fat 1/2

1/3 cup red wine vinegar
1/3 cup oil
1 onion, minced
1 teaspoon salt
2 teaspoons dried parsley, crumbled

1 teaspoon prepared mustard
1 teaspoon brown sugar
2 6-ounce cans button mushrooms, drained

Combine vinegar, oil, onion, salt, parsley, mustard and brown sugar in saucepan. Bring to a boil. Add mushrooms. Simmer over low heat for 5 to 6 minutes. Chill, covered, stirring occasionally. Drain mushrooms; place in serving dish.

Dot Chrismon

Mom O'Rourke's Spinach Balls

Yield:
60 servings
Utensil:
baking sheet
Approx Per
Serving:
Cal 40
Prot 1 g
Carbo 2 g
Fiber <1 g
T Fat 3 g
Chol 34 mg
Sod 101 mg

Dietary
Exchanges:
Milk 0
Vegetable 0
Fruit 0
Bread/Starch 0
Meat 0; Fat 1

2 10-ounce packages frozen chopped spinach
¾ cup melted butter
2 onions, minced
½ cup grated Parmesan cheese
6 eggs, beaten
1 teaspoon Accent
1 teaspoon garlic salt
1 teaspoon pepper
2 cups herb-seasoned stuffing mix

Cook spinach using package directions; drain well. Combine spinach, butter, onions, Parmesan cheese, eggs, Accent, garlic salt, pepper and stuffing mix in large bowl; mix well. Shape into 1-inch balls. Place on non-stick baking sheet. Bake at 350 degrees for 10 to 15 minutes or until golden brown. May be frozen before baking.

Marion S. Haerle, Greensboro

Vegetable Pizzas

Yield:
70 servings
Utensil:
2 baking sheets
Approx Per
Serving:
Cal 73
Prot 1 g
Carbo 4 g
Fiber <1 g
T Fat 6 g
Chol 9 mg
Sod 120 mg

Dietary
Exchanges:
Milk 0
Vegetable 0
Fruit 0
Bread/Starch 0
Meat 0; Fat 1½

2 8-count cans refrigerator crescent rolls
16 ounces cream cheese, softened
1 cup mayonnaise
1 envelope ranch salad dressing mix
Flowerets of 1 bunch broccoli, chopped
Flowerets of 1 head cauliflower, chopped
¾ cup minced green onions
2 cups chopped tomatoes

Place dough on 2 lightly greased 10x15-inch baking sheets; press to cover. Bake at 400 degrees for 10 minutes; cool. Combine cream cheese, mayonnaise and salad dressing mix in mixer bowl; beat on low speed until smooth. Spread over crusts. Sprinkle broccoli, cauliflower, green onions and tomatoes over cream cheese. Cut into 2-inch squares. May be refrigerated, tightly covered, for 24 hours. May also top with green, red or yellow chopped bell peppers or sliced mushrooms.

Phyllis Lennon

Vietnamese Eggrolls

Yield:
12 servings
Utensil:
wok
**Approx Per
Serving:**
Cal 126
Prot 12 g
Carbo 4 g
Fiber 1 g
T Fat 6 g
Chol 78 mg
Sod 221 mg

**Dietary
Exchanges:**
Milk 0
Vegetable 1/2
Fruit 0
Bread/Starch 0
Meat 1 1/2; Fat 1/2

8 ounces ground beef
8 ounces ground pork
8 ounces shrimp,
  peeled, chopped
2 cloves of garlic, minced
1 1/2 tablespoons sugar
1 teaspoon salt
1/2 teaspoon pepper
2 tablespoons oil
1 clove of garlic, crushed
1 cup shredded carrots
2 onions, finely chopped
12 egg roll wrappers
1 egg yolk, slightly
  beaten
Oil for deep frying

Combine first 7 ingredients in bowl; mix well. Let stand for 15 minutes. Stir-fry garlic in 2 tablespoons oil in wok for 1 minute. Add meat mixture. Stir-fry for 5 minutes until browned; drain. Add carrots and onions. Stir-fry for 1 minute. Let stand until cool. Unfold egg roll wrappers. Spoon 2 tablespoons mixture along lower half of each wrapper; lift up lower edge, fold over filling. Tuck in edges at both ends; roll up. Brush flaps with egg yolk; press firmly to seal. Deep-fry egg rolls in wok over medium-high heat until golden brown on all sides.

Nutritional information does not include oil for deep frying.

Khuong Huynh, Twin City

Zucchini Appetizers

Yield:
48 servings
Utensil:
baking pan
**Approx Per
Serving:**
Cal 45
Prot 1 g
Carbo 2 g
Fiber <1 g
T Fat 3 g
Chol 24 mg
Sod 99 mg

**Dietary
Exchanges:**
Milk 0
Vegetable 0
Fruit 0
Bread/Starch 0
Meat 0; Fat 1/2

4 eggs, slightly beaten
1/2 cup oil
3 cups shredded
  zucchini
1 cup baking mix
1/2 cup finely chopped
  onion
1/2 cup grated
  Parmesan cheese
2 tablespoons parsley
1 teaspoon salt
1/2 teaspoon oregano
1 clove of garlic, minced
1/8 teaspoon pepper

Combine eggs and oil in bowl; mix well. Add zucchini, baking mix, onion, Parmesan cheese, parsley, salt, oregano, garlic and pepper; mix well. Pour into greased 9x13-inch baking pan. Bake at 350 degrees for 30 minutes. Cut into 1x2-inch rectangles.

Norma Briggs, Graham

Coconut Almond Milk

Yield:
7 servings
Utensil:
blender
Approx Per
Serving:
Cal 86
Prot 3 g
Carbo 3 g
Fiber 2 g
T Fat 8 g
Chol 0 mg
Sod 37 mg

Dietary
Exchanges:
Milk 0
Vegetable 0
Fruit 0
Bread/Starch 0
Meat 1/2; Fat 1 1/2

2/3 cup almonds, blanched
1/3 cup unsweetened coconut
1 3/4 cups cold water
1/8 teaspoon vanilla extract
1/8 teaspoon salt
1 3/4 cups (about) water

Combine almonds, coconut and 1 3/4 cups water in blender container; process until smooth. Strain liquid into bowl. Pour in additional water to make 3 1/2 cups; stir well. Chill until serving time.

Kathleen S. Yax, Mebane

Pineapple Sherbet Float

Yield:
2 servings
Utensil:
pitcher
Approx Per
Serving:
Cal 229
Prot 1 g
Carbo 42 g
Fiber 0 g
T Fat 2 g
Chol 9 mg
Sod 95 mg

Dietary
Exchanges:
Milk 0
Vegetable 0
Fruit 0
Bread/Starch 2 1/2
Meat 0; Fat 1/2

1 1/4 cups pineapple sherbet
1/2 cup dry white wine
1/2 cup ginger ale

Combine sherbet, wine and ginger ale in pitcher. Stir gently until sherbet is partially melted. Serve in tall glasses.

Martha M. Wheeler, Chapin, South Carolina

CHERRY PUNCH

Yield:
64 servings
Utensil:
punch bowl
Approx Per
Serving:
Cal 42
Prot <1 g
Carbo 11 g
Fiber <1 g
T Fat <1 g
Chol 0 mg
Sod 2 mg

Dietary
Exchanges:
Milk 0
Vegetable 0
Fruit 0
Bread/Starch 0
Meat 0; Fat 0

1 envelope
   cherry-flavored
   drink mix
2 cups sugar
4¼ quarts water
1 18-ounce can
   pineapple juice

1 6-ounce can frozen
   orange juice
   concentrate, thawed
1 1-quart bottle of
   ginger ale, chilled

Combine cherry-flavored drink mix, sugar, water, pineapple juice and orange juice concentrate in punch bowl; stir well. Chill in refrigerator. Stir in ginger ale before serving.

Mrs. Coy M. Vance, Raleigh

CRANBERRY PUNCH

Yield:
32 servings
Utensil:
large saucepan
Approx Per
Serving:
Cal 82
Prot <1 g
Carbo 22 g
Fiber 1 g
T Fat <1 g
Chol 0 mg
Sod <1 mg

Dietary
Exchanges:
Milk 0
Vegetable 0
Fruit ½
Bread/Starch 0
Meat 0; Fat 0

1½ pounds cranberries
2 quarts water
6 whole cloves

3 cups sugar
½ cup lemon juice
1 cup orange juice

Combine cranberries, water and cloves in large saucepan. Cook over high heat until cranberries are soft. Strain liquid into bowl. Add sugar, lemon juice and orange juice; mix well. Serve hot or cold.

Mary Pickett, Winston-Salem

EASY PUNCH

2 envelopes unsweetened strawberry-flavored drink mix
1 quart boiling water
2 cups sugar
1 quart cold water
1 46-ounce can pineapple juice
1 1-quart bottle of ginger ale

Combine strawberry-flavored drink mix with boiling water in saucepan. Stir in sugar. Remove from heat. Pour into 1-gallon container. Add cold water and pineapple juice; mix well. Chill in refrigerator. Add ginger ale before serving.

B.S. Cuthrell, Winston-Salem

PINEAPPLE PUNCH

2 64-ounce cans pineapple juice
1 gallon water
4 cups sugar
1 1-ounce bottle of almond extract
2 1-quart bottles of ginger ale, chilled

Combine pineapple juice, water, sugar and almond extract in punch bowl; stir well. Chill in refrigerator. Add ginger ale before serving; stir well. May freeze part of mixture to float in bowl.

Dot Fesperman, Winston-Salem

SOUTHERN-STYLE PUNCH

Yield:
24 servings
Utensil:
punch bowl
Approx Per
Serving:
Cal 142
Prot 1 g
Carbo 31 g
Fiber <1 g
T Fat <1 g
Chol 0 mg
Sod 9 mg

Dietary
Exchanges:
Milk 0
Vegetable 0
Fruit 1½
Bread/Starch 0
Meat 0; Fat 0

1 48-ounce bottle of cranberry juice
1 12-ounce can frozen lemonade concentrate, thawed
1 46-ounce can pineapple juice
1 2-liter bottle of ginger ale
1 cup Southern Comfort

Combine cranberry juice, lemonade concentrate, pineapple juice, ginger ale and Southern Comfort in punch bowl; mix well. Chill in refrigerator. Serve over crushed ice.

Dottie (Slater) Fambrough, Gadsden, Alabama

STRAWBERRY PUNCH

Yield:
48 servings
Utensil:
punch bowl
Approx Per
Serving:
Cal 73
Prot <1 g
Carbo 19 g
Fiber <1 g
T Fat <1 g
Chol 0 mg
Sod 5 mg

Dietary
Exchanges:
Milk 0
Vegetable 0
Fruit ½
Bread/Starch 0
Meat 0; Fat 0

1½ quarts water
2 cups sugar
2½ cups orange juice
½ cup lemon juice
4 cups unsweetened pineapple juice
2 10-ounce packages frozen strawberries, thawed
2 1-quart bottles of lemon-lime soda

Bring water to a boil in large saucepan. Add sugar, stirring until dissolved. Stir in orange juice, lemon juice, pineapple juice and strawberries with juice. Pour into large container; freeze until firm. Thaw in punch bowl 1 hour before serving. Add lemon-lime soda; stir until slushy.

Betty Hawkins, Burlington

Tropical Ice

Yield:
24 servings
Utensil:
large bowl
Approx Per
Serving:
Cal 32
Prot <1 g
Carbo 8 g
Fiber 1 g
T Fat <1 g
Chol 0 mg
Sod 1 mg

Dietary
Exchanges:
Milk 0
Vegetable 0
Fruit 1/2
Bread/Starch 0
Meat 0; Fat 0

2½ cups unsweetened orange juice
1 20-ounce can unsweetened crushed pineapple
1 tablespoon lemon juice
2 cups mashed bananas
¼ cup powdered artificial sweetner
1 1-quart bottle of reduced-calorie ginger ale

Combine orange juice, crushed pineapple with juice, lemon juice, bananas and artificial sweetner in large bowl; stir well. Freeze until firm. Thaw in punch bowl. Add ginger ale; stir until slushy. Garnish with fresh strawberries.

Janet Mills, Winston-Salem

No Shortcuts Russian Tea

Yield:
20 servings
Utensil:
6-quart kettle
Approx Per
Serving:
Cal 101
Prot 1 g
Carbo 26 g
Fiber <1 g
T Fat <1 g
Chol 0 mg
Sod 3 mg

Dietary
Exchanges:
Milk 0
Vegetable 0
Fruit 1
Bread/Starch 0
Meat 0; Fat 0

6 cups water
¾ to 1 cup sugar
2 cinnamon sticks
1 tablespoon whole cloves
1 tablespoon whole allspice
4 cups strong tea
1 12-ounce can frozen orange juice concentrate, thawed
1 6-ounce can frozen lemonade concentrate, thawed
3 cups pineapple juice

Combine water, sugar, cinnamon, cloves and allspice in kettle. Bring to a boil. Cook for 5 minutes, stirring occasionally. Strain mixture to remove spices. Add tea, orange juice concentrate, lemonade concentrate and pineapple juice; mix well. Serve hot.

Lynn Kiger, Rural Hall

SPICED APPLE CIDER

Yield:
20 servings
Utensil:
percolator
Approx Per
Serving:
Cal 63
Prot <1 g
Carbo 7 g
Fiber <1 g
T Fat <1 g
Chol 0 mg
Sod 26 mg

Dietary
Exchanges:
Milk 0
Vegetable 0
Fruit 0
Bread/Starch 0
Meat 0; Fat 0

1 teaspoon whole
  cloves
3 cinnamon sticks
1 teaspoon whole
  allspice

½ cup packed brown
  sugar
1 cup orange juice
¼ teaspoon salt
2 quarts apple cider

Place cloves, cinnamon, allspice and sugar in percolator basket. Mix orange juice, salt and apple cider in percolator. Perk as for coffee. Refrigerate unused portion.

Jean H. Mahaffey, Winston-Salem

WASSAIL

Yield:
20 servings
Utensil:
large saucepan
Approx Per
Serving:
Cal 240
Prot <1 g
Carbo 61 g
Fiber 1 g
T Fat <1 g
Chol 0 mg
Sod 8 mg

Dietary
Exchanges:
Milk 0
Vegetable 0
Fruit 2½
Bread/Starch 0
Meat 0; Fat 0

1 gallon apple juice
1   48-ounce can
  pineapple juice
6 tablespoons lemon
  juice

1 tablespoon cinnamon
2 cups dark honey

Combine apple juice, pineapple juice, lemon juice and cinnamon in large saucepan; mix well. Bring to a boil, stirring occasionally. Remove from heat. Add honey, stirring well. Serve hot.

Doris Whitesell

INDIA TEA

Yield:
20 servings
Utensil:
large saucepan
*Approx Per
Serving:*
Cal 83
Prot <1 g
Carbo 22 g
Fiber <1 g
T Fat <1 g
Chol 0 mg
Sod 1 mg

*Dietary
Exchanges:*
Milk 0
Vegetable 0
Fruit 1/2
Bread/Starch 0
Meat 0; Fat 0

2 quarts water
6 tablespoons thawed
  lemon juice
  concentrate
1¹/₂ cups sugar
2 cups strong tea

3 cups pineapple juice
1 teaspoon vanilla
  extract
1 teaspoon almond
  extract

Bring water to a boil in large saucepan. Remove from heat. Add sugar, stirring until dissolved. Stir in tea, pineapple juice, vanilla and almond extracts. Simmer over low heat for 30 minutes.

Gale Owens, Greensboro

INSTANT RUSSIAN TEA MIX

Yield:
70 servings
Utensil:
bowl
*Approx Per
Serving:*
Cal 44
Prot 0 g
Carbo 11 g
Fiber 0 g
T Fat 0 g
Chol 0 mg
Sod 3 mg

*Dietary
Exchanges:*
Milk 0
Vegetable 0
Fruit 0
Bread/Starch 0
Meat 0; Fat 0

2 cups orange-flavored
  breakfast drink mix
1 3-ounce package
  sweetened
  lemonade mix

¹/₂ cup instant tea
1¹/₂ cups sugar
¹/₂ teaspoon ground
  cloves
1 teaspoon cinnamon

Combine powdered breakfast drink mix, lemonade mix, tea powder, sugar, cloves and cinnamon in bowl; stir well. Add 2 rounded teaspoons of mix to one cup hot water to serve.

Connie Kelly, Mocksville

SOUPS

Mom's Borsch

1 pound beef chuck
3 quarts water
1 6-ounce can tomato
   paste
Salt and pepper to taste
12 ounces beets,
   peeled, grated
1 cup shredded carrots
3 cups shredded
   cabbage
1/4 cup minced onion
1 tablespoon dillseed
1/8 teaspoon minced
   garlic
1 to 2 tablespoons
   lemon juice

Cut beef into 1-inch pieces. Bring beef and water to a boil in stockpot; skim surface. Stir in tomato paste, salt and pepper. Simmer for 1 1/2 hours. Add beets, carrots, cabbage, onion, dillseed and garlic. Simmer for 45 minutes longer. Stir in lemon juice. Ladle into soup bowls. Garnish with sour cream.

Helen Genaille

Broccoli and Cheese Soup

3/4 cup chopped onion
2 tablespoons corn oil
6 cups water
6 chicken bouillon
   cubes
8 ounces uncooked
   fine egg noodles
1 teaspoon salt
1/8 teaspoon garlic
   powder
2 10-ounce packages
   frozen chopped
   broccoli
6 cups milk
16 ounces Velveeta
   cheese, chopped
Pepper to taste

Sauté onion in oil in stockpot over medium heat for 3 to 4 minutes. Add water and bouillon cubes. Bring to a boil, stirring occasionally. Add noodles and salt gradually, allowing soup to return to a boil. Cook for 3 minutes. Add garlic powder and broccoli. Cook for 4 minutes. Stir in milk, cheese and pepper. Cook just until cheese melts and soup is heated through; do not boil.

Betty King, Mebane

CREAMY BROCCOLI SOUP

Yield:
4 servings
Utensil:
saucepan
**Approx Per
Serving:**
Cal 280
Prot 9 g
Carbo 19 g
Fiber 4 g
T Fat 20 g
Chol 53 mg
Sod 760 mg

**Dietary
Exchanges:**
Milk 1/2
Vegetable 1 1/2
Fruit 0
Bread/Starch 1 1/2
Meat 0; Fat 5

3 cups broccoli
flowerets
1 medium onion,
chopped
1 carrot, shredded
1/4 cup butter

2 cups milk
1 10-ounce can cream
of chicken soup
White pepper and
paprika to taste

Sauté broccoli, onion and carrot in butter in large saucepan. Stir in milk and soup. Cook just until heated through. Sprinkle with pepper and paprika.

Jo Ann Felker, Long Beach

CREAMY BROCCOLI AU GRATIN SOUP

Yield:
6 servings
Utensil:
saucepan
**Approx Per
Serving:**
Cal 156
Prot 7 g
Carbo 9 g
Fiber <1 g
T Fat 10 g
Chol 31 mg
Sod 364 mg

**Dietary
Exchanges:**
Milk 1/2
Vegetable 0
Fruit 0
Bread/Starch 1/2
Meat 1/2; Fat 2

1/2 cup chopped onion
2 tablespoons butter
1 3/4 cups water
1 4 1/2-ounce package
broccoli and rice au
gratin mix
1/4 cup flour

1/4 teaspoon dry mustard
1 3/4 cups chicken broth
2 cups milk
1/2 cup shredded
Cheddar cheese
1 green onion, cut into
thin strips

Sauté onion in butter in saucepan. Add water and broccoli-rice mix. Bring to a boil; reduce heat. Simmer, covered, for 20 minutes. Mix flour and dry mustard in small bowl. Stir in 1/2 cup chicken broth gradually. Add to soup with remaining broth and milk. Heat to the simmering point, stirring occasionally. Cook until thickened, stirring occasionally. Stir in cheese. Ladle into soup bowls. Top with green onion.

Nutritional information does not include broccoli and rice au gratin mix.

Aura Lee Wilson, Burlington

Brunswick Stew

Yield:
12 servings
Utensil:
stockpot
Approx Per Serving:
Cal 305
Prot 22 g
Carbo 48 g
Fiber 8 g
T Fat 4 g
Chol 36 mg
Sod 448 mg

Dietary Exchanges:
Milk 0
Vegetable 1
Fruit 0
Bread/Starch 3
Meat 1½; Fat 0

6 chicken breasts, skinned
3 16-ounce cans lima beans
2 16-ounce packages frozen corn
3 cups chopped potatoes
4 cups canned tomatoes
2 cups chopped onions
3 tablespoons sugar
3 dashes of liquid smoke
¼ cup flour
1 cup water
Salt to taste

Rinse chicken well. Combine with water to cover in 8-quart stockpot. Cook until tender. Remove chicken, reserving broth. Cool chicken and broth. Chop chicken into bite-sized pieces. Remove fat from broth. Add enough water to broth to measure 1 quart. Add chicken and vegetables. Simmer for 30 minutes, stirring frequently. Add sugar and liquid smoke. Stir in mixture of flour and 1 cup water. Cook until thickened, stirring constantly. Season to taste.

Margaret P. Moore, King

Best-Ever Brunswick Stew

Yield:
24 servings
Utensil:
stockpot
Approx Per Serving:
Cal 460
Prot 27 g
Carbo 58 g
Fiber 5 g
T Fat 15 g
Chol 55 mg
Sod 1393 mg

Dietary Exchanges:
Milk 0
Vegetable 2
Fruit 0
Bread/Starch 2½
Meat 2½; Fat 3

1 3-pound chicken
1 pound cubed pork
2 pounds stew beef
2 hot peppers
1 14-ounce bottle of hot catsup
1 18-ounce bottle of hickory smoke-flavored barbecue sauce with onion bits
3 28-ounce cans crushed tomatoes in tomato purée
Hot sauce to taste
1 tablespoon Worcestershire sauce
1 6-ounce can tomato paste
2 teaspoons salt
Pepper to taste
1 cup margarine
3 16-ounce cans Shoe Peg corn, drained
3 16-ounce cans green butter beans
4 large onions, sliced
5 pounds potatoes, peeled, chopped

Cook chicken, pork and beef in water to cover in 16-quart stockpot until tender. Add hot peppers. Remove and chop chicken, discarding skin and bones; return to stockpot. Add remaining ingredients except potatoes. Simmer for 1½ hours. Add potatoes. Simmer until potatoes are tender.

Betty Perkinson, Burlington

New England Clam Chowder

Yield:
6 servings
Utensil:
saucepan
Approx Per
Serving:
Cal 150
Prot 7 g
Carbo 16 g
Fiber 1 g
T Fat 7 g
Chol 42 mg
Sod 271 mg

Dietary
Exchanges:
Milk 1/2
Vegetable 1/2
Fruit 0
Bread/Starch 1/2
Meat 1/2; Fat 1 1/2

1 small onion, chopped
1/2 cup chopped celery
2 tablespoons butter
2 cups chopped
  potatoes
2 cups water

1/2 teaspoon salt
1/4 teaspoon pepper
2 cups milk
1 7-ounce can minced
  clams
Paprika to taste

Sauté onion and celery in butter in large saucepan until tender but not brown. Add potatoes, water, salt and pepper. Simmer, covered, for 15 minutes or until potatoes are tender. Stir in milk and clams. Heat to serving temperature. Serve in warmed bowls. Sprinkle with paprika.

Sarah L. Tagert, Greensboro

Best-Ever Corn Chowder

Yield:
6 servings
Utensil:
saucepan
Approx Per
Serving:
Cal 248
Prot 9 g
Carbo 39 g
Fiber 2 g
T Fat 8 g
Chol 21 mg
Sod 1036 mg

Dietary
Exchanges:
Milk 1/2
Vegetable 1/2
Fruit 0
Bread/Starch 2
Meat 1/2; Fat 1 1/2

5 slices bacon
1 12-ounce can whole
  kernel corn
1 medium onion, sliced
1 cup chopped potatoes
1/2 cup chopped carrots
1/2 cup chopped celery

1/2 teaspoon salt
Pepper to taste
1 10-ounce can cream
  of celery soup
2 cups milk
1 16-ounce can
  cream-style corn

Fry bacon in saucepan until crisp; remove bacon, reserving drippings. Drain whole kernel corn, reserving liquid. Add enough water to reserved liquid to measure 1/2 cup. Add to drippings in saucepan. Add onion, potatoes, carrots, celery, salt and pepper. Simmer, covered, for 15 minutes. Stir in soup, milk, drained corn and cream-style corn. Simmer until heated through. Ladle into soup bowls. Crumble bacon over servings.

Helen Genaille

Gazpacho

Yield:
6 servings
Utensil:
large bowl
Approx Per Serving:
Cal 122
Prot 3 g
Carbo 17 g
Fiber 5 g
T Fat 6 g
Chol 0 mg
Sod 642 mg

Dietary Exchanges:
Milk 0
Vegetable 3
Fruit 0
Bread/Starch 0
Meat 0; Fat 1

2 cucumbers, chopped
2 tomatoes, chopped
1 green bell pepper, chopped
1 bunch green onions, chopped
3 stalks celery, chopped
2 carrots, shredded
3 tablespoons chopped parsley
4 cups (or more) vegetable juice cocktail

2 tablespoons olive oil
2 tablespoons red wine vinegar
1 tablespoon Paul Newman's salad dressing
1 tablespoon lemon juice
1 clove of garlic, crushed
Worcestershire sauce to taste
1 teaspoon cumin

Combine cucumbers, tomatoes, green pepper, green onions, celery, carrots and parsley in large bowl. Add vegetable juice; mix well. Add olive oil, vinegar, salad dressing, lemon juice, garlic, Worcestershire sauce and cumin; mix well. Chill for 2 hours. Serve cold.

Nancy Garner, Burlington

Hearty Beef and Vegetable Chowder

Yield:
8 servings
Utensil:
saucepan
Approx Per Serving:
Cal 206
Prot 14 g
Carbo 17 g
Fiber 2 g
T Fat 10 g
Chol 37 mg
Sod 848 mg

Dietary Exchanges:
Milk 0
Vegetable 2
Fruit 0
Bread/Starch 1/2
Meat 1 1/2; Fat 1

1 pound ground beef
1 cup chopped onion
2 tablespoons margarine
1 16-ounce can tomatoes, chopped
2 cups vegetable juice cocktail
2 cups hot water
2 beef bouillon cubes
1/2 teaspoon Worcestershire sauce

1 cup sliced celery
1 bay leaf
1 teaspoon salt
1/8 teaspoon pepper
1 cup uncooked fine noodles
1 10-ounce package frozen mixed vegetables
1/4 to 1/2 teaspoon thyme

Brown ground beef with onion in margarine in 3-quart saucepan, stirring until ground beef is crumbly; drain. Add tomatoes, vegetable juice, water, bouillon, Worcestershire sauce, celery, bay leaf, salt and pepper. Bring to a boil; reduce heat. Simmer, covered, for 30 minutes. Add noodles, mixed vegetables and thyme. Bring to a boil; reduce heat. Simmer, covered, for 15 minutes longer. Remove bay leaf.

Francie Huffman, Winston-Salem

GROUND BEEF AND VEGETABLE SOUP

1½ pounds ground beef
2 onions, chopped
1⅓ cups chopped okra
1 10-ounce can Shoe Peg corn
⅔ cup butter beans
1 16-ounce can tomatoes, chopped
2 10-ounce cans tomato soup
1½ soup cans water
½ teaspoon chili powder
¼ teaspoon oregano
Garlic salt, salt and pepper to taste

Combine ground beef, onions, okra, corn, butter beans, tomatoes, soup and water in large saucepan. Add chili powder, oregano, garlic salt, salt and pepper. Bring to a boil; reduce heat. Simmer for 1½ to 2 hours, stirring occasionally. May use fresh, frozen or canned vegetables as preferred.

Martha S. Tingen, Graham

LENTIL SOUP

½ cup minced onion
⅓ cup minced celery
2 cloves of garlic, minced
3 tablespoons butter
1 cup chopped ham
2 cups tomato sauce
½ teaspoon oregano
Salt and pepper to taste
4 cups beef broth
2 cups water
1 cup dried lentils
8 teaspoons butter

Sauté onion, celery and garlic in 3 tablespoons butter in saucepan until tender. Add ham. Sauté for 5 minutes. Add tomato sauce, oregano, salt and pepper. Simmer for 5 minutes. Stir in broth, water and lentils. Simmer, covered, for 1 hour or until lentils are tender. Place 1 teaspoon butter in each serving bowl. Ladle soup into bowls. Garnish with Parmesan cheese.

June Totterweich, Greensboro

French Onion Soup

Yield:
2 servings
Utensil:
saucepan
Approx Per
Serving:
Cal 500
Prot 29 g
Carbo 53 g
Fiber 2 g
T Fat 20 g
Chol 45 mg
Sod 2262 mg

Dietary
Exchanges:
Milk 0
Vegetable 1
Fruit 0
Bread/Starch 3½
Meat 3; Fat 2

1 medium onion, chopped
2 10-ounce cans French onion soup
4 slices French bread
2 ounces Parmesan cheese
2 ounces mozzarella cheese, shredded

Combine onion and soup in saucepan. Cook for 15 minutes. Toast French bread on both sides. Place 1 slice in each of 2 oven-proof bowls. Spoon soup into bowls. Sprinkle with half the Parmesan cheese; add remaining bread slices. Top with mozzarella cheese and remaining Parmesan cheese. Bake at 400 degrees for 10 to 15 minutes or until cheese is bubbly.

Robin Hall, Greensboro

Potato Soup

Yield:
4 servings
Utensil:
saucepan
Approx Per
Serving:
Cal 440
Prot 11 g
Carbo 31 g
Fiber 3 g
T Fat 31 g
Chol 94 mg
Sod 222 mg

Dietary
Exchanges:
Milk 1
Vegetable ½
Fruit 0
Bread/Starch 1
Meat ½; Fat 5½

4 slices bacon, chopped
2 large potatoes, chopped
1 onion, chopped
Garlic salt and pepper to taste
2 stalks celery, chopped
1 quart half and half

Cook bacon until very brown and crisp in skillet; drain. Combine potatoes and onion with garlic salt, pepper and enough water to just cover in saucepan. Cook for 1 to 1½ hours or until very tender. Add celery and bacon. Cook for 20 minutes. Stir in half and half. Heat just to the simmering point.

Ellman Grubb, Springdale, Arkansas

CREAMY POTATO SOUP

Yield:
4 servings
Utensil:
saucepan
**Approx Per
Serving:**
Cal 173
Prot 5 g
Carbo 31 g
Fiber 2 g
T Fat 4 g
Chol 10 mg
Sod 268 mg

**Dietary
Exchanges:**
Milk 0
Vegetable 1/2
Fruit 0
Bread/Starch 1 1/2
Meat 0; Fat 1/2

3/4 cup chopped onion
2 teaspoons butter
1 10-ounce can
   chicken broth
1 cup water
Salt and pepper to taste

4 cups chopped peeled
   potatoes
1/2 cup milk
1 teaspoon parsley
   flakes

Sauté onion in butter in saucepan. Add broth, water, salt, pepper and potatoes. Simmer, covered, for 20 to 25 minutes or until potatoes are tender. Purée half the mixture in blender; return to saucepan. Stir in milk and parsley flakes. Heat to serving temperature.

Jessie Grandinetti

ITALIAN SAUSAGE AND ZUCCHINI SOUP

Yield:
8 servings
Utensil:
saucepan
**Approx Per
Serving:**
Cal 158
Prot 9 g
Carbo 16 g
Fiber 4 g
T Fat 8 g
Chol 21 mg
Sod 843 mg

**Dietary
Exchanges:**
Milk 0
Vegetable 3
Fruit 0
Bread/Starch 0
Meat 1; Fat 1

1 pound Italian
   sausage
2 cups sliced celery
2 28-ounce cans
   tomatoes, chopped
1 cup chopped onion
1 teaspoon oregano
1 teaspoon Italian
   seasoning
1 teaspoon basil

1/4 teaspoon garlic
   powder
1 teaspoon salt
2 pounds small
   zucchini, sliced 1/2
   inch thick
2 medium green bell
   peppers, cut into
   1/2-inch pieces

Remove casing from sausage. Brown in saucepan, stirring until crumbly. Add celery. Sauté until tender; drain. Add tomatoes, onion, oregano, Italian seasoning, basil, garlic powder and salt; mix well. Simmer, covered, for 20 minutes. Add zucchini and green peppers. Simmer, covered, for 20 minutes or until vegetables are tender. May add water and/or red wine during cooking if needed for desired consistency. May brown sausage in skillet and then cook soup in slow cooker if preferred.

Kathy Boyd, Winston-Salem

Squash Soup

Yield:
4 servings
Utensil:
saucepan
Approx Per
Serving:
Cal 121
Prot 6 g
Carbo 15 g
Fiber 2 g
T Fat 5 g
Chol 15 mg
Sod 529 mg

Dietary
Exchanges:
Milk 1/2
Vegetable 11/2
Fruit 0
Bread/Starch 1/2
Meat 0; Fat 1

2 squash, sliced
1 white onion, chopped
1 10-ounce can potato
   soup

1 cup milk
1 cup chicken broth
Salt and pepper to
   taste

Place squash and onion in a small amount of water in saucepan. Cook just until tender. Purée mixture in blender. Return to saucepan. Purée mixture of potato soup and milk in blender. Stir into squash mixture. Add chicken broth, salt and pepper; mix well. Cook over low heat until heated through, stirring occasionally. Garnish with paprika.

Theresa S. Edwards, Kernersville

Low-Calorie Creamy Tomato Soup

Yield:
4 servings
Utensil:
saucepan
Approx Per
Serving:
Cal 183
Prot 9 g
Carbo 34 g
Fiber 4 g
T Fat 2 g
Chol 4 mg
Sod 554 mg

Dietary
Exchanges:
Milk 1/2
Vegetable 21/2
Fruit 0
Bread/Starch 1
Meat 1/2; Fat 0

1 potato, chopped
2 carrots, chopped
2 stalks celery,
   chopped
1 medium onion,
   chopped
2 bay leaves
11/2 teaspoons basil
3/4 teaspoons oregano
1/4 teaspoon pepper

1/4 teaspoon chili
   powder
11/2 cups chicken stock
1 16-ounce can
   tomatoes
2 tablespoons tomato
   paste
1/3 cup orzo or other
   tiny pasta, cooked
1 cup low-fat yogurt

Combine potato, carrots, celery, onion, bay leaves, basil, oregano, pepper, chili powder and chicken stock in large saucepan; mix well. Bring to a boil; reduce heat. Simmer, covered, for 10 minutes or until vegetables are tender. Stir in undrained tomatoes, tomato paste and pasta. Simmer for 5 minutes or until heated through. Remove from heat; discard bay leaves. Stir in yogurt. Serve immediately.

Clyde Padgett, Winston-Salem

TOMATO SOUP

Yield:
8 servings
Utensil:
saucepan
Approx Per
Serving:
Cal 102
Prot 3 g
Carbo 7 g
Fiber 1 g
T Fat 7 g
Chol 8 mg
Sod 513 mg

Dietary
Exchanges:
Milk 0
Vegetable 1
Fruit 0
Bread/Starch 0
Meat 1/2; Fat 1 1/2

1 onion, chopped
1 stalk celery, chopped
1 carrot, chopped
2 tablespoons butter
2 tablespoons olive oil
1 28-ounce can
   tomatoes, crushed
2 14-ounce cans
   chicken broth
2 tablespoons chopped
   fresh basil
2 tablespoons chopped
   parsley

Sauté onion, celery and carrot in butter and olive oil in 2-quart saucepan for 8 to 10 minutes or until tender. Add tomatoes and broth. Bring to a boil; reduce heat. Simmer for 30 minutes. Add basil and parsley. Simmer for 10 minutes longer. May substitute 1 tablespoon each dried basil and parsley for fresh herbs.

Virginia Vargas, Pfafftown

TURKEY CHOWDER

Yield:
6 servings
Utensil:
saucepan
Approx Per
Serving:
Cal 220
Prot 15 g
Carbo 19 g
Fiber 1 g
T Fat 9 g
Chol 25 mg
Sod 1895 mg

Dietary
Exchanges:
Milk 0
Vegetable 0
Bread/Starch 2
Meat 1 1/2
Fat 2 1/2

2 cups chopped
   potatoes
4 teaspoons minced
   onion
6 cups turkey stock
1 teaspoon salt
1 teaspoon white pepper
1 10-ounce can cream
   of celery soup
1 10-ounce can cream
   of mushroom soup
1 cup chopped cooked
   turkey
1/2 cup crumbled
   crisp-fried bacon
1/4 cup chopped
   parsley

Combine potatoes, onion, turkey stock, salt and white pepper in 3 1/2-quart saucepan. Bring to a boil; reduce heat. Simmer, covered, for 20 minutes or until potatoes are tender; remove from heat. Stir in soups, turkey, bacon and parsley; mix well. Heat to serving temperature.

Jerry Jarrell, Jamestown

WA'HAN'PI

Yield:
12 servings
Utensil:
saucepan
Approx Per
Serving:
Cal 299
Prot 22 g
Carbo 36 g
Fiber 9 g
T Fat 8 g
Chol 45 mg
Sod 46 mg

Dietary
Exchanges:
Milk 0
Vegetable 0
Fruit 0
Bread/Starch 2¹/₂
Meat 2¹/₂; Fat 0

2 cups dried corn
2 cups dried pinto beans
2 pounds chopped pork
6 potatoes, chopped
1 large onion, chopped
Salt and pepper to taste

Combine corn and beans with water to cover in saucepan. Soak overnight. Add pork. Simmer for 3 to 3¹/₂ hours. Add potatoes, onion, salt and pepper. Simmer for 30 minutes longer or until potatoes are tender. Serve hot with fry bread.

Nutritional information does not include dried corn.

Edna Cassidy

CRACKED WHEAT SOUP

Yield:
8 servings
Utensil:
stockpot
Approx Per
Serving:
Cal 197
Prot 6 g
Carbo 35 g
Fiber 8 g
T Fat 4 g
Chol 3 mg
Sod 1537 mg

Dietary
Exchanges:
Milk 0
Vegetable ¹/₂
Fruit 0
Bread/Starch 2
Meat 0; Fat 1

1 10-ounce can chicken broth
2 cups cracked wheat
1 tablespoon oil
1 medium onion, chopped
14 cups hot water
3 chicken bouillon cubes
4 teaspoons salt
¹/₄ cup sour cream

Chill chicken broth overnight. Skim fat from top of broth. Sauté cracked wheat in oil in skillet for 5 to 7 minutes or until light brown. Combine with chicken broth, onion, water, bouillon and salt in large stockpot. Bring to a boil; reduce heat. Simmer, covered, for 50 minutes. Stir in sour cream. Serve immediately. Garnish servings with nutmeg. Add water to reheat. May substitute beef broth or onion soup and beef bouillon for chicken broth and chicken bouillon.

Gertrude Gould, Winston-Salem

SALADS

APPLE SALAD

Yield:
12 servings
Utensil:
large bowl
Approx Per
Serving:
Cal 405
Prot 19 g
Carbo 39 g
Fiber 2 g
T Fat 20 g
Chol 25 mg
Sod 86 mg

Dietary
Exchanges:
Milk ½
Vegetable 0
Fruit 1
Bread/Starch 0
Meat 0; Fat 4½

1 20-ounce can crushed pineapple
2 3-ounce packages lemon gelatin
1 tablespoon sugar
2 cups boiling water
2 cups cold water
2 cups chopped apples
2 bananas, chopped
1 cup chopped pecans
1 egg, beaten
¼ cup sugar
1 tablespoon flour
16 ounces whipped topping
2 tablespoons coconut

Drain pineapple, reserving 1 cup juice. Dissolve gelatin and 1 tablespoon sugar in boiling water in bowl. Stir in cold water. Chill until partially set. Fold in apples, bananas, pecans and pineapple. Pour into serving dish. Chill until firm. Combine egg, remaining ¼ cup sugar, flour and reserved pineapple juice in saucepan. Cook over medium heat until thickened, stirring constantly. Let stand until cool. Fold in whipped topping; spread over congealed layer. Sprinkle with coconut.

Polly Simpson, Greensboro

APRICOT SALAD

Yield:
8 servings
Utensil:
saucepan
Approx Per
Serving:
Cal 292
Prot 14 g
Carbo 28 g
Fiber 1 g
T Fat 15 g
Chol 1 mg
Sod 185 mg

Dietary
Exchanges:
Milk ½
Vegetable 0
Fruit 1
Bread/Starch 0
Meat 0; Fat 3

1 16-ounce can fruit cocktail
1 3-ounce package apricot gelatin
½ teaspoon salt
1 tablespoon sugar
2 tablespoons lemon juice
½ teaspoon almond extract
8 ounces whipped topping
½ cup chopped pecans

Drain fruit cocktail, reserving juice. Bring reserved juice to a boil in saucepan. Add gelatin, salt and sugar. Stir until dissolved. Chill until partially set. Add lemon juice, almond extract and fruit cocktail; mix well. Fold in whipped topping and pecans gently. Pour into 4-cup mold. Chill until set. Unmold onto serving plate.

Frances Thompson, Winston-Salem

BLUEBERRY SALAD

Yield:
8 servings
Utensil:
saucepan
Approx Per
Serving:
Cal 427
Prot 7 g
Carbo 40 g
Fiber 3 g
T Fat 29 g
Chol 31 mg
Sod 183 mg

Dietary
Exchanges:
Milk 0
Vegetable 0
Fruit 1
Bread/Starch 1/2
Meat 0; Fat 8

1 16-ounce can blueberries
1 8-ounce can crushed pineapple
1 3-ounce package grape gelatin
8 ounces cream cheese, softened
1/2 cup sugar
2 cups reduced-calorie sour cream
1 cup pecans

Drain blueberries and pineapple, reserving juice. Add enough water to reserved juice to measure 2 cups. Bring to a boil in saucepan. Stir in gelatin until dissolved. Add blueberries and pineapple; mix well. Pour into serving bowl. Refrigerate until set. Whip cream cheese, sugar and sour cream in bowl until smooth; fold in pecans. Spread over congealed layer. Chill until serving time.

Nancy Garner, Burlington

CHERRY SALAD

Yield:
10 servings
Utensil:
saucepan
Approx Per
Serving:
Cal 204
Prot 9 g
Carbo 36 g
Fiber 1 g
T Fat 4 g
Chol 0 mg
Sod 38 mg

Dietary
Exchanges:
Milk 0
Vegetable 0
Fruit 1/2
Bread/Starch 1/2
Meat 0; Fat 1

1 16-ounce can Bing cherries
1 cup water
1 cup sugar
1 3-ounce package cherry gelatin
1 envelope unflavored gelatin
Juice of 1 lemon
Zest of 1 lemon
Juice of 1 orange
Zest of 1 orange
1/2 cup chopped pecans
1/2 cup crushed pineapple

Drain cherries, reserving juice. Bring reserved juice and water to a boil in saucepan. Add sugar, cherry gelatin, unflavored gelatin, lemon juice, lemon zest, orange juice and orange zest. Stir until gelatin is dissolved. Chill until partially set. Add pecans, pineapple with juice and cherries; mix well. Pour into 8-inch square dish. Chill until serving time.

Minta Coeyman, Greensboro

FROSTED CRANBERRY SQUARES

Yield:
9 servings
Utensil:
9-inch square dish
Approx Per
Serving:
Cal 377
Prot 5 g
Carbo 52 g
Fiber 1 g
T Fat 18 g
Chol 32 mg
Sod 178 mg

Dietary
Exchanges:
Milk 0
Vegetable 0
Fruit 2
Bread/Starch 1¹/₂
Meat 0; Fat 4¹/₂

1²/₃ cups crushed
  pineapple
2 3-ounce packages
  lemon gelatin
1 cup ginger ale
1 16-ounce can jellied
  cranberry sauce

8 ounces cream cheese,
  softened
1 envelope whipped
  topping mix
¹/₂ cup chopped pecans
1 tablespoon butter,
  softened

Drain pineapple, reserving juice. Add enough water to reserved juice to measure 1 cup. Bring to a boil in saucepan. Stir in gelatin until dissolved. Let stand until cool. Stir in ginger ale. Chill until partially set. Combine pineapple and cranberry sauce in bowl. Fold into gelatin mixture. Spoon into 9-inch square glass dish. Chill until firm. Beat cream cheese in bowl until fluffy. Prepare whipped topping mix using package directions. Fold in cream cheese. Spread over congealed layer. Combine pecans and butter in small baking pan. Bake at 350 degrees for 10 minutes. Sprinkle cooled pecans over top. Chill until serving time. Cut into squares and serve on lettuce-lined plates.

Wilma B. Farabee, Lexington

CRANBERRY-PINEAPPLE SALAD

Yield:
8 servings
Utensil:
bowl
Approx Per
Serving:
Cal 343
Prot 4 g
Carbo 57 g
Fiber 3 g
T Fat 13 g
Chol 0 mg
Sod.116 mg

Dietary
Exchanges:
Milk 0
Vegetable 0
Fruit 2
Bread/Starch 1¹/₂
Meat 0; Fat 4¹/₂

1 6-ounce package
  cherry gelatin
2 cups boiling water
1 cup cold water
1 16-ounce can whole
  cranberry sauce

1 cup chopped pecans
1 8-ounce can
  crushed pineapple,
  drained
1 3-ounce can coconut

Dissolve gelatin in boiling water in bowl. Stir in cold water. Chill until partially set. Fold in cranberry sauce, pecans, pineapple and coconut. Pour into serving bowl. Chill until firm.

Barbara Johnson, Graham

CRANBERRY-APPLE SALAD

Yield:
10 servings
Utensil:
8-cup mold
Approx Per Serving:
Cal 441
Prot 3 g
Carbo 64 g
Fiber 2 g
T Fat 22 g
Chol 13 mg
Sod 310 mg

Dietary Exchanges:
Milk 0
Vegetable 0
Fruit 3
Bread/Starch 1
Meat 0; Fat 5

2 16-ounce cans whole cranberry sauce
2 cups boiling water
2 3-ounce packages strawberry gelatin
2 tablespoons lemon juice
1/2 teaspoon salt
1 cup mayonnaise
2 cups chopped apples
1/2 cup walnuts

Melt cranberry sauce in saucepan over medium heat. Drain, reserving liquid. Combine reserved liquid, water and gelatin in bowl. Stir until gelatin is dissolved. Add lemon juice and salt; mix well. Chill until partially set. Add mayonnaise; beat until smooth. Fold in cranberries, apples and walnuts. Pour into 8-cup mold. Chill overnight. Unmold onto serving plate.

Sara M. Jones, Greensboro

CRANBERRY-BANANA SALAD

Yield:
8 servings
Utensil:
6-cup mold
Approx Per Serving:
Cal 228
Prot 2 g
Carbo 48 g
Fiber 3 g
T Fat 5 g
Chol 0 mg
Sod 52 mg

Dietary Exchanges:
Milk 0
Vegetable 0
Fruit 2 1/2
Bread/Starch 1/2
Meat 0; Fat 1 1/2

1 3-ounce package cherry gelatin
1 1/2 cups boiling water
1 8-ounce can crushed pineapple
1 16-ounce jar cranberry-orange relish
2 bananas, sliced
1/2 cup chopped pecans

Dissolve gelatin in boiling water in bowl. Cool slightly. Add pineapple with juice, relish, bananas and pecans. Pour into 6-cup mold. Chill until firm. Unmold onto lettuce-lined plate.

S. M. Apple, Burlington

CRANBERRY-ORANGE SALAD

Yield:
9 servings
Utensil:
7-cup compote
Approx Per Serving:
Cal 224
Prot 3 g
Carbo 36 g
Fiber 2 g
T Fat 9 g
Chol 18 mg
Sod 66 mg

Dietary Exchanges:
Milk 0
Vegetable 0
Fruit 1
Bread/Starch 1
Meat 0; Fat 2

2 3-ounce packages raspberry gelatin
1/2 cup whipping cream, whipped
2 teaspoons grated orange zest
1 peeled orange, ground
2 cups cranberries, ground
2 unpeeled tart apples, ground
1/3 cup sugar
1/2 cup chopped pecans
1/3 cup crushed pineapple
1/3 cup seedless red grapes, cut into halves

Prepare gelatin using package directions. Chill until partially set. Fold in whipped cream gently. Combine orange zest, orange, cranberries, apples, sugar, pecans, pineapple with juice and grapes in large bowl; mix well. Fold in gelatin mixture gently. Spoon into 7-cup compote. Chill for 4 hours. Garnish with orange slices, fresh berries or mint sprig. May substitute whole cranberry sauce for fresh cranberries by adding sauce to slightly set gelatin.

Helen A. Howard, Pfafftown

ESKIMO SALAD

Yield:
12 servings
Utensil:
large bowl
Approx Per Serving:
Cal 279
Prot 6 g
Carbo 32 g
Fiber 2 g
T Fat 16 g
Chol 11 mg
Sod 151 mg

Dietary Exchanges:
Milk 0
Vegetable 0
Fruit 1
Bread/Starch 0
Meat 1/2; Fat 41/2

1 20-ounce can crushed pineapple, drained
11/2 cups cottage cheese
1 20-ounce can fruit cocktail, drained
3 cups miniature marshmallows
1 3-ounce can coconut
11/2 cups chopped pecans
3/4 cup sour cream
1/8 teaspoon salt
1/2 cup (about) pineapple juice

Combine pineapple, cottage cheese, fruit cocktail, marshmallows, coconut, pecans, sour cream and salt in large bowl. Stir in enough pineapple juice to make of desired consistency. Chill for 24 hours for enhanced flavor. May store in refrigerator for up to 1 week.

Mavis Peterson, Elon College

Fruit Salad

Yield:
12 servings
Utensil:
large bowl
Approx Per
Serving:
Cal 152
Prot 1 g
Carbo 39 g
Fiber 3 g
T Fat <1 g
Chol 0 mg
Sod 70 mg

Dietary
Exchanges:
Milk 0
Vegetable 0
Fruit 2
Bread/Starch 1/2
Meat 0; Fat 0

1 20-ounce can pineapple chunks
1 16-ounce can sliced peaches, drained
1 11-ounce can mandarin oranges, drained
2 cups fresh strawberries, sliced
4 bananas, sliced
1 4-ounce package vanilla instant pudding mix
3 tablespoons instant orange-flavored drink mix

Combine pineapple chunks with juice, peaches, mandarin oranges, strawberries and bananas in large bowl. Stir in dry pudding mix and orange-flavored powder; mix well. Spoon into serving bowl. Chill in refrigerator.

Jean Jarrett, Thomasville

Fruit Cocktail Salad

Yield:
10 servings
Utensil:
large bowl
Approx Per
Serving:
Cal 260
Prot 2 g
Carbo 48 g
Fiber 1 g
T Fat 8 g
Chol 10 mg
Sod 44 mg

Dietary
Exchanges:
Milk 0
Vegetable 0
Fruit 1
Bread/Starch 0
Meat 0; Fat 3

1 cup sour cream
1 cup sugar
1 20-ounce can pineapple chunks, drained
1 16-ounce can fruit cocktail, drained
1 cup coconut
2 cups miniature marshmallows

Blend sour cream and sugar in large bowl. Add pineapple chunks, fruit cocktail, coconut and marshmallows; mix well. Spoon into serving bowl. Chill before serving. Garnish with pecans and cherries.

Zane Gerringer, Elon College

FRUITY SURPRISE SALAD

Yield:
12 servings
Utensil:
glass dish
Approx Per
Serving:
Cal 322
Prot 9 g
Carbo 41 g
Fiber 2 g
T Fat 15 g
Chol 5 mg
Sod 215 mg

Dietary
Exchanges:
Milk 0
Vegetable 0
Fruit ½
Bread/Starch 1
Meat ½; Fat 4

2 3-ounce packages strawberry gelatin
1¼ cups boiling water
1 cup pineapple chunks, drained
1 cup fruit cocktail, drained
1 cup miniature marshmallows
1 cup coconut
2 large bananas, sliced
¾ cup chopped pecans
8 ounces whipped topping
12 ounces cottage cheese

Dissolve gelatin in boiling water in large bowl. Add pineapple chunks, fruit cocktail, marshmallows, coconut, bananas, pecans, whipped topping and cottage cheese; mix well. Spoon into 9x13-inch glass dish. Chill before serving.

Karla Moses, Denton

FRUIT COMPOTE

Yield:
6 servings
Utensil:
large skillet
Approx Per
Serving:
Cal 215
Prot 1 g
Carbo 38 g
Fiber 2 g
T Fat 8 g
Chol 0 mg
Sod 92 mg

Dietary
Exchanges:
Milk 0
Vegetable 0
Fruit 1½
Bread/Starch 0
Meat 0; Fat 2

¼ cup margarine
¾ cup confectioners' sugar
2 teaspoons grated orange rind
1 teaspoon cornstarch
⅓ cup orange juice
2 tablespoons lemon juice
1 cup sliced bananas
1 cup fresh pineapple chunks
1 cup cherries
1 cup blueberries

Melt margarine in large skillet. Add confectioners' sugar, orange rind, cornstarch, orange juice and lemon juice. Cook until slightly thickened, stirring constantly. Fold in bananas, pineapple chunks, cherries and blueberries. Simmer until fruit is warm. Spoon into compote. Serve immediately.

Ruth Kent Eslinger, Winston-Salem

COLD SPICED FRUIT

Yield:
15 servings
Utensil:
serving bowl
Approx Per
Serving:
Cal 174
Prot 1 g
Carbo 46 g
Fiber 2 g
T Fat <1 g
Chol 0 mg
Sod 25 mg

Dietary
Exchanges:
Milk 0
Vegetable 0
Fruit 2
Bread/Starch 1/2
Meat 0; Fat 0

1 20-ounce can pineapple chunks
1 16-ounce can sliced peaches
1 16-ounce can apricots
2 unpeeled oranges, sliced, seeded
1 cup sugar
1/2 cup vinegar
3 cinnamon sticks
5 whole cloves
1 3-ounce package cherry gelatin
1 29-ounce can pears, drained

Drain pineapple, reserving juice. Drain peaches and apricots, reserving half the juices. Cut orange slices into halves. Place orange slices in saucepan; cover with water. Simmer until rind is tender; drain, reserving liquid. Chop oranges. Simmer reserved orange liquid, reserved fruit juices, sugar, vinegar, spices and gelatin in medium saucepan for 30 minutes. Combine pineapple chunks, peaches, apricots, oranges and pears in 9-cup serving bowl. Pour hot juice mixture over fruit. Refrigerate for 24 hours.

Ellie Key, Graham

HOLIDAY SALAD WITH SOUR CREAM DRESSING

Yield:
10 servings
Utensil:
serving dish
Approx Per
Serving:
Cal 169
Prot 3 g
Carbo 30 g
Fiber 1 g
T Fat 6 g
Chol 1 mg
Sod 80 mg

Dietary
Exchanges:
Milk 0
Vegetable 0
Fruit 1
Bread/Starch 1
Meat 0; Fat 1 1/2

1 cup applesauce
1 6-ounce package raspberry gelatin
1 cup orange juice
2 8-ounce cans crushed pineapple, drained
1 teaspoon grated lemon rind
1/2 cup chopped pecans
1 teaspoon grated orange rind
1/4 cup reduced-calorie sour cream
1/4 cup light mayonnaise
1 tablespoon honey
1/8 teaspoon curry powder

Bring applesauce to a boil in saucepan. Dissolve gelatin in applesauce. Add orange juice, crushed pineapple, pecans, lemon rind and orange rind; mix well. Pour into serving dish. Chill until set. Whip sour cream, mayonnaise, honey and curry powder in bowl. Spread over congealed layer. May need to thin dressing with milk.

Frances Thompson, Winston-Salem

ORANGE GELATIN SALAD

Yield:
12 servings
Utensil:
serving dish
Approx Per
Serving:
Cal 191
Prot 5 g
Carbo 29 g
Fiber <1 g
T Fat 7 g
Chol 2 mg
Sod 100 mg

Dietary
Exchanges:
Milk ½
Vegetable 0
Fruit 0
Bread/Starch 1
Meat 0; Fat 1½

1 6-ounce package
   orange gelatin
2 cups boiling water
1 cup marshmallows
1 cup buttermilk

1 8-ounce can
   crushed pineapple
8 ounces whipped
   topping

Dissolve gelatin in boiling water in bowl. Add marshmallows; mix well. Cool slightly. Stir in buttermilk and pineapple. Chill until partially set. Fold in whipped topping. Pour into 9x12-inch serving dish. Chill until serving time.

Mrs. David R. Koontz, Burlington

ORANGE CONGEALED SALAD

Yield:
6 servings
Utensil:
serving bowl
Approx Per
Serving:
Cal 336
Prot 15 g
Carbo 39 g
Fiber <1 g
T Fat 15 g
Chol 7 mg
Sod 339 mg

Dietary
Exchanges:
Milk ½
Vegetable 0
Fruit ½
Bread/Starch 1
Meat 1; Fat 2½

1 3-ounce package
   orange gelatin
8 ounces whipped
   topping
12 ounces low-fat
   cottage cheese

1 8-ounce can
   juice-pack crushed
   pineapple, drained

Fold gelatin into whipped topping in bowl. Add cottage cheese and pineapple, stirring to mix. Spoon into serving bowl. Chill, covered, overnight. May substitute any flavor gelatin.

Eleanor Brooks

Congealed Mandarin Orange Salad

Yield:
8 servings
Utensil:
6-cup ring mold
Approx Per Serving:
Cal 248
Prot 3 g
Carbo 37 g
Fiber 1 g
T Fat 11 g
Chol 8 mg
Sod 153 mg

Dietary Exchanges:
Milk 0
Vegetable ½
Fruit 1
Bread/Starch 1
Meat 0; Fat 2½

2 8-ounce cans crushed pineapple
1 11-ounce can mandarin oranges
2 3-ounce packages orange gelatin
1½ cups hot tea
1 8-ounce can water chestnuts, drained
½ cup mayonnaise
3 tablespoons orange juice
1 tablespoon grated orange rind

Drain pineapple and oranges, reserving juices. Add enough water to reserved juices to measure 1½ cups. Dissolve gelatin in hot tea in bowl. Add reserved juices with water. Chill until partially set. Chop water chestnuts. Fold pineapple, oranges and water chestnuts into gelatin. Spoon into lightly greased 6-cup ring mold. Chill, covered, until firm. Unmold onto lettuce-lined plate. Whip mayonnaise, orange juice and grated orange rind in small bowl. Serve with congealed salad.

Martha M. Wheeler, Chapin, South Carolina

Peach Salad

Yield:
24 servings
Utensil:
glass dish
Approx Per Serving:
Cal 112
Prot 3 g
Carbo 15 g
Fiber <1 g
T Fat 5 g
Chol 1 mg
Sod 60 mg

Dietary Exchanges:
Milk 0
Vegetable 0
Fruit 0
Bread/Starch ½
Meat 0; Fat 1

1 8-ounce can crushed pineapple
2 3-ounce packages peach gelatin
3 tablespoons sugar
8 ounces whipped topping
2 cups buttermilk
½ cup chopped pecans

Combine pineapple with juice, gelatin and sugar in saucepan. Bring to a boil over medium heat, stirring to dissolve gelatin. Let stand until cool. Stir in whipped topping, buttermilk and pecans. Spoon into 9x13-inch glass dish. Chill until set.

Etta Fulp, Kernersville

PHOENIX SALAD

Yield:
10 servings
Utensil:
glass dish
Approx Per
Serving:
Cal 322
Prot 7 g
Carbo 48 g
Fiber 2 g
T Fat 13 g
Chol 56 mg
Sod 107 mg

Dietary
Exchanges:
Milk 0
Vegetable 0
Fruit 1
Bread/Starch 1
Meat 0; Fat 2½

2 3-ounce packages lemon gelatin
2 cups boiling water
1 cup cold water
2 large apples, chopped
1 20-ounce can crushed pineapple
½ cup chopped pecans
2 tablespoons lemon juice
2 eggs, beaten
½ cup sugar
8 ounces whipped topping

Dissolve gelatin in boiling water in bowl. Add cold water. Chill until partially set. Fold in apples, pineapple with juice and pecans. Pour into 8x12-inch glass dish. Chill until set. Combine lemon juice, eggs and sugar in glass bowl. Microwave on High for 4 to 5 minutes, stirring 4 times. Let stand until cool. Fold in whipped topping. Spread over congealed layer. Chill until serving time.

Jack G. Nance, Winston-Salem

PINEAPPLE-CHEESE SALAD

Yield:
6 servings
Utensil:
serving bowl
Approx Per
Serving:
Cal 370
Prot 14 g
Carbo 38 g
Fiber 1 g
T Fat 19 g
Chol 10 mg
Sod 336 mg

Dietary
Exchanges:
Milk ½
Vegetable 0
Fruit ½
Bread/Starch 1
Meat 1; Fat 3½

1 8-ounce can crushed pineapple
1 3-ounce package lime gelatin
2 cups whipped topping
1½ cups cottage cheese
¼ cup pecans

Bring pineapple with juice to a boil in saucepan. Boil for 2 minutes. Add gelatin. Cook for 2 minutes longer, stirring constantly. Let stand until cool. Stir in whipped topping, cottage cheese and pecans. Spoon into serving bowl. Chill until serving time.

Mrs. Atlas T. Newsome, Wilson

SEAFOAM SALAD

Yield:
6 servings
Utensil:
4-cup mold
Approx Per Serving:
Cal 417
Prot 9 g
Carbo 45 g
Fiber 1 g
T Fat 24 g
Chol 34 mg
Sod 201 mg

Dietary Exchanges:
Milk 1/2
Vegetable 0
Fruit 1
Bread/Starch 1
Meat 0; Fat 5

1 20-ounce can pears
1 3-ounce package
   lime gelatin
2 tablespoons milk

6 ounces cream cheese,
   softened
1 envelope whipped
   topping mix

Drain pears, reserving juice. Mash pears. Bring reserved juice to a boil in saucepan. Dissolve gelatin in juice. Blend milk and cream cheese in bowl. Stir in gelatin mixture. Add mashed pears; mix well. Prepare whipped topping mix using package directions. Fold into gelatin mixture. Pour into 4-cup mold. Chill until set. Unmold onto serving plate.

Ruth C. Cline, Winston-Salem

STRAWBERRY DELIGHT SALAD

Yield:
12 servings
Utensil:
glass dish
Approx Per Serving:
Cal 253
Prot 4 g
Carbo 31 g
Fiber 2 g
T Fat 14 g
Chol 29 mg
Sod 113 mg

Dietary Exchanges:
Milk 0
Vegetable 0
Fruit 1/2
Bread/Starch 1
Meat 0; Fat 3 1/2

2 3-ounce packages
   strawberry gelatin
2 cups boiling water
1 16-ounce package
   frozen strawberries
2 8-ounce cans
   crushed pineapple

8 ounces cream cheese,
   softened
1/2 cup sugar
1 cup sour cream
1/2 teaspoon vanilla
   extract
1/2 cup chopped pecans

Dissolve gelatin in boiling water in large bowl. Add strawberries, stirring until thawed. Stir in crushed pineapple with juice. Pour into 8x12-inch glass dish. Chill for 2 hours to overnight. Whip cream cheese and sugar in bowl until fluffy. Blend in sour cream and vanilla. Spread over congealed layer. Sprinkle with pecans. Chill before serving.

Carol Sawyer, Whitsett

STRAWBERRY-PRETZEL SALAD

Yield:
12 servings
Utensil:
baking dish
Approx Per
Serving:
Cal 461
Prot 8 g
Carbo 54 g
Fiber 1 g
T Fat 26 g
Chol 22 mg
Sod 496 mg

Dietary
Exchanges:
Milk 0
Vegetable 0
Fruit 1
Bread/Starch 1½
Meat 0; Fat 6

¾ cup margarine,
  softened
3 tablespoons sugar
2½ cups coarsely
  crushed pretzels
1 6-ounce package
  strawberry gelatin

2 cups boiling water
1 cup cold water
3 cups strawberries
1 cup sugar
8 ounces cream cheese
8 ounces whipped
  topping

Combine ¾ cup margarine, 3 tablespoons sugar and pretzels in bowl; mix well. Press into greased 9x13-inch baking dish. Bake at 350 degrees for 10 minutes. Let stand until cool. Dissolve gelatin in boiling water in large bowl. Add cold water. Stir in strawberries. Chill until partially set. Cream remaining 1 cup sugar and cream cheese in mixer bowl until smooth. Fold in whipped topping. Spread over cooled pretzel crust. Pour gelatin mixture over cream cheese layer. Chill until set.

Rebecca Matthews, Clemmons

STRAWBERRY CONGEALED SALAD

Yield:
8 servings
Utensil:
glass dish
Approx Per
Serving:
Cal 443
Prot 9 g
Carbo 50 g
Fiber 2 g
T Fat 25 g
Chol 33 mg
Sod 204 mg

Dietary
Exchanges:
Milk ½
Vegetable 0
Fruit 1
Bread/Starch 1
Meat 0; Fat 6

1 6-ounce package
  strawberry gelatin
1 cup boiling water
2 cups strawberries
1 16-ounce can
  crushed pineapple
1 cup miniature
  marshmallows

8 ounces cream cheese,
  softened
2 cups whipped
  topping
½ cup chopped pecans

Dissolve gelatin in boiling water in large bowl. Add strawberries and pineapple with juice; mix well. Pour into 8x12-inch glass dish. Top with marshmallows. Chill overnight. Combine cream cheese and whipped topping in bowl. Whip until smooth. Spread over congealed layer. Sprinkle with pecans. Chill in refrigerator.

Bonnie Helsabeck

DATE WALDORF SALAD

Yield:
12 servings
Utensil:
large bowl
Approx Per
Serving:
Cal 208
Prot 3 g
Carbo 23 g
Fiber 3 g
T Fat 13 g
Chol 6 mg
Sod 75 mg

Dietary
Exchanges:
Milk 0
Vegetable 0
Fruit 1
Bread/Starch 0
Meat 0; Fat 0

Sections and juice of 2 oranges
4 apples, coarsely chopped
2/3 cup pitted dates, chopped
2/3 cup sliced celery
1/2 cup chopped walnuts
1/2 cup mayonnaise
1 cup whipped topping

Combine orange sections, orange juice, apples, dates, celery and walnuts in large bowl; toss gently. Whip mayonnaise and whipped topping in small bowl. Pour over fruit; toss to coat. Spoon coated fruit into lettuce-lined bowl. Chill in refrigerator.

Fran Grinstead, Snow Camp

WATERGATE SALAD

Yield:
6 servings
Utensil:
large bowl
Approx Per
Serving:
Cal 588
Prot 11 g
Carbo 73 g
Fiber 2 g
T Fat 31 g
Chol 4 mg
Sod 216 mg

Dietary
Exchanges:
Milk 1/2
Vegetable 0
Fruit 1
Bread/Starch 1
Meat 0; Fat 6 1/2

1 3-ounce package pistachio instant pudding mix
16 ounces whipped topping
1 20-ounce can crushed pineapple
1 1/2 cups miniature marshmallows
1/2 cup chopped pecans

Combine pudding mix, whipped topping, pineapple with juice, marshmallows and pecans in large bowl; mix well. Chill for several hours to overnight. Serve on lettuce-lined plate.

Thelma L. Wilson, Winston-Salem

GALE'S BEACH PASTA AND ROAST BEEF SALAD

Yield:
4 servings
Utensil:
large bowl
Approx Per Serving:
Cal 987
Prot 56 g
Carbo 87 g
Fiber 9 g
T Fat 45 g
Chol 114 mg
Sod 238 mg

Dietary Exchanges:
Milk 0
Vegetable 1
Fruit 0
Bread/Starch 6½
Meat 5; Fat 5½

1 16-ounce package "veggie pasta"
2 green onions, chopped
1 carrot, thinly sliced
1 stalk celery, chopped
1 tomato, chopped
4 large mushrooms, thinly sliced
6 slices roast beef, chopped
2 tablespoons Dijon mustard
2 tablespoons red wine vinegar
½ cup olive oil
1 tablespoon dill dip seasoning mix

Cook pasta using package directions; drain. Combine with green onions, carrot, celery, tomato, mushrooms and roast beef in large bowl; mix well. Blend mustard and vinegar in small bowl. Add oil and dill seasoning, stirring well. Pour over salad; toss gently to coat.

Gale Owens, Greensboro

ALABAMA CHICKEN SALAD

Yield:
8 servings
Utensil:
large bowl
Approx Per Serving:
Cal 731
Prot 22 g
Carbo 36 g
Fiber 3 g
T Fat 57 g
Chol 80 mg
Sod 604 mg

Dietary Exchanges:
Milk 0
Vegetable 0
Fruit 1
Bread/Starch 1
Meat 3; Fat 11½

4 cups chopped cooked chicken
2 teaspoons oil
2 teaspoons orange juice
2 teaspoons vinegar
1 teaspoon salt
3 cups cooked rice
1½ cups green seedless grapes
1 13-ounce can crushed pineapple, drained
1 11-ounce can mandarin oranges, drained
1 cup toasted slivered almonds
2 cups mayonnaise

Combine chicken, oil, orange juice, vinegar and salt in large bowl; set aside. Combine cooked rice, grapes, pineapple, mandarin oranges, almonds and mayonnaise in medium bowl; mix well. Add to chicken mixture; stir well. Serve on lettuce-lined salad plates. May substitute 1 cup light mayonnaise mixed with 1 cup yogurt for 2 cups mayonnaise.

Jean Creed May, Greensboro

CURRIED CHICKEN AND ORANGE SALAD

Yield:
8 servings
Utensil:
large bowl
Approx Per
Serving:
Cal 270
Prot 12 g
Carbo 10 g
Fiber 2 g
T Fat 22 g
Chol 37 mg
Sod 169 mg

Dietary
Exchanges:
Milk 0
Vegetable 0
Fruit ½
Bread/Starch 0
Meat 1½; Fat 4

3 chicken breasts, cooked, cubed
1 2-ounce can black olives, drained, sliced
1 2-ounce package toasted slivered almonds
½ cup chopped red onion
1 11-ounce can mandarin oranges
½ cup plus 2 tablespoons mayonnaise
1 tablespoon lemon juice
1 teaspoon curry powder

Combine chicken, olives, almonds and onion in medium bowl. Drain mandarin oranges, reserving 2 tablespoons juice and 8 orange slices. Combine reserved orange juice, mayonnaise, lemon juice and curry powder in small bowl; mix well. Pour over chicken mixture, stirring gently. Add mandarin oranges; toss gently. Chill, covered, for 1 hour. Serve on lettuce-lined serving plates. Garnish with reserved mandarin orange slices.

Elaine Ruth Morrison, Hobe Sound, Florida

FRUITED CHICKEN SALAD

Yield:
5 servings
Utensil:
large bowl
Approx Per
Serving:
Cal 362
Prot 30 g
Carbo 18 g
Fiber 2 g
T Fat 20 g
Chol 90 mg
Sod 543 mg

Dietary
Exchanges:
Vegetable ½
Fruit 1
Bread/Starch 0
Meat 3½
Fat 2½

4 cups chopped cooked chicken breasts
2 cups chopped celery
2 cups seedless grape halves
¼ cup slivered almonds
1 cup drained unsweetened crushed pineapple
1 teaspoon salt
½ cup sour cream
2 tablespoons mayonnaise

Combine chicken, celery, grapes, almonds, pineapple and salt in large bowl. Blend sour cream and mayonnaise in small bowl. Add to chicken mixture; stir well. Chill in refrigerator. Serve on lettuce-lined serving plate.

Lorraine Taylor, Greensboro

CHICKEN SALAD AND RICE-A-RONI

Yield:
8 servings
Utensil:
large bowl
**Approx Per
Serving:**
Cal 299
Prot 18 g
Carbo 21 g
Fiber 3 g
T Fat 17 g
Chol 50 mg
Sod 504 mg

**Dietary
Exchanges:**
Milk 0
Vegetable 1½
Fruit 0
Bread/Starch 1
Meat 2; Fat 2½

1 5-ounce package chicken-flavored Rice-A-Roni
2 9-ounce jars marinated artichoke hearts
2 whole cooked chicken breasts, boned, chopped
¾ cup chopped celery
6 green onions, chopped
½ green bell pepper, chopped
12 stuffed green olives, sliced
½ cup mayonnaise
1 teaspoon curry powder

Prepare rice using package directions; drain. Drain and chop artichokes, reserving juice. Combine rice, artichokes and chicken in large bowl. Add celery, green onions, green pepper and olives; mix well. Combine mayonnaise, curry powder and reserved artichoke juice in small bowl; mix well. Pour over chicken mixture; mix well. Serve on lettuce-lined serving plates.

Elaine Ruth Morrison, Hobe Sound, Florida

CHOPPED EGG MOLD

Yield:
6 servings
Utensil:
3-cup mold
**Approx Per
Serving:**
Cal 309
Prot 13 g
Carbo 3 g
Fiber 1 g
T Fat 27 g
Chol 590 mg
Sod 848 mg

**Dietary
Exchanges:**
Milk 0
Vegetable ½
Fruit 0
Bread/Starch 0
Meat 2; Fat 4½

12 hard-boiled eggs, chopped
½ cup melted butter
1½ teaspoons salt
2 tablespoons prepared mustard
1 onion, finely chopped
1 tablespoon half and half
½ teaspoon poppy seed
½ teaspoon caraway seed

Combine eggs, butter, salt, mustard, onion, half and half, poppy seed and caraway seed in bowl; mix well. Spoon into 3-cup mold. Chill in refrigerator until firm. Unmold onto serving plate.

Mrs. Coy M. Vance, Raleigh

Macaroni Salad

1 8-ounce package macaroni
¼ cup French salad dressing
1 cup mayonnaise
¾ cup sliced olives
1 onion, finely chopped
2 tomatoes, chopped
1 cup shredded sharp Cheddar cheese
1 teaspoon salt
¼ teaspoon pepper

Cook macaroni using package directions; drain well. Pour in large salad bowl. Add salad dressing; stir well. Chill in refrigerator for 30 minutes. Add mayonnaise, olives, onion, tomatoes, Cheddar cheese, salt and pepper; mix well. Serve chilled.

Lottie Dix, Greensboro

Macaroni-Cheese-Bacon Salad

1 8-ounce package macaroni and cheese dinner
4 hard-boiled eggs, sliced
¼ cup chopped green bell pepper
6 slices crisp-fried bacon, crumbled
2 tablespoons chopped onion
Salt and pepper to taste
¼ cup (about) mayonnaise

Prepare macaroni and cheese dinner using package directions; let stand until cool. Combine with sliced eggs, green pepper, bacon, onion, salt and pepper in large bowl; mix well. Add mayonnaise, stirring well to moisten.

Dot Smith, Haw River

Pasta Salad

1 8-ounce package sea shell macaroni
1 6-ounce package salami, chopped
·1 6-ounce package Swiss cheese, cubed
1 cup cherry tomato halves
2 green bell peppers, chopped
1/2 cup chopped celery
1/2 cup chopped black olives
3/4 cup Italian salad dressing
1/4 teaspoon celery seed

Cook macaroni using package directions; drain. Combine with salami, Swiss cheese, tomatoes, green peppers, celery and black olives in large bowl; mix well. Add Italian salad dressing and celery seed; stir well to moisten. Chill in refrigerator overnight.

Doris Boyles, Winston-Salem

Spaghetti Salad

1 16-ounce package spaghetti
2 8-ounce bottles of Italian salad dressing
1 3-ounce jar Salad Supreme seasoning
1 tomato, peeled, chopped
1 cucumber, peeled, seeded, chopped
1 purple onion, chopped

Break spaghetti into thirds. Cook using package directions; drain. Combine with Italian salad dressing, salad seasoning, tomato, cucumber and onion in large bowl; mix well. Chill for 2 hours before serving, stirring occasionally.

Nutritional information does not include Salad Supreme seasoning.

Betty Kye Bailey, Winston-Salem

Lemon-Rice Salad with Peanuts

Yield:
6 servings
Utensil:
large bowl
Approx Per Serving:
Cal 360
Prot 7 g
Carbo 40 g
Fiber 2 g
T Fat 20 g
Chol 0 mg
Sod 983 mg

Dietary Exchanges:
Milk 0
Vegetable 0
Fruit 0
Bread/Starch 2½
Meat ½; Fat 3½

4 quarts water
1 tablespoon salt
1½ cups uncooked long-grain rice
½ cup unsalted dry-roasted peanuts, coarsely chopped
3 green onions, chopped
½ cup minced fresh parsley
¾ teaspoon grated lemon zest
3 tablespoons lemon juice
Salt and pepper to taste
6 tablespoons olive oil

Bring water with salt to a boil in saucepan. Add rice. Cook over high heat for 10 minutes. Drain into colander; place colander over large saucepan of boiling water. Steam, covered, for 15 minutes or until fluffy and dry. Combine with peanuts, green onions and parsley in large bowl; mix well. Combine lemon zest, lemon juice, salt and pepper in small bowl. Whisk in oil, blending well. Pour over rice mixture; mix well. Chill in refrigerator before serving.

Joe Tarnowsky, Greensboro

Rice Salad

Yield:
4 servings
Utensil:
medium bowl
Approx Per Serving:
Cal 304
Prot 6 g
Carbo 41 g
Fiber 5 g
T Fat 14 g
Chol 8 mg
Sod 761 mg

Dietary Exchanges:
Milk 0
Vegetable 3
Fruit 0
Bread/Starch 2
Meat 0; Fat 3

1 5-ounce package chicken-flavored Rice-A-Roni
8 stuffed green olives, sliced
½ green bell pepper, chopped
1 bunch green onions, minced
¼ cup mayonnaise
¼ teaspoon curry powder
Salt and pepper to taste
2 9-ounce jars artichoke hearts

Prepare rice using package directions; drain and cool. Combine with olives, green pepper, green onions, mayonnaise, curry powder, salt and pepper in medium bowl; mix well. Drain and chop artichokes, reserving liquid. Pour enough reserved liquid over rice to moisten; stir well. Add chopped artichokes; mix well. Chill in refrigerator before serving.

Dot Chrismon

TUNA SALAD

Yield:
6 servings
Utensil:
large bowl
Approx Per
Serving:
Cal 540
Prot 22 g
Carbo 53 g
Fiber 4 g
T Fat 26 g
Chol 24 mg
Sod 435 mg

Dietary
Exchanges:
Milk 0
Vegetable 1/2
Fruit 0
Bread/Starch 3 1/2
Meat 1 1/2; Fat 5

1   12-ounce package macaroni
1   9-ounce can tuna, drained
1   8-ounce can green peas, drained
1 onion, chopped
1   2-ounce jar chopped pimento, drained
2 sweet pickles, chopped
3/4 cup mayonnaise
Salt and pepper to taste

Cook macaroni using package directions; drain. Combine macaroni with tuna, peas, onion, pimento and pickles in large bowl; mix well. Add mayonnaise, salt and pepper; stir well to moisten. Chill in refrigerator before serving.

Mary Howell, Snow Camp

LIGHT TACO SALAD

Yield:
6 servings
Utensil:
skillet
Approx Per
Serving:
Cal 508
Prot 32 g
Carbo 42 g
Fiber 3 g
T Fat 25 g
Chol 64 mg
Sod 1497 mg

Dietary
Exchanges:
Milk 0
Vegetable 2
Bread/Starch 1 1/2
Meat 3 1/2
Fat 4 1/2

1 pound ground turkey
1 tablespoon olive oil
1 onion, chopped
1/2 teaspoon garlic powder
1 envelope taco seasoning mix
2 drops of Tabasco sauce
1   15-ounce can tomato sauce
2 to 3 tomatoes, chopped
2 cups shredded Mexican cheese
1 head lettuce, shredded
6 taco shell bowls
6 tablespoons reduced-calorie sour cream
1   2-ounce can chopped black olives

Brown ground turkey in oil in skillet, stirring until crumbly; drain. Add onion and garlic powder. Cook until onion is tender. Add taco seasoning, Tabasco sauce and tomato sauce. Simmer over low heat for 30 minutes. Layer 3 tablespoons filling, tomatoes and cheese in lettuce-lined shells. Top each with 1 tablespoon sour cream and 1 teaspoon olives. Serve while filling is warm.

Nancy Garner, Burlington

SHRIMP SALAD

Yield:
12 servings
Utensil:
large bowl
Approx Per
Serving:
Cal 549
Prot 33 g
Carbo 35 g
Fiber 3 g
T Fat 30 g
Chol 377 mg
Sod 586 mg

Dietary
Exchanges:
Milk 0
Vegetable 1/2
Fruit 0
Bread/Starch 2
Meat 3; Fat 6

1 16-ounce package elbow macaroni
3 pounds cooked, peeled shrimp
1 cup mayonnaise-type salad dressing
6 hard-boiled eggs, chopped
2 green bell peppers, chopped
4 green onions, finely chopped
3 cucumbers, thinly sliced
1 6-ounce jar mushroom pieces
Salt and pepper to taste
1 cup mayonnaise-type salad dressing
1/4 cup catsup
2 tablespoons prepared mustard
2 tablespoons prepared horseradish

Cook macaroni using package directions; drain. Let stand until cooled. Combine with shrimp in large bowl. Add 1 cup salad dressing, stirring well to moisten. Add next 7 ingredients; mix well. Blend 1 cup salad dressing, catsup, mustard and horseradish in small bowl. Add to macaroni mixture; stir well. Chill before serving. May store in refrigerator for up to 4 days.

Phyllis Lennon

MARINATED ASPARAGUS

Yield:
6 servings
Utensil:
bowl
Approx Per
Serving:
Cal 332
Prot 3 g
Carbo 22 g
Fiber 2 g
T Fat 28 g
Chol 0 mg
Sod 500 mg

Dietary
Exchanges:
Milk 0
Vegetable 1 1/2
Fruit 0
Bread/Starch 0
Meat 0; Fat 5 1/2

2 14-ounce cans asparagus, drained
1 green bell pepper, chopped
1 bunch green onions, chopped
1 stalk celery, finely chopped
1/2 cup wine vinegar
1/2 cup sugar
1/2 clove of garlic
1/4 teaspoon paprika
3/4 cup oil

Combine asparagus, green pepper, green onions and celery in bowl. Mix vinegar, sugar, garlic and paprika together in small bowl. Add oil, stirring vigorously. Pour over asparagus; stir gently. Marinate in refrigerator for 4 to 5 hours.

Phyllis Lennon

PETE'S GREEN BEAN SALAD

Yield:
2 servings
Utensil:
medium bowl
**Approx Per
Serving:**
Cal 412
Prot 15 g
Carbo 16 g
Fiber 2 g
T Fat 34 g
Chol 58 mg
Sod 1283 mg

**Dietary
Exchanges:**
Milk 0
Vegetable 2
Bread/Starch 0
Meat 2½
Fat 5½

2 cups cooked green beans
4 hot dogs, chopped
3 green onions, chopped

3 teaspoons wine vinegar
¼ cup white vinegar

Combine green beans, hot dogs and green onions in medium bowl; mix well. Mix wine vinegar and white vinegar in small cup. Pour over green beans, stirring well.

"Pete" Jones, Winston-Salem

MARINATED BROCCOLI

Yield:
8 servings
Utensil:
bowl
**Approx Per
Serving:**
Cal 406
Prot 4 g
Carbo 11 g
Fiber 5 g
T Fat 41 g
Chol 0 mg
Sod 537 mg

**Dietary
Exchanges:**
Milk 0
Vegetable 1½
Fruit 0
Bread/Starch 0
Meat 0; Fat 8

1 cup cider vinegar
1 tablespoon sugar
1 tablespoon dill seed
1 tablespoon Accent
1 teaspoon salt

1 teaspoon pepper
1 teaspoon garlic salt
1½ cups oil
Flowerets of 3 bunches broccoli

Mix vinegar, sugar, dill seed, Accent, salt, pepper and garlic salt in bowl. Stir in oil. Pour marinade over broccoli in bowl. Chill, covered, for 24 hours, basting occasionally with marinade. Drain before serving.

Nutritional information includes entire amount of marinade.

Fay B. Tuttle

BROCCOLI SALAD

Yield:
8 servings
Utensil:
medium bowl
Approx Per
Serving:
Cal 207
Prot 5 g
Carbo 8 g
Fiber 1 g
T Fat 18 g
Chol 145 mg
Sod 324 mg

Dietary
Exchanges:
Milk 0
Vegetable 1/2
Fruit 1/2
Bread/Starch 0
Meat 1/2; Fat 31/2

Flowerets of 1 bunch broccoli
1 tablespoon (heaping) chopped onion
4 hard-boiled eggs, chopped
1/3 cup raisins
1/4 cup bacon bits
1/2 teaspoon sugar
1/2 cup mayonnaise
2 teaspoons lemon juice
1 tablespoon vinegar
2 tablespoons oil
1/2 teaspoon salt
1/4 teaspoon pepper

Combine broccoli, onion, eggs, raisins and bacon bits in medium bowl. Mix sugar, mayonnaise, lemon juice, vinegar, oil, salt and pepper in small bowl; stir well. Pour over broccoli; mix well to coat. Marinate in refrigerator for 6 to 8 hours.

Alice K. Neese, Elon College

BROCCOLI AND CAULIFLOWER SALAD

Yield:
8 servings
Utensil:
bowl
Approx Per
Serving:
Cal 100
Prot 4 g
Carbo 4 g
Fiber 2 g
T Fat 8 g
Chol 142 mg
Sod 196 mg

Dietary
Exchanges:
Milk 0
Vegetable 1/2
Fruit 0
Bread/Starch 0
Meat 1/2; Fat 11/2

Flowerets of 1 bunch broccoli, chopped
Flowerets of 1 head cauliflower, chopped
1 bunch green onions, chopped
4 hard-boiled eggs, chopped
15 green olives, sliced
1 tablespoon lemon juice
Salt and pepper to taste
1/2 cup reduced-calorie mayonnaise

Combine broccoli, cauliflower, green onions, eggs and olives in bowl; stir well. Blend lemon juice, salt, pepper and mayonnaise in small bowl. Pour over broccoli; mix well. Chill in refrigerator before serving.

Nancy Garner, Burlington

Marinated Vegetables

Yield:
6 servings
Utensil:
saucepan
**Approx Per
Serving:**
Cal 296
Prot 2 g
Carbo 14 g
Fiber 4 g
T Fat 27 g
Chol 0 mg
Sod 32 mg

**Dietary
Exchanges:**
Milk 0
Vegetable 1½
Fruit 0
Bread/Starch 0
Meat 0; Fat 5½

Flowerets of 1 bunch
  broccoli
Flowerets of 1 head
  cauliflower
4 carrots, thinly sliced
1 cup cherry tomatoes
3 tablespoons lemon
  juice

2 tablespoons sugar
3 tablespoons red
  wine vinegar
¾ teaspoon chervil
¼ teaspoon oregano
¼ teaspoon red pepper
¾ cup olive oil

Place broccoli, cauliflower and carrots in saucepan containing 1 inch boiling water. Reduce heat. Simmer for 10 minutes; drain. Combine with tomatoes in large bowl. Mix lemon juice, sugar, vinegar, chervil, oregano, red pepper and oil in small bowl. Pour over vegetables. Chill, covered, for 24 hours, stirring occasionally.

Fay B. Tuttle

Merle's Four "C" Salad

Yield:
8 servings
Utensil:
7-cup salad mold
**Approx Per
Serving:**
Cal 159
Prot 4 g
Carbo 15 g
Fiber 1 g
T Fat 10 g
Chol 31 mg
Sod 141 mg

**Dietary
Exchanges:**
Milk 0
Vegetable ½
Fruit 0
Bread/Starch ½
Meat 0; Fat 2½

1 cup finely shredded
  cabbage
1 cup grated carrots
1 cup chopped celery
1   3-ounce package
  lime gelatin

1 cup boiling water
8 ounces cream cheese,
  softened
7 ounces ginger ale

Combine cabbage, carrots and celery in large bowl. Chill, covered, in refrigerator. Dissolve gelatin in boiling water in bowl. Beat cream cheese until fluffy. Add to gelatin mixture, stirring until smooth. Add ginger ale. Chill in refrigerator until partially set. Add vegetables to gelatin mixture; mix well. Spoon into 7-cup salad mold. Chill until firm. Unmold onto serving plate.

Mrs. Roy T. Rhue, Newport

CHINESE SALAD

Yield:
8 servings
Utensil:
salad bowl
Approx Per
Serving:
Cal 261
Prot 6 g
Carbo 19 g
Fiber 2 g
T Fat 19 g
Chol 10 mg
Sod 602 mg

Dietary
Exchanges:
Milk 0
Vegetable 1
Fruit 0
Bread/Starch ½
Meat ½; Fat 4

1 8-ounce can water chestnuts, drained
1 5-ounce can chow mein noodles
1 small head cabbage, shredded
½ cup almond slivers
1 4-ounce package small mushrooms, chopped
4 green onions, chopped
½ cup mayonnaise
¼ cup soy sauce

Toast water chestnuts and noodles. Combine with cabbage, almonds, mushrooms and green onions in salad bowl; mix well. Stir in mixture of mayonnaise and soy sauce. Chill until serving time.

Luci B. Wilson, Winston-Salem

SWEET AND SOUR SLAW

Yield:
12 servings
Utensil:
large bowl
Approx Per
Serving:
Cal 127
Prot <1 g
Carbo 35 g
Fiber 1 g
T Fat <1 g
Chol 0 mg
Sod 986 mg

Dietary
Exchanges:
Milk 0
Vegetable ½
Fruit 0
Bread/Starch 0
Meat 0; Fat 0

½ head cabbage, shredded
½ cup shredded carrot
½ cup chopped green bell pepper
½ cup chopped celery
¼ cup chopped onion
1 clove of garlic, minced
2 tablespoons salt
2 cups sugar
1 cup cider vinegar
1 cup water

Combine cabbage, carrot, green pepper, celery, onion and garlic in large bowl; mix well. Sprinkle with salt. Cover with cold water. Chill, tightly covered, for 1 hour; drain. Mix sugar, vinegar and 1 cup water in saucepan. Bring to a boil, stirring to dissolve sugar. Let stand until cool. Pour over salad mixture; toss well. Refrigerate for 4 to 6 hours, stirring occasionally. May keep for up to one month in refrigerator.

Mrs. J.C. Kuley, Bethania

FREEZER COLESLAW

1 head cabbage,
  shredded
1 teaspoon salt
1 carrot, shredded
1 green bell pepper,
  chopped

1 cup vinegar
1/4 cup water
1 cup sugar
1 teaspoon dry mustard
1 teaspoon celery seed

Sprinkle cabbage with salt in large bowl. Let stand for 30 minutes; squeeze out excess moisture. Add carrot and green pepper. Mix vinegar, water, sugar, mustard and celery seed in saucepan. Bring to a boil. Boil for 1 minute, stirring constantly; cool. Pour over salad mixture; toss well. Spoon into airtight containers. Store in freezer.

Mary Pickett, Winston-Salem

LEXINGTON BARBECUE SLAW

4 cups chopped
  cabbage
1/4 cup sugar
1/2 teaspoon black
  pepper

Dash of red pepper
1 teaspoon salt
1/3 cup catsup
2 tablespoons white
  vinegar

Combine cabbage, sugar, black pepper, red pepper and salt in large bowl. Add catsup and vinegar; toss well to mix. Chill, covered, in refrigerator for 2 to 3 hours.

Mildred B. Johnson

MARINATED CUCUMBER SALAD

Yield:
8 servings
Utensil:
small bowl
Approx Per Serving:
Cal 42
Prot 2 g
Carbo 11 g
Fiber 3 g
T Fat <1 g
Chol 0 mg
Sod 5 mg

Dietary Exchanges:
Milk 0
Vegetable 1½
Fruit 0
Bread/Starch 0
Meat 0; Fat 0

4 cucumbers, thinly sliced
1 red bell pepper, finely chopped
3 white onions, thinly sliced
1 cup white vinegar
2 tablespoons water

Combine cucumbers, red pepper and onions in bowl. Mix vinegar and water in small bowl. Pour over cucumber mixture. Marinate in refrigerator overnight.

Ruby Hudspeth, Yadkinville

CUCUMBER SALAD

Yield:
8 servings
Utensil:
bowl
Approx Per Serving:
Cal 40
Prot 1 g
Carbo 4 g
Fiber 2 g
T Fat 3 g
Chol 2 mg
Sod 275 mg

Dietary Exchanges:
Milk 0
Vegetable ½
Fruit 0
Bread/Starch 0
Meat 0; Fat ½

1 teaspoon salt
3 cucumbers, peeled, sliced
2 tablespoons mayonnaise
1 teaspoon Dijon mustard
1 clove of garlic, crushed
Dash of white pepper
1 tablespoon chopped fresh dill

Sprinkle salt over cucumbers in colander; toss well. Drain for 30 minutes; rinse, pat dry. Combine mayonnaise, mustard, garlic and white pepper in bowl; stir well. Add cucumbers; toss well. Sprinkle with dill. Chill, covered, for 2 to 3 hours. Remove garlic before serving.

Mrs. J.C. Kuley, Bethania

CHRISTMAS SALAD

Yield:
8 servings
Utensil:
glass container
Approx Per
Serving:
Cal 223
Prot 3 g
Carbo 59 g
Fiber 2 g
T Fat <1 g
Chol 0 mg
Sod 504 mg

Dietary
Exchanges:
Milk 0
Vegetable 2
Fruit 0
Bread/Starch 0
Meat 0; Fat 0

1 20-ounce can sauerkraut, drained
1 20-ounce can bean sprouts, drained
1 2-ounce jar chopped pimento, drained
2 cups chopped celery
1 large onion, chopped
1 green bell pepper, chopped
2 cups sugar
3/4 cup vinegar

Combine sauerkraut, bean sprouts and pimento in bowl; mix well. Add celery, onion and green pepper; stir well. Add sugar and vinegar; mix well. Spoon mixture into 1/2-gallon glass container. Chill, covered, for 2 days in refrigerator; do not stir.

Jane Dalton, Winston-Salem

SAUERKRAUT SALAD

Yield:
12 servings
Utensil:
large bowl
Approx Per
Serving:
Cal 161
Prot 1 g
Carbo 29 g
Fiber 1 g
T Fat 6 g
Chol 0 mg
Sod 513 mg

Dietary
Exchanges:
Milk 0
Vegetable 1 1/2
Fruit 0
Bread/Starch 0
Meat 0; Fat 1

2 16-ounce cans sauerkraut, drained
1 cup chopped celery
1 cup chopped green onions
1 8-ounce can water chestnuts, drained, sliced
1/4 cup grated carrot
1 cup chopped green bell pepper
2 tablespoons chopped pimento
2/3 cup vinegar
1/3 cup oil
1/3 cup water
1 1/4 cups sugar

Combine sauerkraut, celery, green onions, water chestnuts, carrot, green pepper and pimento in large bowl; mix well. Mix vinegar, oil, water and sugar in small bowl; stir vigorously. Pour over sauerkraut mixture, stirring to coat. Chill, covered, overnight.

Bettie Duggins, Kernersville

KIT'S SPINACH SALAD

Yield:
8 servings
Utensil:
serving dish
Approx Per
Serving:
Cal 299
Prot 8 g
Carbo 16 g
Fiber 2 g
T Fat 24 g
Chol 22 mg
Sod 627 mg

Dietary
Exchanges:
Milk 0
Vegetable 1
Fruit 0
Bread/Starch 1/2
Meat 1; Fat 5

1 3-ounce package lime gelatin
1 cup boiling water
1 cucumber, chopped
2 stalks celery, chopped
1 1/3 cups cottage cheese
1 onion, chopped
1 teaspoon salt
1 10-ounce package frozen chopped spinach, thawed, drained
1 cup mayonnaise
3 tablespoons vinegar

Dissolve gelatin in boiling water in large bowl. Add cucumber, celery, cottage cheese, onion, salt, spinach, mayonnaise and vinegar; mix well. Spoon into 7x12-inch serving dish or mold. Chill until firm. Unmold onto serving plate.

Martha H. Hashinger, Greensboro

SEVEN-LAYER SALAD

Yield:
12 servings
Utensil:
9x13-inch dish
Approx Per
Serving:
Cal 257
Prot 6 g
Carbo 10 g
Fiber 2 g
T Fat 22 g
Chol 24 mg
Sod 424 mg

Dietary
Exchanges:
Milk 0
Vegetable 1/2
Fruit 0
Bread/Starch 1/2
Meat 1/2; Fat 5

1 cup mayonnaise
1 cup sour cream
1/2 head lettuce, torn
1 cup chopped green pepper
1 large onion, sliced
1 16-ounce can peas, drained
1/2 cup shredded Cheddar cheese
1 3-ounce jar bacon bits

Blend mayonnaise and sour cream in small bowl. Layer lettuce, green pepper, onion, peas, sour cream mixture, cheese and bacon bits in 9x13-inch dish. Chill, covered, for 24 hours.

Doris Whitesell

LAYERED SALAD

Yield:
12 servings
Utensil:
9x13-inch dish
**Approx Per
Serving:**
Cal 417
Prot 14 g
Carbo 12 g
Fiber 2 g
T Fat 35 g
Chol 181 mg
Sod 700 mg

**Dietary
Exchanges:**
Milk 0
Vegetable 1/2
Bread/Starch 1/2
Meat 1 1/2
Fat 7 1/2

1/2 head romaine
  lettuce
6 hard-boiled eggs,
  sliced
1 cup shredded Swiss
  cheese
1 pound spinach, torn
1 10-ounce package
  frozen tiny peas,
  thawed, drained

1 red onion, sliced
  into rings
1 pound bacon,
  crisp-fried,
  crumbled
1 cup mayonnaise
1 cup salad dressing
1 teaspoon sugar
1 cup shredded
  Cheddar cheese

Layer lettuce leaves, sliced eggs, 1/4 cup Swiss cheese, spinach, 1/4 cup Swiss cheese, peas, 1/4 cup Swiss cheese, onion rings, 1/4 cup Swiss cheese and bacon in 9x13-inch dish. Combine mayonnaise, salad dressing and sugar in small bowl; blend well. Spread over top of salad sealing to edges. Sprinkle Cheddar cheese over top. Chill, covered, for several hours. Cut into squares to serve.

Mary Kiser

LUCKY BLACK-EYED PEA SALAD

Yield:
6 servings
Utensil:
large bowl
**Approx Per
Serving:**
Cal 258
Prot 13 g
Carbo 32 g
Fiber 10 g
T Fat 11 g
Chol 0 mg
Sod 403 mg

**Dietary
Exchanges:**
Milk 0
Vegetable 1/2
Fruit 0
Bread/Starch 2
Meat 0; Fat 2 1/2

2 15-ounce cans
  black-eyed peas,
  drained
1/2 cup chopped red
  bell pepper
1/2 cup chopped green
  bell pepper
1/2 cup thinly sliced
  celery

1/2 cup sliced black
  olives
1/4 cup minced green
  onions
1/4 cup Italian salad
  dressing
1/4 cup chili sauce
2 tablespoons bacon bits

Combine black-eyed peas, red pepper, green pepper, celery, olives and green onions in large bowl. Stir in mixture of salad dressing and chili sauce. Chill, covered, overnight. Top with bacon bits before serving. May substitute taco sauce for chili sauce.

Betty J. Brandt, Ocala, Florida

Potato Salad

Yield:
10 servings
Utensil:
large bowl
Approx Per
Serving:
Cal 200
Prot 4 g
Carbo 23 g
Fiber 2 g
T Fat 11 g
Chol 64 mg
Sod 418 mg

Dietary
Exchanges:
Milk 0
Vegetable 0
Fruit 0
Bread/Starch 1
Meat 1/2; Fat 2

5 cups cooked, cubed
  potatoes
2 hard-boiled eggs,
  chopped
1/2 cup sweet pickle
  cubes
1/2 cup chopped onion
1/2 cup chopped celery

1/2 cup chopped tomato
1/4 cup cubed Swiss
  cheese
1/2 cup mayonnaise
2 teaspoons sugar
1/2 teaspoon pepper
1 teaspoon salt
Dash of paprika

Combine hot potatoes, eggs, pickle cubes, onion, celery, tomato and Swiss cheese in large bowl. Mix mayonnaise, sugar, pepper and salt in small bowl. Add to potato mixture, stirring gently. Sprinkle with paprika. Serve warm.

Alice Ellis, Advance

Perfect Potato Salad

Yield:
4 servings
Utensil:
large bowl
Approx Per
Serving:
Cal 453
Prot 6 g
Carbo 29 g
Fiber 1 g
T Fat 36 g
Chol 161 mg
Sod 898 mg

Dietary
Exchanges:
Milk 0
Vegetable 1/2
Fruit 0
Bread/Starch 1
Meat 1/2; Fat 8

3 potatoes, cooked,
  peeled
1 teaspoon sugar
1 teaspoon vinegar
1/2 cup sliced celery
1/3 cup finely chopped
  onion
1 teaspoon salt

1/4 cup chopped sweet
  pickles
1 teaspoon celery seed
3/4 cup mayonnaise
2 hard-boiled eggs,
  sliced
Dash of paprika

Cut potatoes into quarters; slice quarters to 1/4-inch thickness. Place in large bowl. Sprinkle sugar and vinegar over potatoes. Add celery, onion, salt, pickles and celery seed to potato mixture; mix well. Stir in mayonnaise to coat. Add eggs, stirring gently. Sprinkle with paprika. Chill, covered, for 3 to 4 hours.

Ruby E. Sprinkle, Winston-Salem

MAINE POTATO SALAD

Yield:
8 servings
Utensil:
large bowl
Approx Per
Serving:
Cal 246
Prot 4 g
Carbo 23 g
Fiber 2 g
T Fat 16 g
Chol 83 mg
Sod 134 mg

Dietary
Exchanges:
Milk 0
Vegetable 1/2
Fruit 0
Bread/Starch 1
Meat 1/2; Fat 31/2

6 potatoes, cooked,
  peeled, cubed
1 onion, finely
  chopped
1/4 cup chopped red
  bell pepper
1/2 cup sour cream

1/2 cup mayonnaise
1 tablespoon prepared
  mustard
1 teaspoon celery seed
2 hard-boiled eggs,
  chopped

Combine potatoes, onion and red pepper in large bowl. Mix sour cream, mayonnaise, mustard and celery seed in small bowl. Add to potato mixture, stirring well. Top with chopped eggs. Chill in refrigerator.

Sarah L. Tagert, Greensboro

SCANDINAVIAN SALAD

Yield:
6 servings
Utensil:
1/2-gallon jar
Approx Per
Serving:
Cal 415
Prot 6 g
Carbo 64 g
Fiber 6 g
T Fat 19 g
Chol 0 mg
Sod 403 mg

Dietary
Exchanges:
Milk 0
Vegetable 2
Fruit 0
Bread/Starch 1/2
Meat 0; Fat 31/2

1 16-ounce can Le
   Sueur peas, drained
1 16-ounce can
   French-style green
   beans, drained
1 bunch celery,
   chopped
1 bunch green onions,
   sliced
1 onion, chopped

1 2-ounce jar
   chopped pimento,
   drained
11/4 cups sugar
1 cup vinegar
2 tablespoons water
1/2 cup oil
1/2 teaspoon paprika
1/2 teaspoon salt

Combine peas, beans, celery, green onions, onion and pimento in 1/2-gallon jar. Mix sugar, vinegar, water, oil, paprika and salt together, stirring until smooth. Pour over vegetables; toss to mix well. Chill, covered, for 24 hours or more. May store in refrigerator for 2 weeks or longer.

Mary Rudisill, Hendersonville

Korean Salad

Yield:
4 servings
Utensil:
blender
Approx Per
Serving:
Cal 742
Prot 9 g
Carbo 53 g
Fiber 7 g
T Fat 59 g
Chol 7 mg
Sod 622 mg

Dietary
Exchanges:
Milk 0
Vegetable 4
Bread/Starch 0
Meat ½
Fat 11½

1 pound fresh spinach, torn
1 8-ounce can water chestnuts, drained, sliced
5 slices crisp-fried bacon, crumbled
1 16-ounce can bean sprouts, drained
½ cup sugar
⅓ cup catsup
⅓ cup vinegar
1 cup oil
5 tablespoons Worcestershire sauce
1 onion, quartered

Combine spinach, water chestnuts, bacon and bean sprouts in salad bowl. Combine sugar, catsup, vinegar, oil, Worcestershire sauce and onion in blender container. Process at high speed until smooth. Pour over salad before serving; toss gently to coat.

Patricia Radisch, Kernersville

Marinated Cherry Tomatoes

Yield:
8 servings
Utensil:
bowl
Approx Per
Serving:
Cal 140
Prot 1 g
Carbo 7 g
Fiber 2 g
T Fat 14 g
Chol 0 mg
Sod 375 mg

Dietary
Exchanges:
Milk 0
Vegetable 1
Fruit 0
Bread/Starch 0
Meat 0; Fat 3

3 pints cherry tomatoes
3 bunches green onions, sliced
1 cup red wine vinegar
1½ teaspoons oregano
1½ teaspoons basil leaves
1½ teaspoons salt
¾ teaspoon pepper
½ cup olive oil

Slice tomatoes into halves. Combine with green onions in bowl. Mix vinegar, oregano, basil, salt and pepper in small bowl. Stir in oil. Pour over tomatoes. Chill, covered, for 3 to 4 hours.

Nancy Garner, Burlington

BLEU CHEESE SALAD DRESSING

Yield:
184 servings
Utensil:
large bowl
**Approx Per
Serving:**
Cal 76
Prot 1 g
Carbo <1 g
Fiber <1 g
T Fat 8 g
Chol 7 mg
Sod 112 mg

**Dietary
Exchanges:**
Milk 0
Vegetable 0
Fruit 0
Bread/Starch 0
Meat 0; Fat 2

2 quarts mayonnaise
¾ pound bleu cheese,
  crumbled
2 teaspoons
  Worcestershire sauce
2 teaspoons salt
2 cups ounces tomato
  juice
1 teaspoon brown
  sugar

Combine mayonnaise, bleu cheese, Worcestershire sauce, salt, tomato juice and brown sugar in large bowl; mix well. Pour into large covered container. Store in refrigerator.

Mrs. Eugene G. Wilson, Winston-Salem

LOW-CALORIE FRENCH DRESSING

Yield:
64 servings
Utensil:
blender
**Approx Per
Serving:**
Cal 18
Prot <1 g
Carbo 3 g
Fiber <1 g
T Fat 1 g
Chol 0 mg
Sod 104 mg

**Dietary
Exchanges:**
Milk 0
Vegetable 0
Fruit 0
Bread/Starch 0
Meat 0; Fat 0

1 10-ounce can
  tomato soup
1 cup water
½ cup sugar
½ cup vinegar
2 tablespoons
  prepared mustard
1 tablespoon pepper
1 teaspoon salt
1 large onion, cut into
  quarters
2 tablespoons
  Worcestershire sauce
1 teaspoon garlic salt
¼ cup oil

Pour soup into blender container. Rinse soup can with 1 cup water; add to soup. Process at low speed for 15 seconds. Add sugar, vinegar, mustard, pepper, salt, onion, Worcestershire sauce, garlic salt and oil. Process at high speed for 1 minute. Store in refrigerator.

Lottie Dix, Greensboro

Sunny Italy Italian Salad Dressing

Yield:
32 servings
Utensil:
1-quart jar
Approx Per
Serving:
Cal 50
Prot 0 g
Carbo 2 g
Fiber <1 g
T Fat 5 g
Chol 0 mg
Sod 56 mg

Dietary
Exchanges:
Milk 0
Vegetable 0
Fruit 0
Bread/Starch 0
Meat 0; Fat 1

¼ cup sugar
½ cup water
3 tablespoons olive oil
1 tablespoon red wine vinegar
1 8-ounce bottle of creamy Italian salad dressing
⅛ teaspoon paprika

Dissolve sugar in water in 1-quart jar. Add olive oil, vinegar, salad dressing and paprika; cover and shake vigorously. Chill for 4 hours before serving. Store in refrigerator. Garnish salad with Salad Delight seasoning when served.

Sharon M. Fanelli, Gibsonville

Poppy Seed Dressing

Yield:
32 servings
Utensil:
blender
Approx Per
Serving:
Cal 80
Prot <1 g
Carbo 5 g
Fiber <1 g
T Fat 7 g
Chol 0 mg
Sod 61 mg

Dietary
Exchanges:
Milk 0
Vegetable 0
Fruit 0
Bread/Starch 0
Meat 0; Fat 1½

¾ cup sugar
⅓ cup cider vinegar
1 teaspoon salt
1 teaspoon finely grated onion
1 teaspoon dry mustard
1 cup oil
1 tablespoon poppy seed

Combine sugar, vinegar, salt, onion and mustard in blender container. Process at high speed until sugar is dissolved. Add oil in fine stream, processing constantly at high speed until completely blended. Stir in poppy seed. Store, covered, in refrigerator. Stir before serving.

Jean Newnam, Elon College

Russian Salad Dressing

Yield:
64 servings
Utensil:
1-quart jar
Approx Per Serving:
Cal 42
Prot <1 g
Carbo 3 g
Fiber <1 g
T Fat 3 g
Chol 0 mg
Sod 77 mg

Dietary Exchanges:
Milk 0
Vegetable 0
Fruit 0
Bread/Starch 0
Meat 0; Fat 1

1 cup oil
3/4 cup sugar
1 cup cider vinegar
2 tablespoons chopped green bell pepper
2 tablespoons chopped onion
1 tablespoon chopped pimento
1 10-ounce can tomato soup
1 1/2 teaspoons salt
1 tablespoon dry mustard
1 clove of garlic, minced

Combine oil, sugar, vinegar, green pepper, onion, pimento, soup, salt, mustard and garlic in 1-quart jar; shake vigorously. Chill before serving. May store in refrigerator for up to 1 month.

Mrs. J. C. Kuley, Bethania

Cooked Russian Dressing

Yield:
100 servings
Utensil:
large saucepan
Approx Per Serving:
Cal 16
Prot <1 g
Carbo 3 g
Fiber <1 g
T Fat <1 g
Chol 14 mg
Sod 53 mg

Dietary Exchanges:
Milk 0
Vegetable 0
Fruit 0
Bread/Starch 0
Meat 0; Fat 0

1 cup sugar
2 eggs, beaten
3/4 teaspoon pepper
1 tablespoon flour
2 tablespoons prepared mustard
1 cup vinegar
1 cup chopped onion
1 cup chopped green bell pepper
1 stalk celery, chopped
3 hard-boiled eggs, chopped
1 12-ounce bottle of chili sauce

Combine sugar, beaten eggs, pepper, flour, mustard, vinegar, onion, green pepper, celery, chopped eggs and chili sauce in large saucepan. Cook over medium heat until thickened, stirring constantly. Chill, covered, in refrigerator.

Thelma L. Wilson, Winston-Salem

MEATS

EYE OF ROUND ROAST BEEF

½ cup Worcestershire sauce
½ cup soy sauce
1 3-pound eye of round roast
2 cups sour cream
1 cup mayonnaise
2 tablespoons fresh white horseradish
1 tablespoon hot pepper sauce
½ teaspoon salt
½ cup Creole mustard
⅛ teaspoon sugar

Combine Worcestershire sauce and soy sauce in roasting bag; mix well. Add roast. Marinate in refrigerator for 3 days; drain. Combine sour cream, mayonnaise, horseradish, pepper sauce, salt, mustard and sugar in bowl; mix well. Chill, covered, overnight. Place roast in roaster. Bake at 275 degrees for 1 hour. Reduce temperature to 150 degrees. Bake for 2½ hours or to desired degree of doneness. Let stand for 10 minutes before slicing paper thin. Serve with horseradish sauce.

Jewel Smith, Clemmons

BAKED BEEF TENDERLOIN

1 4-pound beef tenderloin
Salt and pepper to taste
½ cup chopped onion
½ cup butter
½ cup cooking wine
½ cup mushrooms

Sprinkle beef with salt and pepper. Place in baking pan. Sauté onion in butter in skillet. Spoon over beef. Bake at 450 degrees for 20 minutes. Add wine and mushrooms. Reduce oven temperature to 300 degrees. Bake for 20 minutes longer. Slice to serve.

Fran Klingerman, Greensboro

BEST ROAST

Yield:
6 servings
Utensil:
roasting pan
Approx Per
Serving:
Cal 378
Prot 38 g
Carbo 5 g
Fiber <1 g
T Fat 22 g
Chol 109 mg
Sod 774 mg

Dietary
Exchanges:
Milk 0
Vegetable 0
Bread/Starch 1
Meat 5
Fat 3

1 3-pound boneless
chuck roast
Garlic salt and pepper
to taste
1/2 envelope onion
soup mix
1 10-ounce can cream
of mushroom soup

Place roast on large square of heavy-duty foil.
Sprinkle with garlic salt, pepper and soup mix.
Spread mushroom soup over top. Seal foil tightly;
place in roasting pan. Roast at 350 degrees for 1
hour and 15 minutes.

B. S. Cuthrell, Winston-Salem

POT ROAST

Yield:
6 servings
Utensil:
baking dish
Approx Per
Serving:
Cal 409;
Prot 44 g
Carbo 26 g
Fiber 5 g
T Fat 14 g
Chol 120 mg
Sod 433 mg

Dietary
Exchanges:
Milk 0
Vegetable 2 1/2
Fruit 0
Bread/Starch 1/2
Meat 5 1/2; Fat 0

1 3-pound beef roast,
trimmed
Juice of 1 lemon
2 medium onions,
thinly sliced
6 small carrots
2 medium potatoes,
cut into quarters
1 clove of garlic,
minced
1 teaspoon dry mustard
1 teaspoon ginger
1 teaspoon thyme
4 stalks celery,
chopped
1 small green bell
pepper, chopped
2 cups tomato juice or
vegetable juice
cocktail

Place roast in shallow dish. Squeeze lemon juice
over roast; pierce with fork. Marinate, covered, in
refrigerator overnight. Place roast in baking dish.
Arrange onions, carrots and potatoes around roast.
Sprinkle with garlic, dry mustard, ginger and
thyme. Top with celery and green pepper. Pour
tomato juice around roast. Roast, covered, for 3
hours or until very tender.

Mrs. Carlton Tuttle, Germantown

WESTERN POT ROAST

Yield:
8 servings
Utensil:
saucepan
Approx Per
Serving:
Cal 281
Prot 31 g
Carbo 11 g
Fiber <1 g
T Fat 12 g
Chol 90 mg
Sod 818 mg

Dietary
Exchanges:
Milk 0
Vegetable ½
Fruit 0
Bread/Starch 0
Meat 4; Fat ½

1   3-pound chuck roast
1 tablespoon oil
1 cup chopped onion
¼ cup Worcestershire
    sauce
2 tablespoons cider
    vinegar
1 cup catsup
1½ teaspoons salt

Brown beef in oil in heavy saucepan. Remove roast. Sauté onion in drippings in saucepan. Return roast to saucepan. Combine Worcestershire sauce, vinegar, catsup and salt in bowl; mix well. Pour over roast. Simmer, covered, for 2½ to 3 hours or until tender.

Ruth S. Curl, Liberty

CHINESE BEEF

Yield:
4 servings
Utensil:
skillet
Approx Per
Serving:
Cal 234
Prot 24 g
Carbo 9 g
Fiber 3 g
T Fat 12 g
Chol 60 mg
Sod 817 mg

Dietary
Exchanges:
Milk 0
Vegetable 1½
Fruit 0
Bread/Starch 0
Meat 3; Fat ½

1   1-pound flank steak
1 clove of garlic,
    chopped
⅛ teaspoon ginger
½ teaspoon salt
Pepper to taste
1 tablespoon oil
2 tablespoons soy
    sauce
¼ teaspoon sugar
1 tomato, cut into
    quarters
1 green bell pepper,
    chopped
1   16-ounce can bean
    sprouts, drained
1½ teaspoons
    cornstarch
2 tablespoons water

Cut steak into thin strips cross grain. Sprinkle with garlic, ginger, salt and pepper. Brown lightly in oil in skillet. Add soy sauce and sugar. Cook for 5 minutes. Add tomato, green pepper and bean sprouts. Heat until bubbly. Cook, covered, for 5 minutes. Blend cornstarch with water in bowl. Stir into skillet. Cook until thickened, stirring constantly.

Helen A. Howard, Pfafftown

Oven-Barbecued Swiss Steak

Yield:
6 servings
Utensil:
Dutch oven
**Approx Per
Serving:**
Cal 240
Prot 30 g
Carbo 16 g
Fiber 1 g
T Fat 6 g
Chol 72 mg
Sod 933 mg

**Dietary
Exchanges:**
Milk 0
Vegetable 1½
Fruit 0
Bread/Starch ½
Meat 3½; Fat 0

⅓ cup flour
1 teaspoon salt
¼ teaspoon pepper
1 2-pound round or
  chuck steak
1 tablespoon
  Worcestershire sauce
1 tablespoon vinegar
2 8-ounce cans
  seasoned tomato
  sauce
1 tablespoon sugar
Pepper sauce to taste
1 medium onion, sliced

Mix flour, salt and pepper in bowl. Sprinkle over steak, coating well. Brown slowly on both sides in lightly greased Dutch oven; drain. Combine Worcestershire sauce, vinegar, tomato sauce, sugar and pepper sauce in bowl; mix well. Pour over steak. Add onion. Bake, covered, at 350 degrees for 1 hour to 1 hour and 15 minutes or until tender.

Marie B. Ball, Winston-Salem

Steak Chow Mein

Yield:
8 servings
Utensil:
saucepan
**Approx Per
Serving:**
Cal 288
Prot 26 g
Carbo 20 g
Fiber 3 g
T Fat 12 g
Chol 62 mg
Sod 333 mg

**Dietary
Exchanges:**
Milk 0
Vegetable 1½
Fruit 0
Bread/Starch 1
Meat 2½; Fat 1

2 pounds round steak,
  cubed
2 large onions,
  chopped
2 tablespoons soy
  sauce
Salt and pepper to
  taste
1 teaspoon chili powder
5 stalks celery, chopped
½ cup chopped green
  bell pepper
2 16-ounce cans bean
  sprouts
1 6-ounce can chow
  mein noodles

Brown steak and onions with soy sauce, salt and pepper in nonstick skillet sprayed with nonstick cooking spray. Simmer, covered, for 2 hours or until steak is tender. Combine with chili powder and celery in saucepan. Cook for 30 minutes. Add green pepper and bean sprouts. Simmer for 2 hours or longer. Serve over noodles. May serve over rice and top with noodles if preferred.

Eleanor Brooks

SOUTHERN-STYLE ORIENTAL DELIGHT

1 2-pound flank steak
2 pounds chicken breast filets
1 6-ounce bottle of Allegro marinade
1 ounce light soy sauce
2 ounces red cooking wine
2 cups long grain and wild rice mix
1 tablespoon oil
4 cups water
1 tablespoon oil
1 6-ounce can water chestnuts
1 6-ounce can bamboo shoots
1 12-ounce can Chinese vegetables
Freshly ground pepper to taste

Cut beef into 1-inch cubes. Rinse chicken and pat dry. Cut chicken into 1-inch pieces. Combine marinade, soy sauce and wine in bowl. Add beef and chicken; mix well. Marinate in refrigerator for 2 hours. Add enough water to cover meat; mix well. Marinate in refrigerator overnight. Cook rice with 1 tablespoon oil in water in saucepan for 20 minutes or until tender. Drain beef and chicken, reserving marinade. Stir-fry beef and chicken in 1 tablespoon oil in wok. Drain and rinse water chestnuts, bamboo shoots and Chinese vegetables. Add to wok with rice and desired amount of reserved marinade. Season with pepper.

Nutritional information includes entire amount of marinade.

W. A. Gilchrist, Jr., High Point

OVEN BEEF STEW

Yield:
4 servings
Utensil:
baking dish
Approx Per
Serving:
Cal 340
Prot 24 g
Carbo 30 g
Fiber 5 g
T Fat 14 g
Chol 60 mg
Sod 654 mg

Dietary
Exchanges:
Milk 0
Vegetable 2½
Fruit 0
Bread/Starch 1
Meat 3; Fat 1½

1 pound lean beef cubes
2 tablespoons oil
1 potato, chopped
3 carrots, chopped
2 onions, chopped
2 6-ounce cans tomato juice
1 tablespoon soy sauce
1 tablespoon sugar
2 tablespoons cornstarch
1 bay leaf
Salt and pepper to taste

Brown beef on all sides in oil in skillet; drain. Combine with potato, carrots and onions in 1-quart baking dish. Combine tomato juice, soy sauce, sugar, cornstarch, bay leaf, salt and pepper in bowl; mix well. Pour into baking dish. Bake, covered, at 250 degrees for 3 hours or longer. Remove bay leaf.

Frances Thompson, Winston-Salem

BEEF STROGANOFF

Yield:
6 servings
Utensil:
saucepan
Approx Per
Serving:
Cal 328
Prot 23 g
Carbo 9 g
Fiber <1 g
T Fat 22 g
Chol 78 mg
Sod 831 mg

Dietary
Exchanges:
Milk 0
Vegetable 0
Bread/Starch 1½
Meat 2½
Fat 5½

1½ pounds stew beef
1 10-ounce can cream of mushroom soup
1 10-ounce can golden mushroom soup
1 cup sour cream

Combine beef, soups and sour cream in saucepan. Simmer for 2 hours or until beef is tender, stirring frequently. Serve over rice or noodles.

Julia O. Baity, Mocksville

BEEF TERIYAKI

Yield:
2 servings
Utensil:
grill
**Approx Per
Serving:**
Cal 581
Prot 69 g
Carbo 27 g
Fiber 1 g
T Fat 21 g
Chol 180 mg
Sod 6594 mg

**Dietary
Exchanges:**
Milk 0
Vegetable ½
Fruit 0
Bread/Starch 0
Meat 8½; Fat 0

1½ pounds flank steak
½ cup soy sauce
1 cup beef bouillon
½ cup finely chopped
  onion
2 tablespoons lemon
  juice

2 tablespoons honey
½ teaspoon garlic
  powder
1 teaspoon seasoned
  salt
1 teaspoon salt

Cut beef into 1½-inch pieces. Combine soy sauce, bouillon, onion, lemon juice, honey, garlic powder, seasoned salt and salt in small bowl; mix well. Add beef. Marinate in refrigerator for 24 hours; drain. Thread beef onto skewers. Grill over hot coals for 6 to 8 minutes or until done to taste, turning to brown all sides.

Nutritional information includes entire amount of marinade.

Ellman C. Grubb, Springdale, Arkansas

CORNED BEEF CASSEROLE

Yield:
6 servings
Utensil:
dish
**Approx Per
Serving:**
Cal 404
Prot 22 g
Carbo 7 g
Fiber 1 g
T Fat 32 g
Chol 80 mg
Sod 1319 mg

**Dietary
Exchanges:**
Milk 0
Vegetable 1
Bread/Starch 0
Meat 3½
Fat 5½

1 12-ounce can corned
   beef, crumbled
1 16-ounce can
   sauerkraut
½ cup mayonnaise,
   drained

¼ cup Thousand
   Island salad
   dressing
1 large tomato, sliced
1 cup shredded Swiss
   cheese

Layer corned beef and sauerkraut in microwave-safe dish. Mix mayonnaise and salad dressing in bowl. Spread over layers. Top with tomato slices; sprinkle with cheese. Microwave on High for 15 minutes.

Nancy Garner, Burlington

New England Boiled Dinner

2½ to 3 pound boneless corned beef brisket
2 cloves of garlic, cut into halves
1 tablespoon mixed whole pickling spice
9 small onions
6 medium carrots
4 medium potatoes
2 turnips
1 small cabbage

Place beef brisket in large saucepan with just enough water to cover. Tie garlic halves and pickling spice in cheesecloth bag. Cut 1 onion into quarters. Add spice bag and onion quarters to saucepan. Simmer, covered, for 1½ hours. Cut carrots and potatoes into halves. Peel and cube turnips. Add remaining whole onions, carrots, potatoes and turnips to saucepan. Simmer, covered, for 30 minutes. Cut cabbage into 8 wedges. Add to saucepan. Simmer, uncovered, for 15 minutes longer. Carve brisket cross grain into thin slices, starting at pointed end.

Emmaline Lindsay, Greensboro

Barbucup

1 pound ground beef
½ cup barbecue sauce
2 tablespoons brown sugar
1 tablespoon dried minced onion
2 10-count cans refrigerator biscuits
1 cup shredded Cheddar cheese

Brown ground beef in skillet, stirring until crumbly; drain. Combine ground beef, barbecue sauce, brown sugar and onion in bowl; mix well. Separate biscuits; place in muffin cups. Press to form cups. Spoon ground beef mixture into cups. Sprinkle with cheese. Bake at 400 degrees for 12 minutes.

Patsy M. Davis

BARBECUED HAMBURGERS

1 cup soft bread
   crumbs
1/2 cup milk
1 1/2 pounds ground
   beef
2 tablespoons oil
2 small onions,
   peeled, sliced

1/2 teaspoon salt
Dash of pepper
3 tablespoons
   Worcestershire sauce
2 tablespoons vinegar
1/4 cup sugar
3/4 cup catsup

Combine bread crumbs, milk and ground beef in bowl; mix well. Shape into 6 patties. Brown beef patties on both sides in hot oil in skillet. Separate onion slices into rings; place over beef patties. Combine salt, pepper, Worcestershire sauce, vinegar, sugar and catsup in bowl; mix well. Pour over beef patties. Simmer, covered, for 15 minutes. Remove beef patties to serving plate. Spoon sauce over beef patties. Garnish with additional onion rings.

Jean W. Andrews, Graham

EASY CAJUN CASSEROLE

1 1/2 pounds ground
   beef
3 large potatoes,
   peeled
2 onions, finely
   chopped
2 stalks celery, finely
   chopped

1/2 cup uncooked rice
1 16-ounce can red
   kidney beans,
   drained
Salt and pepper to
   taste
2 10-ounce cans
   tomato soup

Brown ground beef in skillet, stirring until crumbly; drain. Spray deep casserole with nonstick cooking spray. Slice potatoes. Layer potatoes, onions, ground beef, celery, rice, red beans, salt and pepper in casserole. Pour tomato soup over all. Bake, covered, at 375 degrees for 2 hours.

Craig Davis, Greensboro

CASSEROLE SURPRISE

Yield:
8 servings
Utensil:
large skillet
Approx Per Serving:
Cal 263
Prot 17 g
Carbo 10 g
Fiber 1 g
T Fat 17 g
Chol 58 mg
Sod 638 mg

Dietary Exchanges:
Milk 0
Vegetable ½
Fruit 0
Bread/Starch 1
Meat 2½; Fat 3

1 pound ground beef
Salt to taste
1 large potato, peeled
¼ head cabbage, shredded
2 carrots, shredded
1 medium onion, chopped
1 10-ounce can cream of mushroom soup
6 slices American cheese

Crumble ¾ of the ground beef in skillet. Sprinkle with salt. Slice potatoes. Layer potatoes, cabbage, carrots, onion and remaining ¼ of the ground beef in skillet. Pour in soup, spreading over layers. Top with cheese slices. Cook over medium heat for 30 to 40 minutes or until ground beef is brown, stirring occasionally.

Frances King

HARVEST CASSEROLE

Yield:
24 servings
Utensil:
large casserole
Approx Per Serving:
Cal 269
Prot 17 g
Carbo 12 g
Fiber <1 g
T Fat 17 g
Chol 55 mg
Sod 558 mg

Dietary Exchanges:
Milk 0
Vegetable 0
Fruit 0
Bread/Starch 1
Meat 2; Fat 3

3 pounds lean ground beef
1 large onion, chopped
2 cups chopped celery
1 tablespoon margarine
8 ounces egg noodles, cooked
1 12-ounce can evaporated milk
3 10-ounce cans cream of mushroom soup
¾ pound Velveeta cheese, crumbled

Brown ground beef with onion in skillet, stirring until crumbly; drain. Sauté celery in margarine in skillet. Combine ground beef mixture, celery, egg noodles, evaporated milk, soup and cheese in large bowl; mix well. Spoon into large casserole. Bake at 350 degrees for 1 hour or until hot and bubbly. Sprinkle top with additional cheese. May freeze before or after baking.

Fran Grinstead, Snow Camp

Meal in One

Yield:
6 servings
Utensil:
shallow casserole
Approx Per
Serving:
Cal 474
Prot 29 g
Carbo 34 g
Fiber 2 g
T Fat 25 g
Chol 91 mg
Sod 1195 mg

Dietary
Exchanges:
Milk 0
Vegetable 1
Fruit 0
Bread/Starch 2½
Meat 3½; Fat 4

1½ pounds lean ground beef
½ cup chopped onion
1 9-ounce package frozen cut green beans
1 cup cooked sliced carrots
1 10-ounce can cream of mushroom soup
1 10-ounce can tomato soup
½ cup water
½ teaspoon coarse ground black pepper
3 cups mashed, cooked potatoes
¾ cup shredded Cheddar cheese

Brown ground beef with onion in skillet, stirring until crumbly; drain. Cook green beans using package directions; drain. Combine ground beef, beans, carrots, mushroom soup, tomato soup, water and black pepper in bowl; mix well. Spoon into shallow casserole. Spoon potatoes in diagonal lines on top. Sprinkle with cheese. Bake at 350 degrees for 30 minutes.

Barbara N. Grieser, Greensboro

Pinto Bean Casserole

Yield:
8 servings
Utensil:
casserole
Approx Per
Serving:
Cal 286
Prot 20 g
Carbo 40 g
Fiber 5 g
T Fat 5 g
Chol 38 mg
Sod 279 mg

Dietary
Exchanges:
Milk 0
Vegetable ½
Fruit 0
Bread/Starch 2½
Meat 2; Fat 0

1 pound ground beef
1 15-ounce can pinto beans
4 large potatoes, sliced, cooked
1 large onion, thinly sliced
Salt to taste
1 10-ounce can tomato soup
½ soup can water
1 green bell pepper, thinly sliced

Brown ground beef in skillet, stirring until crumbly; do not drain. Layer beans, ground beef, potatoes and onion in 2½-quart casserole. Sprinkle with salt. Pour mixture of tomato soup and water over all. Top with green pepper. Bake, covered with foil, at 350 degrees for 1 hour.

Jeanette M. Boggs, Graham

CHILI

Yield:
4 servings
Utensil:
saucepan
Approx Per
Serving:
Cal 313
Prot 23 g
Carbo 16 g
Fiber <1 g
T Fat 18 g
Chol 74 mg
Sod 1327 mg

Dietary
Exchanges:
Milk 0
Vegetable 0
Fruit 0
Bread/Starch ½
Meat 3; Fat 1½

1 pound ground beef
1 tablespoon mustard
1 tablespoon vinegar
1 tablespoon
   Worcestershire sauce
¼ cup catsup
2 tablespoons chili
   powder
1 10-ounce can
   tomato soup
1 soup can water
1 teaspoon salt

Combine ground beef, mustard, vinegar, Worcestershire sauce, catsup, chili powder, tomato soup, water and salt in saucepan. Simmer for 1 hour.

Pat L. Burke, Burlington

CHILI CASSEROLE

Yield:
12 servings
Utensil:
casserole
Approx Per
Serving:
Cal 158
Prot 9 g
Carbo 11 g
Fiber 1 g
T Fat 9 g
Chol 25 mg
Sod 328 mg

Dietary
Exchanges:
Milk 0
Vegetable 1
Fruit 0
Bread/Starch ½
Meat 1; Fat 1

2 large onions,
   chopped
2 green bell peppers,
   sliced
3 tablespoons
   shortening
1 pound ground beef
2 16-ounce cans
   tomatoes
1 cup cooked rice
1 teaspoon chili powder
1 teaspoon salt
Dash of red pepper
1 cup bread crumbs

Sauté onions and green pepper in shortening in skillet. Add ground beef. Cook until ground beef is brown, stirring frequently; drain. Add tomatoes, rice, chili powder, salt and red pepper; mix well. Spoon into greased 9x13-inch casserole. Top with bread crumbs. Bake at 350 degrees for 30 minutes.

Lou Bullard, Winston-Salem

GREAT CHILI CON CARNE

2 pounds ground beef
1 pound cubed beef
1/2 large onion, finely chopped
1 28-ounce can stewed tomatoes
1/2 cup medium picante sauce
1/2 6-ounce can tomato paste
1 to 2 cups water
3 jalapeño peppers, finely chopped
4 to 5 tablespoons chili powder
1 teaspoon garlic powder
1 teaspoon cumin
1 teaspoon salt
1 teaspoon pepper
2 16-ounce cans pinto beans

Cook ground beef and cubed beef in skillet until almost brown, stirring frequently. Add onion. Cook until meat is brown; drain. Add stewed tomatoes, picante sauce, tomato paste, water, jalapeño peppers, chili powder, garlic powder, cumin, salt, pepper and pinto beans. Bring to a full boil. Reduce heat. Simmer for 30 to 40 minutes, stirring frequently and adding water for desired consistency.

G. H. Campbell, Greensboro

EASY CHILI FOR HOT DOGS

1 pound lean ground beef
1/4 cup oil
1 6-ounce can tomato paste
1 cup water
1/4 teaspoon salt
1/8 teaspoon sugar
1 tablespoon vinegar
1 tablespoon mustard
2 tablespoons catsup
1/2 cup chopped onion
1 teaspoon (or more) chili powder

Combine ground beef, oil, tomato paste, water, salt, sugar, vinegar, mustard, catsup and onion in large saucepan. Simmer over low heat for 4 to 5 hours, stirring frequently. Add chili powder. Cook until very thick with a rich brown color, stirring frequently. This is delicious over hot dogs or hamburgers and freezes well.

Penny Monk, Burlington

POLISH CHILI

2 pounds ground sirloin tip beef
2 large onions, chopped
1 stalk celery, chopped
2 16-ounce cans tomatoes, chopped
2 16-ounce cans dark red kidney beans
2 16-ounce cans white Shoe Peg corn, drained
2 cups tomato juice
1 tablespoon chili powder
1 tablespoon Worcestershire sauce
1 cup catsup

Brown beef in skillet, stirring until crumbly; drain. Add onions and celery. Cook for 15 minutes, stirring frequently. Add tomatoes, kidney beans, corn, tomato juice, chili powder, Worcestershire sauce and catsup. Cook, uncovered, for 1 hour, stirring occasionally. May cover and keep warm over low heat until serving time. Freezes well.

Jesse R. Meredith, Thomasville

THREE-BEAN CHILI

2 pounds ground beef
1 large onion, chopped
1 large green bell pepper, chopped
1 16-ounce can kidney beans
1 16-ounce can pinto beans
1 16-ounce can small green lima beans
1 16-ounce bottle of barbecue sauce
1 tablespoon mustard
1½ teaspoons molasses
1 teaspoon chili powder
1 tablespoon Worcestershire sauce
1 teaspoon salt
1 teaspoon pepper

Brown ground beef with onion and green pepper in skillet, stirring frequently; drain. Combine ground beef mixture, kidney beans, pinto beans, lima beans, barbecue sauce, mustard, molasses, chili powder, Worcestershire sauce, salt and pepper in large saucepan. Simmer for 1 hour. May also be baked, covered, at 350 degrees for 1 hour.

Ruby Hicks

CHINESE BEEF

1 pound ground chuck
1½ cups chopped
  onions
2 tablespoons oil
2 cups finely sliced
  celery
2 cups beef broth
1 16-ounce can bean
  sprouts, drained

2 tablespoons
  cornstarch
2 tablespoons soy
  sauce
4 cups cooked
  buttered noodles

Brown ground chuck with onions in oil in skillet, stirring frequently; drain. Add celery and beef broth. Simmer over low heat for 10 minutes, stirring frequently. Add bean sprouts. Mix cornstarch and soy sauce in bowl. Stir into ground chuck mixture. Cook until thickened, stirring constantly. Spoon over buttered noodles.

Nancy M. Farris, Burlington

EASY GOULASH

1 pound ground beef
1 medium onion,
  chopped
1 medium green bell
  pepper, chopped
2 16-ounce cans
  tomatoes, chopped

Sliced mushrooms to
  taste
Salt and pepper to
  taste
8 ounces macaroni,
  cooked

Brown ground beef with onion and green pepper in skillet, stirring frequently; drain. Add tomatoes and mushrooms. Simmer for 10 to 15 minutes or until vegetables are tender. Add salt, pepper and macaroni; mix well. Cook until of serving temperature. May add tomato juice or water for desired consistency.

Ramona P. Cheek, Graham

ENCHILADA CASSEROLE CON ESPINACAS

Yield:
12 servings
Utensil:
shallow casserole
Approx Per Serving:
Cal 539
Prot 25 g
Carbo 33 g
Fiber 1 g
T Fat 35 g
Chol 99 mg
Sod 867 mg

Dietary Exchanges:
Milk 0
Vegetable 1
Fruit 0
Bread/Starch 2
Meat 3; Fat 7

1 12-ounce package frozen chopped spinach
2 pounds ground chuck
1 large onion, finely chopped
1 16-ounce can tomatoes, chopped
Salt and pepper to taste
1 10-ounce can golden mushroom soup
1 10-ounce can cream of mushroom soup
1 cup sour cream
1/4 cup milk
1/2 teaspoon garlic powder
12 to 16 flour tortillas
1/2 cup (or more) melted butter
2 4-ounce cans chopped green chilies
8 ounces mild Cheddar cheese, shredded

Cook spinach using package directions; drain. Cook ground chuck in skillet, stirring until crumbly; drain. Add onion, tomatoes, spinach, salt and pepper; mix well. Combine soups, sour cream, milk and garlic powder in bowl; mix well. Dip half the tortillas in melted butter. Arrange on bottom and up sides of large shallow casserole. Spoon ground chuck mixture over tortillas. Sprinkle with chopped chilies. Reserve 1/2 cup cheese. Sprinkle remaining cheese over chilies. Dip remaining tortillas in melted butter; spread over top of layers. Add sour cream sauce, spreading over surface. Chill, covered with plastic wrap, overnight. Sprinkle with reserved cheese. Bake at 325 degrees for 35 to 45 minutes or until hot and bubbly.

Peggy Strauss, Graham

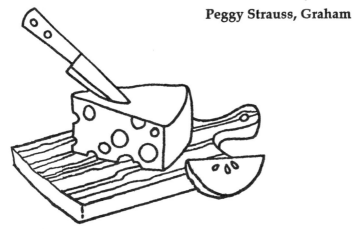

Western Hash

Yield:
6 servings
Utensil:
large skillet
*Approx Per
Serving:*
Cal 388
Prot 25 g
Carbo 20 g
Fiber 2 g
T Fat 23 g
Chol 86 mg
Sod 971 mg

*Dietary
Exchanges:*
Milk 0
Vegetable 1½
Fruit 0
Bread/Starch 1
Meat 3½; Fat 3

1 pound ground beef
1 cup chopped green
  bell pepper
½ cup chopped onion
½ cup uncooked rice
½ teaspoon salt
1 28-ounce can
   tomatoes, chopped
½ teaspoon basil
Pepper to taste
8 ounces Velveeta
  cheese, sliced

Brown ground beef in large skillet, stirring until crumbly; drain. Add green pepper, onion and rice. Cook for 2 minutes, stirring constantly. Add salt, tomatoes, basil and pepper. Simmer, covered, for 25 minutes. Top with cheese. Heat until cheese is melted.

Stella Fleming, Winston-Salem

Lasagna

Yield:
8 servings
Utensil:
casserole
*Approx Per
Serving:*
Cal 672
Prot 42 g
Carbo 35 g
Fiber 1 g
T Fat 41 g
Chol 129 mg
Sod 1643 mg

*Dietary
Exchanges:*
Milk 0
Vegetable 2
Fruit 0
Bread/Starch 1½
Meat 5½; Fat 5

1 pound ground beef
¾ cup chopped onion
2 tablespoons oil
1 16-ounce can
   tomatoes, chopped
2 6-ounce cans
   tomato paste
2 cups water
2 teaspoons salt
1 teaspoon sugar
1 teaspoon garlic powder
½ teaspoon pepper
½ teaspoon oregano
8 ounces lasagna
  noodles, cooked
16 ounces Cheddar
   cheese, shredded
8 ounces mozzarella
  cheese, shredded
1 cup Parmesan cheese

Brown ground beef with onion in oil in skillet, stirring until crumbly; drain. Add tomatoes, tomato paste, water, salt, sugar, garlic powder, pepper and oregano. Simmer, uncovered, for 30 minutes, stirring occasionally. Layer 1 cup ground beef sauce in 9x13-inch casserole. Alternate layers of lasagna noodles, sauce, Cheddar cheese, mozzarella cheese and Parmesan cheese, ending with cheese. Bake at 350 degrees for 40 to 50 minutes or until light brown and bubbly. Let stand for 15 minutes before serving.

Sarah L. Finley, Graham

COTTAGE LASAGNA

Yield:
8 servings
Utensil:
casserole
Approx Per Serving:
Cal 553
Prot 42 g
Carbo 32 g
Fiber 1 g
T Fat 28 g
Chol 168 mg
Sod 1595 mg

Dietary Exchanges:
Milk 0
Vegetable 1/2
Fruit 0
Bread/Starch 2
Meat 6; Fat 2

1 pound ground beef
1 teaspoon garlic salt
1 tablespoon parsley flakes
1 tablespoon basil
1½ teaspoons salt
2 cups chopped tomatoes
10 ounces lasagna noodles
3 cups cottage cheese
1 teaspoon salt
½ teaspoon pepper
2 eggs, beaten
2 tablespoons parsley flakes
½ cup Parmesan cheese
16 ounces mozzarella cheese, shredded

Brown ground beef in skillet, stirring until crumbly; drain. Add next 5 ingredients. Simmer, covered, for 30 minutes, stirring occasionally. Cook noodles in salted water using package directions; drain. Rinse in cold water. Combine cottage cheese and next 5 ingredients in bowl; mix well. Layer noodles, cottage cheese mixture, mozzarella cheese and ground beef sauce ½ at a time in 9x13-inch casserole. Bake at 375 degrees for 30 minutes.

Charlotte Ingle, Burlington

RICOTTA LASAGNA

Yield:
8 servings
Utensil:
casserole
Approx Per Serving:
Cal 741
Prot 50 g
Carbo 37 g
Fiber 1 g
T Fat 44 g
Chol 157 mg
Sod 1479 mg

Dietary Exchanges:
Milk 0
Vegetable 2
Fruit 0
Bread/Starch 1½
Meat 7; Fat 4½

2 pounds ground beef
1 cup chopped onion
2 tablespoons oil
1 16-ounce can tomatoes, chopped
2 6-ounce cans tomato paste
2 cups water
2 teaspoons salt
1 teaspoon sugar
1 teaspoon garlic powder
½ teaspoon pepper
1 teaspoon oregano
8 ounces lasagna noodles
16 ounces ricotta cheese
16 ounces mozzarella cheese, shredded
1 cup Parmesan cheese

Brown ground beef with onion in oil in skillet, stirring until crumbly; drain. Add next 8 ingredients. Simmer, uncovered, for 30 minutes, stirring occasionally. Cook lasagna noodles using package directions; drain. Layer 1 cup ground beef sauce in 9x13-inch casserole. Alternate layers of lasagna noodles, ground beef sauce, ricotta cheese, mozzarella cheese and Parmesan cheese, ending with cheese. Bake at 350 degrees for 40 to 50 minutes or until light brown and bubbly. Let stand for 15 minutes. Cut into squares.

Barbara A. Stewart, Graham

BARBECUED MEATBALLS

Yield:
4 servings
Utensil:
casserole
Approx Per
Serving:
Cal 510
Prot 31 g
Carbo 47 g
Fiber <1 g
T Fat 23 g
Chol 161 mg
Sod 1190 mg

Dietary
Exchanges:
Milk 1/2
Vegetable 1/2
Bread/Starch 1 1/2
Meat 3 1/2
Fat 2 1/2

1 pound ground beef
1 cup evaporated milk
1 cup bread crumbs
1 egg, beaten
3 tablespoons sugar
1/2 cup catsup
1 teaspoon salt
1 1/2 tablespoons
    Worcestershire sauce
1/4 cup vinegar
1/2 cup chopped green
    bell pepper
1/2 cup chopped onion

Combine ground beef, evaporated milk, bread crumbs and egg in bowl; mix well. Shape into meatballs. Place meatballs in casserole. Combine sugar, catsup, salt, Worcestershire sauce and vinegar in bowl; mix well. Stir in green pepper and onion. Pour over meatballs. Bake at 400 degrees for 45 minutes.

Pat L. Burke, Burlington

BARBECUED MEATBALLS II

Yield:
4 servings
Utensil:
cast-iron skillet
Approx Per
Serving:
Cal 413
Prot 26 g
Carbo 39 g
Fiber <1 g
T Fat 18 g
Chol 78 mg
Sod 1222 mg

Dietary
Exchanges:
Milk 0
Vegetable 1/2
Fruit 0
Bread/Starch 1 1/2
Meat 3; Fat 2

1 pound ground beef
1 cup bread crumbs
1/2 cup milk
1/2 cup chopped green
    bell pepper
1/2 cup chopped onion
1/2 cup vinegar
3/4 cup catsup
1 tablespoon sugar
1 teaspoon salt
1 teaspoon black
    pepper

Combine ground beef, bread crumbs and milk in bowl; mix well. Shape into balls. Place in cast-iron skillet. Bake at 350 degrees until browned; drain. Add mixture of remaining ingredients. Bake for 30 minutes longer.

Betty A. Day, Winston-Salem

MEATBALLS IN CHIPS

2 pounds ground chuck
1 egg, beaten
1 onion, chopped
1 tablespoon finely
   chopped parsley
1 teaspoon caraway
   seed
1 teaspoon garlic
   powder
1 16-ounce package
   potato chips, finely
   crushed
1 tablespoon melted
   margarine

Combine ground chuck, egg, onion, parsley, caraway seed and garlic powder in bowl; mix well. Shape into balls. Roll in crushed potato chips to coat. Brown several at a time in margarine in large skillet over medium heat, stirring gently; drain.

Dorothy S. Batten, Lexington

SANDY'S MEATBALLS

2 pounds ground beef
1 5-ounce can
   evaporated milk
1 small onion, finely
   chopped
2 teaspoons
   Worcestershire sauce
Salt and pepper to
   taste
2 cups catsup
1 cup packed light
   brown sugar
2 tablespoons
   Worcestershire sauce

Combine ground beef, evaporated milk, onion, Worcestershire sauce, salt and pepper in bowl; mix well. Shape into 1-inch meatballs. Place in baking dish. Bake at 400 degrees for 15 minutes; drain. Combine catsup, brown sugar and Worcestershire sauce in saucepan; mix well. Add meatballs. Simmer until sauce is thickened, stirring frequently. These are good served on noodles, rice or creamed potatoes.

Norma Hall, Mebane

SWEDISH MEATBALLS

Yield:
8 servings
Utensil:
skillet
Approx Per Serving:
Cal 451
Prot 27 g
Carbo 28 g
Fiber 1 g
T Fat 25 g
Chol 145 mg
Sod 890 mg

Dietary Exchanges:
Milk 0
Vegetable 0
Bread/Starch 2
Meat 3½
Fat 3½

½ cup oats
1½ cups fine bread crumbs
½ cup milk
½ cup minced onion
½ cup minced celery
½ cup applesauce
2 tablespoons lemon juice
1 teaspoon grated lemon rind
2 eggs, beaten
1½ teaspoons salt
¼ teaspoon pepper
½ teaspoon nutmeg
2 pounds ground beef
2 tablespoons oil
¾ cup water
¼ cup flour
1 10-ounce can cream of mushroom soup
1 cup water

Combine oats, bread crumbs and milk in mixer bowl; mix well. Add onion, celery, applesauce, lemon juice, lemon rind, eggs, salt, pepper and nutmeg; beat well. Add ground beef a small amount at a time, beating for 7 minutes or until fluffy. Shape into meatballs with wet hands. Place in large shallow container. Chill in refrigerator. Brown meatballs several at a time in oil in skillet; remove meatballs to bowl. Return all meatballs to skillet. Add ¾ cup water. Simmer for 5 minutes, stirring gently. Remove meatballs to bowl. Cool pan drippings. Add flour to cooled pan drippings, stirring to mix. Add mushroom soup and remaining 1 cup water. Cook until thickened, stirring constantly. Add meatballs. Simmer for 5 minutes.

Mary H. Harden, Graham

SWEET AND SOUR MEATBALLS

Yield:
8 servings
Utensil:
skillet
Approx Per
Serving:
Cal 292
Prot 20 g
Carbo 22 g
Fiber 1 g
T Fat 14 g
Chol 91 mg
Sod 846 mg

Dietary
Exchanges:
Milk 0
Vegetable 1/2
Fruit 0
Bread/Starch 1
Meat 2¹/₂; Fat 1

1¹/₄ cups bread crumbs
1¹/₂ pounds ground
beef
1 egg, beaten
1 tablespoon instant
minced onion
1¹/₂ teaspoons salt
¹/₄ teaspoon pepper
¹/₄ cup milk
1 green bell pepper,
thinly sliced

1 red bell pepper,
thinly sliced
1 medium onion,
thinly sliced
1 tablespoon flour
³/₄ cup chili sauce
¹/₂ cup water
1¹/₂ teaspoons light
brown sugar
¹/₂ teaspoon dry
mustard

Combine first 7 ingredients in bowl; mix well. Shape into 2-inch meatballs. Brown in skillet; remove. Drain most of pan drippings. Sauté vegetables in remaining pan drippings; remove. Stir flour into pan drippings. Heat until bubbly, stirring constantly. Add chili sauce and water. Cook until thickened, stirring constantly. Stir in brown sugar and mustard. Add meatballs and vegetables. Simmer, covered, for 20 minutes.

Pat Anderton, Winston-Salem

ITALIAN PEAS AND MEATBALLS

Yield:
6 servings
Utensil:
large skillet
Approx Per
Serving:
Cal 221
Prot 13 g
Carbo 38 g
Fiber 9 g
T Fat 3 g
Chol 47 mg
Sod 963 mg

Dietary
Exchanges:
Milk 0
Vegetable 1/2
Fruit 0
Bread/Starch 2¹/₂
Meat 1/2; Fat 0

8 ounces ground chuck
1 egg, beaten
¹/₂ teaspoon salt
1 tablespoon parsley
flakes
¹/₂ cup seasoned bread
crumbs

3 16-ounce cans peas,
undrained
1 8-ounce can tomato
sauce
¹/₂ teaspoon oregano
2 cloves of garlic,
minced

Combine ground chuck, egg, salt, parsley flakes and bread crumbs in bowl; mix well. Shape into small meatballs. Brown meatballs in large skillet; drain. Add peas, tomato sauce, oregano and garlic. Simmer for 45 minutes.

Jessie Grandinetti

TANGY SWEET AND SOUR MEATBALLS

Yield:
8 servings
Utensil:
skillet
Approx Per
Serving:
Cal 105
Prot 12 g
Carbo 5 g
Fiber <1 g
T Fat 4 g
Chol 30 mg
Sod 517 mg

Dietary
Exchanges:
Milk 0
Vegetable 1/2
Fruit 0
Bread/Starch 0
Meat 1 1/2; Fat 0

1 pound ground round
1/4 cup chopped onion
2 tablespoons finely
chopped parsley
1 tablespoon prepared
mustard
1 clove of garlic, minced
2 teaspoons
Worcestershire sauce
1 teaspoon oregano
1 egg white
2 tablespoons bread
crumbs
1 8-ounce can tomato
sauce
3/4 cup water
2 tablespoons soy sauce
2 tablespoons lemon
juice
2 envelopes artificial
sweetener

Combine ground round and next 8 ingredients in bowl; mix well. Shape into 1-inch meatballs. Brown in skillet sprayed with nonstick cooking spray; drain. Add tomato sauce, water, soy sauce and lemon juice. Simmer for 20 minutes. Remove from heat. Remove meatballs to serving dish. Add artificial sweetener to sauce; mix well. Pour over meatballs.

Janet Mills, Winston-Salem

DIET MEAT LOAF

Yield:
2 servings
Utensil:
casserole
Approx Per
Serving:
Cal 306
Prot 37 g
Carbo 11 g
Fiber 3 g
T Fat 12 g
Chol 105 mg
Sod 342 mg

Dietary
Exchanges:
Milk 0
Vegetable 2
Fruit 0
Bread/Starch 0
Meat 5; Fat 0

14 ounces extra lean
ground beef
4 ounces carrots, grated
2 ounces celery, finely
chopped
1 ounce green onions,
finely chopped
1/4 green bell pepper,
finely chopped
1/2 cup tomato juice
Salt, pepper and garlic
powder to taste

Spray 8x8-inch casserole with nonstick cooking spray. Combine ground beef, carrots, celery, green onions, green pepper, tomato juice and seasonings in bowl; mix well. Press into casserole. Bake at 350 degrees for 1 hour and 10 minutes; drain. Cool slightly before slicing.

Bonnie Henrich, Winston-Salem

CHEESY MEAT LOAF

Yield:
6 servings
Utensil:
loaf pan
**Approx Per
Serving:**
Cal 411
Prot 25 g
Carbo 34 g
Fiber 1 g
T Fat 19 g
Chol 157 mg
Sod 785 mg

**Dietary
Exchanges:**
Milk 0
Vegetable 1/2
Fruit 0
Bread/Starch 1 1/2
Meat 3; Fat 2 1/2

1 pound ground beef
2 eggs, beaten
2 cups bread crumbs
1/2 cup catsup
1 large onion, chopped
1/2 cup chopped green
    bell pepper
1/2 cup milk
2 tablespoons
    Worcestershire sauce
Salt and pepper to
    taste
1/2 teaspoon chili
    powder
2 or 3 slices American
    cheese

Combine ground beef, eggs, bread crumbs, catsup, onion, green pepper, milk, Worcestershire sauce, salt, pepper and chili powder in bowl; mix well. Press into greased loaf pan. Bake at 350 degrees for 1 hour or until brown; drain. Place cheese on top. Bake for 5 minutes longer or until cheese is melted.

Ruby R. Hudspeth, Yadkinville

CHILI MEAT LOAF

Yield:
8 servings
Utensil:
loaf pan
**Approx Per
Serving:**
Cal 315
Prot 23 g
Carbo 17 g
Fiber 1 g
T Fat 17 g
Chol 134 mg
Sod 806 mg

**Dietary
Exchanges:**
Milk 0
Vegetable 1/2
Fruit 0
Bread/Starch 1
Meat 3; Fat 2

1 1/2 pounds ground
    beef
2 teaspoons salt
1/2 teaspoon pepper
2 slices bread,
    crumbled
1 cup oats
1 onion, chopped
1   10-ounce can hot
    dog chili
1 teaspoon garlic powder
1 tablespoon
    Worcestershire sauce
2 teaspoons sage
2 eggs
1 cup milk

Combine ground beef, salt, pepper, bread, oats, onion, chili, garlic powder, Worcestershire sauce, sage, eggs and milk in bowl; mix lightly. Press into 5x9-inch loaf pan. Bake at 350 degrees for 1 hour or until brown.

Nell J. Miller, Winston-Salem

JUICY MEAT LOAF

1 pound ground beef
¹/2 pound ground pork
1 cup fresh bread
  crumbs
1 medium onion,
  chopped
1 egg, beaten
1¹/2 teaspoons salt
¹/4 teaspoon pepper
1 8-ounce can tomato
  sauce
2 tablespoons mustard
2 tablespoons vinegar
2 tablespoons brown
  sugar

Combine ground beef, ground pork, bread crumbs, onion, egg, salt and pepper in bowl. Add ¹/2 of the tomato sauce, reserving remaining sauce. Mix meat loaf lightly. Press into 6x10-inch casserole. Bake at 325 degrees for 35 to 45 minutes. Combine reserved tomato sauce, mustard, vinegar and brown sugar in saucepan. Simmer until slightly thickened, stirring constantly. Baste meat loaf with sauce. Bake for 25 to 30 minutes longer, basting occasionally.

Macie McElroy, Graham

SAUSAGE AND BEEF MEAT LOAF

¹/2 pound sausage
1 pound ground chuck
1 cup undrained
  cooked tomatoes
2 tablespoons chopped
  onion
1 egg
¹/4 teaspoon pepper
¹/4 teaspoon sage
1 teaspoon salt
1 cup cracker crumbs

Combine sausage, ground chuck, tomatoes, onion, egg, pepper, sage, salt and cracker crumbs in bowl; mix well. Press into 5x9-inch loaf pan. Bake at 375 degrees for 45 minutes.

Constance P. Toelkes, Winston-Salem

POP SHAW'S MEAT LOAF

2 pounds lean ground beef
1 pound lean ground pork
1 green bell pepper, chopped
1 onion, chopped
6 tablespoons melted butter
2 eggs, beaten
1 cup cracker crumbs
1 1/2 cups milk
1 cup catsup
1 teaspoon salt
1/4 teaspoon black pepper
1 teaspoon sage
1/2 teaspoon poultry seasoning
2 slices bacon

Combine ground beef and pork in bowl; mix well. Add green pepper, onion, butter, eggs, cracker crumbs, milk, catsup, salt, black pepper, sage and poultry seasoning; mix well. Shape into loaf in 3-inch deep casserole. Place bacon on top. Place in cold oven. Bake at 350 degrees for 1 1/2 hours or until brown.

Earl Shaw, Greensboro

MOSTACCIOLI

1 1/2 to 2 pounds ground beef
1/2 cup chopped onion
2 8-ounce cans tomato sauce
1 6-ounce can sliced mushrooms
1 10-ounce can Cheddar cheese soup
Garlic salt to taste
Salt and pepper to taste
16 ounces mostaccioli
4 ounces Swiss cheese, cubed
8 ounces mozzarella cheese

Brown ground beef with onion in skillet, stirring until crumbly; drain. Add next 6 ingredients. Simmer for 15 minutes, stirring frequently. Cook pasta using package directions; drain. Combine ground beef sauce, pasta and Swiss cheese in bowl; mix well. Cut 2 ounces mozzarella cheese into long thin slices; cut remaining 6 ounces mozzarella cheese into cubes. Add cubes to mixture; mix well. Spoon into large casserole. Top with slices of mozzarella cheese. Bake, covered, at 425 degrees for 20 minutes or until cheese is melted.

Edythe C. Kelly, Greensboro

EASY STUFFED PEPPERS

Yield:
6 servings
Utensil:
saucepan
Approx Per Serving:
Cal 239
Prot 17 g
Carbo 14 g
Fiber 1 g
T Fat 13 g
Chol 95 mg
Sod 587 mg

Dietary Exchanges:
Milk 0
Vegetable 1
Fruit 0
Bread/Starch 1/2
Meat 2 1/2; Fat 1

6 medium green bell
  peppers
1 pound ground beef
2 tablespoons grated
  onion
1 cup soft bread crumbs

1 egg, slightly beaten
1/2 teaspoon salt
1 10-ounce can
  tomato soup
Salt and pepper to
  taste

Cut off tops of peppers, discarding seeds and membranes; invert to drain. Combine ground beef, onion, bread crumbs, egg, 1/2 teaspoon salt and half the soup in bowl; mix well. Spoon into peppers. Place in saucepan; add 1 to 1 1/2 inches salted water. Simmer, covered, for 30 minutes or until peppers are tender; drain. Place on serving plate. Heat remaining soup to serving temperature. Pour over peppers.

Alice Ellis, Advance

IMPOSSIBLE CHEESEBURGER PIE

Yield:
6 servings
Utensil:
pie plate
Approx Per Serving:
Cal 396
Prot 26 g
Carbo 19 g
Fiber 1 g
T Fat 24 g
Chol 214 mg
Sod 590 mg

Dietary Exchanges:
Milk 1/2
Vegetable 1
Fruit 0
Bread/Starch 1/2
Meat 3 1/2; Fat 3

1 pound ground beef
1 1/2 cups chopped
  onions
1/2 teaspoon salt
1/4 teaspoon pepper
1 1/2 cups milk

3/4 cup baking mix
3 eggs
2 tomatoes, sliced
1 cup shredded
  Cheddar cheese

Brown ground beef with onions in skillet, stirring until ground beef is crumbly; drain. Stir in salt and pepper. Spread in greased deep pie plate. Combine milk, baking mix and eggs in mixer bowl or blender container. Beat for 1 minute or process for 15 seconds. Pour over beef mixture in pie plate. Bake at 400 degrees for 25 minutes. Top with tomatoes; sprinkle with cheese. Bake for 5 to 8 minutes longer or until knife inserted in center comes out clean.

Kathleen H. Bartes, Burlington

HAMBURGER QUICHE

Yield:
6 servings
Utensil:
pie plate
Approx Per
Serving:
Cal 468
Prot 22 g
Carbo 20 g
Fiber <1 g
T Fat 33 g
Chol 166 mg
Sod 680 mg

Dietary
Exchanges:
Milk 0
Vegetable ½
Fruit 0
Bread/Starch 1
Meat 3; Fat 5

8 ounces lean ground beef
½ cup chopped onion
½ cup chopped green bell pepper
1 tablespoon butter
3 tablespoons flour
½ teaspoon garlic salt
¼ teaspoon pepper
2 eggs
1 cup milk
1 teaspoon Worcestershire sauce
2 cups shredded sharp Cheddar cheese
1 unbaked 9-inch deep-dish pie shell

Brown ground beef with onion and green pepper in butter in skillet, stirring frequently; drain. Stir in mixture of flour, garlic salt and pepper. Combine eggs, milk, Worcestershire sauce and half the cheese in bowl; mix well. Add to beef mixture; mix well. Spoon into pie shell. Sprinkle with remaining cheese. Bake at 400 degrees for 25 to 30 minutes or until done to taste.

Jeanna Baxter, High Point

CRUSTLESS HAMBURGER QUICHE

Yield:
8 servings
Utensil:
pie plate
Approx Per
Serving:
Cal 294
Prot 15 g
Carbo 4 g
Fiber <1 g
T Fat 25 g
Chol 185 mg
Sod 292 mg

Dietary
Exchanges:
Milk 0
Vegetable 0
Fruit 0
Bread/Starch 0
Meat 2; Fat 4

8 ounces ground beef
1 small onion, chopped
1 cup shredded Cheddar cheese
4 eggs, beaten
½ cup mayonnaise
Salt and pepper to taste
½ cup evaporated milk
¼ cup Parmesan cheese

Brown ground beef in skillet, stirring until crumbly; drain. Spoon into 10-inch pie plate. Sprinkle with onion and Cheddar cheese. Beat eggs with mayonnaise, salt and pepper in bowl; add evaporated milk. Pour over ground beef. Sprinkle with Parmesan cheese. Bake at 325 degrees for 35 to 40 minutes or until brown.

Mrs. Coy M. Vance, Raleigh

ITALIAN MEAT PIE

Yield:
6 servings
Utensil:
pie plate
Approx Per
Serving:
Cal 305
Prot 19 g
Carbo 19 g
Fiber <1 g
T Fat 17 g
Chol 49 mg
Sod 431 mg

Dietary
Exchanges:
Milk 0
Vegetable 0
Fruit 0
Bread/Starch 1
Meat 2½; Fat 2

12 ounces extra-lean
    ground beef
½ cup chopped green
    bell pepper
2 teaspoons cornstarch
¾ cup water
1   6-ounce can tomato
    paste
¼ cup onion flakes

½ teaspoon oregano
¼ teaspoon each garlic
    powder, onion
    powder and pepper
⅓ cup Parmesan cheese
1   9 or 10-inch deep-
    dish pie shell
1 cup shredded
    mozzarella cheese

Brown ground beef in nonstick skillet; drain. Add green pepper. Cook for 2 minutes, stirring constantly. Dissolve cornstarch in water in cup. Add with next 6 ingredients to sauce. Simmer, covered, for 10 minutes. Sprinkle half the Parmesan cheese into pie shell. Layer half the sauce and half the mozzarella cheese on top. Layer remaining sauce and remaining Parmesan cheese over mozzarella cheese. Place on baking sheet. Bake at 400 degrees for 15 minutes. Sprinkle with remaining mozzarella cheese. Bake for 5 minutes.

Mrs. E. F. Rowe, Winston-Salem

POTLUCK CASSEROLE

Yield:
8 servings
Utensil:
baking dish
Approx Per
Serving:
Cal 348
Prot 22 g
Carbo 33 g
Fiber 4 g
T Fat 14 g
Chol 56 mg
Sod 916 mg

Dietary
Exchanges:
Milk 0
Vegetable 1
Fruit 0
Bread/Starch 2
Meat 2; Fat 1½

1½ cups uncooked
    elbow macaroni
Salt to taste
1 pound ground beef
2 medium onions,
    chopped
2   8-ounce cans
    tomato sauce

1   16-ounce can
    kidney beans
½ teaspoon chili
    powder
1 teaspoon salt
1¼ cups shredded
    Cheddar cheese

Cook macaroni in salted boiling water in saucepan until tender; drain. Brown ground beef with onions in skillet, stirring frequently; drain. Add tomato sauce. Simmer for 5 minutes. Add macaroni, beans, chili powder, 1 teaspoon salt and 1 cup cheese; mix well. Spoon into 2-quart baking dish. Sprinkle with remaining ¼ cup cheese. Bake at 375 degrees for 25 to 30 minutes or until bubbly.

Sarah L. Tagert, Greensboro

Russian Noodles

Yield:
6 servings
Utensil:
large skillet
Approx Per
Serving:
Cal 371
Prot 20 g
Carbo 27 g
Fiber 1 g
T Fat 20 g
Chol 66 mg
Sod 1113 mg

Dietary
Exchanges:
Milk 0
Vegetable 1
Fruit 0
Bread/Starch 1½
Meat 2; Fat 3½

1 pound ground beef
1 cup chopped onion
3 cups uncooked
  medium noodles
2 6-ounce cans
  tomato juice
1 tablespoon
  Worcestershire sauce
1½ teaspoons celery salt
1 teaspoon salt
Pepper to taste
¼ cup chopped green
  bell pepper
1 cup sour cream
1 3-ounce can sliced
  mushrooms, drained

Brown ground beef lightly in large skillet, stirring until crumbly; drain. Add onion. Cook until onion is tender but not brown. Sprinkle noodles over beef mixture. Combine tomato juice, Worcestershire sauce, celery salt, salt and pepper in bowl; mix well. Pour over noodles. Bring to a boil; reduce heat. Simmer for 20 minutes. Add green pepper. Simmer, covered, for 10 minutes or until noodles are tender. Stir in sour cream and mushrooms. Heat just to serving temperature.

Helen A. Howard, Pfafftown

Easy Baked Spaghetti

Yield:
6 servings
Utensil:
baking dish
Approx Per
Serving:
Cal 346
Prot 20 g
Carbo 33 g
Fiber 2 g
T Fat 15 g
Chol 54 mg
Sod 494 mg

Dietary
Exchanges:
Milk 0
Vegetable 0
Bread/Starch 2½
Meat 2½
Fat 1½

1 7-ounce package
  spaghetti
8 ounces ground beef
⅓ cup chopped onion
⅓ cup chopped green
  bell pepper
⅓ cup chopped
  mushrooms
1 10-ounce can
  tomato soup
Mrs. Dash seasoning
  to taste
8 ounces mozzarella
  cheese, shredded

Cook spaghetti using package directions; drain. Spoon into greased 9x13-inch baking dish. Brown ground beef in nonstick skillet, stirring until crumbly; drain. Add onion, green pepper and mushrooms; mix well. Stir in soup and seasoning. Spoon over spaghetti; top with cheese. Bake at 325 degrees for 10 to 15 minutes or until cheese melts.

Peggy Kiger, Pfafftown

BEEF SPAGHETTI CASSEROLE

Yield:
10 servings
Utensil:
baking dish
Approx Per
Serving:
Cal 486
Prot 29 g
Carbo 24 g
Fiber 1 g
T Fat 31 g
Chol 110 mg
Sod 569 mg

Dietary
Exchanges:
Milk 0
Vegetable 1/2
Fruit 0
Bread/Starch 1 1/2
Meat 3 1/2; Fat 5

2 pounds ground beef
1 small onion, chopped
8 ounces cream cheese, softened
1 cup cottage cheese
1 cup sour cream
1 8-ounce package spaghetti, cooked
2 8-ounce cans tomato sauce
1 cup shredded sharp Cheddar cheese

Brown ground beef with onion in skillet, stirring until crumbly; drain. Spoon into 9x13-inch baking dish. Combine cream cheese, cottage cheese and sour cream in bowl; mix well. Spread over ground beef layer. Spoon spaghetti over cream cheese mixture. Pour tomato sauce over layers, piercing layers with knife to mix lightly. Top with Cheddar cheese. Bake at 350 degrees for 30 minutes or until heated through and cheese melts.

Mrs. D. S. Coeyman, Greensboro

ITALIAN SPAGHETTI SAUCE

Yield:
12 servings
Utensil:
saucepan
Approx Per
Serving:
Cal 306
Prot 24 g
Carbo 17 g
Fiber 1 g
T Fat 17 g
Chol 74 mg
Sod 935 mg

Dietary
Exchanges:
Milk 0
Vegetable 1
Fruit 0
Bread/Starch 1/2
Meat 3; Fat 1 1/2

3 pounds ground chuck
1 cup finely chopped celery
1 1/2 green bell peppers, finely chopped
2 large onions, finely chopped
3 cups tomato juice
3 6-ounce cans tomato paste
1/2 cup catsup
3 tablespoons chili powder
1 tablespoon salt
1 teaspoon each red pepper and black pepper

Oil bottom of 4-quart saucepan. Brown ground chuck in prepared saucepan, stirring until crumbly. Add celery, green peppers and onions. Cook for 10 minutes, stirring frequently; drain. Add tomato juice, tomato paste, catsup, chili powder, salt, red pepper and black pepper; mix well. Simmer for 4 hours. Serve over spaghetti. May add garlic salt and oregano if desired.

Margia Thomas, Burlington

VERMICELLI WITH ITALIAN MEATBALLS

12 ounces lean ground beef
8 ounces ground veal
²/₃ cup fine dry bread crumbs
1 small onion, finely chopped
1 egg
¹/₄ cup Parmesan cheese
¹/₂ teaspoon salt
¹/₈ teaspoon pepper
1 tablespoon oil
Sweet Tomato Sauce
1   16-ounce package vermicelli, cooked

Combine ground beef, ground veal, bread crumbs, onion, egg, Parmesan cheese, ¹/₂ teaspoon salt and ¹/₈ teaspoon pepper in bowl; mix well. Shape into balls. Roll in oil, coating well. Brown on all sides in skillet; drain. Add meatballs to Sweet Tomato Sauce in large saucepan. Simmer for 30 minutes or until thickened to desired consistency. Spoon over vermicelli. Garnish with additional Parmesan cheese. May use all ground beef if preferred.

Sweet Tomato Sauce

¹/₂ cup chopped onion
1 clove of garlic, minced
2 tablespoons olive oil
4 cups water
1   28-ounce can tomatoes, chopped
2   6-ounce cans tomato paste
1 tablespoon sugar
1 teaspoon oregano
¹/₂ teaspoon basil
1 large bay leaf
1 teaspoon salt
¹/₂ teaspoon pepper

Sauté onion and garlic in olive oil in heavy saucepan. Stir in water, tomatoes, tomato paste, sugar, oregano, basil, bay leaf, 1 teaspoon salt and ¹/₂ teaspoon pepper. Bring to a boil, stirring occasionally; reduce heat. Simmer for 1 hour or longer. Remove bay leaf.

Ruth Kent Eslinger, Winston-Salem

SPAGHETTI SAUCE

Yield:
8 servings
Utensil:
saucepan
**Approx Per
Serving:**
Cal 220
Prot 18 g
Carbo 10 g
Fiber 1 g
T Fat 12 g
Chol 56 mg
Sod 1065 mg

**Dietary
Exchanges:**
Milk 0
Vegetable 1
Fruit 0
Bread/Starch ½
Meat 2½; Fat 1

1½ pounds ground chuck
1 medium onion, chopped
1 small green bell pepper, chopped
1 6-ounce can tomato paste
1 8-ounce can tomato sauce
2 cups stewed tomatoes
2 tablespoons oregano
Garlic salt to taste
1 tablespoon salt
Red pepper to taste

Combine ground chuck with a small amount of water in heavy 6-quart saucepan. Brown, stirring until crumbly; drain. Add onion and green pepper. Stir in tomato paste and tomato sauce. Rinse tomato paste and tomato sauce cans with ½ can water each; stir into ground chuck mixture. Add tomatoes, oregano, garlic salt, salt and red pepper; mix well. Simmer for 1½ hours, skimming grease from surface. Serve over spaghetti.

Polly Martin, Burlington

QUICK HAMBURGER STROGANOFF

Yield:
6 servings
Utensil:
saucepan
**Approx Per
Serving:**
Cal 298
Prot 17 g
Carbo 8 g
Fiber <1 g
T Fat 22 g
Chol 67 mg
Sod 790 mg

**Dietary
Exchanges:**
Milk 0
Vegetable ½
Fruit 0
Bread/Starch 1
Meat 2; Fat 4½

1 pound ground beef
1 10-ounce can cream of mushroom or cream of chicken soup
1 soup can water
1 teaspoon garlic salt
½ teaspoon pepper
2 envelopes butter-flavored noodles and sauce mix
3 cups water
¼ cup minced onion
1 4-ounce can sliced mushrooms
1 cup sour cream

Brown ground beef in large saucepan, stirring until crumbly; drain. Add soup, soup can water, garlic salt and pepper. Stir in noodles and sauce mix, 3 cups water, onion and mushrooms. Simmer for 10 to 15 minutes or until noodles are tender; remove from heat. Fold in sour cream. Serve immediately.

Nutritional information does not include noodles and sauce mix.

Pat Anderton, Winston-Salem

SUNDAY SPECIAL CASSEROLE

1 pound lean ground beef
1 small onion, chopped
1   10-ounce can cream of chicken soup
½ soup can water
1   16-ounce package frozen Tater Tots

Brown ground beef with onion in skillet, stirring until ground beef is crumbly; drain. Spoon into 9x9-inch baking dish. Mix soup with water in bowl. Spread over ground beef mixture; top with Tater Tots. Bake at 350 degrees for 30 minutes. May add topping of buttered bread crumbs if desired.

Johnsie Estes, Winston-Salem

OVERNIGHT BRUNCH EGGS

1 pound Smithfield ham sausage
12 eggs
2 tablespoons milk
¾ cup Sherry
1   10-ounce can cream of celery soup
2 cups shredded extra sharp Cheddar cheese

Brown sausage in skillet, stirring until crumbly; drain. Beat eggs with milk in mixer bowl. Scramble eggs in pan drippings until soft cooked. Combine Sherry and soup in saucepan. Heat until well blended, stirring constantly. Layer eggs, sausage, soup and cheese ½ at a time in 9x13-inch casserole;. Chill, covered, in refrigerator overnight. Bake, uncovered, at 375 degrees for 30 to 40 minutes or until brown and bubbly.

Deloris L. Peterson, Greensboro

CHEESE AND HAM STRATA

¾ cup sliced mushrooms
¼ cup sliced green onions
½ pound cooked ham cubes
8 ounces Velveeta cheese, cubed
4 cups ¾-inch bread cubes
1 cup milk
4 eggs, beaten

Sauté mushrooms and green onions in nonstick skillet until tender. Cool. Combine ham, cheese and bread cubes in bowl; mix well. Stir in vegetables. Place in greased 8-inch square casserole. Mix milk and eggs in bowl. Pour over ham mixture. Chill, covered, for several hours. Bake, uncovered, at 350 degrees for 50 to 55 minutes or until golden brown. Let stand 10 minutes before serving.

Dorothy D. Burroughs

HAM LOAF

1 pound ground smoked ham
1 pound ground pork
2 eggs, beaten
1 cup cracker crumbs
1 cup milk
1 cup water
1 cup vinegar
1 cup packed brown sugar
2 tablespoons dry mustard

Combine ham, pork and eggs in bowl; mix well. Mix cracker crumbs and milk in small bowl. Stir into ham mixture. Shape into loaf; place in 7x11-inch loaf pan. Combine water, vinegar, brown sugar and mustard in saucepan. Simmer for 30 minutes or until thickened, stirring frequently. Baste ham loaf. Bake at 325 degrees for 1 hour and 30 minutes, basting every 30 minutes. Heat remaining sauce to serving temperature. Invert ham loaf to serving plate. Serve with remaining sauce.

Kathy Boyd, Winston-Salem

HAM AND POTATO CASSEROLE

<table>
<tr><td>

Yield:
12 servings
Utensil:
casserole
Approx Per Serving:
Cal 154
Prot 9 g
Carbo 11 g
Fiber 1 g
T Fat 8 g
Chol 25 mg
Sod 609 mg

</td></tr>
<tr><td>

Dietary Exchanges:
Milk 0
Vegetable 0
Fruit 0
Bread/Starch 1
Meat 1; Fat 1½

</td></tr>
</table>

¼ cup chopped onion
2 tablespoons margarine
1 10-ounce can cream of chicken soup
½ cup milk
3 ounces Cheddar cheese, shredded
2 tablespoons chopped pimento
2 tablespoons chopped green bell pepper
3 cups cooked potato cubes
2 cups chopped cooked ham

Sauté onion in margarine in skillet until soft. Add soup, milk and half the cheese. Cook until cheese is melted, stirring frequently. Stir in pimento, green pepper, potato cubes and ham; mix well. Spoon into 9x13-inch casserole. Sprinkle with remaining cheese. Bake at 350 degrees for 35 minutes.

Kathleen Dabley

SPANISH STIR-FRY

<table>
<tr><td>

Yield:
10 servings
Utensil:
wok
Approx Per Serving:
Cal 427
Prot 27 g
Carbo 33 g
Fiber 4 g
T Fat 21 g
Chol 61 mg
Sod 1832 mg

</td></tr>
<tr><td>

Dietary Exchanges:
Milk 0
Vegetable 2
Fruit 0
Bread/Starch 1½
Meat 3; Fat 2

</td></tr>
</table>

½ cup oil
¾ pound onions, chopped
Mrs. Dash, seasoned salt, thyme, celery flakes, parsley flakes, crushed red pepper to taste
¾ pound carrots, sliced
¾ pound cabbage, chopped
¾ pound green bell peppers, chopped
1 8-ounce can mushrooms
½ pound celery, sliced
½ cup water
Ginger to taste
1 tablespoon cornstarch
1 beef bouillon cube
2¼ pounds baked ham, cubed
5 cups hot cooked rice

Heat 1 tablespoon oil in wok. Add onions and seasonings. Stir-fry until tender. Remove to bowl. Stir-fry next 5 ingredients 1 at a time, adding seasonings and oil as needed; remove to bowl. Combine water, ginger, cornstarch and bouillon cube in saucepan. Cook until thickened, stirring constantly. Combine cooked vegetables, sauce and ham in wok. Stir-fry until of serving temperature. Serve over hot cooked rice.

Jack Holcomb, Belew Creek

SHISH KABOBS TERIYAKI

¼ cup soy sauce
¼ cup vinegar
¼ cup oil
1 clove of garlic, minced
1 teaspoon minced
  fresh ginger
1 pound boneless
  lamb, cut into
  1-inch cubes
4 cherry tomatoes

1 green pepper, cut
  into 1-inch pieces
1 8-ounce can
  pineapple chunks,
  drained
1 8-ounce can whole
  water chestnuts,
  drained
4 cups hot cooked rice
8 fresh mushroom caps

Combine first 5 ingredients in a large shallow non-metallic container. Add lamb. Marinate, covered, in refrigerator for several hours to overnight. Remove lamb from marinade. Alternate lamb, tomatoes, green pepper, pineapple, water chestnuts and mushrooms on skewers. Grill kabobs over medium coals for 5 minutes on each side or until done to taste, basting frequently with marinade. Serve over hot cooked rice; garnish with parsley sprigs. May substitute pork, chicken or beef for lamb.

A. A. Vargas, Pfafftown

BARBECUE PORK

3 pounds pork loin
  roast
½ cup catsup
½ cup vinegar
½ cup water
½ cup Worcestershire
  sauce

¼ cup Texas Pete hot
  pepper sauce
3 tablespoons brown
  sugar
½ teaspoon dry
  mustard
Salt and pepper to taste

Place pork roast in baking pan. Bake at 350 degrees for 3 hours. Remove fat from roast. Slice or chop lean pork. Place in baking pan. Mix catsup, vinegar, water, Worcestershire sauce, Texas Pete sauce, brown sugar, dry mustard, salt and pepper in bowl. Pour over pork. Bake for 1 hour or until dry.

Ronald Belcher, Advance

SLOW COOKER BARBECUE

Yield:
6 servings
Utensil:
slow cooker
Approx Per Serving:
Cal 399
Prot 25 g
Carbo 12 g
Fiber 0 g
T Fat 28 g
Chol 95 mg
Sod 1270 mg

Dietary Exchanges:
Milk 0
Vegetable 0
Bread/Starch 0
Meat 3¹/₂
Fat 3¹/₂

1³/₄ pounds pork loin roast
2 tablespoons sugar
1 tablespoon salt
1 cup vinegar
6 to 8 tablespoons pork roast pan drippings
¹/₄ to ¹/₂ cup catsup
1 tablespoon Worcestershire sauce
Texas Pete hot pepper sauce to taste

Brown pork roast quickly in hot skillet. Place in slow cooker. Mix sugar, salt and vinegar in bowl. Pour over roast. Cook on Low for 10 to 12 hours or until very tender. Remove roast, reserving 6 to 8 tablespoons pan drippings. Cut roast into small pieces. Add catsup, Worcestershire sauce and Texas Pete sauce to pan drippings; mix well. Combine with chopped roast in bowl; toss to mix.

Nancy Boner Parnell, Winston-Salem

CAP'N BRACK'S PORK CHOPS

Yield:
4 servings
Utensil:
skillet
Approx Per Serving:
Cal 379
Prot 33 g
Carbo 16 g
Fiber <1 g
T Fat 20 g
Chol 98 mg
Sod 520 mg

Dietary Exchanges:
Milk 0
Vegetable 0
Fruit 0
Bread/Starch 1
Meat 5; Fat ¹/₂

1 tablespoon prepared mustard
4 ¹/₂-inch center-cut pork chops
¹/₂ cup self-rising flour
1 tablespoon oil
1 10-ounce can chicken with rice soup

Spread mustard on both sides of pork chops; sprinkle with flour. Brown pork chops on both sides in hot oil in skillet. Cook for 10 to 12 minutes. Add soup. Simmer, covered, for 5 to 7 minutes or until pork chops are tender.

Don Braxton, Burlington

CREOLE PORK CHOPS

Yield:
4 servings
Utensil:
10-inch skillet
Approx Per
Serving:
Cal 475
Prot 32 g
Carbo 42 g
Fiber 2 g
T Fat 19 g
Chol 98 mg
Sod 79 mg

Dietary
Exchanges:
Milk 0
Vegetable 1
Fruit 0
Bread/Starch 2½
Meat 4½; Fat ½

4 loin pork chops
Salt and pepper to
 taste
1 tablespoon bacon
 drippings
1¾ cups hot water

1 cup white whole
 grain rice
1 large onion, sliced
1 green bell pepper,
 sliced
1 large tomato, sliced

Trim pork chops; season with salt and pepper. Brown on both sides in bacon drippings in 10-inch skillet. Add water and rice. Layer onion, green pepper and tomato on top. Add additional seasonings if desired. Simmer, covered, for 30 to 35 minutes or until rice and chops are tender and water is absorbed. Fluff rice with fork. Serve with vegetables on top. May use other kinds of rice and substitute canned tomatoes for fresh.

Wendie Brumsey, Greensboro

PORK CHOPS WITH APPLES

Yield:
4 servings
Utensil:
large skillet
Approx Per
Serving:
Cal 331
Prot 29 g
Carbo 19 g
Fiber 3 g
T Fat 16 g
Chol 95 mg
Sod 363 mg

Dietary
Exchanges:
Milk 0
Vegetable ½
Fruit 1
Bread/Starch 0
Meat 4½; Fat 0

4 4-ounce center-cut
 pork chops
1 medium onion,
 chopped
1¼ cups water
¼ teaspoon pepper

1 teaspoon chicken-
 flavored instant
 bouillon
3 medium cooking
 apples
½ teaspoon cinnamon

Trim pork chops. Spray skillet with nonstick cooking spray. Brown pork chops with onion in skillet. Mix water, pepper and instant bouillon in bowl, stirring until bouillon is dissolved. Add to pork chops. Simmer, covered for 15 to 20 minutes. Skim off fat. Peel and slice apples. Add apples and cinnamon to skillet. Simmer, covered, for 15 minutes longer. Serve hot.

Janet Mills, Winston-Salem

BAKED PORK CHOPS AND BAKED BEANS

Yield:
4 servings
Utensil:
casserole
Approx Per
Serving:
Cal 782
Prot 40 g
Carbo 128 g
Fiber 7 g
T Fat 16 g
Chol 95 mg
Sod 1426 mg

Dietary
Exchanges:
Milk 0
Vegetable 1/2
Fruit 0
Bread/Starch 4 1/2
Meat 4 1/2; Fat 0

2 16-ounce cans baked beans
1/2 medium onion, chopped
1 cup packed brown sugar
1/2 cup catsup
1 teaspoon prepared mustard
1/4 cup syrup
1 teaspoon Worcestershire sauce
4 lean center-cut pork chops

Combine baked beans, onion, brown sugar, catsup, mustard, syrup and Worcestershire sauce in 8x10-inch casserole; mix well. Place pork chops on top. Bake, uncovered, at 350 degrees for 1 1/2 hours or until pork chops are brown and tender.

Betty Myers, Graham

PORK CHOP CASSEROLE

Yield:
10 servings
Utensil:
casserole
Approx Per
Serving:
Cal 447
Prot 35 g
Carbo 20 g
Fiber 2 g
T Fat 25 g
Chol 117 mg
Sod 637 mg

Dietary
Exchanges:
Milk 0
Vegetable 0
Fruit 0
Bread/Starch 1 1/2
Meat 5; Fat 2 1/2

10 pork chops
4 or 5 potatoes, sliced
1 large onion, sliced
1 10-ounce can cream of mushroom soup
Salt and pepper to taste
6 to 8 slices American cheese

Place pork chops in 9x13-inch casserole. Layer potatoes, onion, soup, salt, pepper and cheese over pork chops. Bake, covered with foil, at 350 degrees for 1 hour or until pork chops and potatoes are tender.

Carol N. Flynn, Greensboro

Rice and Pork Chops

2 10-ounce cans
  chicken broth
1 cup uncooked rice
2 teaspoons parsley
  flakes
2 teaspoons salt

6 lean pork chops
2 tablespoons oil
6 onion slices
12 apple wedges

Heat broth in saucepan. Mix rice, parsley flakes and salt in 9x13-inch casserole. Add hot broth. Brown pork chops in hot oil in skillet. Arrange over rice mixture. Top each pork chop with onion slice. Add apple wedges. Bake, covered with foil, at 350 degrees for 1 hour.

Norma Hauser

Pork Chops and Rice

4 medium thick pork
  chops
Salt and pepper to
  taste
1 16-ounce package
  long grain and wild
  rice

1 large onion, sliced
2 tomatoes, sliced
1/2 green bell pepper,
  sliced
1 10-ounce can
  chicken broth
1/8 teaspoon thyme

Season pork chops with salt and pepper. Brown in skillet; drain, reserving 2 tablespoons pan drippings. Place rice in greased casserole. Layer pork chops, onion, tomatoes and green pepper over rice. Pour chicken broth over layers; sprinkle with thyme. Add reserved 2 tablespoons pan drippings. Bake at 350 degrees for 1 hour. May substitute drained canned tomatoes for fresh.

Betty Hawkins, Burlington

SAUCY PORK CHOPS

Yield:
4 servings
Utensil:
casserole
Approx Per
Serving:
Cal 309
Prot 30 g
Carbo 16 g
Fiber 1 g
T Fat 14 g
Chol 94 mg
Sod 875 mg

Dietary
Exchanges:
Milk 0
Vegetable 1/2
Fruit 0
Bread/Starch 0
Meat 4 1/2; Fat 0

1/2 cup catsup
1 teaspoon salt
1/2 teaspoon chili powder
1 cup water
1 1/2 teaspoons dry mustard

1 tablespoon brown sugar
4 loin 1 1/2-inch center-cut pork chops
1 lemon, sliced
1 yellow onion, sliced

Mix catsup, salt, chili powder, water, mustard and brown sugar in small bowl. Place pork chops in greased 10x10-inch casserole. Pour in sauce. Place 1 slice of lemon and onion on each pork chop. Bake, covered, at 325 degrees for 2 hours. Remove cover; baste with sauce. Bake for 30 minutes longer. Baste pork chops with sauce before serving.

Mary Jane Daleiden, Greensboro

SPANISH PORK CHOPS

Yield:
6 servings
Utensil:
skillet
Approx Per
Serving:
Cal 279
Prot 28 g
Carbo 7 g
Fiber 0 g
T Fat 15 g
Chol 95 mg
Sod 504 mg

Dietary
Exchanges:
Milk 0
Vegetable 0
Fruit 0
Bread/Starch 0
Meat 4 1/2; Fat 0

6 pork chops
1/4 cup catsup
1 teaspoon dry mustard
1 teaspoon salt

1 teaspoon pepper
1/2 cup water
1/4 cup vinegar
2 tablespoons sugar

Brown pork chops in skillet. Mix catsup, mustard, salt, pepper, water, vinegar and sugar in small bowl. Add to pork chops. Simmer, covered, for 45 minutes.

Jean Watkins, Haw River

STUFFING-TOPPED PORK CHOPS

Yield:
8 servings
Utensil:
baking pan
Approx Per
Serving:
Cal 486
Prot 39 g
Carbo 18 g
Fiber 1 g
T Fat 28 g
Chol 139 mg
Sod 672 mg

Dietary
Exchanges:
Milk 0
Vegetable 0
Fruit 0
Bread/Starch 1
Meat 5½; Fat 2

8 to 10   1-inch pork
   chops
2 cups chicken
   bouillon
1 small onion, chopped
⅓ cup melted butter

4 slices bread,
   crumbled
4 ounces herb-seasoned
   stuffing mix
1 teaspoon parsley
   flakes

Trim pork chops. Place in baking pan. Pour in ¼ cup bouillon. Mix remaining bouillon, onion, butter, bread, stuffing mix and parsley flakes in bowl. Spread over pork chops. Bake, uncovered, at 325 degrees for 1 hour and 15 minutes or until tender.

Mary Frances Naughton, Greensboro

GREEK SOUVLAKIA

Yield:
12 servings
Utensil:
grill
Approx Per
Serving:
Cal 332
Prot 27 g
Carbo 1 g
Fiber <1 g
T Fat 24 g
Chol 93 mg
Sod 724 mg

Dietary
Exchanges:
Milk 0
Vegetable 0
Fruit 0
Bread/Starch 0
Meat 4; Fat 2

½ cup olive oil
½ cup lemon juice
2 cloves of garlic,
   minced
4 teaspoons salt

¼ teaspoon pepper
2 tablespoons oregano
4 pounds 1½-inch
   pork cubes

Combine olive oil, lemon juice, garlic, salt, pepper and oregano in bowl. Place pork cubes in large flat dish. Pour marinade over pork. Marinate, covered, in refrigerator for 3 to 4 days, turning occasionally. Thread onto skewers. Cook on hot grill to desired doneness.

Ruby Hicks

SLOW COOKER ROAST PORK

Yield:
6 servings
Utensil:
slow cooker
Approx Per
Serving:
Cal 547
Prot 57 g
Carbo 18 g
Fiber 1 g
T Fat 26 g
Chol 177 mg
Sod 143 mg

Dietary
Exchanges:
Milk 0
Vegetable 0
Fruit 0
Bread/Starch 1
Meat 8; Fat 0

3 or 4 sweet potatoes
1   3 to 4-pound pork
    loin roast
Kitchen Bouquet to
    taste

Garlic powder to taste
Salt and pepper to
    taste

Place sweet potatoes in slow cooker. Brush roast with Kitchen Bouquet. Sprinkle with garlic powder, salt and pepper. Place over sweet potatoes. Cook, covered, on High for 2 hours. Reduce temperature to Low. Cook for 4 hours longer. Do not remove cover for 4 hours.

Thelma L. Wilson, Winston-Salem

PORK ROAST WITH TANGY SAUCE

Yield:
12 servings
Utensil:
roasting pan
Approx Per
Serving:
Cal 321
Prot 28 g
Carbo 23 g
Fiber 0 g
T Fat 13 g
Chol 89 mg
Sod 447 mg

Dietary
Exchanges:
Milk 0
Vegetable 0
Fruit 0
Bread/Starch 0
Meat 4; Fat 0

1/2 teaspoon salt
1/2 teaspoon garlic salt
1/2 teaspoon chili
    powder
1   4-pound rolled and
    tied pork loin roast

1 cup apple jelly
1 cup catsup
2 tablespoons vinegar
2 teaspoons chili
    powder

Combine salt, garlic salt and 1/2 teaspoon chili powder in small bowl; mix well. Rub roast with mixture. Place roast, fat side up, on rack in shallow roasting pan. Bake in preheated 325-degree oven for 1 hour and 45 minutes. Combine jelly, catsup, vinegar and remaining 2 teaspoons chili powder in saucepan. Bring to a boil. Simmer, uncovered, for 2 minutes, stirring constantly. Baste roast with jelly sauce. Bake for 15 minutes longer or until tender. Let stand for 10 minutes before carving. Serve remaining sauce with roast.

Edith Gerringer, Burlington

SPARERIBS CANTONESE

Yield:
4 servings
Utensil:
slow cooker
**Approx Per
Serving:**
Cal 1433
Prot 90 g
Carbo 59 g
Fiber 0 g
T Fat 90 g
Chol 362 mg
Sod 2343 mg

**Dietary
Exchanges:**
Milk 0
Vegetable 0
Fruit 0
Bread/Starch 0
Meat 13; Fat 10

4 pounds pork ribs
1 cup orange marmalade
1/2 teaspoon ground
ginger
1/2 cup soy sauce
1/2 teaspoon garlic
powder
3/4 cup water

Brown pork ribs in skillet; drain. Mix marmalade, ginger, soy sauce, garlic powder and water in bowl. Place ribs in slow cooker. Add marmalade sauce. Cook on Low for 4 hours or until tender. May bake ribs at 450 degrees for 30 minutes; drain. Add sauce. Bake at 350 degrees for 1 1/2 hours.

Wanda Lemons, Clemmons

BREAKFAST EGGS

Yield:
6 servings
Utensil:
casserole
**Approx Per
Serving:**
Cal 403
Prot 22 g
Carbo 17 g
Fiber 1 g
T Fat 27 g
Chol 334 mg
Sod 1140 mg

**Dietary
Exchanges:**
Milk 1/2
Vegetable 0
Fruit 0
Bread/Starch 1
Meat 2 1/2; Fat 4

1 pound sausage
6 eggs, beaten
6 slices bread, cubed
1/2 cup shredded
Cheddar cheese
2 cups milk
1 teaspoon salt
1 teaspoon mustard
1/2 cup shredded
Cheddar cheese

Brown sausage in skillet, stirring until crumbly; drain. Combine eggs, bread, 1/2 cup cheese, milk, salt, mustard and sausage in bowl; mix well. Pour into greased 7x12-inch casserole. Sprinkle with remaining 1/2 cup cheese. Chill, covered, in refrigerator for 12 hours to overnight. Bake at 350 degrees for 35 minutes or until bubbly.

Lee P. Powell, Clemmons

Bubble and Squeak

Yield:
4 servings
Utensil:
4-quart casserole
**Approx Per
Serving:**
Cal 508
Prot 26 g
Carbo 9 g
Fiber 2 g
T Fat 41 g
Chol 105 mg
Sod 1407 mg

**Dietary
Exchanges:**
Milk 0
Vegetable 1/2
Bread/Starch 1/2
Meat 3 1/2
Fat 6 1/2

1 head cabbage
1 pound link sausage
2 tablespoons margarine
2 tablespoons
  cornstarch
1 1/2 cups water
1 chicken bouillon
  cube
8 ounces Muenster
  cheese slices

Cut cabbage into 6 to 8 wedges. Cook in steamer until tender-crisp; drain. Brown sausage in skillet; drain. Cut into 1/2-inch slices. Melt margarine in saucepan. Add mixture of cornstarch and water. Add bouillon cube. Cook over medium heat until bouillon cube is dissolved and sauce is thickened, stirring constantly. Layer 1/2 of the cabbage wedges, sausage, sauce and cheese slices in buttered 4-quart casserole. Repeat layers, ending with cheese. Bake at 350 degrees for 25 minutes.

Susan Merdeth, Raleigh

Pepperoni Pizzas

Yield:
16 servings
Utensil:
2 pizza pans
**Approx Per
Serving:**
Cal 182
Prot 6 g
Carbo 21 g
Fiber 1 g
T Fat 8 g
Chol 0 mg
Sod 553 mg

**Dietary
Exchanges:**
Milk 0
Vegetable 1/2
Fruit 0
Bread/Starch 1
Meat 1/2; Fat 1 1/2

1 envelope dry yeast
1 cup lukewarm water
1 teaspoon salt
3 cups unbleached flour
2 cloves of garlic, minced
2 tablespoons olive oil
1 16-ounce can plum
  tomatoes, drained
1 teaspoon oregano
1 8-ounce can tomato
  sauce
1 teaspoon basil
Salt and pepper to taste
1 8-ounce package
  sliced pepperoni

Dissolve yeast in water in bowl. Add salt and flour; mix well. Knead on floured surface for 10 minutes. Place in lightly greased bowl. Cover with towel. Let rise for 1 hour. Sauté garlic in oil in saucepan over medium heat for 1 minute. Chop tomatoes. Add with next 6 ingredients to garlic. Simmer for 30 minutes or until thickened, stirring frequently. Oil 2 pizza pans; sprinkle with cornmeal. Divide dough into 2 portions. Roll each into circle; place on prepared pans. Spread sauce over dough. Layer pepperoni slices over sauce. Bake in preheated 475-degree oven for 10 to 15 minutes or until crust is brown.

Marion S. Haerle, Greensboro

Red Beans and Rice

Yield:
6 servings
Utensil:
large saucepan
**Approx Per
Serving:**
Cal 597
Prot 30 g
Carbo 93 g
Fiber 20 g
T Fat 12 g
Chol 30 mg
Sod 630 mg

**Dietary
Exchanges:**
Milk 0
Vegetable 1½
Bread/Starch 5½
Meat 2½
Fat 1½

1 pound dry red beans
1 cup chopped onion
1 cup sliced celery
½ cup chopped green
  bell pepper
1 pound link sausage,
  sliced
1 bay leaf
1 teaspoon garlic
  powder
Tabasco sauce to taste
Salt and pepper to
  taste
1 16-ounce can
  tomatoes, chopped
6 cups cooked rice

Soak beans using package directions; drain. Place in large saucepan with water to half the depth of beans. Bring to a boil. Sauté onion, celery and green pepper in nonstick skillet until tender. Add to beans. Add sausage, bay leaf, garlic powder, Tabasco sauce, salt, pepper and tomatoes. Simmer for 2 hours or until beans are tender, stirring occasionally. Mash beans against side of pan to thicken. Serve over rice.

Teresa Crispino, High Point

Breakfast Casserole

Yield:
6 servings
Utensil:
casserole
**Approx Per
Serving:**
Cal 403
Prot 22 g
Carbo 17 g
Fiber 1 g
T Fat 27 g
Chol 334 mg
Sod 1140 mg

**Dietary
Exchanges:**
Milk ½
Vegetable 0
Fruit 0
Bread/Starch 1
Meat 2½; Fat 4

1 pound sausage
6 slices bread, crusts
  trimmed
6 eggs, beaten
1 teaspoon salt
1 teaspoon dry mustard
1 cup shredded
  Cheddar cheese
2 cups milk

Brown sausage in skillet, stirring until crumbly; drain. Cool. Cut bread into cubes. Combine sausage, eggs, bread, salt, mustard, cheese and milk in bowl; mix well. Pour into buttered 9x9-inch casserole. Bake at 350 degrees for 45 minutes. May be refrigerated overnight before cooking.

Agnes C. Morgan, Burlington

RICE AND SAUSAGE CASSEROLE

Yield:
8 servings
Utensil:
casserole
Approx Per Serving:
Cal 240
Prot 9 g
Carbo 27 g
Fiber 1 g
T Fat 11 g
Chol 25 mg
Sod 1221 mg

Dietary Exchanges:
Milk 0
Vegetable 1/2
Fruit 0
Bread/Starch 2
Meat 1; Fat 2

1 pound lean sausage
1 onion, chopped
3 or 4 stalks celery, chopped
4 bouillon cubes
4 cups boiling water
1 cup uncooked rice
1 10-ounce can cream of chicken soup
1 8-ounce can sliced water chestnuts

Brown sausage in skillet, stirring until crumbly; drain, reserving pan drippings. Sauté onion and celery in pan drippings until tender. Stir bouillon cubes into boiling water until dissolved. Combine sausage, vegetables, bouillon, rice and soup in casserole; mix well. Chill, covered, in refrigerator overnight. Skim grease from casserole. Stir in water chestnuts. Bake at 325 degrees for 1½ hours.

Dorothy Holcomb

SAUERKRAUT AND POLISH SAUSAGE

Yield:
6 servings
Utensil:
deep casserole
Approx Per Serving:
Cal 170
Prot 8 g
Carbo 8 g
Fiber 0 g
T Fat 12 g
Chol 28 mg
Sod 1507 mg

Dietary Exchanges:
Milk 0
Vegetable 1½
Fruit 0
Bread/Starch 0
Meat 1; Fat 2

1 pound kielbasa Polish sausage
2 16-ounce cans sauerkraut
5 slices crisp-fried bacon, crumbled
Caraway seed to taste

Cook sausage in boiling water to cover in saucepan for 20 minutes; drain, reserving cooking water. Rinse sauerkraut; drain well. Slice sausage diagonally into ¼-inch slices. Combine sauerkraut, crumbled bacon and caraway seed in deep casserole; mix well. Place sausage slices on top. Pour reserved cooking water over all. Bake at 350 degrees for 30 minutes.

Ellman Grubb, Springdale, Arkansas

SAUSAGE AND RICE CASSEROLE

Yield:
8 servings
Utensil:
casserole
Approx Per
Serving:
Cal 217
Prot 10 g
Carbo 15 g
Fiber 1 g
T Fat 13 g
Chol 34 mg
Sod 625 mg

Dietary
Exchanges:
Milk 0
Vegetable ½
Fruit 0
Bread/Starch 1½
Meat 1; Fat 2

¾ pound sausage
1 medium onion,
   finely chopped
½ green bell pepper,
   chopped

2 cups cooked rice
1   10-ounce can cream
   of chicken soup
1 cup shredded sharp
   Cheddar cheese

Brown sausage with onion and green pepper in skillet, stirring until crumbly; drain. Layer rice, sausage, soup and cheese in 9x13-inch casserole. Bake at 350 degrees for 25 minutes or until bubbly.

Kathleen Oakley

VENISON PIE

Yield:
8 servings
Utensil:
skillet
Approx Per
Serving:
Cal 256
Prot 20 g
Carbo 23 g
Fiber 1 g
T Fat 10 g
Chol 22 mg
Sod 967 mg

Dietary
Exchanges:
Milk 0
Vegetable 1
Bread/Starch 1
Meat 2½
Fat 1½

1 pound ground
   venison
1 cup chopped onion
1 cup chopped green
   bell pepper
2   8-ounce cans
   tomato sauce
1   12-ounce can
   yellow corn, drained
1 clove of garlic

1 tablespoon sugar
1 teaspoon salt
2 teaspoons chili
   powder
6 ounces sharp
   Cheddar cheese,
   chopped
1   6-ounce package
   corn muffin mix

Brown venison with onion and green pepper in 2-quart cast-iron skillet, stirring frequently. Add tomato sauce, corn, garlic, sugar, salt and chili powder; mix well. Simmer for 20 to 25 minutes or until thickened, stirring frequently. Stir in cheese. Cook until cheese is melted. Prepare corn muffin mix using package directions. Spoon batter over all. Bake at 375 degrees for 40 minutes or until corn bread tests done.

Jimmy Thompson, Mebane

POULTRY

BUFFET CHICKEN

Yield:
8 servings
Utensil:
baking dish
Approx Per
Serving:
Cal 323
Prot 29 g
Carbo 21 g
Fiber 0 g
T Fat 13 g
Chol 72 mg
Sod 514 mg

Dietary
Exchanges:
Milk 0
Vegetable 0
Fruit 0
Bread/Starch 1½
Meat 3; Fat 1½

8 chicken breast filets   **¼ cup melted**
8 ounces stuffing mix   **margarine**

Rinse chicken and pat dry. Pound flat with meat mallet. Prepare stuffing mix using package directions. Spoon mixture onto filets; fold to enclose filling. Place in baking dish; brush with melted margarine. Bake at 325 degrees for 1 hour, brushing with margarine every 15 minutes. Garnish servings with cranberry sauce cut into desired shapes.

Ellie Key, Graham

APRICOT CHICKEN

Yield:
6 servings
Utensil:
baking dish
Approx Per
Serving:
Cal 485
Prot 27 g
Carbo 34 g
Fiber <1 g
T Fat 26 g
Chol 72 mg
Sod 980 mg

Dietary
Exchanges:
Milk 0
Vegetable 0
Fruit 0
Bread/Starch ½
Meat 3; Fat 5

6 chicken breasts   **1 8-ounce jar apricot**
¼ cup white wine   **preserves**
1 8-ounce bottle of   **1 envelope onion soup**
**   Russian salad**   **mix**
**   dressing**

Rinse chicken and pat dry; place in baking dish. Combine wine, salad dressing, preserves and soup mix in saucepan. Heat until bubbly, stirring to mix well. Pour over chicken. Bake, covered, at 350 degrees for 45 minutes. Bake, uncovered, for 15 minutes longer.

Nancy Garner, Burlington

BAKED CHICKEN BREASTS

Yield:
4 servings
Utensil:
baking dish
Approx Per Serving:
Cal 477
Prot 32 g
Carbo 48 g
Fiber 1 g
T Fat 16 g
Chol 79 mg
Sod 1198 mg

Dietary Exchanges:
Milk 0
Vegetable 0
Fruit 0
Bread/Starch 5
Meat 3; Fat 4

1 10-ounce can cream of mushroom soup
1 10-ounce can cream of chicken soup
1½ cups water
1 cup uncooked rice
4 chicken breasts

Mix soups and water in bowl. Spread in baking dish. Sprinkle rice over soups. Rinse chicken and pat dry. Arrange over rice. Bake at 350 degrees for 1½ hours.

B. S. Cuthrell, Winston-Salem

CREAMY BAKED CHICKEN BREASTS

Yield:
4 servings
Utensil:
baking dish
Approx Per Serving:
Cal 767
Prot 70 g
Carbo 13 g
Fiber <1 g
T Fat 45 g
Chol 202 mg
Sod 1099 mg

Dietary Exchanges:
Milk 0
Vegetable 0
Fruit 0
Bread/Starch 1½
Meat 9½; Fat 6

8 chicken breast filets
8 4x4-inch slices Swiss cheese
1 10-ounce can cream of chicken soup
½ cup white wine
1 cup herb-seasoned stuffing mix
¼ cup melted margarine

Rinse chicken and pat dry. Arrange in lightly greased 10x10-baking dish. Top with cheese slices. Combine soup with wine in bowl; mix well. Spoon evenly over chicken. Sprinkle with stuffing mix; drizzle with margarine. Bake at 350 degrees for 55 to 60 minutes or until done to taste.

Audrey H. Jackson, Winston-Salem

BAKED CHICKEN WITH RICE

1 cup uncooked rice
1 envelope onion soup
  mix
6 chicken breasts,
  skinned

1 10-ounce can cream
   of mushroom soup
1 soup can water
¹/₈ teaspoon pepper

Sprinkle rice evenly in 9x9-inch nonstick baking dish or baking dish sprayed with nonstick cooking spray. Sprinkle ¹/₄ of the soup mix over rice. Rinse chicken and pat dry. Arrange over layers; top with remaining soup mix. Combine mushroom soup, water and pepper in bowl; mix well. Spoon over chicken. Bake, covered with foil, at 325 degrees for 2 hours. May use cream of celery or cream of chicken soup if preferred.

Janet Mills, Winston-Salem

BAKED CHICKEN AND SAUERKRAUT

8 chicken breast filets
1 teaspoon salt
¹/₂ teaspoon pepper
1 16-ounce can
   sauerkraut, drained

4 large slices Swiss
  cheese
1¹/₄ cups Thousand
   Island salad
   dressing

Rinse chicken and pat dry. Arrange in greased 9x9-inch baking dish; sprinkle with salt and pepper. Layer sauerkraut, cheese and salad dressing over chicken. Bake, covered with foil, at 325 degrees for 1¹/₂ hours or until chicken is fork-tender. Garnish with parsley.

Mrs. John Raum, Winston-Salem

BREAST OF CHICKEN

1/4 cup flour
1/4 teaspoon paprika
1/4 teaspoon pepper
2 chicken breast filets
1/4 cup margarine
1/2 cup white or Marsala cooking wine
1 cup sliced mushrooms
2 tablespoons minced parsley

Mix flour with paprika and pepper in bowl. Rinse chicken and pat dry. Sprinkle with flour mixture, coating well. Cook in margarine in skillet until golden brown on both sides and cooked through. Remove to oven-proof platter. Keep warm in 200-degree oven. Pour wine into skillet, stirring to deglaze. Add mushrooms. Cook until wine is reduced by 1/2. Add any juices from chicken platter. Pour over chicken. Sprinkle with parsley.

Janet Mills, Winston-Salem

CHICKEN CACCIATORE

1 31/2-pound chicken, cut up
3 tablespoons olive oil
1/4 cup unsalted butter
1/2 cup minced parsley
1 teaspoon rosemary
6 large mushrooms, chopped
2 large tomatoes, peeled, chopped
Freshly ground pepper to taste

Rinse chicken and pat dry. Sauté in olive oil in heavy skillet until golden brown. Transfer to covered baking dish. Add butter to drippings in skillet. Sauté parsley in butter for 5 minutes. Stir in rosemary and mushrooms. Stir in tomatoes. Cook, covered, for 5 minutes. Spoon over chicken; sprinkle with pepper. Bake, covered, at 350 degrees for 35 to 40 minutes or until chicken is tender. Serve over pasta which has been tossed with olive oil.

Nutritional information does not include pasta.

Pauline B. Hart, Clemmons

Cajun Chicken Breasts

Yield:
4 servings
Yield:
grill
Approx Per
Serving:
Cal 427
Prot 34 g
Carbo <1 g
Fiber 0 g
T Fat 32 g
Chol 96 mg
Sod 386 mg

Dietary
Exchanges:
Milk 0
Vegetable 0
Bread/Starch 0
Meat 4½
Fat 4½

1½ pounds chicken breast filets
½ cup melted margarine

2 teaspoons (about) Cajun seasoning

Rinse chicken and pat dry. Brush with margarine; sprinkle with seasoning. Grill until done to taste, turning frequently and basting with margarine. May broil if preferred. May substitute fish for chicken.

Nutritional information does not include Cajun seasoning.

Aura Lee Wilson, Burlington

Chicken Cheese Bake

Yield:
2 servings
Utensil:
baking dish
Approx Per
Serving:
Cal 640
Prot 51 g
Carbo 23 g
Fiber <1 g
T Fat 35 g
Chol 130 mg
Sod 2025 mg

Dietary
Exchanges:
Milk 0
Vegetable 0
Fruit 0
Bread/Starch 3½
Meat 6½; Fat 7

2 large chicken breast filets
1   10-ounce can cream of mushroom soup
¼ cup white wine
3 ounces Monterey Jack cheese, shredded

2 ounces Parmesan cheese
Freshly ground pepper to taste

Rinse chicken and pat dry; place in 9x9-inch baking dish. Mix soup and wine in bowl. Pour over chicken. Top with Monterey Jack cheese. Bake at 400 degrees for 30 minutes. Sprinkle with Parmesan cheese and pepper.

Robin Hall, Greensboro

COUNTRY CHICKEN

1/2 cup dry bread crumbs
1/4 cup Parmesan cheese
1 tablespoon chopped parsley
1/4 teaspoon salt
1/8 teaspoon pepper
8 chicken breast filets
1/2 cup milk
2 tablespoons butter

Combine bread crumbs, cheese, parsley, salt and pepper in bowl. Rinse chicken and pat dry. Dip in milk, then in crumb mixture, coating well. Cook in butter in large skillet for 5 to 7 minutes on each side or until golden brown and done to taste.

Jeanna Baxter, High Point

CREAMED CHICKEN IN PATTY SHELLS

1/4 cup margarine
8 medium chicken breasts
Salt and pepper to taste
1 large onion, chopped
1/2 cup margarine
1 10-ounce can cream of chicken soup
1/2 10-ounce can cream of celery soup
1/2 to 1 soup can water
Salt and pepper to taste
1 2-ounce jar chopped pimento
12 puff pastry patty shells, baked

Melt 1/4 cup margarine in baking dish. Rinse chicken and pat dry. Sprinkle with salt and pepper. Place in margarine in baking dish. Bake, covered, at 325 degrees for 1 hour. Chop into 1-inch pieces, discarding skin and bones. Sauté onion in 1/2 cup margarine in saucepan. Add soups, chicken, water, salt and pepper; mix well. Simmer for 15 minutes. Stir in pimento. Spoon into patty shells.

Penny Monk, Burlington

Slow Cooker Chicken

Yield:
10 servings
Utensil:
slow cooker
Approx Per
Serving:
Cal 248
Prot 29 g
Carbo 5 g
Fiber <1 g
T Fat 12 g
Chol 79 mg
Sod 607 mg

Dietary
Exchanges:
Milk 0
Vegetable 0
Bread/Starch 1
Meat 3½
Fat 1½

5 whole chicken breasts
Juice of 2 lemons
Paprika, celery salt, salt and pepper to taste

1 10-ounce can cream of mushroom soup
1 10-ounce can cream of celery soup
½ cup Parmesan cheese

Rinse chicken and pat dry. Season with lemon juice, paprika, celery salt, salt and pepper. Place in slow cooker. Combine soups in medium bowl; mix well. Spoon over chicken. Sprinkle with cheese. Cook on Low for 6 to 8 hours or until done to taste. Serve over rice. May add ½ cup dry Sherry or white wine if desired.

Thelma L. Wilson, Winston-Salem

Chicken Delight

Yield:
6 servings
Utensil:
baking dish
Approx Per
Serving:
Cal 489
Prot 27 g
Carbo 37 g
Fiber 1 g
T Fat 26 g
Chol 72 mg
Sod 993 mg

Dietary
Exchanges:
Milk 0
Vegetable 0
Fruit 2
Bread/Starch ½
Meat 3; Fat 5

6 chicken breast filets
1 8-ounce bottle of Catalina salad dressing

1 16-ounce can whole cranberry sauce
1 envelope onion soup mix

Rinse chicken and pat dry. Arrange in 9x13-inch baking dish. Combine salad dressing, cranberry sauce and soup mix in bowl; mix well. Spoon over chicken. Bake at 300 degrees for 1½ hours. Serve over rice.

Dot Fesperman, Winston-Salem

CHICKEN DIABLO

Yield:
4 servings
Utensil:
baking pan
Approx Per Serving:
Cal 335
Prot 51 g
Carbo 0 g
Fiber 0 g
T Fat 13 g
Chol 144 mg
Sod 1097 mg

Dietary Exchanges:
Milk 0
Vegetable 0
Fruit 0
Bread/Starch 0
Meat 6½; Fat 0

1 3-pound chicken
1 teaspoon garlic
  powder
2 teaspoons MSG
2 teaspoons salt
2 teaspoons pepper

Cut chicken into 12 small portions, discarding skin; rinse and pat dry. Place on greased foil in 1-inch deep baking pan. Combine garlic powder, MSG, salt and pepper in small jar or shaker; mix well. Sprinkle on chicken, turning to season well. Bake at 500 degrees for 10 to 22 minutes or until done to taste.

Pat Radisch, Kernersville

DOUBLE CRISPY CHICKEN

Yield:
6 servings
Utensil:
baking pan
Approx Per Serving:
Cal 503
Prot 41 g
Carbo 43 g
Fiber 1 g
T Fat 17 g
Chol 147 mg
Sod 630 mg

Dietary Exchanges:
Milk 0
Vegetable 0
Bread/Starch 2½
Meat 4½
Fat 1½

1 egg
1 cup milk
1 cup flour
½ teaspoon salt
¼ teaspoon pepper
1 3-pound chicken,
  cut up
7 cups cornflakes,
  crushed
3 tablespoons melted
  margarine

Beat egg and milk in small mixer bowl. Add flour, salt and pepper; mix until smooth. Rinse chicken and pat dry. Dip in batter; coat well with cornflake crumbs. Arrange skin side up in single layer in foil-lined baking pan. Drizzle with margarine. Bake at 350 degrees for 1 hour or until chicken is tender.

Lela Smith, Germanton

DIXIE CHICKEN

½ cup yellow
  cornmeal
½ cup flour
1 teaspoon salt
¼ teaspoon pepper

1 2½-pound chicken,
  cut up
½ cup buttermilk
½ cup melted
  margarine

Combine cornmeal, flour, salt and pepper in bowl; mix well. Rinse chicken and pat dry. Dip in buttermilk; coat well with flour mixture. Arrange in single layer in buttered baking pan. Drizzle with melted margarine. Bake at 375 to 400 degrees for 1 hour or until done to taste.

Norma Hall, Mebane

EASY COMPANY CHICKEN

1 4-ounce jar chipped
  beef
6 chicken breast filets
6 slices bacon

1 10-ounce can cream
  of mushroom soup
1 cup light sour cream

Sprinkle half the chipped beef in baking dish. Rinse chicken and pat dry. Wrap 1 slice bacon around each filet. Arrange in prepared dish. Top with remaining beef. Combine soup and sour cream in bowl; mix well. Spoon over layers. Bake, covered, at 350 degrees for 1 hour.

Nancy Garner, Burlington

FAST AND EASY CHICKEN

4 large chicken breasts
Mrs. Dash seasoning
   to taste
2 tablespoons oil

1 10-ounce can cream
   of chicken soup
⅓ cup water

Rinse chicken and pat dry. Sprinkle with seasoning. Brown on both sides in oil in skillet; reduce heat to medium. Cook, covered, for 7 minutes or until done to taste. Spoon soup over chicken. Pour water over top. Simmer for 8 to 10 minutes. Serve with rice or stove-top stuffing.

Peggy Y. Kiger, Pfafftown

ITALIAN CHICKEN

4 chicken breasts,
  skinned
1 15-ounce jar
   spaghetti sauce

1½ cups Parmesan
  cheese
1 cup shredded
  Cheddar cheese

Arrange chicken meaty side down in 9x13-inch baking dish. Pour half the spaghetti sauce over chicken; sprinkle with half the Parmesan cheese. Bake, covered, at 400 degrees for 20 minutes. Turn chicken over. Top with remaining spaghetti sauce and Parmesan cheese. Bake, covered, for 20 minutes. Add Cheddar cheese. Bake, uncovered, for 10 minutes longer.

Colleen Blackwood, Elon College

JADE TREE CHICKEN

Yield:
4 servings
Utensil:
skillet
Approx Per
Serving:
Cal 304
Prot 23 g
Carbo 10 g
Fiber 3 g
T Fat 19 g
Chol 54 mg
Sod 1236 mg

Dietary
Exchanges:
Milk 0
Vegetable 1½
Bread/Starch 0
Meat 2½
Fat 2½

2 tablespoons soy sauce
1 tablespoon oil
1 teaspoon cornstarch
Garlic powder to taste
½ teaspoon sugar
¼ teaspoon salt
¼ teaspoon red pepper
3 chicken breast filets
2 cups broccoli flowerets
1 cup sliced celery
1 onion, cut into 8
   wedges
3 tablespoons oil
2 tablespoons soy sauce
1 teaspoon cornstarch
2 tablespoons dry
   Sherry
¼ cup cold water

Combine first 7 ingredients in large bowl; mix well. Rinse chicken and pat dry. Cut into bite-sized pieces. Add to marinade; mix well. Marinate, covered, in refrigerator for 20 minutes. Stir-fry broccoli, celery and onion in 3 tablespoons oil in skillet for 6 minutes or until tender-crisp. Remove with slotted spoon. Add chicken to skillet. Stir-fry for 5 minutes. Add stir-fried vegetables. Mix remaining ingredients in small bowl;. Pour over chicken mixture. Simmer, uncovered, for 3 minutes, stirring constantly. Serve over rice.

Mrs. Fordie Atkins, Lakeland, Florida

ONION CRISPY CHICKEN

Yield:
4 servings
Utensil:
baking dish
Approx Per
Serving:
Cal 511
Prot 28 g
Carbo 16 g
Fiber 1 g
T Fat 38 g
Chol 72 mg
Sod 436 mg

Dietary
Exchanges:
Milk 0
Vegetable 0
Fruit 0
Bread/Starch 1
Meat 3; Fat 6

4 chicken breast filets
½ cup melted
   margarine
1 tablespoon
   Worcestershire sauce
1 teaspoon dry mustard
Salt and pepper to taste
2 3-ounce cans
   French-fried onions,
   crushed

Rinse chicken and pat dry. Pound with meat mallet to flatten. Combine margarine, Worcestershire sauce, dry mustard, salt and pepper in bowl; mix well. Dip chicken in margarine mixture; coat well with crushed onions. Arrange in buttered 9x9-inch baking dish. Top with any remaining onion crumbs; drizzle with remaining margarine. Bake at 350 degrees for 30 minutes.

M. P. Cromer, Winston-Salem

ORANGE AND LEMON CHICKEN

Yield:
4 servings
Utensil:
baking dish
**Approx Per
Serving:**
Cal 283
Prot 26 g
Carbo 18 g
Fiber 1 g
T Fat 12 g
Chol 72 mg
Sod 63 mg

**Dietary
Exchanges:**
Milk 0
Vegetable 0
Fruit 1
Bread/Starch 0
Meat 3; Fat 1

4 large chicken breast filets
Juice of 4 large oranges
Juice of 3 large lemons
2 tablespoons brown sugar
1½ tablespoons olive oil
¼ teaspoon marjoram
Pepper to taste

Rinse chicken and pat dry. Arrange in 9x13-inch baking dish. Combine orange juice, lemon juice, brown sugar, olive oil, marjoram and pepper in small bowl; mix well. Pour over chicken. Marinate in refrigerator for 24 hours. Bake chicken at 400 degrees for 45 to 50 minutes or until done to taste. Serve with brown or wild rice and asparagus.

Robin Hall, Greensboro

OVEN-FRIED CHICKEN

Yield:
6 servings
Utensil:
baking dish
**Approx Per
Serving:**
Cal 451
Prot 35 g
Carbo 14 g
Fiber 0 g
T Fat 27 g
Chol 96 mg
Sod 875 mg

**Dietary
Exchanges:**
Milk 0
Vegetable 0
Bread/Starch 1
Meat 4½
Fat 3½

1 3-pound chicken, cut up
Salt to taste
½ cup margarine
1 cup baking mix
1 teaspoon paprika
1 teaspoon salt
¼ teaspoon pepper

Rinse chicken, removing skin. Combine with salted water to cover in bowl. Let stand in refrigerator overnight. Drain and pat dry. Melt margarine in foil-lined 9x13-inch baking dish. Combine baking mix, paprika, salt and pepper in bowl. Roll chicken in baking mix, coating well. Arrange in prepared baking dish. Bake at 425 degrees for 35 minutes. Turn chicken. Bake for 15 minutes longer or until done to taste.

Mary M. Gregory, Winston-Salem

OVEN-FRIED SESAME CHICKEN

2 tablespoons flour
3 tablespoons sesame
  seed
1/4 teaspoon pepper
4 chicken breasts,
  skinned

2 tablespoons soy
  sauce
2 tablespoons melted
  reduced-calorie
  margarine

Combine flour, sesame seed and pepper in bowl; mix well. Rinse chicken and pat dry. Dip in soy sauce; coat well with sesame seed mixture. Arrange bone side down in shallow 9x9-inch baking dish. Drizzle with margarine. Bake at 400 degrees for 40 to 45 minutes or until done to taste.

Mrs. M. B. Owens, Burlington

CHICKEN IN PAPRIKA SAUCE

4 pounds cut-up
  chicken
1/4 cup margarine
2 green bell peppers,
  cut into strips
3 medium onions,
  chopped
4 large tomatoes, cut
  into wedges
4 stalks celery,
  chopped

3/4 cup sour cream
1/2 10-ounce can
  cream of mushroom
  soup
1/4 teaspoon
  Worcestershire sauce
1 tablespoon paprika
2 teaspoons salt
1/8 teaspoon red pepper

Rinse chicken and pat dry. Brown on all sides in margarine in large skillet. Add green peppers, onions, tomatoes and celery. Simmer, covered, for 15 minutes. Combine sour cream, soup, Worcestershire sauce, paprika, salt and red pepper in small saucepan; mix well. Heat just to the boiling point over medium heat, stirring constantly. Pour over chicken. Simmer, covered, for 1 hour or until chicken is tender. Serve over rice.

Mabel G. Trent, Elon College

CHICKEN PARISIAN

Yield:
4 servings
Utensil:
baking dish
Approx Per Serving:
Cal 391
Prot 29 g
Carbo 9 g
Fiber 1 g
T Fat 24 g
Chol 98 mg
Sod 685 mg

Dietary Exchanges:
Milk 0
Vegetable 1/2
Fruit 0
Bread/Starch 1 1/2
Meat 3; Fat 5 1/2

4 chicken breast filets
1 10-ounce can cream of mushroom soup
1/2 cup white wine
1 4-ounce can sliced mushrooms, drained
1 cup sour cream

Rinse chicken and pat dry. Arrange in 8x8-inch baking dish. Combine soup, wine and mushrooms in bowl; mix well. Pour over chicken. Bake at 350 degrees for 1 hour to 1 hour and 15 minutes. Remove chicken to serving plate. Stir sour cream into liquid in baking dish. Serve over chicken.

Sharon M. Fanelli, Gibsonville

CHICKEN BREASTS PARMESAN

Yield:
4 servings
Utensil:
skillet
Approx Per Serving:
Cal 259
Prot 30 g
Carbo 6 g
Fiber <1 g
T Fat 12 g
Chol 76 mg
Sod 233 mg

Dietary Exchanges:
Milk 0
Vegetable 0
Fruit 0
Bread/Starch 1/2
Meat 4; Fat 1

4 4-ounce chicken breast filets
1/3 cup fine dry bread crumbs
1 tablespoon minced parsley
2 egg whites
2 teaspoons water
3 tablespoons Parmesan cheese
1 tablespoon olive oil

Rinse chicken and pat dry. Pound to 1/4-inch thickness with meat mallet. Mix bread crumbs and parsley in shallow dish. Beat egg whites with water in bowl. Roll chicken in cheese. Dip in egg whites, then roll in bread crumb mixture, coating well. Place on rack. Chill for 20 minutes. Heat olive oil in heavy 10-inch skillet over medium-high heat for 1 minute. Add chicken. Brown for 3 minutes on each side or until done to taste. Place on warm serving plate; garnish with lemon quarters.

Pat Harwood, Graham

CHICKEN PARMESAN

⅓ cup water
¼ cup Parmesan
  cheese
¼ cup cornflake
  crumbs
1 tablespoon parsley
  flakes
¼ teaspoon garlic
  powder

¼ teaspoon paprika
⅛ teaspoon thyme
¼ teaspoon pepper
4 chicken breasts,
  skinned
1 tablespoon oil
1 tablespoon melted
  margarine
⅓ cup Marsala

Spray baking pan with nonstick cooking spray. Add water to pan. Mix cheese, cornflake crumbs, parsley flakes, garlic powder, paprika, thyme and pepper in bowl. Rinse chicken and pat dry. Roll in cheese mixture, coating well. Arrange in prepared pan. Drizzle with oil and margarine. Bake at 350 degrees for 30 minutes. Pour wine over chicken. Reduce oven temperature to 325 degrees; cover chicken with foil. Bake for 10 minutes; remove foil. Bake for 10 minutes longer.

Norma B. Moore, Burlington

CHICKEN PIE

4 chicken breasts
1 10-ounce can cream
  of chicken soup
1 teaspoon baking
  powder

1 cup self-rising flour
1 cup milk
½ cup melted
  margarine

Rinse chicken and pat dry. Cook in water to cover in saucepan until tender. Drain, reserving 2 cups broth. Chop chicken, discarding bones. Combine chicken, reserved broth and soup in bowl; mix well. Spoon into baking dish. Combine baking powder, flour, milk and margarine in bowl; mix well. Spoon over chicken. Bake at 350 degrees until golden brown.

Mary Kington, Kernersville

CHICKEN POTPIE

2½ pounds chicken breast filets, cooked, chopped
1 16-ounce package frozen mixed vegetables
2 cups chicken broth
2 10-ounce cans cream of chicken soup
1 cup baking mix
1 cup buttermilk
½ cup melted margarine
½ teaspoon pepper

Layer chicken and vegetables in 9x13-inch baking dish. Heat chicken broth and soup in saucepan until bubbly, stirring to mix well. Pour over layers. Combine baking mix, buttermilk, margarine and pepper in bowl; mix until smooth. Spoon evenly over layers. Bake at 350 degrees for 1 hour or until crust is light brown.

Marilyn Lauritzen, Greensboro

CHICKEN AND SAUSAGE PERLOW

3 pounds cut-up chicken
1 pound pork sausage links
2 pounds smoked sausage
1 large onion, chopped
1 large green bell pepper, chopped
8 cups water
½ cup butter
Salt and pepper to taste
4 cups uncooked regular rice

Rinse chicken. Cut sausage links into ½-inch slices; cut smoked sausage into ¼-inch slices. Combine chicken and sausage with onion, green pepper, water, butter, salt and pepper in cast-iron pot. Simmer, covered, for 45 minutes or until chicken is falling from bones. Bring to a boil. Stir in rice; reduce heat. Simmer, covered, for 20 minutes. Stir well, removing chicken bones and skin. Cook for 10 minutes longer or until all liquid is absorbed and rice is tender. Perlow is a dish from the low country where rice is a major menu item. The name is probably derived from pilau or pilaf.

Royce Flynt, King

CHICKEN ROLL-UPS

Yield:
6 servings
Utensil:
baking dish
Approx Per
Serving:
Cal 413
Prot 37 g
Carbo 8 g
Fiber 0 g
T Fat 24 g
Chol 131 mg
Sod 679 mg

Dietary
Exchanges:
Milk 0
Vegetable 0
Fruit 0
Bread/Starch 1/2
Meat 5; Fat 2 1/2

6 chicken breast filets
Garlic salt to taste
6 slices ham
6 slices mozzarella
  cheese
1/2 cup seasoned bread
  crumbs
Pepper to taste
1/4 cup melted butter
1/4 cup dry Sherry

Rinse chicken and pat dry. Pound to 1/4-inch thickness with meat mallet. Sprinkle with garlic salt. Top each filet with slice of ham and cheese. Sprinkle with seasoned bread crumbs and pepper. Roll filets to enclose filling; secure with toothpicks. Place in baking dish. Drizzle with butter and wine. Bake at 350 degrees for 35 minutes or just until tender.

Mavis Peterson, Elon College

CHICKEN SIMON AND GARFUNKLE

Yield:
6 servings
Utensil:
baking dish
Approx Per
Serving:
Cal 494
Prot 35 g
Carbo 15 g
Fiber <1 g
T Fat 30 g
Chol 227 mg
Sod 419 mg

Dietary
Exchanges:
Milk 0
Vegetable 0
Fruit 0
Bread/Starch 1
Meat 4 1/2; Fat 4

6 chicken breast filets
Salt to taste
1/2 cup butter, softened
6 ounces mozzarella
  cheese
1/2 cup flour
2 eggs, beaten
1/2 cup bread crumbs
1 teaspoon parsley
1/4 teaspoon sage
1/4 teaspoon rosemary
1/4 teaspoon thyme
1/2 cup mushrooms
1/2 cup white wine

Rinse chicken and pat dry. Flatten chicken with meat mallet; sprinkle with salt. Spread with butter. Cut cheese into rectangles. Place 1 piece cheese at narrow end of each filet. Roll to enclose. Coat with flour. Dip into eggs and then roll in bread crumbs. Place seam side down in baking dish. Sprinkle with parsley, sage, rosemary, thyme and mushrooms. Bake at 350 degrees for 30 minutes. Add wine. Bake for 15 minutes longer.

Mavis Peterson, Elon College

Spicy Chicken and Pasta

Yield:
6 servings
Utensil:
skillet
Approx Per Serving:
Cal 720
Prot 46 g
Carbo 73 g
Fiber 6 g
T Fat 26 g
Chol 96 mg
Sod 756 mg

Dietary Exchanges:
Milk 0
Vegetable 1½
Fruit 0
Bread/Starch 4½
Meat 4½; Fat 3

3 pounds chicken breasts and thighs, skinned, boned
1 bunch celery
¼ cup plus 3 tablespoons oil
⅓ cup flour
½ teaspoon red pepper
1 medium green bell pepper, chopped
1 medium onion, chopped
1 28-ounce can tomatoes
1¼ teaspoons salt
1 teaspoon sugar
1 teaspoon thyme
2 teaspoons Worcestershire sauce
¼ teaspoon cumin
1 16-ounce package macaroni

Rinse chicken and pat dry. Cut into 14 portions. Chop 1 stalk celery. Cut remaining celery into 2-inch slices. Cook chicken, several pieces at a time, in ¼ cup hot oil in 12-inch skillet, removing to large bowl when brown. Cook sliced celery in pan drippings until light brown and tender-crisp; remove to bowl with chicken. Add 3 tablespoons oil to skillet. Stir in flour and red pepper. Cook over medium heat for 20 minutes or until flour is dark brown but not burned, stirring constantly. Add chopped celery, green pepper and onion. Cook until vegetables are tender-crisp. Add chicken and celery slices to skillet. Add undrained tomatoes, salt, sugar, thyme, Worcestershire sauce and cumin. Bring to a boil over high heat; reduce heat. Simmer, covered, for 25 to 30 minutes or until chicken is very tender, stirring frequently. Cook macaroni using package directions; drain. Stir macaroni into chicken mixture just before serving.

Edith K. Gordon, Pfafftown

MICROWAVE CHICKEN BRUNCH

Yield:
2 servings
Utensil:
dish
Approx Per
Serving:
Cal 374
Prot 28 g
Carbo 2 g
Fiber <1 g
T Fat 27 g
Chol 121 mg
Sod 293 mg

Dietary
Exchanges:
Milk 0
Vegetable 0
Bread/Starch 0
Meat 3½
Fat 4½

2 chicken breasts
2 green onions with
  tops, sliced
2 tablespoons butter
¼ cup sour cream
1 teaspoon lemon juice
2 teaspoons dry Sherry
Salt and pepper to
  taste
2 slices bacon

Rinse chicken and pat dry. Place in microwave-safe dish; cover with plastic wrap. Microwave on High until chicken is tender. Remove chicken to cool. Add green onions and butter to drippings; cover with plastic wrap. Microwave on High for 2 minutes. Add sour cream, lemon juice, Sherry, salt and pepper; mix well. Wrap bacon in paper towels. Place on microwave-safe dish. Microwave on High for 2 to 2½ minutes or until crisp. Cut chicken into strips. Stir into sour cream sauce. Spoon onto serving plate. Crumble bacon over top.

Gloria Stinson, Winston-Salem

MICROWAVE CHICKEN STIR-FRY

Yield:
4 servings
Utensil:
browning dish
Approx Per
Serving:
Cal 346
Prot 31 g
Carbo 8 g
Fiber 2 g
T Fat 21 g
Chol 72 mg
Sod 834 mg

Dietary
Exchanges:
Milk 0
Vegetable ½
Fruit 0
Bread/Starch 0
Meat 4; Fat 3

¼ cup reduced-
  sodium soy sauce
2 tablespoons oil
1 tablespoon dry Sherry
2 whole boneless
  chicken breasts,
  skinned
1 green bell pepper
½ cup sliced almonds
1 medium onion,
  thinly sliced

Combine soy sauce, oil and Sherry in bowl; mix well. Wash chicken and pat dry. Flatten chicken breasts with meat mallet. Cut into ¾ to 1½-inch strips. Add to marinade. Let stand at room temperature for 15 to 30 minutes or in refrigerator overnight. Cut green pepper into ¼-inch strips. Preheat microwave browning dish on High in microwave for 5 minutes. Add chicken, marinade, green pepper and almonds. Stir briskly until sizzling slows. Separate onion into rings. Add to browning dish. Microwave on High for 5½ to 8½ minutes or until chicken is tender and no longer pink, stirring every 2 minutes.

Roseleen Brandon, Yadkinville

CHICKEN AND SNOW PEAS STIR-FRY

Yield:
6 servings
Utensil:
wok
**Approx Per
Serving:**
Cal 308
Prot 22 g
Carbo 31 g
Fiber 4 g
T Fat 10 g
Chol 48 mg
Sod 521 mg

**Dietary
Exchanges:**
Milk 0
Vegetable 1
Fruit 0
Bread/Starch 1½
Meat 2; Fat 1

2 tablespoons soy sauce
3 tablespoons water
1 tablespoon cornstarch
¾ cup chicken stock
¼ cup dry Sherry
2 tablespoons oil
1 clove of garlic, cut
    into halves
1 pound chicken
    breasts, cubed
2 cups sliced celery
1 large onion, cut into
    1-inch pieces
1 green bell pepper,
    coarsely chopped
4 ounces snow peas
8 ounces fresh
    mushrooms, sliced
3 cups cooked rice
2 scallions, chopped

Combine first 5 ingredients in bowl; mix well. Add oil and garlic to hot wok. Brown garlic for 1 minute. Remove garlic and discard. Stir-fry chicken for 3 minutes; push to 1 side. Add celery. Stir-fry for 3 minutes; push to 1 side. Add onion, green pepper and snow peas. Stir-fry for 3 minutes. Add mushrooms. Stir-fry for 3 minutes. Add soy sauce mixture. Cook until sauce is thickened and clear, stirring constantly. Serve over rice. Sprinkle with chopped scallions.

Betty Link, Venice, Florida

CHICKEN STUFF

Utensil:
6 servings
Utensil:
skillet
**Approx Per
Serving:**
Cal 414
Prot 39 g
Carbo 36 g
Fiber 3 g
T Fat 12 g
Chol 96 mg
Sod 418 mg

**Dietary
Exchanges:**
Milk 0
Vegetable 1
Fruit 0
Bread/Starch 2
Meat 4½; Fat ½

1½ cups chopped
    celery
1½ cups chopped
    green bell peppers
1 large onion, sliced
1 cup julienne carrot
1 clove of garlic,
    minced
1 tablespoon olive oil
1 cup sliced
    mushrooms
1 teaspoon ginger
1 teaspoon hot pepper
    sauce
1 tablespoon soy sauce
1   3-pound chicken,
    cooked, chopped
Salt and pepper to
    taste
2 tablespoons flour
1 cup chicken broth
4 cups cooked rice

Sauté celery, green peppers, onion, carrot and garlic in oil in 10-inch skillet for 10 minutes or until vegetables are tender-crisp. Add mushrooms, ginger, hot pepper sauce, soy sauce, chicken, salt and pepper. Blend flour and chicken broth in small bowl. Add to skillet. Simmer until thickened, stirring constantly. Serve over rice.

Ginger King, Graham

Yield:
6 servings
Utensil:
wok
Approx Per Serving:
Cal 787
Prot 30 g
Carbo 27 g
Fiber 2 g
T Fat 64 g
Chol 72 mg
Sod 853 mg

Dietary Exchanges:
Milk 0
Vegetable 1
Fruit 0
Bread/Starch 1/2
Meat 4; Fat 11 1/2

3 whole chicken breasts, cut into strips
1/4 teaspoon salt
2 tablespoons cornstarch
1/2 teaspoon sugar
Cayenne pepper to taste
1 cup peanut oil
1 cup walnuts
1 tablespoon sugar
3 tablespoons peanut oil
1 tablespoon chopped gingerroot
1 tablespoon minced garlic

2 tablespoons sliced scallions
2 red bell peppers, cut into 1-inch triangles
2 carrots, julienne-style
1 cup snow peas
1 bunch watercress, chopped
1/2 cup catsup
4 teaspoons Worcestershire sauce
3 tablespoons sugar
1/2 cup chicken broth
4 teaspoons soy sauce
1/2 teaspoon salt
2 teaspoons sesame oil

Rinse chicken and pat dry. Coat with mixture of 1/4 teaspoon salt, cornstarch, 1/2 teaspoon sugar and cayenne pepper. Brown in 1 cup hot peanut oil in wok. Remove chicken to bowl. Cook walnuts in oil remaining in wok for 15 to 30 seconds; remove to bowl. Add 1 tablespoon sugar; toss to mix. Discard oil in wok. Add 3 tablespoons peanut oil to wok. Stir-fry gingerroot, garlic and scallions for 30 seconds. Add red peppers and carrots. Stir-fry until tender-crisp. Add chicken, snow peas and watercress. Stir-fry until heated through. Mix catsup, Worcestershire sauce, 3 tablespoons sugar, chicken broth, soy sauce, 1/2 teaspoon salt, sesame oil and cayenne pepper in bowl. Add to wok. Cook until thickened, stirring constantly. Add walnuts.

Ruth Kitchens, Winston-Salem

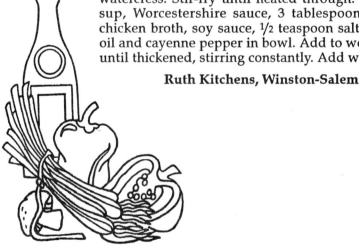

Swiss Chicken Casserole

Yield:
6 servings
Utensil:
baking dish
Approx Per
Serving:
Cal 430
Prot 37 g
Carbo 12 g
Fiber <1 g
T Fat 26 g
Chol 124 mg
Sod 723 mg

Dietary
Exchanges:
Milk 0
Vegetable 0
Fruit 0
Bread/Starch 1¹/2
Meat 5; Fat 3¹/2

6 chicken breast filets
6 4x4-inch Swiss cheese slices
1 10-ounce can cream of chicken soup
¹/4 cup milk
2 cups herb-seasoned stuffing mix
¹/4 cup melted butter

Rinse chicken and pat dry; arrange in lightly greased 8x12-inch baking dish. Top with cheese slices. Combine soup and milk in bowl; mix well. Spoon over chicken; sprinkle with stuffing mix. Drizzle with butter. Bake, covered, at 350 degrees for 50 minutes.

Anna E. Myers, Hillsville, Virginia

Chicken Supreme

Yield:
12 servings
Utensil:
baking dish
Approx Per
Serving:
Cal 529
Prot 61 g
Carbo 14 g
Fiber <1 g
T Fat 24 g
Chol 183 mg
Sod 948 mg

Dietary
Exchanges:
Milk 0
Vegetable 0
Fruit 0
Bread/Starch 1
Meat 7¹/2; Fat 2

2 cups sour cream
¹/4 cup lemon juice
4 teaspoons Worcestershire sauce
4 cloves of garlic, minced
2 teaspoons paprika
2 teaspoons celery salt
2 teaspoons salt
¹/2 teaspoon pepper
12 chicken breast filets
1 cup bread crumbs
1 cup cornflake crumbs
¹/2 cup butter
¹/2 cup shortening

Combine first 8 ingredients in bowl; mix well. Rinse chicken and pat dry. Add to sour cream mixture, coating well. Marinate in refrigerator overnight. Drain chicken. Roll in mixture of bread crumbs and cornflake crumbs, coating well. Arrange in shallow baking dish. Melt butter with shortening in saucepan. Spoon half the butter mixture over chicken. Bake at 350 degrees for 45 minutes. Spoon remaining butter over chicken. Bake for 10 to 15 minutes longer or until brown and done to taste. Serve with rice pilaf.

Nutritional information includes entire amount of marinade.

Judy Vandervelde, Burlington

Chicken with Wild Rice

Yield:
8 servings
Utensil:
baking pan
Approx Per
Serving:
Cal 434
Prot 34 g
Carbo 43 g
Fiber 1 g
T Fat 13 g
Chol 73 mg
Sod 1526 mg

Dietary
Exchanges:
Milk 0
Vegetable 0
Fruit 0
Bread/Starch 4
Meat 3; Fat 2½

2 6-ounce packages wild rice
2 10-ounce cans cream of mushroom soup
2½ cups water
8 chicken breasts
2 envelopes onion soup mix
¾ cup white wine

Sprinkle rice in greased shallow baking pan. Add soup and water. Rinse chicken and pat dry; arrange in prepared pan. Sprinkle with onion soup mix. Bake, covered with foil, at 350 degrees for 1 hour. Add wine. Bake for 30 minutes longer.

Mary H. Pitts, Winston-Salem

Chicken and Broccoli Casserole

Yield:
6 servings
Utensil:
baking pan
Approx Per
Serving:
Cal 310
Prot 21 g
Carbo 20 g
Fiber 5 g
T Fat 17 g
Chol 51 mg
Sod 1003 mg

Dietary
Exchanges:
Milk 0
Vegetable 1½
Fruit 0
Bread/Starch 2
Meat 2; Fat 3

2 10-ounce packages frozen broccoli
1 medium onion, chopped
1 cup grated carrot
2 10-ounce cans cream of chicken soup
2 cups chopped cooked chicken
1 cup herb-seasoned stuffing mix
2 tablespoons melted margarine
¾ cup shredded Cheddar cheese
Salt and pepper to taste

Cook broccoli using package directions until tender-crisp; drain. Combine with onion, carrot and soup in saucepan; mix well. Heat until bubbly. Add chicken. Heat until bubbly. Spoon into greased 8x8-inch baking pan. Combine stuffing mix, margarine, cheese, salt and pepper in bowl; mix well. Sprinkle over chicken. Bake at 350 degrees for 25 to 30 minutes or until brown and done to taste.

Rosa Richardson, Winston-Salem

CHICKEN DIVAN

Yield:
8 servings
Utensil:
baking dish
Approx Per
Serving:
Cal 299
Prot 21 g
Carbo 10 g
Fiber 3 g
T Fat 20 g
Chol 69 mg
Sod 423 mg

Dietary
Exchanges:
Milk 0
Vegetable 1
Bread/Starch 0
Meat 2½
Fat 3½

2 10-ounce packages frozen broccoli
2 whole chicken breasts, cooked, chopped
1 10-ounce can cream of chicken soup
¼ cup milk
1 cup sour cream
2 tablespoons Sherry
Garlic salt to taste
1 cup shredded sharp Cheddar cheese
½ cup slivered almonds

Cook broccoli using package directions; drain. Layer broccoli and chicken in 9x13-inch baking dish. Combine soup, milk, sour cream, wine and garlic salt in bowl; mix well. Spoon over chicken. Sprinkle with cheese; top with almonds. Bake at 350 degrees for 30 to 35 minutes or until heated through.

Alice N. Wells, Winston-Salem

CURRIED CHICKEN AND BROCCOLI CASSEROLE

Yield:
8 servings
Utensil:
baking dish
Approx Per
Serving:
Cal 445
Prot 30 g
Carbo 12 g
Fiber 3 g
T Fat 31 g
Chol 104 mg
Sod 796 mg

Dietary
Exchanges:
Milk 0
Vegetable 1
Bread/Starch 1½
Meat 3½
Fat 5½

2 10-ounce packages frozen broccoli
6 chicken breasts, cooked, chopped
2 10-ounce cans cream of chicken soup
1½ cups reduced-calorie mayonnaise
2 teaspoons lemon juice
1 teaspoon curry powder
2 cups shredded sharp Cheddar cheese

Cook broccoli using package directions; drain. Layer broccoli and chicken in baking dish. Combine soup, mayonnaise, lemon juice and curry powder in saucepan. Heat until bubbly. Pour over layers. Sprinkle with cheese. Bake at 350 degrees for 20 to 30 minutes or until heated through.

Eleanor Brooks

CHICKEN CASSEROLE

Yield:
8 servings
Utensil:
baking dish
Approx Per
Serving:
Cal 459
Prot 34 g
Carbo 19 g
Fiber 1 g
T Fat 27 g
Chol 165 mg
Sod 775 mg

Dietary
Exchanges:
Milk ½
Vegetable 0
Fruit 0
Bread/Starch 1½
Meat 3½; Fat 5

1 3-pound chicken
½ cup chopped green
   bell pepper
½ cup chopped celery
¼ cup chopped
   pimento
½ cup mayonnaise
8 slices bread, cubed

2 cups milk
2 eggs, beaten
½ teaspoon salt
Pepper to taste
1 10-ounce can golden
   mushroom soup
½ cup shredded
   Cheddar cheese

Rinse chicken inside and out. Cook in water to cover in saucepan until tender; drain. Chop chicken, discarding skin and bones. Combine chicken, green pepper, celery, pimento and mayonnaise in bowl; mix well. Layer half the bread, chicken mixture and remaining bread in greased baking dish. Combine milk, eggs, salt and pepper in bowl; mix well. Pour over layers. Chill overnight. Spread soup over top; sprinkle with cheese. Bake at 325 degrees for 1 hour.

Dot Hutchens, Clemmons

EASY CHICKEN CASSEROLE

Yield:
8 servings
Utensil:
baking dish
Approx Per
Serving:
Cal 318
Prot 12 g
Carbo 10 g
Fiber <1 g
T Fat 26 g
Chol 139 mg
Sod 500 mg

Dietary
Exchanges:
Milk 0
Vegetable ½
Bread/Starch 1
Meat 1½
Fat 5½

2 cups chopped
   cooked chicken
   breasts
1 10-ounce can cream
   of mushroom soup
3 hard-boiled eggs,
   sliced

1 cup chopped celery
¾ cup mayonnaise
1 cup thinly sliced
   water chestnuts
2 cups crushed potato
   chips

Combine chicken, soup, eggs, celery, mayonnaise, water chestnuts and half the potato chips in bowl; mix well. Spoon into shallow 1½-quart baking dish. Top with remaining potato chips. Bake at 350 degrees for 20 to 25 minutes or until brown and bubbly.

Lillian Buie, Winston-Salem

CHICKEN AND RICE CASSEROLE

Yield:
10 servings
Utensil:
baking dish
Approx Per
Serving:
Cal 315
Prot 12 g
Carbo 24 g
Fiber 2 g
T Fat 19 g
Chol 24 mg
Sod 679 mg

Dietary
Exchanges:
Milk 0
Vegetable 1/2
Fruit 0
Bread/Starch 2
Meat 11/2; Fat 4

2 cups chopped celery
1/4 cup chopped onion
1/4 cup margarine
2 cups cooked rice
2 cups chopped
   cooked chicken
1 7-ounce can sliced
   water chestnuts,
   drained
2 10-ounce cans
   cream of chicken
   soup
1 cup water
1 cup crushed
   cornflakes
3 tablespoons melted
   margarine
1 cup sliced almonds

Sauté celery and onion lightly in 1/4 cup margarine in skillet. Add rice, chicken, water chestnuts, soup and water; mix well. Spoon into 9x13-inch baking dish. Top with mixture of cornflakes and 3 tablespoons melted margarine; sprinkle with almonds. Bake at 350 degrees for 45 minutes.

A Pioneer

CHICKEN SQUARES

Yield:
8 servings
Utensil:
baking sheet
Approx Per
Serving:
Cal 343
Prot 18 g
Carbo 19 g
Fiber <1 g
T Fat 21 g
Chol 72 mg
Sod 656 mg

Dietary
Exchanges:
Milk 0
Vegetable 0
Bread/Starch 11/2
Meat 11/2
Fat 41/2

4 chicken breasts
8 ounces cream cheese,
   softened
2 tablespoons melted
   margarine
2 tablespoons milk
1 tablespoon minced
   onion
1/4 teaspoon salt
1/8 teaspoon pepper
1 8-count can
   crescent rolls
1 10-ounce can cream
   of chicken soup
1/4 cup milk

Rinse chicken well. Cook in water to cover in saucepan until tender; drain. Chop chicken, discarding skin and bones. Blend cream cheese and margarine in bowl. Add chicken, 2 tablespoons milk, onion, salt and pepper; mix well. Separate roll dough into triangles. Spoon chicken mixture into center of each triangle. Bring up corners to enclose filling; seal edges. Place on baking sheet. Bake at 350 degrees for 20 minutes or until golden brown. Combine soup and 1/4 cup milk in saucepan. Cook until heated through. Serve with chicken squares.

B. S. Cuthrell, Winston-Salem

CHINESE CHICKEN CASSEROLE

Yield:
10 servings
Utensil:
baking dish
Approx Per Serving:
Cal 316
Prot 15 g
Carbo 25 g
Fiber 2 g
T Fat 18 g
Chol 33 mg
Sod 769 mg

Dietary Exchanges:
Milk 0
Vegetable 1¹/₂
Fruit 0
Bread/Starch 2
Meat 1¹/₂; Fat 4

1 6-ounce can Chinese noodles
3 cups chopped cooked chicken
1 10-ounce can cream of chicken soup
1 10-ounce can cream of mushroom soup
1 10-ounce can cream of celery soup
1 16-ounce can mixed chop suey vegetables, drained
1 7-ounce can sliced water chestnuts, drained
¹/₄ cup slivered almonds
¹/₄ cup melted margarine

Sprinkle half the noodles in deep 9x13-inch baking dish. Combine chicken, soups, mixed vegetables, water chestnuts and almonds in bowl; mix well. Spoon into prepared dish. Mix remaining noodles with margarine in bowl. Sprinkle over casserole. Bake at 350 degrees for 35 to 45 minutes or until heated through.

Edith Gerringer, Burlington

CHICKEN CURRY CASSEROLE

Yield:
10 servings
Utensil:
baking dish
Approx Per Serving:
Cal 534
Prot 15 g
Carbo 28 g
Fiber 1 g
T Fat 41 g
Chol 71 mg
Sod 894 mg

Dietary Exchanges:
Milk 0
Vegetable 0
Fruit 0
Bread/Starch 2¹/₂
Meat 1¹/₂; Fat 9

3 cups chopped cooked chicken
2 cups (or more) cooked rice
2 cups chopped celery
2 tablespoons chopped onion
2 10-ounce cans cream of chicken soup
1¹/₂ cups mayonnaise
Curry powder to taste
2 cups crushed cornflakes
¹/₄ cup slivered almonds
6 tablespoons melted butter

Combine chicken, rice, celery, onion, soup, mayonnaise and curry powder in bowl; mix well. Spoon into 9x13-inch baking dish. Combine cornflakes, almonds and butter in bowl; mix well. Sprinkle over casserole. Bake at 350 degrees for 30 minutes or until bubbly.

LaRue Benson, Burlington

KING RANCH CHICKEN

1 3-pound chicken
1 8-count package soft corn tortillas
1 cup chopped onion
1 cup chopped green bell pepper
1 clove of garlic, minced
1 tablespoon olive oil
1 10-ounce can cream of mushroom soup
1 10-ounce can cream of chicken soup
1 10-ounce can Ro-Tel tomatoes with green chilies
1 teaspoon oregano
1 teaspoon cumin
2 cups shredded Cheddar cheese

Rinse chicken inside and out. Cook in water to cover in saucepan until tender. Drain, reserving 1 cup broth. Chop chicken, discarding skin and bones. Cut tortillas into bite-sized pieces. Layer tortillas and chicken in 9x13-inch baking dish. Pour reserved broth over layers. Sauté onion, green pepper and garlic in olive oil in saucepan. Stir in next 5 ingredients. Cook until heated through. Pour over layers. Top with cheese. Bake at 350 degrees for 20 minutes or until bubbly.

Ginger King, Graham

POPPY SEED CHICKEN

6 chicken breasts
1 10-ounce can cream of celery soup
1 10-ounce can cream of mushroom soup
1 cup sour cream
1/4 cup slivered almonds
1 stack butter crackers, crushed
2 tablespoons poppy seed
6 tablespoons melted butter

Rinse chicken well. Cook in water to cover in saucepan until tender; drain. Chop chicken, discarding skin and bones. Combine chicken with soups, sour cream and almonds in bowl; mix well. Spoon into 9x13-inch baking dish. Combine cracker crumbs, poppy seed and butter in bowl; mix well. Sprinkle over casserole. Bake at 350 degrees for 45 minutes. May substitute 1 can water chestnuts for almonds if preferred.

Barbara Joyce, Burlington

JULIA'S HOT CHICKEN SALAD

2 cups chopped
cooked chicken
2 cups chopped celery
3 tablespoons minced
onion
1/2 cup almonds
3 tablespoons lemon
juice
3/4 cup mayonnaise

1 4-ounce can sliced
mushrooms, drained
1/2 teaspoon salt
1/2 teaspoon pepper
1 10-ounce can cream
of chicken soup
1 cup crushed potato
chips

Combine chicken, celery, onion, almonds, lemon juice, mayonnaise, mushrooms, salt and pepper in bowl; mix well. Spoon into 8x8-inch baking dish. Spoon soup over top; sprinkle with potato chips. Bake at 300 degrees for 30 minutes or until heated through.

Jerry Jarrell, Jamestown

CHICKEN WITH SAUSAGE AND MUSHROOMS

1 3-pound chicken
1 pound hot sausage
1 6-ounce package
long grain and wild
rice mix

1/4 cup milk
1 10-ounce can cream
of mushroom soup
1 8-ounce can sliced
mushrooms

Rinse chicken inside and out. Cook in water to cover until tender; drain. Cut into large pieces. Brown sausage in skillet, stirring until crumbly; drain. Cook rice using package directions. Combine milk and soup in bowl; mix well. Add chicken, sausage, rice and undrained mushrooms; mix well. Spoon into 2 to 3-quart baking dish. Bake at 350 degrees for 30 minutes.

Fran Grinstead, Snow Camp

CHICKEN SPAGHETTI

Yield:
12 servings
Utensil:
baking dish
Approx Per
Serving:
Cal 397
Prot 31 g
Carbo 37 g
Fiber 3 g
T Fat 15 g
Chol 69 mg
Sod 513 mg

Dietary
Exchanges:
Milk 0
Vegetable 1
Fruit 0
Bread/Starch 2½
Meat 3; Fat 2

4 pounds chicken
1 16-ounce package spaghetti
8 ounces bacon
3 large onions, chopped
1 28-ounce can tomatoes
1 7-ounce jar olives, drained, chopped
1 cup cream of mushroom soup

Rinse chicken well. Cook in water to cover in saucepan until tender. Drain, reserving broth. Chop chicken, discarding skin and bones. Cook spaghetti in reserved broth in saucepan until done to taste; drain. Cook bacon in skillet until crisp. Remove and crumble bacon; reserve drippings. Sauté onions in reserved drippings in skillet. Add tomatoes, olives and soup; mix well. Cook until heated through. Add chicken and bacon; mix well. Alternate layers of chicken mixture and spaghetti in large baking dish or 2 small baking dishes. Bake at 350 degrees until light brown. Garnish with Parmesan cheese.

Thelma Wilson, Winston-Salem

CHICKEN TETRAZZINI

Yield:
10 servings
Utensil:
baking dish
Approx Per
Serving:
Cal 364
Prot 28 g
Carbo 30 g
Fiber 1 g
T Fat 14 g
Chol 73 mg
Sod 697 mg

Dietary
Exchanges:
Milk 0
Vegetable 0
Fruit 0
Bread/Starch 3
Meat 3; Fat 2½

4 large chicken breasts
1 10-ounce package thin spaghetti
1 10-ounce can cream of mushroom soup
1 10-ounce can cream of chicken soup
1 2-ounce can chopped pimento, drained
½ cup milk
½ teaspoon salt
½ teaspoon pepper
½ cup shredded Cheddar cheese
½ cup toasted bread crumbs
5 teaspoons butter

Rinse chicken well. Cook in water to cover in saucepan until tender. Drain, reserving broth. Chop chicken, discarding skin and bones. Cook spaghetti in reserved broth for 6 minutes; remove from heat. Let stand until additional liquid is absorbed and spaghetti is tender; drain. Combine chicken, soups, pimento, milk, salt and pepper in bowl; mix well. Alternate layers of chicken mixture and spaghetti in baking dish. Top with cheese and bread crumbs; dot with butter. Bake at 350 degrees for 30 minutes.

Deborah M. Bryan, Elon College

Busy-Day Turkey Casserole

Yield:
4 servings
Utensil:
baking dish
Approx Per
Serving:
Cal 372
Prot 23 g
Carbo 25 g
Fiber 3 g
T Fat 21 g
Chol 42 mg
Sod 640 mg

Dietary
Exchanges:
Milk 0
Vegetable 1/2
Fruit 0
Bread/Starch 2
Meat 2 1/2; Fat 5

1 7-ounce can turkey
1/2 cup chopped celery
1 small onion, minced
1/2 cup chopped
   almonds
1/4 cup evaporated milk

1 10-ounce can cream
   of mushroom soup
Salt and pepper to
   taste
1 3-ounce can chow
   mein noodles

Combine turkey, celery, onion, almonds, evaporated milk, soup, salt, pepper and half the noodles in bowl; mix well. Spoon into greased baking dish. Top with remaining noodles. Bake at 325 degrees for 45 minutes. Garnish with parsley. May substitute chicken, tuna or ham for turkey and cashews for almonds.

R. Sharpe, Greensboro

Turkey Chili con Carne

Yield:
4 servings
Utensil:
saucepan
Approx Per
Serving:
Cal 329
Prot 35 g
Carbo 32 g
Fiber 9 g
T Fat 7 g
Chol 59 mg
Sod 668 mg

Dietary
Exchanges:
Milk 0
Vegetable 2
Fruit 0
Bread/Starch 1 1/2
Meat 3; Fat 1/2

1 pound ground turkey
2 medium onions,
   chopped
1 tablespoon canola oil
2 cups canned
   tomatoes

2 cups cooked kidney
   beans
2 teaspoons chili
   powder
1/4 teaspoon pepper

Brown ground turkey with onions in oil in saucepan, stirring until turkey is crumbly; drain. Add tomatoes, beans, chili powder and pepper; mix well. Simmer for 30 minutes.

Peggy B. Smith, Burlington

TURKEY LOAF

Yield:
8 servings
Utensil:
loaf pan
Approx Per
Serving:
Cal 178
Prot 27 g
Carbo 7 g
Fiber 1 g
T Fat 4 g
Chol 93 mg
Sod 153 mg

Dietary
Exchanges:
Milk 0
Vegetable ½
Fruit 0
Bread/Starch ½
Meat 3; Fat 0

2 pounds ground turkey
1 cup shredded carrots
½ cup chopped celery
½ cup chopped onion
¼ cup minced parsley
½ cup quick-cooking oats
1 egg
¼ cup water
1 teaspoon Worcestershire sauce
½ teaspoon sage, thyme, marjoram and oregano
½ teaspoon pepper
¼ cup catsup
¾ teaspoon dry mustard

Combine turkey, carrots, celery, onion, parsley, oats, egg, water, Worcestershire sauce, sage, thyme, marjoram, oregano and pepper in bowl; mix well. Pack into 5x9-inch loaf pan. Combine catsup and dry mustard in small bowl. Spoon over loaf. Bake at 350 degrees for 45 minutes. Invert onto serving plate.

Mrs. Carlton Tuttle, Germanton

TURKEY MOLE

Yield:
6 servings
Utensil:
skillet
Approx Per
Serving:
Cal 165
Prot 19 g
Carbo 12 g
Fiber 1 g
T Fat 5 g
Chol 39 mg
Sod 397 mg

Dietary
Exchanges:
Milk 0
Vegetable 0
Fruit 0
Bread/Starch ½
Meat 2; Fat ½

1 pound ground turkey
½ cup sliced celery
¼ cup chopped onion
1 clove of garlic, minced
1 tablespoon oil
1 8-ounce can whole kernel corn, drained
3 tablespoons flour
1 teaspoon sugar
2 teaspoons baking cocoa
1½ to 2 teaspoons chili powder
⅛ teaspoon apple pie spice
¼ teaspoon salt
¼ teaspoon pepper
1¼ cups beef broth

Cook turkey, celery, onion and garlic in oil in skillet, stirring until turkey is crumbly and vegetables are tender; drain. Stir in corn, flour, sugar, cocoa, chili powder, apple pie spice, salt and pepper. Add beef broth; mix well. Cook until thickened, stirring constantly. Cook for 1 minute longer, stirring constantly. Serve with tortilla chips, sliced avocado, chopped tomato, chopped green pepper, sour cream or other toppings of choice.

Nutritional information does not include toppings.

Ellen M. Mercier, Greensboro

TURKEY AND NOODLE CASSEROLE

6 ounces uncooked medium noodles
1 10-ounce can cream of chicken soup
1 5-ounce can evaporated milk
¼ teaspoon salt
1½ cups shredded process cheese
1 cup chopped celery
2 cups chopped cooked turkey
¼ cup chopped green bell pepper
¼ cup chopped pimento
½ cup bread crumbs
2 tablespoons melted butter
½ cup slivered almonds

Cook noodles using package directions; drain. Shape into nest in greased 2-quart baking dish. Combine soup, evaporated milk and salt in saucepan. Cook until heated through, stirring constantly. Stir in cheese until melted. Add celery, turkey, green pepper and pimento; mix well. Spoon into noodle nest. Top with mixture of bread crumbs and butter; sprinkle with almonds. Bake at 400 degrees for 20 minutes.

Doreen Smith, West End

TURKEY STROGANOFF

2 pounds ground turkey
1 tablespoon olive oil
½ teaspoon garlic powder
2 teaspoons salt
Pepper to taste
4 cups tomato sauce
1 4-ounce can mushrooms, drained
2 cups low-fat sour cream
1 cup cottage cheese
1 bunch green onions, sliced
1 16-ounce package wide noodles, cooked
1 cup shredded sharp Cheddar cheese

Brown ground turkey in olive oil, stirring until crumbly; drain. Add garlic powder, salt and pepper. Stir in tomato sauce and mushrooms. Simmer for several minutes. Combine next 3 ingredients in bowl. Let stand for several minutes. Reserve a small amount of turkey mixture. Alternate layers of noodles, remaining turkey mixture and cheese mixture in rectangular baking dish sprayed with nonstick cooking spray until all ingredients are used. Top with reserved turkey mixture and cheese. Bake at 350 degrees for 15 to 20 minutes or until bubbly.

Nancy Garner, Burlington

SEAFOOD

BAKED PARMESAN FISH

Yield:
4 servings
Utensil:
baking dish
Approx Per
Serving:
Cal 415
Prot 36 g
Carbo 3 g
Fiber <1 g
T Fat 27 g
Chol 159 mg
Sod 509 mg

Dietary
Exchanges:
Milk 0
Vegetable 0
Fruit 0
Bread/Starch 0
Meat 4; Fat 5

½ cup butter
1½ pounds flounder
Salt and pepper to
   taste
½ cup lemon juice
½ cup white wine
¼ cup Parmesan
   cheese
Paprika to taste

Melt butter in 9x13-inch baking dish in 400-degree oven. Season fish with salt and pepper. Place in butter in prepared dish, turning to coat well. Bake at 400 degrees for 10 to 15 minutes or until fish flakes easily, reducing oven temperature to 350 to 375 degrees if butter browns too quickly. Pour mixture of lemon juice and wine over fish. Sprinkle with cheese and paprika. Broil for 5 minutes.

Mrs. Ray Taylor, Winston-Salem

CRUSTY FLOUNDER

Yield:
2 servings
Utensil:
baking dish
Approx Per
Serving:
Cal 365
Prot 46 g
Carbo 24 g
Fiber 0 g
T Fat 9 g
Chol 123 mg
Sod 577 mg

Dietary
Exchanges:
Milk 0
Vegetable 0
Fruit 0
Bread/Starch 1½
Meat 5; Fat 1

1 pound fresh or
   frozen flounder
   filets
2 ounces cornmeal
½ teaspoon paprika
¼ teaspoon garlic salt
¼ cup malt vinegar
2 tablespoons melted
   light margarine

Rinse fish filets and pat dry. Combine cornmeal, paprika and garlic salt in bowl; mix well. Dip fish into vinegar; coat with cornmeal mixture. Arrange in small baking dish. Sprinkle with remaining cornmeal mixture; drizzle with margarine. Bake at 450 degrees for 20 to 25 minutes or until filets are golden brown and flake easily.

Lon B. Burnette, Winston-Salem

FLOUNDER WITH VEGETABLES

¼ cup melted
  margarine
2 tablespoons lemon
  juice
½ teaspoon dillweed
4 frozen flounder filets

8 ¼-inch onion slices
2 medium potatoes
2 medium carrots
1 16-ounce can
  French-style green
  beans, drained

Combine margarine, lemon juice and dillweed in small bowl; mix well. Place fish filets in baking dish. Drizzle with margarine mixture. Top with onion slices. Peel potatoes and cut lengthwise into ¼ inch strips. Cut carrots into ⅛-inch slices. Place potatoes and carrots around fish. Top with beans. Cover with foil. Bake at 425 degrees for 30 to 35 minutes or until vegetables are tender.

Patricia B. Osborne, Greensboro

FRIED FISH

1 egg
⅓ cup prepared
  mustard
½ teaspoon seasoned
  salt

4 fish filets
1 cup instant potato
  flakes
Oil for frying

Combine egg, mustard and seasoned salt in bowl; mix well. Dip fish in egg mixture; coat well with potato flakes. Fry in hot oil in skillet until golden brown on both sides.

Nutritional information does not include oil for frying.

Betty Melvin

ICELAND FISH WITH PASTA

<table>
<tr><td>

Yield:
2 servings
Utensil:
sauté pan
Approx Per
Serving:
Cal 747
Prot 50 g
Carbo 100 g
Fiber 8 g
T Fat 16 g
Chol 92 mg
Sod 622 mg

Dietary
Exchanges:
Milk 0
Vegetable 2½
Bread/Starch 6½
Meat 3½
Fat 2½

</td></tr>
</table>

1 small onion, minced
2 tablespoons
  margarine
2 6-ounce firm
  whitefish filets,
  skin removed
Juice of ½ lemon
3 tablespoons chopped
  fresh parsley
1 teaspoon basil
1 teaspoon oregano
½ teaspoon red
  pepper flakes
1 14-ounce can Italian-
  style tomatoes,
  coarsely chopped
8 ounces pasta, cooked

Sauté onion in margarine in sauté pan over medium heat for 3 minutes. Add fish filets. Strain lemon juice over fish. Simmer, covered, for 10 minutes for each inch of thickness. Remove fish to plate. Add parsley, basil, oregano, red pepper and tomatoes to sauté pan. Simmer for 5 minutes or until slightly thickened. Spoon pasta onto serving plates. Place fish on pasta; spoon sauce over top. Serve with steamed broccoli.

Doris Whitesell

SALMON WITH WINE AND CAPERS

<table>
<tr><td>

Yield:
4 servings
Utensil:
skillet
Approx Per
Serving:
Cal 329
Prot 38 g
Carbo 4 g
Fiber <1 g
T Fat 11 g
Chol 67 mg
Sod 185 mg

Dietary
Exchanges:
Milk 0
Vegetable 0
Fruit 0
Bread/Starch ½
Meat 5; Fat 0

</td></tr>
</table>

1½ cups white wine
4 salmon steaks
1 tablespoon (about)
  Dijon mustard
2 tablespoons Wondra
  flour
1 tablespoon capers

Bring wine to a simmer in skillet. Add salmon steaks. Simmer, covered, until salmon flakes easily. Remove fish to warm plate. Remove and discard skin and bones. Stir mustard into wine in skillet. Stir in flour until smooth. Cook until slightly thickened, stirring constantly. Stir in capers. Spoon over fish.

Elaine Ruth Morrison, Hobe Sound, Florida

SALMON PATTIES AND CREAM SAUCE WITH PEAS

2 tablespoons butter
2 tablespoons flour
1/2 cup half and half
1/2 cup chicken broth
1/2 cup drained canned
  peas
1/4 teaspoon salt
Pepper to taste
1 16-ounce can salmon
1 egg
1/3 cup minced onion
1/2 cup flour
1 1/2 teaspoons baking
  powder
1 1/2 cups shortening
  for frying

Melt butter in saucepan. Blend in 2 tablespoons flour. Stir in half and half and broth. Cook until thickened, stirring constantly. Add peas, salt and pepper. Keep warm. Drain salmon, reserving 2 tablespoons liquid. Mix salmon, egg and onion in bowl. Stir in 1/2 cup flour. Add mixture of baking powder and salmon liquid; mix well. Shape into patties. Fry in hot shortening in skillet for 5 minutes or until brown on both sides. Spoon sauce over patties.

Nutritional information does not include shortening for frying.

Mavis Peterson, Elon College

STUFFED FISH FILETS

1 cup stove-top
  stuffing mix
4 orange roughy filets
Olive oil cooking
  spray to taste
Lemon-dill seasoning
  and paprika to taste
2 tablespoons white
  wine
2 tablespoons water

Prepare stuffing mix using package directions, substituting margarine for butter. Spoon onto fish filets. Roll to enclose filling. Arrange in baking dish sprayed with nonstick olive oil cooking spray. Spray fish with olive oil cooking spray; sprinkle with lemon-dill seasoning and paprika. Add mixture of wine and water to dish. Bake at 350 degrees just until fish flakes easily, basting with pan juices if necessary to keep fish from drying out. May substitute lemon juice for wine if preferred.

Elaine Ruth Morrison, Hobe Sound, Florida

BARBECUED BLUEFIN TUNA

Yield:
6 servings
Utensil:
grill
Approx Per
Serving:
Cal 592
Prot 45 g
Carbo 37 g
Fiber 1 g
T Fat 31 g
Chol 78 mg
Sod 1462 mg

Dietary
Exchanges:
Milk 0
Vegetable 1/2
Fruit 1/2
Bread/Starch 1/2
Meat 5; Fat 41/2

2 cups fresh orange
   juice
1/2 cup soy sauce
1 cup red wine vinegar
1/2 cup olive oil
1 onion, chopped
4 cloves of garlic,
   minced
1   6-ounce can tomato
   paste
1/2 cup sugar
1 teaspoon red pepper
   flakes

1 tablespoon cumin
11/2 tablespoons whole
   mixed pickling spice
1 teaspoon pepper
6   6-ounce bluefin
   tuna steaks, 1 inch
   thick
2 tablespoons
   unsalted butter
Pepper to taste

Whisk orange juice, soy sauce, vinegar, olive oil, onion, garlic, tomato paste, sugar, red pepper flakes, cumin, pickling spice and 1 teaspoon pepper together in bowl. Arrange tuna steaks in single layer in dish. Add orange juice mixture. Marinate, covered, in refrigerator overnight to 24 hours. Drain, reserving marinade. Grill fish on lightly oiled rack 3 to 5 inches from coals for 3 minutes on each side. Place steaks in baking dish. Spoon 1 tablespoon reserved marinade over each steak. Bake at 375 degrees for 4 to 5 minutes or just until done to taste. Top with butter and pepper.

Nutritional information includes entire amount of marinade.

Joseph R. Tarnowsky, Greensboro

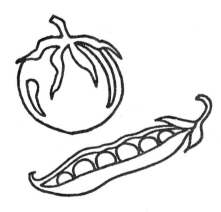

SCALLOPED TUNA

Yield:
6 servings
Utensil:
baking dish
Approx Per
Serving:
Cal 374
Prot 20 g
Carbo 21 g
Fiber 2 g
T Fat 24 g
Chol 75 mg
Sod 1620 mg

Dietary
Exchanges:
Milk 1/2
Vegetable 0
Fruit 0
Bread/Starch 1 1/2
Meat 2; Fat 5

1/4 cup melted butter
1/4 cup flour
2 cups milk
1/2 teaspoon salt
1 cup shredded
   American cheese
3/4 cup sliced stuffed
   olives
1/2 cup minced green
   bell pepper

1 6-ounce can
   water-pack tuna,
   flaked
2 cups soft coarse
   bread crumbs
3/4 cup cornflake
   crumbs
1/2 cup shredded
   American cheese

Blend butter and flour in saucepan. Stir in milk and salt. Cook until thickened, stirring constantly; cool slightly. Add 1 cup cheese, olives, green pepper and tuna; mix well. Layer bread crumbs and tuna 1/2 a time in buttered baking dish. Top with cornflakes and remaining 1/2 cup cheese. Bake at 325 to 350 degrees for 20 to 30 minutes or until heated through.

Mrs. V. B. Williamson, Graham

CHEESY TUNA CASSEROLE

Yield:
10 servings
Utensil:
baking dish
Approx Per
Serving:
Cal 253
Prot 18 g
Carbo 24 g
Fiber 1 g
T Fat 9 g
Chol 34 mg
Sod 801 mg

Dietary
Exchanges:
Milk 0
Vegetable 0
Fruit 0
Bread/Starch 2
Meat 1 1/2; Fat 2

1 8-ounce package
   noodles
2 6-ounce cans
   water-pack tuna
1 8-ounce can peas
3/4 cup milk
1 10-ounce can cream
   of celery soup

1 10-ounce can cream
   of chicken soup
1 cup shredded
   Cheddar cheese
1/4 teaspoon dry
   mustard
1/2 teaspoon onion salt

Cook noodles using package directions; drain. Combine tuna, peas, milk, soups, cheese, dry mustard and onion salt in bowl; mix well. Stir in noodles. Spoon into 9x13-inch baking dish. Bake at 350 degrees for 35 minutes.

Connie Kelly, Mocksville

TUNA CASSEROLE

<table>
<tr><td>

Yield:
4 servings
Utensil:
baking dish
Approx Per
Serving:
Cal 386
Prot 16 g
Carbo 17 g
Fiber 2 g
T Fat 29 g
Chol 22 mg
Sod 808 mg

</td></tr>
</table>

1 10-ounce can cream of mushroom soup
1/2 cup milk
1 6-ounce can water-pack tuna, drained

1 cup drained canned peas
1 cup crushed potato chips

Blend soup and milk in bowl. Add tuna, peas and 3/4 cup potato chips; mix well. Spoon into baking dish. Top with remaining 1/4 cup chips. Bake at 350 degrees for 25 minutes.

Kathryn Howerton

Dietary
Exchanges:
Milk 0
Vegetable 0
Bread/Starch 1 1/2
Meat 1 1/2
Fat 8 1/2

AUNT RUTH'S CRAB CAKES

Yield:
6 servings
Utensil:
skillet
Approx Per
Serving:
Cal 120
Prot 13 g
Carbo 7 g
Fiber <1 g
T Fat 4 g
Chol 86 mg
Sod 331 mg

1/4 cup finely chopped onion
1 tablespoon butter
1 pound backfin or lump crab meat
1 egg, slightly beaten
1 tablespoon prepared mustard

1 tablespoon prepared horseradish
Tabasco sauce to taste
1 tablespoon minced parsley
1/2 cup bread crumbs
Oil for browning

Sauté onion in butter in skillet until tender but not brown; cool. Combine crab meat, egg, mustard, horseradish, Tabasco sauce and parsley in bowl; mix gently, taking care not to break up crab meat. Add onion and 1/4 cup bread crumbs or enough to bind. Shape into 6 cakes. Roll in remaining bread crumbs. Chill for 30 minutes. Brown in hot oil in skillet until golden brown and heated through. Drain on paper towel.

Nutritional information does not include oil for browning.

Elaine Ruth Morrison, Hobe Sound, Florida

Dietary
Exchanges:
Milk 0
Vegetable 0
Fruit 0
Bread/Starch 1/2
Meat 1 1/2; Fat 1/2

CRAB CAKES

Yield:
4 servings
Utensil:
skillet
Approx Per
Serving:
Cal 227
Prot 22 g
Carbo 15 g
Fiber <1 g
T Fat 8 g
Chol 167 mg
Sod 589 mg

Dietary
Exchanges:
Milk 0
Vegetable 0
Fruit 0
Bread/Starch 1
Meat 2¹/₂; Fat 1

1 pound crab meat
1 egg
³/₄ to 1 cup cracker meal
1 teaspoon to 1 tablespoon horseradish
2 teaspoons chopped parsley
1 teaspoon mustard
1 tablespoon mayonnaise
1 teaspoon pepper
Oil for browning

Combine crab meat, egg, cracker meal, horseradish, parsley, mustard, mayonnaise and pepper in bowl; mix well. Shape into 4 cakes. Brown on both sides in hot oil in skillet. Drain on paper towel.

Nutritional information does not include oil for browning.

Teresa Crispino, High Point

BAKED CRAB CASSEROLE

Yield:
8 servings
Utensil:
casserole
Approx Per
Serving:
Cal 214
Prot 16 g
Carbo 12 g
Fiber 1 g
T Fat 10 g
Chol 156 mg
Sod 749 mg

Dietary
Exchanges:
Milk 0
Vegetable ¹/₂
Fruit 0
Bread/Starch ¹/₂
Meat 2; Fat 2

1 large onion, minced
¹/₂ cup minced celery
1 small green bell pepper, minced
¹/₄ cup butter
1¹/₄ pounds crab meat
1 cup Italian bread crumbs
2 eggs, well beaten
1 tablespoon lemon juice
1 tablespoon mustard
1 tablespoon mayonnaise
¹/₄ teaspoon garlic salt
¹/₄ teaspoon Beau Monde seasoning
¹/₄ teaspoon Greek seasoning
¹/₂ teaspoon salt
¹/₄ teaspoon pepper
Tabasco sauce to taste

Sauté onion, celery and green pepper in butter in skillet for 5 minutes or until glazed but not browned. Combine crab meat and bread crumbs in bowl; mix well. Stir in sautéed vegetables. Add eggs; mix well. Add remaining ingredients; mix well. Pack into well greased casserole. Bake at 400 degrees for 20 to 25 minutes or until lightly browned. May substitute well greased seafood shells for casserole.

Colle Toenes, Cedar Hill, Missouri

CRAB MEAT LASAGNA ROLL-UPS

Yield:
6 servings
Utensil:
baking dish
Approx Per Serving:
Cal 288
Prot 21 g
Carbo 32 g
Fiber 0 g
T Fat 8 g
Chol 75 mg
Sod 968 mg

Dietary Exchanges:
Milk 0
Vegetable 1
Fruit 0
Bread/Starch 1½
Meat 3; Fat ½

6 lasagna noodles
8 ounces imitation crab meat
1 cup low-fat cottage cheese
¼ cup Parmesan cheese
1 egg
1 tablespoon parsley flakes
¼ teaspoon onion powder
1 15-ounce can Italian-style tomato sauce
1 cup shredded mozzarella cheese

Cook noodles using package directions. Rinse in cold water and drain well; pat dry. Combine crab meat, cottage cheese, Parmesan cheese, egg, parsley flakes and onion powder in bowl; mix well with fork. Spread on noodles; roll to enclose filling. Place seam side down in 9x9-inch baking dish. Pour tomato sauce over roll-ups. Bake, covered, at 375 degrees for 30 minutes. Sprinkle with mozzarella cheese. Let stand, covered, until mozzarella cheese begins to melt. May prepare and chill for up to 2 days; bake for 50 minutes.

Martha M. Wheeler, Chapin, South Carolina

ANN CRAWFORD'S ETOUFFEE

Yield:
4 servings
Utensil:
saucepan
Approx Per Serving:
Cal 413
Prot 21 g
Carbo 15 g
Fiber 1 g
T Fat 30 g
Chol 131 mg
Sod 2229 mg

Dietary Exchanges:
Milk 0
Vegetable ½
Fruit 0
Bread/Starch 1
Meat 2; Fat 6

½ cup chopped yellow onion
3 stalks celery, chopped
4 green onions, chopped
½ cup margarine
2 10-ounce cans cream of celery soup
1 teaspoon sweet basil
1 teaspoon paprika
¼ to ½ teaspoon cayenne pepper
3 bay leaves
2 tablespoons soy sauce
2 tablespoons Worcestershire sauce
8 ounces crab meat, cooked
8 ounces peeled shrimp, cooked

Sauté onion, celery and green onions in margarine in saucepan. Add soup, basil, paprika, cayenne pepper, bay leaves, soy sauce and Worcestershire sauce; mix well. Simmer for 1 hour or longer, stirring occasionally. Add crab meat and shrimp. Simmer for 30 minutes. Remove bay leaves. Serve with rice and Tabasco sauce. May add or substitute crawfish or chicken.

Jerry Jarrell, Jamestown

BAKED OYSTERS

Yield:
6 servings
Utensil:
6 ramekins
Approx Per
Serving:
Cal 164
Prot 8 g
Carbo 9 g
Fiber <1 g
T Fat 11 g
Chol 146 mg
Sod 336 mg

Dietary
Exchanges:
Milk 0
Vegetable 0
Fruit 0
Bread/Starch 1/2
Meat 1; Fat 2

1 pint fresh oysters
1¼ cups (about) milk
1 tablespoon butter
2 tablespoons flour
½ teaspoon each salt
 and paprika
¼ teaspoon pepper

2 egg yolks, beaten
1 tablespoon lemon juice
1 tablespoon chopped
 parsley
2 tablespoons butter
½ cup fresh fine
 bread crumbs

Cook undrained oysters in saucepan until edges begin to curl; drain, reserving liquid. Add enough milk to reserved liquid to measure 1½ cups. Melt 1 tablespoon butter in same saucepan. Blend in dry ingredients; remove from heat. Stir in milk mixture. Cook until thickened, stirring constantly. Stir ¼ cup hot mixture into egg yolks; stir egg yolks into hot mixture. Cook until thickened, stirring constantly; do not boil. Add oysters, lemon juice and parsley. Cook for 1 minute. Spoon into buttered ramekins. Top with mixture of butter and bread crumbs. Bake at 375 degrees for 20 minutes. Garnish with lemon wedges.

Jo Walker, Winston-Salem

BAKED SCALLOPS

Yield:
2 servings
Utensil:
baking dish
Approx Per
Serving:
Cal 790
Prot 28 g
Carbo 29 g
Fiber 0 g
T Fat 62 g
Chol 168 mg
Sod 1311 mg

Dietary
Exchanges:
Milk 0
Vegetable 0
Fruit 0
Bread/Starch 1½
Meat 3; Fat 13½

12 ounces sea scallops
Salt and pepper to
 taste
1 ounce Sherry

1 cup herb-flavored
 stuffing
½ cup melted butter

Cut scallops into halves. Place in single layer in buttered 6x10-inch baking dish. Sprinkle with salt and pepper. Drizzle with wine. Top with mixture of stuffing and butter. Bake at 375 degrees for 15 minutes.

Ella Getchell, Greensboro

SCALLOPS AND SHRIMP MORNAY

Yield:
2 servings
Utensil:
2 ramekins
Approx Per Serving:
Cal 388
Prot 36 g
Carbo 12 g
Fiber 1 g
T Fat 17 g
Chol 168 mg
Sod 938 mg

Dietary Exchanges:
Milk 1/2
Vegetable 1/2
Fruit 0
Bread/Starch 1/2
Meat 41/2; Fat 3

1/2 cup dry white wine
3/4 cup water
1/4 teaspoon onion flakes
1/4 teaspoon salt
Black pepper to taste
8 ounces bay scallops
4 ounces medium shrimp, peeled, deveined
1/2 cup sliced fresh mushrooms

1 tablespoon butter
11/2 tablespoons flour
1/2 cup milk
1/4 teaspoon salt
1/8 teaspoon white pepper
1/2 cup shredded Swiss cheese
2 tablespoons chopped parsley

Combine wine, water, onion flakes, 1/4 teaspoon salt and black pepper in medium saucepan. Simmer for 5 minutes. Add scallops, shrimp and mushrooms. Simmer, covered, for 5 minutes. Remove scallops, shrimp and mushrooms to bowl with slotted spoon. Boil remaining liquid for 10 minutes or until reduced to 1/2 cup. Melt butter in heavy saucepan over low heat. Stir in flour. Cook for 1 minute, stirring constantly. Add mixture of reduced cooking liquid and milk gradually. Cook until thickened and bubbly, stirring constantly. Add 1/4 teaspoon salt, white pepper and cheese, stirring until cheese melts; remove from heat. Add scallops, shrimp and mushrooms. Spoon into 2 greased ramekins. Bake at 375 degrees for 15 to 20 minutes or until heated through. Sprinkle with parsley.

Alice M. Lempp, Jamestown

SHRIMP AND SCALLOP NOODLE CASSEROLE

Yield:
6 servings
Utensil:
baking dish
Approx Per
Serving:
Cal 412
Prot 22 g
Carbo 36 g
Fiber 2 g
T Fat 22 g
Chol 86 mg
Sod 1173 mg

Dietary
Exchanges:
Milk 1/2
Vegetable 0
Fruit 0
Bread/Starch 2
Meat 1 1/2; Fat 4

8 ounces medium shrimp, peeled
8 ounces sea scallops
3 3-ounce packages shrimp-flavored ramen noodles
1/8 teaspoon lemon pepper
1/4 teaspoon garlic salt
1/8 teaspoon seasoned salt
1/4 cup melted margarine
2 tablespoons cornstarch
1 1/3 cups milk
1/2 cup shredded Cheddar cheese
Paprika to taste

Cook shrimp and scallops in boiling water in saucepan for just 1 1/2 minutes; drain. Cook noodles using package directions; remove from heat. Stir in contents of flavor packets, and next 3 ingredients. Spoon into 8x12-inch baking dish. Blend margarine, cornstarch and milk in saucepan. Cook over low heat until thickened and smooth, stirring constantly. Stir in cheese. Spoon over noodles. Top with shrimp and scallops; mix gently. Sprinkle with paprika. Bake at 325 degrees for 12 minutes or until heated through.

Peggy Gimmon, Winston-Salem

SHRIMP STUFFED WITH SCALLOPS

Yield:
6 servings
Utensil:
baking dish
Approx Per
Serving:
Cal 259
Prot 21 g
Carbo 7 g
Fiber <1 g
T Fat 15 g
Chol 165 mg
Sod 491 mg

Dietary
Exchanges:
Milk 0
Vegetable 0
Fruit 0
Bread/Starch 1/2
Meat 2 1/2; Fat 3

18 5-inch shrimp, peeled, cleaned
3/4 cup chopped scallops
1/2 teaspoon paprika
6 tablespoons butter
1/2 cup cracker meal
3 tablespoons crushed potato chips
5 tablespoons Parmesan cheese
3 tablespoons dry Sherry

Butterfly shrimp. Spoon scallops into shrimp, replacing sides to enclose filling. Place in baking dish with a small amount of water. Sauté paprika in butter in skillet over low heat for 10 minutes. Add cracker meal, potato chips and cheese; mix well. Spoon over shrimp. Bake at 350 degrees for 20 to 25 minutes or until done to taste. Drizzle with wine. Garnish with lemon wedges.

June Totterweich, Greensboro

Marinated Shrimp

Yield:
2 servings
Utensil:
bowl
Approx Per Serving:
Cal 1254
Prot 40 g
Carbo 28 g
Fiber 3 g
T Fat 111 g
Chol 354 mg
Sod 1846 mg

Dietary Exchanges:
Milk 0
Vegetable 2
Fruit 0
Bread/Starch 0
Meat 4; Fat 22

1 pound shrimp, cooked, peeled
2 medium purple onions, sliced into rings
2 to 3 bay leaves
1 cup oil
1/4 cup cider vinegar
1/4 cup catsup
2 tablespoons Worcestershire sauce
2 teaspoons sugar
1/4 teaspoon dry mustard
1 teaspoon salt
Red pepper to taste

Layer shrimp, onions and bay leaves in bowl. Combine oil, vinegar, catsup, Worcestershire sauce, sugar, dry mustard, salt and red pepper in small bowl; mix well. Pour over layers. Marinate in refrigerator for up to 2 days.

Nutritional information includes entire amount of marinade.

Thelma Wilson, Winston-Salem

Cajun Shrimp

Yield:
4 servings
Utensil:
saucepan
Approx Per Serving:
Cal 518
Prot 39 g
Carbo 2 g
Fiber 0 g
T Fat 39 g
Chol 454 mg
Sod 1041 mg

Dietary Exchanges:
Milk 0
Vegetable 0
Fruit 0
Bread/Starch 0
Meat 4; Fat 8

1/2 teaspoon each thyme, rosemary, oregano and salt
1/2 teaspoon crushed red pepper
1/4 teaspoon each cayenne pepper and black pepper
1 1/2 teaspoons minced garlic
1/2 cup plus 5 tablespoons butter
1 teaspoon Worcestershire sauce
2 pounds peeled shrimp
1/2 cup beer

Mix thyme, rosemary, oregano, salt, red pepper, cayenne pepper and black pepper in small bowl. Sauté garlic in butter in saucepan. Add Worcestershire sauce and seasoning mixture. Stir in shrimp. Cook until shrimp are pink. Stir in beer. Cook until done to taste; do not overcook. Serve with French bread.

F. W. "Ace" Ragan, Jr., Lexington

SCRUMPTIOUS SHRIMP

½ cup oil
¾ cup vinegar
2 cups water
1 envelope Italian
  salad dressing mix
1 teaspoon salt

1 large white onion,
  thinly sliced into
  rings
2 pounds cooked
  peeled shrimp

Combine oil, vinegar, water, salad dressing mix and salt in airtight container. Add onion and shrimp; mix well. Chill, covered, overnight. Drain and place in serving dish.

Nutritional information includes entire amount of marinade.

Betty W. Duncan, Winston-Salem

SHRIMP CREOLE

1 large green bell
  pepper, sliced
1 large onion, sliced
1 small clove of garlic,
  minced
2 tablespoons
  shortening
1 10-ounce can
  tomato soup

⅓ cup water
2 teaspoons lemon
  juice
Tabasco sauce to taste
¼ teaspoon salt
Pepper to taste
1 pound shrimp,
  peeled, cooked
3 cups cooked rice

Cook green pepper, onion and garlic in shortening in covered skillet over low heat until tender. Stir in soup, water, lemon juice, Tabasco sauce, salt and pepper. Add shrimp. Cook for 10 minutes, stirring often. Serve over rice.

Doris Whitesell

SHRIMP AND HAM CREOLE

Yield:
6 servings
Utensil:
saucepan
Approx Per Serving:
Cal 210
Prot 23 g
Carbo 8 g
Fiber 1 g
T Fat 8 g
Chol 164 mg
Sod 514 mg

Dietary Exchanges:
Milk 0
Vegetable 1
Bread/Starch 0
Meat 2½
Fat 1½

1 large onion, chopped
1 green bell pepper, chopped
2 tablespoons olive oil
2 tablespoons catsup
8 ounces sliced fresh mushrooms
1 cup milk
½ teaspoon garlic powder
1 teaspoon Worcestershire sauce
½ cup Old Bay seasoning
Salt and pepper to taste
4 ounces cooked ham, chopped
½ cup white wine
1 pound cooked peeled shrimp

Sauté onion and green pepper in olive oil in heavy saucepan; cool slightly. Add catsup, mushrooms and milk. Heat over medium-low heat. Stir in seasonings. Add ham and wine; reduce heat. Simmer for 15 to 20 minutes or to desired consistency. Add shrimp. Cook for 2 to 3 minutes or just until heated through. Serve over rice.

Nutritional information does not include Old Bay seasoning.

Nancy Garner, Burlington

SHRIMP AND CHICKEN KABOBS

Yield:
6 servings
Utensil:
deep skillet
Approx Per Serving:
Cal 320
Prot 31 g
Carbo 39 g
Fiber 2 g
T Fat 5 g
Chol 202 mg
Sod 227 mg

Dietary Exchanges:
Milk 0
Vegetable 0
Fruit 1
Bread/Starch 0
Meat 3½; Fat 0

¾ cup jalapeño jelly
2 tablespoons fresh lemon juice
36 jumbo shrimp
1½ chicken breast filets
1 pineapple
Salt and pepper to taste

Soak wooden skewers in water for 30 minutes. Combine jalapeño jelly and lemon juice in small saucepan. Heat over medium heat until jelly melts, stirring to mix well. Peel and devein shrimp, leaving tails. Cut chicken into ¾-inch pieces. Cut pineapple into ¾-inch pieces. Drain skewers. Thread shrimp, chicken and pineapple onto skewers. Place a few at a time in boiling salted water in deep skillet. Cook for 6 minutes; drain well. Brush with jelly mixture; season with salt and pepper. Place on oiled rack 5 to 6 inches over hot coals. Cook for 1 to 2 minutes, turning until golden brown.

Joe Tarnowsky, Greensboro

SWEET AND SOUR SHRIMP

1 cup chicken broth
2/3 cup pineapple juice
1/4 cup vinegar
2 tablespoons soy
 sauce

2 tablespoons cornstarch
2 tablespoons sugar
7 ounces snow peas
1 pound small shrimp,
 peeled

Combine chicken broth, pineapple juice, vinegar, soy sauce, cornstarch and sugar in saucepan; mix well. Cook for 5 to 10 minutes or until thickened, stirring constantly. Add snow peas and shrimp. Simmer for 8 minutes. Serve over fried rice or noodles.

Juanita Stone, Graham

SEAFOOD CASSEROLE

1 clove of garlic, crushed
1/4 cup melted margarine
4 ounces scallops
4 ounces peeled
 deveined shrimp
5 1/3 ounces imitation
 crab meat
1 4-ounce can lobster
1/2 cup sliced
 mushrooms

3 tablespoons flour
2 cups low-fat milk
White pepper to taste
4 hard-boiled eggs,
 chopped
1/2 cup shredded
 Cheddar cheese
1/2 cup shredded
 low-fat Swiss cheese
1 cup bread crumbs

Sauté garlic in 1 tablespoon margarine in saucepan. Add seafood and mushrooms. Sauté lightly; remove from heat. Discard garlic. Blend 2 tablespoons margarine and flour in double boiler. Add milk. Cook over hot water until thickened, stirring constantly. Add pepper. Add sautéed seafood, eggs and cheeses; mix well. Spoon into 1 1/2-quart baking dish. Sprinkle with mixture of bread crumbs and 1 tablespoon margarine. Bake at 325 degrees for 30 to 45 minutes or until golden brown.

Mrs. J. C. Kuley, Bethania

- Be sure that the fish you buy is fresh. It will smell fishy, but it should smell clean and fresh as well. Gills should be pink to red, eyes should be firm and bulging, and flesh firm and elastic.

- Fresh shrimp will have a mild odor and firm meat.

- Purchase only live crab and lobsters. Tails of live lobsters will curl under when picked up.

- Fresh scallops should have a sweet odor and firm white flesh. They should be free of liquid when bought in packages.

- Shells of live clams, mussels and oysters should be tightly closed or, if slightly open, should close immediately when lightly tapped. Open shells indicate that the shellfish is dead and should not be eaten.

- Shucked oysters should be plump and naturally creamy in color.

- Store seafood in the coldest part of the refrigerator for up to 2 days. To keep it from flavoring other food in the refrigerator, wrap it in foil and store in container with a tight-fitting cover.

- Rinse seafood before using and pat dry.

- As a general rule, cook seafood for 10 minutes for each inch of thickness, whatever the cooking method chosen. For example, poach a 4-inch piece of salmon for 40 minutes; sauté 1/2-inch filet for 5 minutes; and broil a 1 1/2-inch steak for 7 1/2 minutes on each side.

- You should never microwave frozen fish without defrosting it first; it will be tasteless, dry and unevenly cooked. Do not even thaw seafood in the microwave.

- Some fish is "leaner" than others. "Lean" fish include: bluefish, ocean catfish, cod, flounder, grouper, haddock, halibut, ocean perch, red snapper, sole, swordfish and turbot. "Fat" fish include: amberjack, carp, freshwater catfish, mackerel, mullet, salmon, tuna and whitefish. Red salmon has a higher oil content than pink salmon.

VEGETABLES

GOLDEN-TOPPED ASPARAGUS CASSEROLE

Yield:
12 servings
Utensil:
baking dish
Approx Per
Serving:
Cal 190
Prot 10 g
Carbo 9 g
Fiber 1 g
T Fat 13 g
Chol 136 mg
Sod 855 mg

Dietary
Exchanges:
Milk 0
Vegetable 1/2
Fruit 0
Bread/Starch 1
Meat 1; Fat 21/2

2 16-ounce cans asparagus spears, drained
5 hard-boiled eggs, sliced
1 4-ounce jar pimento strips, drained
2 10-ounce cans cream of mushroom soup
8 slices sharp Cheddar cheese
1/2 cup cracker crumbs

Layer asparagus, eggs, pimento strips and soup in greased 8x12-inch baking dish. Top with cheese slices and cracker crumbs. Bake at 325 degrees for 40 minutes.

Thelma L. Wilson, Winston-Salem

LAYERED ASPARAGUS CASSEROLE

Yield:
6 servings
Utensil:
baking dish
Approx Per
Serving:
Cal 475
Prot 13 g
Carbo 43 g
Fiber 1 g
T Fat 29 g
Chol 112 mg
Sod 1356 mg

Dietary
Exchanges:
Milk 0
Vegetable 1/2
Fruit 0
Bread/Starch 1
Meat 1; Fat 21/2

1 12-ounce package round butter crackers
1 16-ounce can asparagus spears, drained
1 10-ounce can cream of mushroom soup
2 hard-boiled eggs, chopped
1 2-ounce jar chopped pimento, drained
1 cup shredded Cheddar cheese

Layer crackers, asparagus, soup, chopped eggs and pimento 1/2 at a time in greased 8-inch square baking dish. Top with shredded cheese. Bake at 350 degrees for 20 to 30 minutes or until bubbly.

Kathleen Bartes, Graham

CREAMY ASPARAGUS CASSEROLE

2 tablespoons butter
2 tablespoons flour
1/4 teaspoon salt
1/4 teaspoon white
  pepper
12/3 cups milk
2 cups asparagus, cut
  into 1-inch pieces

3 hard-boiled eggs,
  sliced
8 slices Cheddar
  cheese
11/2 cups buttered
  cracker crumbs

Melt butter in saucepan over medium heat. Add flour, salt and white pepper; stir well. Stir in milk gradually. Cook over low heat until thickened, stirring constantly. Alternate layers of asparagus, eggs and Cheddar cheese in greased 11/2-quart baking dish until all ingredients are used. Pour white sauce over layers. Top with cracker crumbs. Bake at 350 degrees for 20 minutes.

Chris Wyatt, Lexington

STIR-FRIED ASPARAGUS

3/4 pound fresh
  asparagus
2 tablespoons oil
4 mushrooms, sliced
1 bunch green onions,
  sliced
1/2 green bell pepper,
  cut into thin strips

1 8-ounce can water
  chestnuts, drained
3/4 cup chicken broth
1 tablespoon
  cornstarch
2 tablespoons soy
  sauce

Trim asparagus; slice diagonally into 1/2-inch slices. Heat oil in wok. Add mushrooms. Stir-fry until lightly browned. Add asparagus, green onions and green pepper. Stir-fry for 2 to 3 minutes. Add water chestnuts. Stir-fry for 1 to 2 minutes. Blend chicken broth, cornstarch and soy sauce in small bowl. Pour over mixture, stirring until thickened. Reduce heat. Simmer, covered, for 2 to 3 minutes longer or until vegetables are tender-crisp. Arrange on serving plate; serve immediately. May also add 1 cup chopped chicken or pork.

Juanita Stone, Graham

ASPARAGUS-PEA CASSEROLE

1 16-ounce can asparagus spears
1 16-ounce can tiny peas, drained
1 10-ounce can cream of mushroom soup
1 cup shredded Cheddar cheese
1 cup cornflake crumbs

Drain asparagus, reserving 1/3 cup liquid. Layer peas, asparagus, soup and cheese in greased 11/2-quart baking dish. Sprinkle with reserved asparagus liquid. Top with cornflake crumbs. Bake at 350 degrees for 1 hour.

Ruth Kent Eslinger, Winston-Salem

LAYERED ASPARAGUS-PEA-EGG CASSEROLE

1 16-ounce can asparagus spears
1 16-ounce can tiny peas, drained
3 hard-boiled eggs, sliced
1 10-ounce can cream of mushroom soup
3/4 cup shredded Cheddar cheese
3/4 cup bread crumbs
2 tablespoons melted margarine

Drain asparagus, reserving juice. Alternate layers of peas, sliced eggs and asparagus in greased 11/2-quart baking dish. Mix reserved asparagus juice with soup; stir well. Pour over layers. Sprinkle with cheese. Toss bread crumbs with melted margarine in small bowl. Sprinkle over layers. Bake at 275 degrees for 20 to 30 minutes or until bubbly.

Sarah L. Finley, Graham

SLOW COOKER BAKED BEANS

Yield:
10 servings
Utensil:
slow cooker
Approx Per
Serving:
Cal 248
Prot 13 g
Carbo 32 g
Fiber 5 g
T Fat 8 g
Chol 37 mg
Sod 670 mg

Dietary
Exchanges:
Milk 0
Vegetable 1/2
Fruit 0
Bread/Starch 1
Meat 11/2; Fat 1

1 pound ground beef
1 green bell pepper, chopped
1 onion, chopped
1 cup catsup

1 28-ounce can pork and beans
1/2 cup molasses
3 slices crisp-fried bacon, crumbled

Brown ground beef in skillet, stirring until crumbly; drain. Combine with green pepper, onion, catsup, pork and beans, molasses and bacon in slow cooker. Cook on High for 2 to 3 hours or until bubbly, stirring occasionally.

Zane G. Gerringer, Elon College

BAKED PORK AND BEANS

Yield:
12 servings
Utensil:
baking dish
Approx Per
Serving:
Cal 240
Prot 8 g
Carbo 50 g
Fiber 7 g
T Fat 3 g
Chol 12 mg
Sod 855 mg

Dietary
Exchanges:
Milk 0
Vegetable 0
Fruit 0
Bread/Starch 11/2
Meat 1/2; Fat 1/2

2 28-ounce cans pork and beans
1 cup chopped celery
1/2 cup chopped green bell pepper

1/2 cup chopped onion
1 cup packed brown sugar
1 cup catsup
6 slices bacon

Combine pork and beans, celery, green pepper, onion, brown sugar and catsup in baking dish; mix well. Arrange bacon slices on top. Bake at 325 degrees for 2 hours.

Kathryn Howerton

Barbecued Beans

1 pound ground beef
2 onions, chopped
1 16-ounce can
   kidney beans
1 16-ounce can pork
   and beans
1 16-ounce can lima
   beans
1 28-ounce can
   tomatoes
¹/4 cup vinegar
¹/2 cup catsup
¹/2 cup packed brown
   sugar
1 teaspoon prepared
   mustard
¹/2 teaspoon pepper
1 teaspoon chili
   powder

Brown ground beef and onions in skillet, stirring frequently; drain. Combine with beans, tomatoes, vinegar, catsup, brown sugar, mustard, pepper and chili powder in slow cooker; mix well. Cook on Low for 5 to 6 hours or until bubbly. Serve with corn bread and coleslaw.

Edythe Kelly, Greensboro

Heart-Healthy Pinto Beans

1 pound dried beans
¹/4 cup white vinegar
¹/4 cup red wine
1 tablespoon olive oil
1 teaspoon salt
2 quarts water

Soak beans for 2 hours to overnight; drain. Cover beans with water in large saucepan; add white vinegar. Bring to a boil; drain and rinse. Combine beans, red wine, olive oil and salt with 2 quarts water in large saucepan. Cook over medium heat for 3 hours or until beans are tender.

Jean Creed May, Greensboro

GREEN BEANS AND TATERS

Yield:
6 servings
Utensil:
skillet
Approx Per Serving:
Cal 92
Prot 2 g
Carbo 17 g
Fiber 2 g
T Fat 3 g
Chol 0 mg
Sod 5 mg

Dietary Exchanges:
Milk 0
Vegetable 1¹/2
Fruit 0
Bread/Starch ¹/2
Meat 0; Fat ¹/2

2 medium red potatoes, peeled, sliced
¹/2 onion, chopped
1 tablespoon olive oil
1 16-ounce can unsalted green beans
¹/4 cup cider vinegar
1 teaspoon sugar
¹/2 teaspoon dry mustard
Pepper to taste

Sauté potatoes and onion in hot oil in skillet until golden brown. Drain beans, reserving 2 tablespoons juice; add to potatoes. Mix vinegar, sugar, mustard and reserved bean juice in small bowl. Pour over beans and potatoes. Cook over medium heat until liquid is almost absorbed, stirring occasionally. Season with pepper. Garnish with parsley.

Mrs. J.C. Kuley, Bethania

MARINATED BEANS AND PEAS

Yield:
12 servings
Utensil:
bowl
Approx Per Serving:
Cal 136
Prot 2 g
Carbo 20 g
Fiber 2 g
T Fat 6 g
Chol 0 mg
Sod 341 mg

Dietary Exchanges:
Milk 0
Vegetable ¹/2
Fruit 0
Bread/Starch 1
Meat 0; Fat 1

³/4 cup sugar
²/3 cup vinegar
1 teaspoon celery seed
1 teaspoon salt
¹/3 cup oil
1 onion, chopped
1 16-ounce can peas
1 16-ounce can French-style green beans

Mix sugar, vinegar, celery seed, salt, oil and onion in large bowl; stir well. Add peas and beans to marinade. Chill in refrigerator for several hours.

Jean H. Mahaffey, Winston-Salem

GREEN BEAN CASSEROLE

Yield:
8 servings
Utensil:
casserole
Approx Per
Serving:
Cal 178
Prot 6 g
Carbo 13 g
Fiber 2 g
T Fat 12 g
Chol 25 mg
Sod 681 mg

Dietary
Exchanges:
Milk 0
Vegetable 1
Bread/Starch 1
Meat 1/2
Fat 2 1/2

2 15-ounce cans French-style green beans
1 medium onion, finely chopped
2 tablespoons butter
1 10-ounce can cream of chicken soup
4 ounces shredded sharp cheese
1 3-ounce can French-fried onion rings

Heat green beans in saucepan. Sauté onion in butter in skillet. Stir in soup and cheese. Cook until cheese melts, stirring constantly. Alternate layers of green beans and soup mixture in 1 1/2-quart casserole. Bake at 350 degrees for 15 minutes. Sprinkle onion rings over top. Bake for 5 minutes.

Shirley Salmons, Clemmons

GREEN BEAN AND CORN CASSEROLE

Yield:
8 servings
Utensil:
baking dish
Approx Per
Serving:
Cal 354
Prot 9 g
Carbo 35 g
Fiber 3 g
T Fat 21 g
Chol 44 mg
Sod 1103 mg

Dietary
Exchanges:
Milk 0
Vegetable 1
Fruit 0
Bread/Starch 1 1/2
Meat 1/2; Fat 4

2 16-ounce cans French-style green beans, drained
1 16-ounce can Shoe Peg corn, drained
1 10-ounce can cream of celery soup
1/2 cup sour cream
1/2 cup shredded Cheddar cheese
1/2 onion, chopped
2 cups cracker crumbs
1/2 cup melted butter
1/2 cup toasted slivered almonds

Combine beans and corn in buttered 8x12-inch baking dish. Mix soup, sour cream, cheese and onion in small bowl. Spread over bean mixture. Combine cracker crumbs with melted butter. Sprinkle over soup mixture; top with almonds. Bake at 350 degrees for 35 minutes. May substitute cream of mushroom soup for cream of celery soup.

Ramona P. Cheek, Graham

GREEN BEAN AND YOGURT CASSEROLE

Yield:
6 servings
Utensil:
baking dish
Approx Per Serving:
Cal 63
Prot 3 g
Carbo 6 g
Fiber 1 g
T Fat 3 g
Chol 4 mg
Sod 417 mg

Dietary Exchanges:
Milk 0
Vegetable 1/2
Fruit 0
Bread/Starch 0
Meat 0; Fat 1/2

1 16-ounce can French-style green beans
1 tablespoon chopped onion
1 tablespoon margarine
1 tablespoon flour
1/2 teaspoon salt
1/4 teaspoon pepper
1/2 cup unsweetened low-fat yogurt
1/4 cup shredded low-fat American cheese

Bring beans to a boil in saucepan. Remove from heat; drain. Place beans in 1-quart baking dish sprayed with nonstick cooking spray; keep warm. Sauté onion in margarine in saucepan until tender. Add flour, salt and pepper. Cook over low heat for 1 minute, stirring constantly. Remove from heat; stir in yogurt gradually. Spread yogurt mixture over beans. Sprinkle with cheese. Broil 3 to 4 inches from heat source until cheese melts.

Janet Mills, Winston-Salem

SANDS CHILI BEANS

Yield:
16 servings
Utensil:
saucepan
Approx Per Serving:
Cal 144
Prot 10 g
Carbo 16 g
Fiber 3 g
T Fat 5 g
Chol 19 mg
Sod 600 mg

Dietary Exchanges:
Milk 0
Vegetable 1
Fruit 0
Bread/Starch 1/2
Meat 1; Fat 1/2

1 onion, chopped
1 green bell pepper, chopped
1 4-ounce can mushrooms, drained
1 tablespoon margarine
1 pound ground beef
2 16-ounce cans tomato sauce
1 16-ounce can whole tomatoes
Chili powder to taste
Black pepper to taste
Crushed red pepper to taste
2 16-ounce cans kidney beans

Sauté onion, green pepper and mushrooms in margarine in large skillet. Add ground beef. Cook until grown beef is browned, stirring frequently; drain. Combine tomato sauce and whole tomatoes in 4-quart saucepan. Add chili powder, black pepper and red pepper. Stir in ground beef mixture. Simmer, covered, for 30 minutes, stirring occasionally. Add kidney beans 30 minutes before serving.

Ricky Sands, Walnut Cove

BAKED LIMA BEANS AND PEAS

2 10-ounce packages
   frozen baby lima
   beans, thawed
2 10-ounce packages
   frozen peas, thawed
1 teaspoon dried basil

1 teaspoon salt
4 green onions, minced
4 tablespoons butter
3 tablespoons water
5 to 6 large lettuce
   leaves

Mix lima beans and peas in greased 4-quart baking dish. Stir in basil, salt and minced green onions. Dot with butter; sprinkle with water. Arrange lettuce leaves over top. Bake, covered, at 325 degrees for 45 minutes. May add slivered almonds.

Elwood and Patsy Mann

LIMA BEANS IN SOUR CREAM

2 cups fresh lima beans
¼ cup finely chopped
   onion
3 tablespoons finely
   chopped pimento

2 tablespoons melted
   butter
½ cup sour cream
½ teaspoon salt
⅛ teaspoon pepper

Cook lima beans in boiling salted water for 20 minutes or until tender; drain. Sauté onion and pimento in butter in saucepan until tender. Stir in lima beans, sour cream, salt and pepper. Cook over low heat for 15 minutes or until thoroughly heated, stirring constantly.

Betty T. Weber, Pfafftown

REAL CAJUN RED BEANS AND RICE

<table>
<tr><td>

Yield:
12 servings
Utensil:
large saucepan
Approx Per
Serving:
Cal 248
Prot 15 g
Carbo 28 g
Fiber 9 g
T Fat 9 g
Chol 19 mg
Sod 920 mg

Dietary
Exchanges:
Milk 0
Vegetable 1
Bread/Starch 1½
Meat 1½
Fat 1½

</td></tr>
</table>

1 pound dried red beans
½ pound salt pork
3 cups chopped red
   onions
1 bunch green onions,
   chopped
1 cup fresh chopped
   parsley
1 cup chopped green
   bell pepper
2 cloves of garlic,
   minced
1 tablespoon salt
1 teaspoon red pepper
1 teaspoon black pepper
3 dashes of Tabasco
   sauce
1 tablespoon
   Worcestershire sauce
1 6-ounce can tomato
   sauce
¼ teaspoon oregano
¼ teaspoon thyme
1 pound sausage

Cook red beans with salt pork in large saucepan according to package directions. Add remaining ingredients except sausage; stir well. Simmer for 1 hour, stirring occasionally. Slice sausage into ⅛-inch patties; add to beans. Cook for 45 minutes. Let stand until cool. Bring mixture to a boil; reduce heat. Simmer for 30 to 40 minutes or until beans are tender. Serve over cooked rice.

Jerry Jarrell, Jamestown

SAUCY RED BEANS WITH RICE

<table>
<tr><td>

Yield:
4 servings
Utensil:
skillet
Approx Per
Serving:
Cal 231
Prot 10 g
Carbo 47 g
Fiber 8 g
T Fat 1 g
Chol 0 mg
Sod 549 mg

Dietary
Exchanges:
Milk 0
Vegetable 2
Fruit 0
Bread/Starch 2½
Meat 0; Fat 0

</td></tr>
</table>

1 onion, chopped
½ cup sliced celery
1 cup chopped
   zucchini
⅛ teaspoon garlic
   powder
¼ teaspoon oregano
¼ teaspoon thyme
1 16-ounce can
   chopped tomatoes
1 15-ounce can
   kidney beans,
   drained
⅛ teaspoon red pepper
2 cups cooked
   unsalted rice

Spray skillet with nonstick cooking spray. Add onion and celery. Cook, covered, over medium-low heat until tender, stirring occasionally. Add zucchini, garlic powder, oregano and thyme. Cook, uncovered, for 5 minutes, stirring occasionally. Add tomatoes, kidney beans and red pepper. Simmer, uncovered, for 20 minutes longer, stirring occasionally. Serve over ½ cup portions of rice.

Betty W. Warf, Rural Hall

KIDNEY BEAN LOAF

<table>
<tr><td>

Yield:
6 servings
Utensil:
loaf pan
**Approx Per
Serving:**
Cal 376
Prot 18 g
Carbo 34 g
Fiber 6 g
T Fat 20 g
Chol 128 mg
Sod 1270 mg

</td></tr>
<tr><td>

**Dietary
Exchanges:**
Milk 0
Vegetable ½
Bread/Starch 2
Meat 1½
Fat 3½

</td></tr>
</table>

1 onion, chopped
2 tablespoons oil
2 cups cooked kidney
  beans
1 cup soft whole-
  wheat bread crumbs
2 eggs, beaten
2 cups shredded
  American cheese

1 tablespoon catsup
Salt and pepper to
  taste
1 10-ounce can
  tomato soup
1 to 2 tablespoons
  dried minced onion
1 tablespoon brown
  sugar

Sauté chopped onion in oil in skillet. Mash beans in medium bowl. Stir in sautéed onion, bread crumbs, eggs, cheese, catsup, salt and pepper; mix well. Spoon into loaf pan. Bake at 350 degrees for 30 minutes. Combine soup, dried minced onion and brown sugar in small bowl. Spread over loaf. Bake for 10 minutes longer.

Kathleen Yax, Mebane

WELL-DRESSED BROCCOLI CASSEROLE

<table>
<tr><td>

Yield:
8 servings
Utensil:
baking dish
**Approx Per
Serving:**
Cal 323
Prot 10 g
Carbo 10 g
Fiber 3 g
T Fat 28 g
Chol 38 mg
Sod 912 mg

</td></tr>
<tr><td>

**Dietary
Exchanges:**
Milk 0
Vegetable 1
Fruit 0
Bread/Starch 1
Meat 1; Fat 6

</td></tr>
</table>

2 10-ounce packages
  frozen broccoli
1 8-ounce jar Cheez
  Whiz
½ cup mayonnaise

1 10-ounce can cream
  of chicken soup
¼ cup margarine
1 cup herb-seasoned
  stuffing mix

Cook broccoli using package directions; drain. Place in greased 2-quart baking dish. Melt Cheez Whiz in microwave. Blend with mayonnaise and soup in bowl. Pour over broccoli. Dot with margarine. Sprinkle stuffing mix over top. Bake at 350 degrees for 25 minutes.

Polly Martin, Burlington

RITZY BROCCOLI CASSEROLE

2 10-ounce packages frozen chopped broccoli
2 eggs, beaten
1 onion, chopped
1 10-ounce can cream of mushroom soup
1/2 cup mayonnaise
1 cup shredded sharp Cheddar cheese
2 cups butter-flavored cracker crumbs
1/2 cup margarine, melted

Cook broccoli using package directions; drain. Combine eggs, onion, soup, mayonnaise and cheese in bowl; mix well. Add broccoli; mix well. Spoon into greased 8-inch square baking dish. Mix cracker crumbs with melted margarine. Sprinkle over broccoli mixture. Bake at 350 degrees for 45 minutes.

Mavareen P. Cromer, Winston-Salem

MOCK BROCCOLI SOUFFLÉ

2 10-ounce packages frozen chopped broccoli
1 cup buttermilk baking mix
1 cup milk
2 eggs
1/2 teaspoon salt
1 tablespoon minced onion
1 cup shredded Cheddar cheese

Cook broccoli using package directions; drain. Combine baking mix, milk, eggs, salt and onion in mixer bowl; beat well. Stir in broccoli and cheese. Spoon into greased 1 1/2-quart baking dish. Bake at 325 degrees for 1 hour or until knife inserted near center comes out clean.

Dot Fesperman, Winston-Salem

BROCCOLI PUFF

Yield:
6 servings
Utensil:
baking dish
Approx Per
Serving:
Cal 218
Prot 7 g
Carbo 10 g
Fiber 2 g
T Fat 17 g
Chol 68 mg
Sod 572 mg

Dietary
Exchanges:
Milk 0
Vegetable 1/2
Fruit 0
Bread/Starch 1
Meat 1/2; Fat 41/2

1 10-ounce package frozen chopped broccoli
1 10-ounce can cream of mushroom soup
1/2 cup shredded sharp Cheddar cheese
1/4 cup milk
1/4 cup mayonnaise
1 egg, beaten
1/4 cup fine dry bread crumbs
1 tablespoon butter, melted

Cook broccoli using package directions, omitting salt; drain. Place broccoli in greased 6x10-inch baking dish. Combine soup and cheese in bowl. Add milk, mayonnaise and egg, stirring after each addition. Pour over broccoli. Combine bread crumbs and melted butter in bowl. Sprinkle over mixture. Bake at 350 degrees for 45 minutes or until crumbs are lightly browned.

Sarah L. Finley, Graham

LAYERED BROCCOLI CASSEROLE

Yield:
8 servings
Utensil:
baking dish
Approx Per
Serving:
Cal 169
Prot 4 g
Carbo 4 g
Fiber 2 g
T Fat 15 g
Chol 50 mg
Sod 284 mg

Dietary
Exchanges:
Milk 0
Vegetable 1/2
Fruit 0
Bread/Starch 1/2
Meat 1/2; Fat 31/2

1/2 10-ounce can cream of mushroom soup
1/2 cup shredded Cheddar cheese
1/2 cup mayonnaise
1 egg, beaten
1/2 onion, chopped
Salt and pepper to taste
1 10-ounce package frozen broccoli, thawed

Combine soup, cheese, mayonnaise, egg, onion, salt and pepper in bowl; mix well. Pour 1/2 of the mixture into 8-inch square baking dish. Arrange broccoli on top; cover with remaining sauce mixture. May sprinkle with additional cheese. Bake at 350 degrees for 45 minutes.

Sharon M. Fanelli, Gibsonville

Broccoli with Cheese Sauce

Yield:
4 servings
Utensil:
serving dish
Approx Per
Serving:
Cal 228
Prot 8 g
Carbo 10 g
Fiber 3 g
T Fat 18 g
Chol 54 mg
Sod 312 mg

Dietary
Exchanges:
Milk 1/2
Vegetable 1
Fruit 0
Bread/Starch 1/2
Meat 1/2; Fat 31/2

1 10-ounce package frozen broccoli
1/4 cup butter
2 tablespoons flour
1 cup milk
1/8 teaspoon salt
1/8 teaspoon pepper
1/8 teaspoon dry mustard
Dash of paprika
1/2 cup shredded Cheddar cheese

Cook broccoli using package directions; drain. Place butter in 1-quart glass measure. Microwave on High for 30 seconds. Add flour and milk, stirring well after each addition. Microwave for 3 minutes or until thickened, stirring once. Add salt, pepper, mustard, paprika and Cheddar cheese; mix well. Microwave for 2 minutes; stir to blend in cheese. Arrange broccoli in serving dish. Pour cheese sauce over broccoli. Serve immediately.

Mrs. Paul Schneeloch-Adeline, Clemmons

Broccoli Supreme

Yield:
8 servings
Utensil:
baking dish
Approx Per
Serving:
Cal 130
Prot 5 g
Carbo 11 g
Fiber 3 g
T Fat 8 g
Chol 17 mg
Sod 500 mg

Dietary
Exchanges:
Milk 0
Vegetable 1
Fruit 0
Bread/Starch 1
Meat 0; Fat 2

11/2 pounds fresh broccoli, chopped
1 10-ounce can cream of chicken soup
1/2 cup sour cream
1 tablespoon flour
1/2 teaspoon salt
1/8 teaspoon pepper
1/4 cup shredded carrots
1/3 cup chopped onion
3/4 cup herb-seasoned stuffing mix
2 tablespoons butter, melted

Cook broccoli in boiling water for 10 to 12 minutes or until tender; drain. Combine soup, sour cream, flour, salt and pepper in bowl; mix well. Add broccoli, carrots and onion; stir well to coat. Spoon into lightly greased 2-quart baking dish. Combine stuffing mix with melted butter. Sprinkle over broccoli mixture. Bake at 350 degrees for 30 to 35 minutes or until golden brown.

Bettie Duggins, Kernersville

BROCCOLI PARMIGIANA

2 eggs, beaten
1 10-ounce can cream of mushroom soup
2 10-ounce packages frozen broccoli, thawed
1/2 cup milk
1 cup mayonnaise
1 onion, sliced
1 cup Parmesan cheese
1/4 cup margarine
1 1/2 cups herb-seasoned stuffing mix

Combine eggs, soup, broccoli, milk, mayonnaise and onion in bowl; mix well. Spoon into lightly greased 9x14-inch baking dish. Sprinkle cheese over top. Melt margarine in small skillet. Stir in stuffing mix. Sprinkle over cheese layer. Bake at 350 degrees for 35 to 40 minutes or until topping is golden brown.

Agnes David, Winston-Salem

BROCCOLI-CHEESE CASSEROLE

2 10-ounce packages frozen broccoli
2 tablespoons margarine
1 tablespoon flour
1 teaspoon salt
Dash of pepper
1 1/2 cups milk
1 tablespoon Worcestershire sauce
2 cups shredded American cheese
1 cup buttered bread crumbs

Cook broccoli using package directions; drain. Melt margarine in saucepan. Stir in flour. Cook over low heat until bubbly. Add salt, pepper and milk. Cook until thickened, stirring constantly. Remove from heat. Add Worcestershire sauce and cheese; mix well. Layer broccoli and sauce 1/2 at a time in greased 2-quart casserole. Top with buttered bread crumbs. Bake at 350 degrees for 30 minutes or until golden brown.

Doris S. Stout, Snow Camp

EASY BROCCOLI CASSEROLE

Yield:
6 servings
Utensil:
baking dish
Approx Per
Serving:
Cal 426
Prot 12 g
Carbo 17 g
Fiber 4 g
T Fat 36 g
Chol 128 mg
Sod 780 mg

Dietary
Exchanges:
Milk 0
Vegetable 1½
Fruit 0
Bread/Starch 1
Meat 1; Fat 7½

2 10-ounce packages
   frozen broccoli
1 10-ounce can cream
   of mushroom soup
4 ounces sharp
   Cheddar cheese,
   shredded

2 eggs, beaten
¾ cup mayonnaise
1 onion, chopped
½ cup butter-flavored
   cracker crumbs

Cook broccoli using package directions; drain. Combine broccoli, soup, cheese, eggs, mayonnaise and onion in bowl; mix well. Spoon into buttered 2-quart baking dish. Top with cracker crumbs. Bake at 350 degrees for 30 minutes.

Doreen Smith, West End

CREAMY BROCCOLI-RICE CASSEROLE

Yield:
10 servings
Utensil:
baking dish
Approx Per
Serving:
Cal 285
Prot 9 g
Carbo 22 g
Fiber 3 g
T Fat 18 g
Chol 24 mg
Sod 701 mg

Dietary
Exchanges:
Milk 0
Vegetable 1
Fruit 0
Bread/Starch 1½
Meat 1; Fat 3½

½ cup margarine
2 10-ounce packages
   frozen broccoli,
   thawed
1 cup chopped celery
1 onion, chopped

1 cup uncooked rice
8 ounces Velveeta
   cheese, shredded
1 10-ounce can cream
   of chicken soup

Melt margarine in skillet. Add broccoli, celery and onion. Sauté until tender. Cook rice using package directions. Combine with broccoli mixture, cheese and soup in bowl; mix well. Spoon into greased 2-quart baking dish. Bake at 325 degrees for 40 minutes.

Mary Pace

EASY BROCCOLI AND RICE CASSEROLE

Yield:
8 servings
Utensil:
baking dish
Approx Per
Serving:
Cal 296
Prot 10 g
Carbo 25 g
Fiber 2 g
T Fat 18 g
Chol 35 mg
Sod 777 mg

Dietary
Exchanges:
Milk 0
Vegetable 1/2
Fruit 0
Bread/Starch 2
Meat 1; Fat 4

2 tablespoons butter, softened
1 10-ounce can cream of mushroom soup
1 8-ounce jar Cheez Whiz, softened
1 onion, chopped
1 cup water
1 cup uncooked quick-cooking rice
1 10-ounce package frozen broccoli, thawed
2 tablespoons melted margarine

Blend butter, soup and Cheez Whiz in bowl. Add onion, water, rice and broccoli; mix well. Spoon into 9-inch square baking dish. Drizzle 2 tablespoons melted margarine over top. Bake at 350 degrees for 1 hour or until golden brown and bubbly.

Barbara Johnson, Graham

CHEESY BROCCOLI AND RICE CASSEROLE

Yield:
6 servings
Utensil:
baking dish
Approx Per
Serving:
Cal 590
Prot 22 g
Carbo 34 g
Fiber 3 g
T Fat 42 g
Chol 119 mg
Sod 1623 mg

Dietary
Exchanges:
Milk 0
Vegetable 1
Fruit 0
Bread/Starch 2
Meat 2 1/2; Fat 8

1 cup uncooked converted rice
1 10-ounce package frozen chopped broccoli, cooked, drained
1 10 ounce can cream of celery soup
1/2 cup butter, melted
1 onion, chopped
1 16-ounce jar Cheez Whiz

Cook rice according to package directions; drain. Mix with broccoli, soup, butter and onion in bowl; stir well. Add Cheez Whiz; mix well. Spoon into lightly greased 2-quart baking dish. Bake at 350 degrees for 45 minutes to 1 hour or until golden brown and bubbly.

Deborah B. Edwards, Graham

CYNTHIA'S BROCCOLI CASSEROLE

Yield:
6 servings
Utensil:
baking dish
Approx Per
Serving:
Cal 509
Prot 14 g
Carbo 44 g
Fiber 2 g
T Fat 31 g
Chol 78 mg
Sod 1102 mg

Dietary
Exchanges:
Milk 0
Vegetable 1/2
Fruit 0
Bread/Starch 3
Meat 1 1/2; Fat 7

1 10-ounce package frozen chopped broccoli
1 10-ounce can cream of mushroom soup
1/2 cup butter
1 8-ounce jar Cheez Whiz
1 1/2 cups uncooked minute rice

Cook broccoli using package directions; drain. Combine soup, butter and Cheez Whiz in saucepan. Cook over medium heat until cheese is melted, stirring constantly. Add broccoli and rice; mix well. Spoon into greased 1-quart baking dish. Bake, covered, at 350 degrees for 30 minutes.

Cynthia Cook, Winston-Salem

CREAMY CHEDDAR-BROCCOLI CASSEROLE

Yield:
6 servings
Utensil:
baking dish
Approx Per
Serving:
Cal 384
Prot 8 g
Carbo 23 g
Fiber 3 g
T Fat 30 g
Chol 77 mg
Sod 728 mg

Dietary
Exchanges:
Milk 0
Vegetable 1
Fruit 0
Bread/Starch 1 1/2
Meat 1/2; Fat 6 1/2

1 10-ounce package frozen chopped broccoli
1 cup cooked quick-cooking rice
1 onion, chopped
1/2 cup cubed Cheddar cheese
1/2 cup mayonnaise
1 10-ounce can cream of mushroom soup
1 egg, well beaten
1 cup butter-flavored cracker crumbs
2 tablespoons butter

Cook broccoli using package directions; drain. Combine with cooked rice in bowl. Add onion, cheese, mayonnaise, soup and egg, mixing well after each addition. Spoon into lightly greased 1 1/2-quart baking dish. Top with cracker crumbs; dot with butter. Bake at 350 degrees for 30 minutes or until topping is golden brown.

Carlene Clinton, Pfafftown

Broccoli and Pea Casserole

Yield:
12 servings
Utensil:
baking dish
Approx Per
Serving:
Cal 253
Prot 7 g
Carbo 11 g
Fiber 3 g
T Fat 21 g
Chol 69 mg
Sod 630 mg

Dietary
Exchanges:
Milk 0
Vegetable 1/2
Fruit 0
Bread/Starch 1
Meat 1/2; Fat 4 1/2

2 10-ounce packages
frozen chopped
broccoli
1 10-ounce can peas
1 10-ounce can cream
of chicken soup
1 cup mayonnaise
1 teaspoon salt
1/2 teaspoon pepper
1 cup shredded sharp
Cheddar cheese
2 eggs, beaten
1 onion, chopped
1/2 cup cracker crumbs

Cook broccoli using package directions; drain. Place half the broccoli in greased 2-quart casserole; cover with peas. Combine soup, mayonnaise, salt, pepper, cheese, eggs and onion in bowl; mix well. Layer half the soup mixture, remaining broccoli and remaining soup mixture over peas. Sprinkle cracker crumbs over top. Bake at 350 degrees for 30 minutes.

Gloria Barrett, Holden Beach

Brussels Sprouts and Rice

Yield:
6 servings
Utensil:
12-inch skillet
Approx Per
Serving:
Cal 191
Prot 7 g
Carbo 30 g
Fiber 3 g
T Fat 6 g
Chol 16 mg
Sod 746 mg

Dietary
Exchanges:
Milk 0
Vegetable 2
Fruit 0
Bread/Starch 1 1/2
Meat 0; Fat 1

1 10-ounce can cream
of celery soup
1 cup milk
1 cup water
1 tablespoon butter
3/4 teaspoon caraway
seed
1 teaspoon salt
2/3 cup rice
2 10-ounce packages
frozen Brussels
sprouts, thawed

Combine soup, milk, water, butter, caraway seed and salt in 12-inch skillet; mix well. Bring to a boil over medium heat, stirring constantly. Add rice; reduce heat to low. Simmer, covered, for 15 minutes, stirring occasionally. Cut Brussels sprouts into halves. Stir into rice mixture. Simmer for 15 minutes or until tender.

Doreen Smith, West End

CREOLE CABBAGE

Yield:
8 servings
Utensil:
large saucepan
Approx Per
Serving:
Cal 65
Prot 2 g
Carbo 9 g
Fiber 3 g
T Fat 3 g
Chol 0 mg
Sod 621 mg

Dietary
Exchanges:
Milk 0
Vegetable 1½
Fruit 0
Bread/Starch 0
Meat 0; Fat ½

10 cups shredded
  cabbage
1 teaspoon salt
¼ cup sliced onion
2 tablespoons
  margarine
1¾ cups tomatoes

2 tablespoons chopped
  green bell pepper
2 whole cloves
1 small bay leaf
1 teaspoon salt
1½ teaspoons sugar

Combine cabbage and 1 teaspoon salt with 1 inch of water in large saucepan. Boil, covered, until tender; drain. Simmer onion and margarine in skillet for 5 minutes. Add tomatoes, green pepper, cloves, bay leaf, remaining 1 teaspoon salt and sugar; mix well. Simmer for 15 minutes. Remove cloves and bay leaf. Pour tomato mixture over drained cabbage; toss.

Patsy N. Mann, Kernersville

CABBAGE PLATE

Yield:
6 servings
Utensil:
saucepan
Approx Per
Serving:
Cal 125
Prot 1 g
Carbo 11 g
Fiber 3 g
T Fat 9 g
Chol 0 mg
Sod 523 mg

Dietary
Exchanges:
Milk 0
Vegetable 1½
Fruit 0
Bread/Starch 0
Meat 0; Fat 2

3 cups chopped
  cabbage
2 cups sliced carrots
1 cup chopped onion
1 cup chopped celery

1 tablespoon sugar
1½ teaspoons salt
¼ cup oil
2 cups hot water

Combine cabbage, carrots, onion, celery, sugar, salt and oil in 3-quart saucepan; mix well. Add water. Cook, covered, over low heat for 25 minutes or until tender.

Leola M. Vaughn, Stokesdale

HONEY GINGERED CARROTS

Yield:
4 servings
Utensil:
saucepan
Approx Per
Serving:
Cal 125
Prot 1 g
Carbo 17 g
Fiber 3 g
T Fat 6 g
Chol 17 mg
Sod 41 mg

Dietary
Exchanges:
Milk 0
Vegetable 2
Fruit 0
Bread/Starch 0
Meat 0; Fat 1¹/2

1 pound carrots, sliced
2 tablespoons
   unsalted butter,
   melted

1 tablespoon ginger
1 tablespoon minced
   gingerroot
1 tablespoon honey

Combine carrots, butter, ginger and gingerroot in medium saucepan. Cook, covered, over low heat for 12 minutes. Stir in honey; toss to coat. Cook, uncovered, until carrots are of desired tenderness.

Gloria Stinson, Winston-Salem

MARINATED CARROTS

Yield:
8 servings
Utensil:
covered bowl
Approx Per
Serving:
Cal 248
Prot 2 g
Carbo 32 g
Fiber 2 g
T Fat 14 g
Chol 0 mg
Sod 529 mg

Dietary
Exchanges:
Milk 0
Vegetable 1¹/2
Fruit 0
Bread/Starch ¹/2
Meat 0; Fat 3

2 16-ounce cans
   sliced carrots
1 onion, chopped
1 green bell pepper,
   chopped
1 10-ounce can
   tomato soup

¹/2 cup vinegar
¹/2 cup oil
³/4 cup sugar
1 teaspoon prepared
   mustard

Combine carrots, onion and green pepper in bowl. Add mixture of soup, vinegar, oil, sugar and mustard; toss lightly. Marinate, covered, in refrigerator until serving time.

Betty S. Gregory, Greensboro

COPPER PENNIES

Yield:
8 servings
Utensil:
saucepan
Approx Per
Serving:
Cal 294
Prot 2 g
Carbo 46 g
Fiber 4 g
T Fat 15 g
Chol 0 mg
Sod 89 mg

Dietary
Exchanges:
Milk 0
Vegetable 2
Fruit 0
Bread/Starch ½
Meat 0; Fat 3

2 pounds carrots,
   thinly sliced
1 onion, sliced
1 green bell pepper,
   sliced into rings
1 teaspoon
   Worcestershire sauce
1 cup sugar
¾ cup cider vinegar
1 teaspoon dry mustard
1 10-ounce can low-
   sodium tomato soup
½ cup olive oil
⅛ teaspoon salt
Pepper to taste

Cover carrots with lightly salted water in saucepan. Cook over low heat for 15 minutes; drain. Layer carrots, onion and green pepper in non-metal container. Combine Worcestershire sauce, sugar, vinegar, mustard, soup, olive oil, salt and pepper in medium saucepan. Bring to a boil. Pour over layered vegetables. Marinate in refrigerator for 25 hours.

Nancy Garner, Burlington

CORN AND PEA CASSEROLE

Yield:
8 servings
Utensil:
shallow casserole
Approx Per
Serving:
Cal 256
Prot 13 g
Carbo 25 g
Fiber 4 g
T Fat 13 g
Chol 30 mg
Sod 821 mg

Dietary
Exchanges:
Milk 0
Vegetable 0
Fruit 0
Bread/Starch 2
Meat 1; Fat 2½

1 20-ounce can Shoe
   Peg corn
1 20-ounce can tiny
   peas
1 10-ounce can cream
   of mushroom soup
8 ounces Cheddar
   cheese, shredded

Layer corn, peas and soup in shallow 1½-quart casserole. Sprinkle top with cheese. Bake at 350 degrees for 20 minutes.

Lillian Buie, Winston-Salem

Corn Pudding

Yield:
8 servings
Utensil:
baking dish
Approx Per
Serving:
Cal 222
Prot 6 g
Carbo 28 g
Fiber 1 g
T Fat 11 g
Chol 127 mg
Sod 317 mg

Dietary
Exchanges:
Milk 1/2
Vegetable 0
Fruit 0
Bread/Starch 1
Meat 1/2; Fat 2

½ cup sugar
3 tablespoons flour
3 eggs, beaten
2 cups milk

1 17-ounce can whole kernel corn
⅛ teaspoon salt
¼ cup butter

Combine sugar, flour and eggs in medium-sized mixer bowl; beat well. Stir in milk, corn and salt. Melt butter in lightly greased 1¾-quart baking dish. Pour in corn mixture. Bake at 400 degrees for 1 hour or until knife inserted near center comes out clean. Serve immediately.

Marion Pritchett, Greensboro

Mexican Corn Pudding

Yield:
6 servings
Utensil:
baking dish
Approx Per
Serving:
Cal 159
Prot 6 g
Carbo 25 g
Fiber <1 g
T Fat 4 g
Chol 141 mg
Sod 598 mg

Dietary
Exchanges:
Milk 0
Vegetable 0
Fruit 0
Bread/Starch 1½
Meat 1/2; Fat 1/2

1 17-ounce can cream-style corn
3 eggs, slightly beaten
½ cup fine dry cracker crumbs
1 tablespoon grated onion
2 tablespoons chopped green bell pepper

2 tablespoons chopped pimento
½ teaspoon salt
¼ teaspoon pepper
¼ teaspoon dry mustard

Combine corn, eggs, cracker crumbs, onion, green pepper, pimento, salt, pepper and mustard in bowl; mix well. Pour into lightly greased 1-quart baking dish. Bake at 350 degrees for 1 hour or until knife inserted near center comes out clean.

Emmaline Lindsay, Greensboro

SKILLET CORN PUDDING

Yield:
8 servings
Utensil:
cast-iron skillet
Approx Per
Serving:
Cal 83
Prot 2 g
Carbo 14 g
Fiber 1 g
T Fat 3 g
Chol 2 mg
Sod 232 mg

Dietary
Exchanges:
Milk 0
Vegetable 0
Fruit 0
Bread/Starch 1
Meat 0; Fat 1/2

3 cups fresh corn
1/2 cup milk
3 tablespoons flour
1/8 teaspoon salt
Pepper to taste
3 tablespoons
margarine

Combine corn, milk, flour, salt and pepper in bowl; mix well. Melt margarine over medium heat in cast-iron skillet. Pour in corn mixture. Bake at 450 degrees until golden brown.

Mary Pickett, Winston-Salem

CORN MUFFIN COMBO

Yield:
8 servings
Utensil:
baking dish
Approx Per
Serving:
Cal 500
Prot 14 g
Carbo 34 g
Fiber 1 g
T Fat 36 g
Chol 124 mg
Sod 843 mg

Dietary
Exchanges:
Milk 0
Vegetable 1/2
Bread/Starch 2
Meat 11/2
Fat 71/2

1 small onion, chopped
1/2 cup margarine
2 eggs, beaten
1 16-ounce can whole kernel corn
1 16-ounce can cream-style corn
1 7-ounce package corn muffin mix
1 tablespoon chopped green bell pepper
1/8 teaspoon salt
Pepper to taste
2 cups sour cream
2 cups shredded Cheddar cheese

Sauté onion in margarine in skillet. Combine eggs and corn in large bowl; mix gently. Add corn muffin mix, green pepper, sautéed onion, margarine, salt and pepper, stirring after each addition. Pour into greased 9x13-inch baking dish. Spread sour cream over top of corn mixture. Sprinkle with cheese. Bake at 375 degrees for 40 minutes.

B. J. Showerman, Burlington

EASY CORN PUDDING

Yield:
6 servings
Utensil:
baking dish
Approx Per
Serving:
Cal 198
Prot 6 g
Carbo 22 g
Fiber <1 g
T Fat 11 g
Chol 159 mg
Sod 685 mg

Dietary
Exchanges:
Milk 0
Vegetable 0
Fruit 0
Bread/Starch 1
Meat 1/2; Fat 2

2 cups cream-style corn
2 tablespoons flour
1 tablespoon sugar
1 cup milk
1 teaspoon salt
3 tablespoons melted
  butter
3 eggs, beaten

Combine corn, flour, sugar, milk, salt, butter and eggs in bowl; mix well. Pour into greased 1-quart baking dish. Place in shallow baking pan with 1 inch hot water. Bake at 325 degrees for 1½ hours or until firm, stirring twice.

Jessie Grandinetti

BAKED EGGPLANT

Yield:
6 servings
Utensil:
baking dish
Approx Per
Serving:
Cal 110
Prot 4 g
Carbo 16 g
Fiber 4 g
T Fat 4 g
Chol 47 mg
Sod 459 mg

Dietary
Exchanges:
Milk 0
Vegetable 2
Fruit 0
Bread/Starch 1/2
Meat 0; Fat 1

1 large peeled
  eggplant, cut into
  1/2-inch slices
1/2 teaspoon salt
1/8 teaspoon pepper
1 egg, lightly beaten
1/2 cup cracker crumbs
Oil for frying
3/4 cup chopped celery
1 onion, chopped
2 tablespoons water
1/3 cup reduced-calorie
  sour cream
1/2 teaspoon salt
1/8 teaspoon pepper
4 tomatoes, thickly
  sliced

Season eggplant with 1/2 teaspoon salt and 1/8 teaspoon pepper. Dip into egg; coat with crumbs. Brown lightly on both sides in hot oil in skillet; drain. Arrange in shallow 8x12-inch baking dish. Combine celery, onion and water in glass bowl. Microwave on High for 5 minutes. Stir in sour cream and remaining seasonings. Place 1 tomato slice on each eggplant slice. Top each with celery mixture. Bake at 350 degrees for 30 minutes.

Nutritional information does not include oil for frying.

Mary H. Harden, Graham

EGGPLANT AND RICE CASSEROLE

Yield:
6 servings
Utensil:
baking dish
Approx Per Serving:
Cal 137
Prot 4 g
Carbo 19 g
Fiber 1 g
T Fat 5 g
Chol 12 mg
Sod 355 mg

Dietary Exchanges:
Milk 0
Vegetable 1/2
Fruit 0
Bread/Starch 1
Meat 1/2; Fat 1

8 slices eggplant
1/2 cup chopped onion
Oil for frying
1/2 cup rice
1 1/4 cups chicken broth
6 slices peeled tomato
4 basil leaves

1/4 teaspoon salt
2 tablespoons butter
1/4 cup fine bread crumbs
2 tablespoons Parmesan cheese

Brown eggplant and onion lightly in hot oil in skillet; drain. Cook rice in chicken broth using package directions. Layer eggplant, onion, tomato slices, basil leaves, salt and rice 1/2 at a time in baking dish. Dot with butter. Sprinkle with bread crumbs and Parmesan cheese. Bake at 350 degrees for 30 minutes.

Nutritional information does not include oil for frying.

Doris D. Burnette, Graham

EGGPLANT PARMIGIANA

Yield:
6 servings
Utensil:
glass casserole
Approx Per Serving:
Cal 336
Prot 14 g
Carbo 28 g
Fiber 1 g
T Fat 20 g
Chol 45 mg
Sod 966 mg

Dietary Exchanges:
Milk 0
Vegetable 4
Fruit 0
Bread/Starch 0
Meat 2; Fat 2 1/2

1 large eggplant
1 32-ounce jar spaghetti sauce

3 cups shredded mozzarella cheese

Peel and slice eggplant. Alternate layers of eggplant, sauce and cheese in glass casserole, ending with cheese. Microwave on High for 20 minutes or until tender.

Carol G. Smith, Burlington

OATMEAL MUSHROOM PATTIES

<table>
<tr><td>

Yield:
6 servings
Utensil:
baking dish
Approx Per
Serving:
Cal 237
Prot 7 g
Carbo 23 g
Fiber 2 g
T Fat 14 g
Chol 92 mg
Sod 1163 mg

</td></tr>
</table>

Dietary
Exchanges:
Milk 0
Vegetable 0
Fruit 0
Bread/Starch 2
Meat 1/2; Fat 31/2

1 small potato, grated
2 eggs, lightly beaten
1 cup oats
1 4-ounce can
   mushrooms
1 envelope onion soup
   mix
1/2 teaspoon MSG
1/2 teaspoon basil
2 tablespoons oil
1 10-ounce can cream
   of mushroom soup
1 tablespoon soy sauce
1 tablespoon oil

Combine potato, eggs and oats in bowl; mix well. Drain and chop mushrooms, reserving liquid. Add mushrooms, soup mix, MSG and basil to oat mixture. Stir in enough reserved mushroom liquid to make mixture slightly sticky. Shape into patties. Fry in 2 tablespoons hot oil in skillet until golden brown, turning once. Place in lightly greased baking dish. Combine mushroom soup, soy sauce, remaining 1 tablespoon oil and any remaining mushroom liquid in bowl; mix well. Pour over patties. Bake at 350 degrees for 30 minutes.

Kathleen Yax, Mebane

SOUTHERN OKRA

Yield:
6 servings
Utensil:
skillet
Approx Per
Serving:
Cal 82
Prot 2 g
Carbo 10 g
Fiber 2 g
T Fat 5 g
Chol 0 mg
Sod 170 mg

Dietary
Exchanges:
Milk 0
Vegetable 11/2
Fruit 0
Bread/Starch 0
Meat 0; Fat 1

1 cup sliced okra
1 onion, chopped
1 green bell pepper,
   chopped
2 tablespoons oil
3 peeled tomatoes, cut
   into quarters
1 tablespoon sugar
1 teaspoon flour
1/2 teaspoon salt
1/2 teaspoon pepper

Cook okra in boiling salted water in saucepan for 10 minutes; drain. Brown onion and green pepper in hot oil in skillet. Add tomatoes. Cook over low heat for 5 minutes longer. Stir in okra, sugar, flour, salt and pepper. Cook just until vegetables are tender.

Bonnie Cearley, Jefferson

BAKED ONIONS

Yield:
4 servings
Utensil:
glass baking dish
Approx Per Serving:
Cal 88
Prot 2 g
Carbo 12 g
Fiber 3 g
T Fat 4 g
Chol 0 mg
Sod 55 mg

Dietary Exchanges:
Milk 0
Vegetable 2
Fruit 0
Bread/Starch 0
Meat 0; Fat 1

4 Spanish onions, cut into wedges

4 teaspoons margarine

Pepper to taste

Place onions in glass baking dish. Dot with margarine; sprinkle with pepper. Microwave, tightly covered, on High for 12 minutes.

B. S. Cuthrell, Winston-Salem

CREAMED ONIONS

Yield:
4 servings
Utensil:
baking dish
Approx Per Serving:
Cal 149
Prot 3 g
Carbo 10 g
Fiber 1 g
T Fat 11 g
Chol 31 mg
Sod 380 mg

Dietary Exchanges:
Milk 1/2
Vegetable 1
Fruit 0
Bread/Starch 0
Meat 0; Fat 2 1/2

20 pearl onions
2 tablespoons butter
1/2 teaspoon salt
Pepper to taste
1 teaspoon dry mustard
2 tablespoons flour

1 cup milk
2 tablespoons butter-flavored cracker crumbs
1 tablespoon butter

Cook onions in boiling salted water in saucepan for 30 minutes; drain. Let stand until cool. Melt 2 tablespoons butter over low heat in heavy saucepan. Stir in salt, pepper, dry mustard and flour. Add milk. Cook until thickened, stirring constantly. Place onions in baking dish; pour sauce over onions. Top with cracker crumbs; dot with butter. Bake at 350 degrees for 20 to 25 minutes or until bubbly.

Nancy Garner, Burlington

BEER-FRIED ONION RINGS

Yield:
4 servings
Utensil:
deep-fryer
Approx Per Serving:
Cal 259
Prot 7 g
Carbo 50 g
Fiber 4 g
T Fat 1 g
Chol 0 mg
Sod 10 mg

Dietary Exchanges:
Milk 0
Vegetable 2
Fruit 0
Bread/Starch 2½
Meat 0; Fat 0

1 12-ounce can beer
1½ cups flour
4 large onions, sliced
 into ½-inch rings

Oil for frying
Salt to taste

Combine beer and flour in bowl; mix well. Let stand, covered, at room temperature for 3 hours. Dip onion rings into batter. Fry in 2 inches 375-degree oil in deep-fryer until golden brown, turning frequently. Drain on absorbent paper; salt to taste. Keep warm until serving time.

Nutritional information does not include oil for frying.

Jerry Jarrell, Jamestown

SOUR CREAM ONION PIE

Yield:
6 servings
Utensil:
9-inch pie plate
Approx Per Serving:
Cal 402
Prot 8 g
Carbo 30 g
Fiber 2 g
T Fat 28 g
Chol 154 mg
Sod 523 mg

Dietary Exchanges:
Milk 0
Vegetable 1
Fruit 0
Bread/Starch 1½
Meat ½; Fat 6½

1¼ cups flour
¼ teaspoon salt
⅓ cup butter
2 to 3 tablespoons
 water
3 cups thinly sliced
 Spanish onions

2 tablespoons butter
2 tablespoons flour
2 eggs, beaten
1½ cups sour cream
¾ teaspoon salt
¼ teaspoon pepper
¼ teaspoon thyme

Mix 1¼ cups flour and ¼ teaspoon salt in bowl. Cut in ⅓ cup butter until crumbly. Add water 1 tablespoon at a time, mixing until mixture forms ball. Roll into ½-inch thick circle. Fit into 9-inch pie plate. Bake at 425 degrees for 10 minutes. Cook onions in 2 tablespoons butter in saucepan over low heat until softened; do not brown. Sprinkle with 2 table-spoons flour, stirring to coat. Spoon into pie shell. Mix eggs and remaining ingredients in bowl. Pour over onions. Bake at 425 degrees for 10 minutes. Reduce oven temperature to 350 degrees. Bake for 20 minutes longer or until knife inserted near center comes out clean. Garnish with parsley sprigs.

Margaret Martens, Liberty

PEA CASSEROLE

Yield:
10 servings
Utensil:
glass baking dish
Approx Per
Serving:
Cal 143
Prot 4 g
Carbo 24 g
Fiber 2 g
T Fat 4 g
Chol 0 mg
Sod 230 mg

Dietary
Exchanges:
Milk 0
Vegetable 1/2
Fruit 0
Bread/Starch 1 1/2
Meat 1/2; Fat 1/2

1 cup brown rice
3 cups water
1/2 teaspoon salt
1 10-ounce package
  frozen peas
1 cup water chestnuts,
  thinly sliced
1/2 cup chopped onion
1/2 cup chopped celery
1 teaspoon garlic
  powder
1 teaspoon basil
1/2 teaspoon salt
1 4-ounce jar
  pimentos
1/2 cup cashews,
  ground

Combine rice, water and 1/2 teaspoon salt in saucepan. Cook, covered, over low heat for 50 minutes. Drain peas, reserving liquid. Add peas and water chestnuts to rice; mix well. Spoon into 9x13-inch glass baking dish. Sauté onion and celery in skillet sprayed with nonstick cooking spray. Add reserved liquid from peas, garlic powder, basil, remaining 1/2 teaspoon salt, pimentos and ground cashews; mix well. Pour over rice mixture. Bake at 350 degrees for 15 to 25 minutes or until bubbly in center.

Kathleen S. Yax, Mebane

PEAS AND CARROTS

Yield:
4 servings
Utensil:
saucepan
Approx Per
Serving:
Cal 147
Prot 6 g
Carbo 23 g
Fiber 4 g
T Fat 4 g
Chol 12 mg
Sod 175 mg

Dietary
Exchanges:
Milk 0
Vegetable 2
Fruit 0
Bread/Starch 1/2
Meat 1/2; Fat 1/2

1 16-ounce package
  frozen peas with
  pearl onions
1 16-ounce package
  frozen sliced carrots
2 ounces reduced-
  calorie soft cream
  cheese
2 tablespoons milk
1/4 to 1/2 teaspoon
  cracked pepper
1 clove of garlic,
  minced
1/2 cup herb-seasoned
  croutons

Cook peas with onions and carrots in a small amount of water in medium saucepan for 3 to 5 minutes or until just tender; drain. Stir in cream cheese, milk, pepper and garlic. Cook for 2 to 4 minutes longer or until heated through, stirring frequently. Spoon into serving bowl; sprinkle with croutons.

Sarah L. Tagert, Greensboro

Pepper Hash

Yield:
6 servings
Utensil:
baking dish
Approx Per
Serving:
Cal 136
Prot 7 g
Carbo 11 g
Fiber 1 g
T Fat 8 g
Chol 23 mg
Sod 190 mg

Dietary
Exchanges:
Milk 0
Vegetable 1/2
Fruit 0
Bread/Starch 1/2
Meat 1/2; Fat 1

1 cup chopped green bell pepper
1 cup chopped red bell pepper
1 cup chopped onion
1/2 cup milk
3 to 4 drops of Tabasco sauce
1/2 cup seasoned bread crumbs
1 cup shredded sharp Cheddar cheese

Combine green pepper, red pepper, onion, milk, Tabasco sauce, bread crumbs and cheese in baking dish. Bake at 350 degrees for 30 minutes.

Nancy Garner, Burlington

Potato Barbecue Bake

Yield:
6 servings
Utensil:
baking pan
Approx Per
Serving:
Cal 176
Prot 4 g
Carbo 39 g
Fiber 4 g
T Fat 1 g
Chol 0 mg
Sod 347 mg

Dietary
Exchanges:
Milk 0
Vegetable 0
Fruit 0
Bread/Starch 2
Meat 0; Fat 1 1/2

6 potatoes
3/4 cup water
A-1 sauce to taste
Heinz 57 sauce to taste
1 cup barbecue sauce
Garlic powder to taste

Peel potatoes; cut into quarters lengthwise. Spray 9x12-inch baking pan with nonstick cooking spray. Arrange potatoes in pan; add water. Sprinkle with A-1 sauce and Heinz 57 sauce. Cover with barbecue sauce; add garlic powder. Bake, covered tightly with foil, at 400 degrees for 20 minutes.

Uva M. Harper, Winston-Salem

POTATOES-ONIONS-CABBAGE

Yield:
6 servings
Utensil:
glass baking dish
**Approx Per
Serving:**
Cal 175
Prot 3 g
Carbo 33 g
Fiber 4 g
T Fat 4 g
Chol 0 mg
Sod 61 mg

**Dietary
Exchanges:**
Milk 0
Vegetable 1
Fruit 0
Bread/Starch 1½
Meat 0; Fat 1

5 unpeeled potatoes,
  sliced
2 medium onions,
  sliced
¼ head cabbage, sliced

¼ cup water
2 tablespoons
  margarine
Black pepper to taste
Red pepper to taste

Layer potatoes, onions and cabbage in 9x13-inch glass baking dish; add water. Dot with margarine; sprinkle with black and red pepper to taste. Microwave, covered tightly, on High for 20 minutes.

Harriet Albright, Burlington

ONE POTATO CASSEROLE

Yield:
2 servings
Utensil:
baking pan
**Approx Per
Serving:**
Cal 313
Prot 10 g
Carbo 23 g
Fiber 3 g
T Fat 21 g
Chol 60 mg
Sod 297 mg

**Dietary
Exchanges:**
Milk 0
Vegetable 1
Fruit 0
Bread/Starch 1
Meat 1; Fat 4

1 large baking potato
1 large onion, sliced
2 tablespoons melted
  butter

Vegetable seasoning
  to taste
½ cup shredded
  Cheddar cheese

Scrub potato. Cut into ¼-inch slices. Layer potato and onion in greased 8-inch square baking pan. Drizzle with butter; sprinkle with seasoning. Bake, covered, at 350 degrees for 45 minutes. Uncover; sprinkle with cheese. Bake for 10 minutes longer.

Frances Thompson, Winston-Salem

POTATO CROQUETTES

Yield:
12 servings
Utensil:
deep-fryer
Approx Per
Serving:
Cal 243
Prot 8 g
Carbo 45 g
Fiber 4 g
T Fat 4 g
Chol 115 mg
Sod 199 mg

Dietary
Exchanges:
Milk 0
Vegetable 0
Fruit 0
Bread/Starch 3
Meat 1/2; Fat 1/2

4 pounds potatoes
1 cup bread crumbs
2 tablespoons
  Parmesan cheese
5 eggs, beaten

Parsley to taste
1/8 teaspoon salt
1/8 teaspoon pepper
1 cup bread crumbs
Oil for frying

Cook potatoes in water in saucepan until tender. Drain, peel and mash potatoes. Add 1 cup bread crumbs, Parmesan cheese, eggs, parsley, salt and pepper; mix well. Form into croquettes; roll in remaining 1 cup bread crumbs. Fry in hot oil in deep-fryer until golden brown; drain.

Nutritional information does not include oil for frying.

Mary Pickett, Winston-Salem

CHEESE-POTATO CASSEROLE

Yield:
12 servings
Utensil:
baking dish
Approx Per
Serving:
Cal 520
Prot 10 g
Carbo 36 g
Fiber 1 g
T Fat 39 g
Chol 37 mg
Sod 797 mg

Dietary
Exchanges:
Milk 0
Vegetable 0
Fruit 0
Bread/Starch 2
Meat 1/2; Fat 71/2

1 32-ounce package
   frozen hashed
   brown potatoes
1 teaspoon salt
1/2 teaspoon pepper
1/2 cup melted
   margarine
1 10-ounce can cream
   of chicken soup

1 cup chopped onion
2 cups sour cream
2 cups shredded
   Cheddar cheese
2 cups butter-flavored
   cracker crumbs
2 tablespoons melted
   margarine

Thaw potatoes. Combine potatoes, salt, pepper, 1/2 cup margarine, soup, onion, sour cream and cheese in large bowl; mix well. Spoon into 9x13-inch baking dish. Top with cracker crumbs; drizzle with remaining 2 tablespoons margarine. Bake at 350 degrees for 45 to 50 minutes.

Teresa Crispino, High Point

IRISH POTATO CASSEROLE

Yield:
10 servings
Utensil:
casserole
Approx Per
Serving:
Cal 326
Prot 5 g
Carbo 29 g
Fiber 1 g
T Fat 22 g
Chol 60 mg
Sod 376 mg

Dietary
Exchanges:
Milk 0
Vegetable 0
Fruit 0
Bread/Starch 1½
Meat 0; Fat 5½

10 medium potatoes,
   peeled
8 ounces cream cheese,
   softened
1 cup sour cream
½ cup melted butter

¼ cup chopped chives
1 clove of garlic,
   minced
1 teaspoon salt
⅛ teaspoon paprika

Cook potatoes in water in saucepan until tender. Drain and mash. Beat cream cheese in mixer bowl until smooth. Add potatoes, sour cream, butter, chives, garlic and salt; beat just until combined. Spoon into lightly buttered 2-quart casserole; sprinkle with paprika. Refrigerate, covered, overnight. Remove from refrigerator 15 minutes before baking. Bake, uncovered, at 350 degrees for 30 minutes or until thoroughly heated.

Rebecca B. Mathews, Clemmons

PARMESAN BAKED POTATOES

Yield:
2 servings
Utensil:
baking sheet
Approx Per
Serving:
Cal 594
Prot 7 g
Carbo 34 g
Fiber 4 g
T Fat 49 g
Chol 7 mg
Sod 795 mg

Dietary
Exchanges:
Milk 0
Vegetable 0
Fruit 0
Bread/Starch 2
Meat 1; Fat 9½

2 unpeeled potatoes,
   sliced
½ cup melted
   margarine

3 tablespoons
   Parmesan cheese
½ teaspoon paprika

Dip potato slices into margarine to coat. Arrange on shallow baking sheet. Sprinkle both sides with Parmesan cheese and paprika. Bake at 350 degrees for 30 minutes or until fork-tender.

Nancy Garner, Burlington

PORTUGUESE POTATOES

Yield:
12 servings
Utensil:
baking dish
Approx Per
Serving:
Cal 420
Prot 12 g
Carbo 33 g
Fiber 3 g
T Fat 28 g
Chol 77 mg
Sod 742 mg

Dietary
Exchanges:
Milk 0
Vegetable 0
Bread/Starch 2
Meat 1½
Fat 5½

10 medium potatoes
1 pound Velveeta
  cheese, cubed
½ cup chopped
  pimento
½ cup chopped onion
1 teaspoon paprika
1 tablespoon parsley
  flakes
1 teaspoon garlic
  powder
3 slices bread, cubed
1 cup melted butter

Cook unpeeled potatoes in water in saucepan until tender. Drain; cut into cubes. Place in 9x12-inch baking dish. Top with cheese, pimento, onion, paprika, parsley, garlic powder and bread cubes. Drizzle with melted butter. Bake at 350 degrees for 15 minutes.

Gloria H. Brown, High Point

PUB PIE

Yield:
8 servings
Utensil:
10-inch pie plate
Approx Per
Serving:
Cal 469
Prot 15 g
Carbo 30 g
Fiber 2 g
T Fat 32 g
Chol 95 mg
Sod 721 mg

Dietary
Exchanges:
Milk 0
Vegetable ½
Bread/Starch 1½
Meat 1½
Fat 5½

2 large onions, thinly
  sliced
4 tablespoons butter
2 large baking
  potatoes, thinly
  sliced
¼ teaspoon salt
Pepper to taste
¾ pound sharp
  Cheddar cheese,
  shredded
1 recipe 2-crust pie
  pastry
1 egg, beaten
2 tablespoons milk

Sauté onions in 2 tablespoons butter in skillet; do not brown. Let stand until cool. Melt remaining 2 tablespoons butter in skillet; add potatoes, salt and pepper. Cook over medium heat until golden brown and crispy, stirring frequently. Let stand until cool. Layer cheese, onions and potatoes ½ at a time into pastry-lined pie plate. Top with remaining pastry, fluting edge and cutting vents. Brush with egg beaten with milk. Bake at 350 degrees for 30 to 35 minutes or until golden brown. May be served hot or at room temperature.

Jean M. Marlow, East Bend

POTATOES ROMANOFF

Yield:
8 servings
Utensil:
baking dish
Approx Per
Serving:
Cal 287
Prot 14 g
Carbo 28 g
Fiber 3 g
T Fat 13 g
Chol 36 mg
Sod 582 mg

Dietary
Exchanges:
Milk 0
Vegetable 0
Fruit 0
Bread/Starch 1½
Meat 1½; Fat 2

6 large potatoes,
  peeled
2 cups large dry curd
  cottage cheese
1 cup sour cream
2 cloves of garlic,
  minced
1 teaspoon salt
3 scallions, finely
  chopped
1 cup shredded
  Cheddar cheese
⅛ teaspoon paprika

Cook potatoes in water in saucepan until tender. Drain; cut into cubes. Combine potatoes, cottage cheese, sour cream, garlic, salt and scallions in large bowl; mix well. Spoon into greased 2½-quart baking dish. Sprinkle with cheese and paprika. Bake at 350 degrees for 30 minutes.

Doreen Smith, West End

SCALLOPED POTATOES

Yield:
6 servings
Utensil:
glass baking dish
Approx Per
Serving:
Cal 360
Prot 14 g
Carbo 29 g
Fiber 3 g
T Fat 21 g
Chol 51 mg
Sod 682 mg

Dietary
Exchanges:
Milk ½
Vegetable 0
Bread/Starch 1½
Meat 1½
Fat 3½

3 tablespoons
  margarine
2 tablespoons flour
1 teaspoon salt
¼ teaspoon pepper
2 cups milk
4 cups thinly sliced
  potatoes
2 tablespoons minced
  onion
2 cups shredded
  Cheddar cheese

Place margarine in 3-quart glass baking dish. Microwave on High until margarine is melted. Blend in flour, salt and pepper. Stir in milk gradually. Microwave on High for 8 to 10 minutes, stirring after 4 minutes. Add potatoes and onion; mix well. Microwave, covered, on High for 19 minutes. Top with cheese; cover. Let stand for 5 minutes before serving.

Edith Gerringer, Burlington

CHEESE-SCALLOPED POTATOES

3/4 cup milk
1 10-ounce can cream
   of mushroom soup
1 cup shredded
   Cheddar cheese

4 medium potatoes,
   sliced
1/4 cup chopped onion
1/2 teaspoon salt
1/8 teaspoon pepper

Combine milk and soup in 2-quart glass baking dish, stirring to blend. Add cheese, potatoes, onion, salt and pepper; mix well. Microwave, covered, on High for 10 minutes; stir. Microwave, covered, on High for 10 to 15 minutes longer or until potatoes are tender. May sprinkle with Parmesan cheese.

Melanie Vance, Kernersville

SPINACH CASSEROLE

1/2 cup butter
2 tablespoons chopped
   onion
1½ cups water
1 10-ounce package
   frozen chopped
   spinach
1½ cups minute rice

1 10-ounce can cream
   of celery soup
1 8-ounce jar Cheez
   Whiz
1 tablespoon melted
   butter
1/2 cup crushed herb-
   flavored croutons

Bring 1/2 cup butter, onion and water to a boil in medium saucepan; add spinach. Cook for 5 minutes. Remove from heat; add rice. Let stand for 5 minutes. Add soup and Cheez Whiz; mix well. Spoon into 2½-quart baking dish. Drizzle remaining 1 tablespoon melted butter over crushed croutons in small bowl; mix well. Sprinkle buttered crumbs over spinach mixture. Bake at 325 degrees for 45 minutes.

Helen Raab, Aurora, Illinois

SPINACH LASAGNA

1 10-ounce package frozen chopped spinach
1 pound lasagna noodles
8 ounces mozzarella cheese, shredded
4 ounces egg substitute
Easy Tomato Sauce
2½ cups low-fat cottage cheese
½ cup Parmesan cheese

Cook spinach using package directions; drain and rinse in cold water. Cook lasagna noodles using package directions. Combine spinach, mozzarella cheese and egg substitute in bowl; mix well. Coat lasagna pan with nonstick cooking spray. Layer ⅓ of the Easy Tomato Sauce, ½ of the noodles and ½ of the spinach mixture in prepared baking dish. Top with half the remaining sauce, half the cottage cheese and remaining noodles. Layer remaining spinach mixture, cottage cheese and sauce on top. Sprinkle with Parmesan cheese. Bake at 350 degrees for 40 minutes. Let stand for 10 minutes before serving.

Easy Tomato Sauce

1 large onion, chopped
1 green bell pepper, chopped
3 tablespoons olive oil
1 32-ounce jar spaghetti sauce
1 tablespoon oregano
1 6-ounce can salt-free tomato paste
1 bay leaf
½ teaspoon salt
¼ cup parsley flakes

Sauté onion and green pepper in olive oil in heavy skillet for 5 minutes. Add spaghetti sauce, oregano, tomato paste, bay leaf, salt and parsley flakes; stir well. Simmer for 30 minutes; remove bay leaf.

A Pioneer

SPINACH PIE

Yield:
6 servings
Utensil:
baking dish
Approx Per
Serving:
Cal 572
Prot 27 g
Carbo 21 g
Fiber 2 g
T Fat 43 g
Chol 98 mg
Sod 900 mg

Dietary
Exchanges:
Milk 0
Vegetable 1/2
Bread/Starch 1
Meat 31/2
Fat 61/2

1 10-ounce package
   frozen chopped
   spinach
2 eggs, beaten
1/2 teaspoon salt
1/2 cup melted
   margarine
2 tablespoons
   Parmesan cheese
1 pound Monterey
   Jack cheese,
   shredded
1 cup milk
1 cup flour

Cook spinach using package directions; drain. Combine eggs, salt, margarine, Parmesan cheese, spinach, Monterey Jack cheese, milk and flour in large bowl; mix well. Spoon mixture into greased 9x13-inch baking dish. Bake at 350 degrees for 45 minutes. Cool slightly; cut into squares. May use 2 packages spinach with same results.

Dorothy Keck, Burlington

SPINACH ROLL-UPS

Yield:
4 servings
Utensil:
baking dish
Approx Per
Serving:
Cal 475
Prot 27 g
Carbo 61 g
Fiber 2 g
T Fat 15 g
Chol 23 mg
Sod 1259 mg

Dietary
Exchanges:
Milk 0
Vegetable 41/2
Bread/Starch 21/2
Meat 21/2
Fat 11/2

6 lasagna noodles
1 10-ounce package
   frozen chopped
   spinach, thawed
1 onion, chopped
12 ounces cottage
   cheese
1 teaspoon garlic
   powder
2 cups spaghetti sauce
1/2 cup Parmesan
   cheese

Cook noodles using package directions; drain. Combine spinach, onion, cottage cheese and garlic powder in bowl; mix well. Spread 1/6 of the mixture on each noodle; roll up as for jelly roll. Spoon enough spaghetti sauce into 9-inch square baking dish to cover bottom. Place roll-ups in sauce. Pour remaining sauce over roll-ups. Sprinkle with Parmesan cheese. Bake at 350 degrees for 30 minutes.

Nancy Garner, Burlington

BAKED SQUASH CASSEROLE

Yield:
6 servings
Utensil:
baking dish
**Approx Per
Serving:**
Cal 165
Prot 9 g
Carbo 7 g
Fiber 1 g
T Fat 12 g
Chol 122 mg
Sod 261 mg

**Dietary
Exchanges:**
Milk 0
Vegetable ½
Fruit 0
Bread/Starch 0
Meat 1; Fat 2

2 cups cooked squash
1 tablespoon butter
2 tablespoons flour
2 eggs, beaten
1 cup milk

1 cup shredded
   Cheddar cheese
¼ teaspoon salt
Pepper to taste

Combine squash, butter, flour, eggs, milk, cheese, salt and pepper in large bowl; mix well. Spoon into lightly greased 1½-quart baking dish. Bake at 350 degrees for 30 minutes. May top with buttered bread crumbs.

Connie Kelly, Mocksville

GLORIFIED SQUASH

Yield:
6 servings
Utensil:
baking dish
**Approx Per
Serving:**
Cal 234
Prot 9 g
Carbo 38 g
Fiber 2 g
T Fat 6 g
Chol 9 mg
Sod 947 mg

**Dietary
Exchanges:**
Milk 0
Vegetable 1
Fruit 0
Bread/Starch 2½
Meat 0; Fat 1½

4 cups chopped squash
1 small onion, chopped
1 10-ounce can cream
   of chicken soup
¼ cup shredded
   cheese

⅛ teaspoon salt
Pepper to taste
1 8-ounce package
   herb-seasoned
   stuffing mix

Cook squash and onion in boiling water to cover in saucepan just until tender; drain and cool. Add soup, cheese, salt and pepper; mix well. Spoon into lightly greased 1½-quart baking dish. Bake at 325 degrees for 30 minutes. Sprinkle stuffing mix over top of squash mixture. Bake until stuffing mix is browned.

Zane Gerringer, Elon College

SQUASH CASSEROLE

Yield:
6 servings
Utensil:
baking dish
Approx Per
Serving:
Cal 229
Prot 9 g
Carbo 11 g
Fiber 1 g
T Fat 17 g
Chol 122 mg
Sod 617 mg

Dietary
Exchanges:
Milk 0
Vegetable 1/2
Fruit 0
Bread/Starch 1
Meat 1; Fat 3½

10 butter-flavored crackers, crushed
1 cup shredded Cheddar cheese
2 cups cooked chopped squash
2 eggs, beaten
1/3 cup chopped onion
1 10-ounce can cream of mushroom soup
2 tablespoons butter

Combine cracker crumbs and cheese in small bowl; mix well. Reserve a small amount of cheese mixture for topping. Combine remaining cheese mixture, squash, eggs, onion and soup in lightly greased 1½-quart baking dish; mix well. Top with reserved cheese mixture; dot with butter. Bake at 350 degrees for 25 to 30 minutes or until golden brown.

Kathleen Oakley

SQUASH SOUFFLÉ

Yield:
6 servings
Utensil:
baking dish
Approx Per
Serving:
Cal 341
Prot 16 g
Carbo 20 g
Fiber 3 g
T Fat 22 g
Chol 152 mg
Sod 725 mg

Dietary
Exchanges:
Milk 0
Vegetable 1½
Bread/Starch ½
Meat 1½
Fat 3½

2 pounds squash, sliced
1 medium onion, chopped
8 ounces Cheddar cheese, shredded
1 cup milk
2 eggs, beaten
1 teaspoon salt
1/2 teaspoon sugar
3 tablespoons melted butter
3 tablespoons flour
1/2 cup bread crumbs

Cook squash and onion in boiling water in saucepan for 20 minutes; drain. Add cheese, milk, eggs, salt, sugar, butter and flour; mix well. Pour into lightly greased 2-quart baking dish. Bake at 350 degrees for 30 minutes; sprinkle with bread crumbs. Bake for 10 minutes longer.

Jessie Grandinetti

SQUASH SKILLET

Yield:
4 servings
Utensil:
skillet
**Approx Per
Serving:**
Cal 300
Prot 2 g
Carbo 25 g
Fiber 3 g
T Fat 23 g
Chol 61 mg
Sod 448 mg

**Dietary
Exchanges:**
Milk 0
Vegetable 1
Fruit 0
Bread/Starch ½
Meat 0; Fat 5

1 green bell pepper,
  chopped
1 cup chopped onion
½ cup melted
  margarine
¼ cup Worcestershire
  sauce
2 tablespoons sugar

⅛ teaspoon salt
Pepper to taste
1 butternut squash,
  peeled and cut into
  cubes
1 large tomato, peeled
  and chopped

Sauté green pepper and onion in margarine in skillet. Add Worcestershire sauce, sugar, salt and pepper; mix well. Stir in squash. Cook until squash in partially tender; add tomato. Cook until tender.

Helen A. Howard, Pfafftown

SUMMER SQUASH CASSEROLE

Yield:
6 servings
Utensil:
glass baking dish
**Approx Per
Serving:**
Cal 62
Prot 2 g
Carbo 7 g
Fiber 1 g
T Fat 4 g
Chol 0 mg
Sod 48 mg

**Dietary
Exchanges:**
Milk 0
Vegetable ½
Fruit 0
Bread/Starch 0
Meat 0; Fat 1

1 pound chopped
  summer squash
¼ cup chopped onion
¼ cup chopped celery
1 teaspoon packed
  brown sugar

¼ cup water
⅓ cup herb-seasoned
  stuffing mix
½ cup reduced-calorie
  sour cream

Combine squash, onion, celery, brown sugar and water in bowl; mix well. Spoon into lightly greased 1-quart glass baking dish. Microwave, covered, on High for 7 minutes. Let stand for 4 minutes. Stir in stuffing mix and sour cream. Microwave for 3 minutes longer.

Mary H. Harden, Graham

SQUASH FRITTERS

Yield:
6 servings
Utensil:
large skillet
Approx Per
Serving:
Cal 155
Prot 5 g
Carbo 8 g
Fiber 1 g
T Fat 12 g
Chol 95 mg
Sod 454 mg

Dietary
Exchanges:
Milk 0
Vegetable 1/2
Fruit 0
Bread/Starch 1/2
Meat 1/2; Fat 2

1/3 cup baking mix
2 eggs, lightly beaten
1/2 teaspoon salt
1/2 teaspoon pepper
1/4 cup Parmesan
  cheese

2 cups shredded
  yellow squash
2 to 4 tablespoons
  margarine

Combine baking mix and eggs in bowl. Add salt, pepper, Parmesan cheese and squash, stirring well after each addition. Drop by tablespoonfuls into hot margarine in skillet. Cook for 2 to 3 minutes on each side or until brown; drain. May add 1/4 cup finely chopped onion to squash mixture.

Beverly Raley, Graham

PETE'S SQUASH CASSEROLE

Yield:
6 servings
Utensil:
glass baking dish
Approx Per
Serving:
Cal 398
Prot 13 g
Carbo 28 g
Fiber 2 g
T Fat 25 g
Chol 130 mg
Sod 1008 mg

Dietary
Exchanges:
Milk 1/2
Vegetable 1
Fruit 0
Bread/Starch 1
Meat 1; Fat 41/2

2 cups cooked squash,
  drained
6 tablespoons melted
  margarine
2 medium eggs,
  lightly beaten
1 teaspoon salt

1/2 teaspoon pepper
1 cup chopped onion
1 cup shredded
  Cheddar cheese
1 cup evaporated milk
2 cups cracker crumbs

Combine squash, margarine, eggs, salt, pepper, onion, cheese, evaporated milk and cracker crumbs in bowl; mix well. Spoon into lightly greased 2-quart glass baking dish. Bake, covered, at 375 degrees for 40 minutes.

Pete Jones, Winston-Salem

Butternut Squash Casserole

3 cups cooked
  butternut squash
1/2 cup sugar
1/4 cup packed brown
  sugar
1/2 cup milk
1/4 cup melted
  margarine
1 teaspoon cinnamon

1 teaspoon vanilla
  extract
2 eggs, beaten
21/2 tablespoons
  margarine, softened
1/3 cup flour
1 cup packed brown
  sugar
1 cup pecans, chopped

Beat squash in mixer bowl until smooth. Add sugar, 1/4 cup brown sugar, milk, 1/4 cup margarine, cinnamon, vanilla and eggs; beat well. Pour into lightly greased 11/2-quart baking dish. Combine remaining 21/2 tablespoons margarine, flour, remaining 1 cup brown sugar and pecans in small bowl; mix well. Sprinkle over squash mixture. Bake at 350 degrees for 35 minutes.

Audrey H. Jackson, Winston-Salem

Posh Squash

3 cups sliced yellow
  squash
1 cup mayonnaise
1 cup Parmesan cheese
1/2 cup chopped onion
2 eggs, beaten

1/2 teaspoon salt
1/4 teaspoon pepper
1/2 cup soft bread
  crumbs
2 tablespoons melted
  margarine

Cook squash in boiling salted water in saucepan 10 to 15 minutes or until tender. Drain and cool slightly. Combine mayonnaise, Parmesan cheese, onion, eggs, salt and pepper in bowl; mix well. Add squash, mixing thoroughly. Spoon into greased 11/2-quart casserole. Sprinkle top with combination of bread crumbs and margarine. Bake at 350 degrees for 30 minutes.

Mildred T. Smith

SQUASH AND CARROT CASSEROLE

Yield:
8 servings
Utensil:
2-quart casserole
Approx Per
Serving:
Cal 224
Prot 4 g
Carbo 21 g
Fiber 3 g
T Fat 14 g
Chol 3 mg
Sod 629 mg

Dietary
Exchanges:
Milk 0
Vegetable 1½
Fruit 0
Bread/Starch 1½
Meat 0; Fat 3

2 pounds squash, chopped
1 medium onion, chopped
½ cup margarine, softened
4 ounces herb-seasoned stuffing mix
1 10-ounce can cream of chicken soup
2 carrots, shredded

Cook squash and onion in a small amount of water in saucepan until tender. Combine margarine and stuffing mix in bowl; mix well. Reserve half the mixture for topping. Mix soup and carrots in large bowl. Stir in remaining stuffing mixture, squash and onions. Spoon into greased 2-quart casserole; top with reserved stuffing mixture. Bake at 325 degrees for 30 minutes.

Lois Beck

BRANDIED SWEET POTATOES

Yield:
6 servings
Utensil:
baking dish
Approx Per
Serving:
Cal 312
Prot 2 g
Carbo 53 g
Fiber 2 g
T Fat 6 g
Chol 15 mg
Sod 237 mg

Dietary
Exchanges:
Milk 0
Vegetable 0
Fruit 0
Bread/Starch 2
Meat 0; Fat 1½

6 cooked sweet potatoes
1 tablespoon cornstarch
⅓ cup sugar
⅓ cup packed brown sugar
½ cup orange juice
½ cup Brandy
2 teaspoons grated orange rind
½ teaspoon salt
3 tablespoons butter

Cut peeled sweet potatoes into quarters; place in lightly greased 10-inch square baking dish. Blend cornstarch, sugar and brown sugar in saucepan. Add orange juice, Brandy, grated orange rind, salt and butter; mix well. Cook over medium heat until thickened, stirring constantly. Pour over sweet potatoes. Bake at 350 degrees for 30 minutes.

Mary Jane Daleiden, Greensboro

CANDIED SWEET POTATOES

Yield:
6 servings
Utensil:
casserole
Approx Per Serving:
Cal 483
Prot 2 g
Carbo 88 g
Fiber 1 g
T Fat 15 g
Chol 0 mg
Sod 223 mg

Dietary Exchanges:
Milk 0
Vegetable 0
Fruit 0
Bread/Starch 1½
Meat 0; Fat 3

3 to 4 medium sweet potatoes
1 cup sugar
1 cup packed light brown sugar
2 tablespoons flour
½ cup margarine, softened
1 cup cold water
1 teaspoon vanilla extract
½ teaspoon nutmeg

Cook sweet potatoes in water to cover in saucepan until tender; drain. Peel and slice; place in lightly greased 1½-quart casserole. Combine sugar, brown sugar, flour, margarine, water, vanilla and nutmeg in medium saucepan. Bring to a boil; pour over sweet potatoes. Bake at 350 degrees for 30 minutes or until thickened.

Peggy P. Brooks, Burlington

SWEET POTATO CRUNCH

Yield:
4 servings
Utensil:
baking dish
Approx Per Serving:
Cal 1025
Prot 9 g
Carbo 141 g
Fiber 6 g
T Fat 51 g
Chol 152 mg
Sod 619 mg

Dietary Exchanges:
Milk 0
Vegetable 0
Fruit 0
Bread/Starch 3½
Meat ½; Fat 12

1 29-ounce can sweet potatoes, mashed
½ cup sugar
½ teaspoon salt
¼ teaspoon cinnamon
⅓ cup melted butter
¼ cup milk
1 egg
1 teaspoon vanilla extract
1 cup packed brown sugar
⅓ cup butter, softened
⅓ cup flour
1 cup pecans

Combine sweet potatoes, sugar, salt, cinnamon, ⅓ cup butter, milk, egg and vanilla in large bowl; mix well. Spoon into lightly greased 1½-quart baking dish. Combine brown sugar, remaining ⅓ cup butter, flour and pecans in small bowl; mix well. Sprinkle over sweet potato mixture. Bake at 350 degrees for 35 minutes.

Doris Whitesell

Sweet Potato Casserole

Yield:
12 servings
Utensil:
baking dish
Approx Per Serving:
Cal 294
Prot 3 g
Carbo 46 g
Fiber 1 g
T Fat 12 g
Chol 68 mg
Sod 184 mg

Dietary Exchanges:
Milk 0
Vegetable 0
Fruit 0
Bread/Starch 1/2
Meat 0; Fat 2 1/2

3 cups cooked sweet potatoes, mashed
1 cup sugar
2 eggs
1/2 cup milk
1 teaspoon vanilla extract
1/4 cup melted butter
1/2 teaspoon salt
1/4 cup melted butter
1 cup packed brown sugar
1/2 cup flour
1/2 cup chopped pecans

Combine sweet potatoes, sugar, eggs, milk, vanilla, 1/4 cup butter and salt in large bowl; mix well. Spoon into buttered 2-quart baking dish. Mix 1/4 cup melted butter, brown sugar, flour and pecans in small bowl; sprinkle over sweet potato mixture. Bake at 350 degrees for 30 minutes.

Bernice H. Motsinger, Winston-Salem

Hand-Grated Sweet Potato Pudding

Yield:
6 servings
Utensil:
baking dish
Approx Per Serving:
Cal 354
Prot 5 g
Carbo 53 g
Fiber 1 g
T Fat 15 g
Chol 97 mg
Sod 286 mg

Dietary Exchanges:
Milk 0
Vegetable 0
Fruit 0
Bread/Starch 1
Meat 1/2; Fat 3

4 medium sweet potatoes, grated
1 cup sugar
1 teaspoon vanilla extract
1 teaspoon nutmeg
2 large eggs
1 cup milk
1/4 teaspoon salt
6 tablespoons melted margarine

Combine grated sweet potatoes, sugar, vanilla, nutmeg, eggs, milk, salt and margarine in large bowl; stir to mix. Do not use electric mixer. Pour into lightly greased 7x11-inch baking dish. Bake at 400 degrees for 30 minutes.

Roxie Rudd, Prospect Hill

FRIED SWEET POTATOES

Yield:
4 servings
Utensil:
skillet
**Approx Per
Serving:**
Cal 370
Prot 2 g
Carbo 69 g
Fiber 2 g
T Fat 12 g
Chol 0 mg
Sod 163 mg

**Dietary
Exchanges:**
Milk 0
Vegetable 0
Fruit 0
Bread/Starch 1½
Meat 0; Fat 2½

3 medium sweet
  potatoes
¼ cup margarine

1 cup sugar
¼ cup water

Peel and slice sweet potatoes into ½-inch slices. Melt margarine in skillet over medium heat. Fry sweet potato slices in margarine until lightly browned on both sides. Add sugar and water. Cook, covered, until sweet potatoes are done. Remove cover. Cook until liquid is of desired consistency.

Jean Jarrett, Thomasville

HAWAIIAN SWEET POTATOES

Yield:
10 servings
Utensil:
baking pan
**Approx Per
Serving:**
Cal 136
Prot 1 g
Carbo 28 g
Fiber 2 g
T Fat 2 g
Chol 0 mg
Sod 169 mg

**Dietary
Exchanges:**
Milk 0
Vegetable 0
Fruit ½
Bread/Starch ½
Meat 0; Fat ½

10 pineapple slices
2 cups mashed cooked
  sweet potatoes
½ teaspoon salt
2 tablespoons melted
  margarine

¼ cup sugar
1 teaspoon vanilla
  extract
1 cup miniature
  marshmallows

Arrange pineapple slices in 10x13-inch nonstick baking pan. Combine sweet potatoes, salt, margarine, sugar and vanilla in bowl; mix well. Bake at 350 degrees for 10 minutes. Top with marshmallows. Bake for 5 minutes longer or until browned.

Ruth Kent Eslinger, Winston-Salem

OLD-FASHIONED GRATED SWEET POTATO PUDDING

3 cups grated sweet
  potatoes
1 cup grated coconut
1 teaspoon cinnamon
1 cup butter, softened
1 cup sugar

3 tablespoons
  self-rising flour
1/2 cup packed brown
  sugar
2 eggs
1/2 cup evaporated milk

Combine sweet potatoes, coconut and cinnamon in large bowl; mix well. Beat butter, sugar, flour, brown sugar, eggs and evaporated milk in mixer bowl until smooth. Add to sweet potato mixture, stirring to mix. Pour into lightly greased glass casserole. Bake at 350 degrees for 45 minutes.

Mary Pace

REJUVENATED YAMS

3 pounds sweet
  potatoes
1/2 cup margarine,
  softened
1/2 cup pecan pieces
1/2 teaspoon salt

3/4 cup packed light
  brown sugar
3/8 teaspoon nutmeg
1 1/8 teaspoons
  cinnamon
1/2 cup Cream Sherry

Cook sweet potatoes in boiling water in saucepan; drain and cool slightly. Peel and cut into 1/2 to 3/4-inch slices. Arrange in lightly greased 9x13-inch baking dish; spread with margarine. Sprinkle pecans over margarine. Combine salt, brown sugar, nutmeg and cinnamon in small bowl; mix well. Sprinkle brown sugar mixture over pecans; drizzle with Sherry. Bake, covered, at 375 degrees for 35 to 40 minutes or until bubbly.

Mrs. Roy T. Rhue, Newport

SUNDAY SWEET POTATOES

Yield:
8 servings
Utensil:
baking dish
**Approx Per
Serving:**
Cal 581
Prot 5 g
Carbo 70 g
Fiber 3 g
T Fat 33 g
Chol 71 mg
Sod 294 mg

**Dietary
Exchanges:**
Milk 0
Vegetable 0
Fruit 0
Bread/Starch 1
Meat 1/2; Fat 8

3 cups mashed cooked
  sweet potatoes
1/2 cup milk
2 eggs
1 cup sugar
1/3 cup margarine,
  softened
1 teaspoon vanilla
  extract

1 cup chopped pecans
1 cup packed brown
  sugar
1 cup shredded
  coconut
1/3 cup flour
1/2 cup melted
  margarine

Combine sweet potatoes, milk, eggs, sugar, 1/3 cup margarine and vanilla in bowl; mix well. Spoon into lightly greased 9x13-inch baking dish. Combine pecans, brown sugar, coconut and flour in bowl; mix well. Stir in remaining 1/2 cup margarine. Sprinkle over sweet potato mixture. Bake at 375 degrees for 20 minutes or until browned.

Martha M. Wheeler, Chapin, South Carolina

CANDIED YAMS

Yield:
10 servings
Utensil:
baking dish
**Approx Per
Serving:**
Cal 336
Prot 2 g
Carbo 64 g
Fiber 2 g
T Fat 9 g
Chol 25 mg
Sod 109 mg

**Dietary
Exchanges:**
Milk 0
Vegetable 0
Fruit 0
Bread/Starch 11/2
Meat 0; Fat 2

8 medium sweet
  potatoes
1 cup packed brown
  sugar
1 cup sugar
2 tablespoons flour

1 cup water
1/2 cup butter, softened
1 teaspoon vanilla
  extract
1/2 teaspoon nutmeg

Cook sweet potatoes in boiling water to cover in large saucepan until tender. Peel and slice sweet potatoes. Arrange slices in lightly greased 9x13-inch baking dish. Blend brown sugar, sugar and flour in saucepan; stir in water. Add butter, vanilla and nutmeg; mix well. Bring to a boil; pour over sweet potatoes. Bake at 350 degrees for 30 minutes, basting occasionally with syrup.

Nancy Boner Parnell, Winston-Salem

TOMATOES AMANDA

4 slices multi-grain
  bread, toasted
1 medium onion,
  chopped
1 14¹/2-ounce can
  Italian-style
  tomatoes
1 14¹/2-ounce can
  whole tomatoes
²/3 cup sugar
¹/2 teaspoon salt
¹/4 cup packed brown
  sugar
1 tablespoon margarine

Line bottom of lightly greased 2¹/2-quart glass baking dish with toast broken into bite-sized pieces, reserving 1 slice for topping. Place onion in glass bowl. Microwave on High for 2 minutes. Add Italian-style tomatoes, whole tomatoes, sugar, salt and brown sugar; mix well. Pour into glass baking dish. Top with remaining toast pieces; dot with margarine. Microwave on High for 8 minutes. Broil until crispy. May bake at 350 degrees for 45 minutes or until brown around the edges.

Jane Walters, Winston-Salem

LOW-CALORIE BROILED TOMATOES

2 large tomatoes
¹/4 cup low-calorie
  Italian salad
  dressing
2 tablespoons Italian-
  style bread crumbs
2 tablespoons
  Parmesan cheese

Cut tomatoes into halves; place in broiler pan. Pour salad dressing over tomato halves. Sprinkle with bread crumbs and Parmesan cheese. Broil for 5 minutes. Serve immediately.

Nancy Garner, Burlington

ITALIAN ZUCCHINI PIES

4 cups sliced zucchini
1 cup chopped onion
1/4 cup margarine
2 tablespoons parsley
  flakes
3/4 teaspoon salt
1/2 teaspoon pepper
1/4 teaspoon basil

1/4 teaspoon garlic
  powder
1/4 teaspoon oregano
2 eggs, well beaten
2 cups shredded
  mozzarella cheese
2 unbaked 9-inch pie
  shells

Sauté zucchini and onion in margarine in large skillet for 10 minutes or until tender. Stir in parsley, salt, pepper, basil, garlic powder and oregano. Combine eggs and mozzarella cheese in bowl; add to zucchini mixture. Pour into 2 pie shells. Bake at 375 degrees for 20 minutes. Let stand for 10 minutes before serving.

Mrs. Dewey Redding, Pfafftown

ZUCCHINI SURPRISE

3 cups thinly sliced
  zucchini
1 cup baking mix
1/2 cup Parmesan
  cheese
1/2 teaspoon seasoning
  mix
1/2 teaspoon salt

2 tablespoons chopped
  parsley
1/2 to 1 cup chopped
  onion
1 clove of garlic,
  chopped
1/2 cup oil
4 eggs, lightly beaten

Combine zucchini, baking mix, Parmesan cheese, seasoning mix, salt, parsley, onion, garlic, oil and eggs in large bowl; mix well. Spread into greased 9x13-inch baking pan. Bake at 350 degrees for 25 minutes or until golden brown. May cut into 1x2-inch pieces for appetizers.

Lucille P. Johnson, New London

Zucchini Casserole

4 cups sliced unpeeled zucchini
2 eggs, lightly beaten
1 cup plain yogurt
1 cup Parmesan cheese
1/4 cup chopped green bell pepper
1 medium onion, chopped
1/8 teaspoon salt
Pepper to taste
21/2 tablespoons margarine

Boil zucchini in water to cover in saucepan until tender; drain. Let stand until cool. Combine eggs, yogurt, Parmesan cheese, green pepper, onion, salt and pepper in bowl; mix well. Fold in zucchini. Pour into lightly greased 2-quart casserole; dot with margarine. Bake at 350 degrees for 30 minutes. Serve hot or cold.

Donna Marshall, Burlington

Italian Garden Zucchini

1/2 cup butter
2 cups sliced zucchini
1 7-ounce can whole kernel corn, drained
3/4 cup chopped green bell pepper
1/3 cup chopped onion
1 teaspoon sugar
1/2 teaspoon garlic powder
1/2 teaspoon basil
1/2 teaspoon oregano
1/8 teaspoon pepper
1 tomato, chopped

Melt butter in heavy skillet over medium heat; add zucchini, corn, green pepper, onion, sugar, garlic powder, basil, oregano and pepper. Cook for 15 minutes or until vegetables are tender and liquid has evaporated. Stir in tomato. Cook for 5 minutes longer.

Mildred T. Smith

ZUCCHINI LINGUINE

Yield:
8 servings
Utensil:
glass baking dish
Approx Per
Serving:
Cal 378
Prot 19 g
Carbo 35 g
Fiber 3 g
T Fat 19 g
Chol 52 mg
Sod 606 mg

Dietary
Exchanges:
Milk 0
Vegetable 2
Fruit 0
Bread/Starch 1½
Meat 2; Fat 2½

1 large onion, cubed
3 medium zucchini, cubed
1½ tablespoons olive oil
3 16-ounce cans Italian tomatoes
1 6-ounce can tomato paste
⅛ teaspoon salt
1 teaspoon oregano
½ teaspoon basil
½ teaspoon garlic powder
Dash of pepper
4 cups cooked linguine
8 ounces mozzarella cheese, shredded
8 ounces Cheddar cheese, shredded

Sauté onion and zucchini in olive oil in large skillet over medium heat until tender. Add tomatoes, tomato paste, salt, oregano, basil, garlic powder and pepper; stir well. Cook until heated through, stirring frequently; reduce heat to low. Cook for 30 minutes longer. Arrange linguine in lightly greased 9x13-inch glass baking dish. Pour tomato mixture over linguine; sprinkle with mozzarella and Cheddar cheeses. Broil for 2 to 3 minutes or until cheeses are melted and lightly browned.

Teresa Crispino, High Point

VEGETABLE CASSEROLE

Yield:
10 servings
Utensil:
casserole
Approx Per
Serving:
Cal 376
Prot 7 g
Carbo 21 g
Fiber 5 g
T Fat 30 g
Chol 22 mg
Sod 559 mg

Dietary
Exchanges:
Milk 0
Vegetable 1
Fruit 0
Bread/Starch ½
Meat ½; Fat 5½

2 16-ounce cans mixed vegetables, drained
1 cup chopped onion
¾ cup mayonnaise
1 cup shredded Cheddar cheese
1 cup water chestnuts, chopped
1½ cups (about) butter-flavored cracker crumbs
½ cup melted margarine

Combine mixed vegetables, onion, mayonnaise, cheese and water chestnuts in large bowl; mix well. Spoon into lightly greased 2-quart casserole. Sprinkle with cracker crumbs; drizzle with margarine. Bake at 350 degrees for 30 minutes.

Ruth Lowe, Gibsonville

MIXED VEGETABLE CASSEROLE

1 10-ounce package frozen mixed vegetables
½ cup chopped onion
⅔ cup chopped celery
1 cup mayonnaise
2 cups shredded Cheddar cheese
1 cup butter-flavored cracker crumbs
½ cup melted margarine

Combine mixed vegetables, onion and celery in a small amount of water in saucepan. Cook over medium heat for 5 minutes; drain. Combine vegetables with mayonnaise and cheese in large bowl; mix well. Pour into lightly greased 1½-quart casserole. Sprinkle with cracker crumbs; drizzle with margarine. Bake at 350 degrees for 30 minutes.

Carol Sawyer, Whitsett

VEGGIE ROCK CASSEROLE

2 cups sour cream
1 10-ounce can cream of onion soup
1 cup shredded Cheddar cheese
1 cup shredded mozzarella cheese
1 6-ounce can French-fried onions, chopped
2 16-ounce cans baby carrots, drained
1 16-ounce can cut green beans, drained
1 16-ounce can whole kernel corn, drained
1 12-ounce jar whole mushrooms, drained
1 cup shredded Cheddar cheese
1 cup shredded mozzarella cheese

Combine sour cream, soup, 1 cup Cheddar cheese and 1 cup mozzarella cheese in large bowl; mix well. Fold in 1 cup fried onions, reserving remaining fried onions for topping. Add carrots, green beans, corn and mushrooms; mix well. Spread into lightly greased 9x13-inch baking dish. Sprinkle with remaining 1 cup Cheddar cheese and remaining 1 cup mozzarella cheese; top with reserved fried onions. Bake at 325 degrees for 30 minutes.

Anita Rock, High Point

STIR-FRIED VEGETABLES

2 red bell peppers
2 green bell peppers
2 medium zucchini
4 carrots
4 teaspoons olive oil
½ head red cabbage,
thinly sliced
4 teaspoons white
wine vinegar
¼ cup water
¼ teaspoon salt
¼ teaspoon pepper

Slice red peppers, green peppers, zucchini and carrots julienne-style. Stir-fry in hot oil in wok for 5 minutes. Add cabbage, vinegar, water, salt and pepper. Stir-fry for 5 minutes longer.

Mrs. Carlton Tuttle, Germanton

GREEK STIR-FRIED RICE

½ cup broccoli
flowerets
½ cup cauliflowerets
½ cup julienne carrots
2 tablespoons oil
½ cup coarsely
shredded yellow
squash
½ cup julienne
zucchini
½ cup coarsely
shredded red cabbage
1 to 2 teaspoons soy
sauce
1 teaspoon hot sesame
oil
2 cups cooked rice
¼ cup raw unsalted
cashews
Salt and pepper to taste

Blanch broccoli and cauliflower for 2 minutes; drain and keep warm. Stir-fry carrots in 2 tablespoons hot oil until tender-crisp. Add yellow squash, zucchini and cabbage. Cook until tender-crisp. Add soy sauce, 1 teaspoon hot sesame oil, broccoli and cauliflower. Stir in rice gently. Add cashews, salt and pepper. Heat to serving temperature. May add strips of tomato and chopped green onions.

A. Anthony Vargas, Pfafftown

Swiss Vegetable Medley

Yield:
6 servings
Utensil:
baking dish
Approx Per Serving:
Cal 225
Prot 9 g
Carbo 17 g
Fiber 1 g
T Fat 14 g
Chol 24 mg
Sod 481 mg

Dietary Exchanges:
Milk 0
Vegetable 1
Fruit 0
Bread/Starch 1
Meat 1; Fat 3½

1 10-ounce package frozen broccoli, carrots and cauliflower, thawed
1 10-ounce can cream of mushroom soup
½ cup shredded Swiss cheese
⅓ cup sour cream
¼ teaspoon pepper
1 2-ounce jar chopped pimento, drained
1 3-ounce can French-fried onions
½ cup shredded Swiss cheese

Combine mixed vegetables, soup, ½ cup Swiss cheese, sour cream, pepper and pimento in large bowl; mix well. Stir in half the fried onions, reserving remainder for topping. Pour into lightly greased 1-quart baking dish. Bake, covered, at 350 degrees for 30 minutes. Sprinkle with remaining ½ cup Swiss cheese; top with remaining fried onions. Bake, uncovered, for 5 to 7 minutes longer or until bubbly and golden brown.

L. M. Zanky, Burlington

Layered Vegetable Casserole

Yield:
8 servings
Utensil:
casserole
Approx Per Serving:
Cal 169
Prot 10 g
Carbo 6 g
Fiber 2 g
T Fat 12 g
Chol 29 mg
Sod 481 mg

Dietary Exchanges:
Milk 0
Vegetable 1
Fruit 0
Bread/Starch 0
Meat 1½; Fat 2

1 green bell pepper, cut into strips
2 to 3 stalks celery, thinly sliced
1 onion, sliced into rings
1 to 2 zucchini, sliced
1 to 2 tablespoons reduced-calorie margarine
Salt and pepper to taste
4 to 5 slices provolone cheese
½ cup croutons
1 large tomato, sliced
Oregano to taste
4 to 5 slices American cheese
1 cup sliced mushrooms

Layer green pepper, celery, onion, zucchini, margarine, salt, pepper, provolone cheese, croutons, tomato, oregano and American cheese into lightly greased 2-quart casserole; top with mushrooms. Bake at 350 degrees for 30 minutes. Serve immediately.

Nancy Garner, Burlington

SIDE DISHES

SCRAMBLED EGG AND CHEESE PATTIES

Yield:
4 servings
Utensil:
skillet
Approx Per
Serving:
Cal 557
Prot 17 g
Carbo 23 g
Fiber 2 g
T Fat 44 g
Chol 479 mg
Sod 820 mg

Dietary
Exchanges:
Milk 0
Vegetable 1/2
Fruit 0
Bread/Starch 1
Meat 11/2; Fat 10

6 eggs
8 ounces cream cheese, softened
1 envelope chicken broth seasoning
1 onion, grated
3/4 cup finely chopped pecans
1 cup cracker crumbs

Scramble eggs in nonstick skillet. Add cream cheese, stirring until melted. Add chicken broth seasoning, onion, pecans and cracker crumbs; mix well. Chill in refrigerator overnight or until mixture is firm. Shape into patties. Brown on both sides in nonstick skillet. Serve with gravy or tomato sauce.

Kathleen S. Yax, Mebane

FETTUCINI AND BROCCOLI IN PARMESAN SAUCE

Yield:
2 servings
Utensil:
large saucepan
Approx Per
Serving:
Cal 1068
Prot 46 g
Carbo 147 g
Fiber 14 g
T Fat 33 g
Chol 30 mg
Sod 864 mg

Dietary
Exchanges:
Milk 0
Vegetable 21/2
Fruit 0
Bread/Starch 91/2
Meat 3; Fat 6

1   12-ounce package fettucini
3 cups broccoli flowerets
1 cup reduced-calorie sour cream
3/4 cup Parmesan cheese
11/3 cups cherry tomatoes, quartered

Cook pasta using package directions. Add broccoli to pasta. Cook for 5 to 10 minutes or until both are tender. Drain, reserving 1/3 cup cooking liquid. Combine sour cream, cheese and reserved liquid in bowl; stir well. Add pasta, broccoli and tomatoes; mix well. Serve immediately.

Clarissa Brame, Graham

LAYERED MACARONI AND SAUCE

Yield:
8 servings
Utensil:
baking dish
**Approx Per
Serving:**
Cal 455
Prot 15 g
Carbo 52 g
Fiber 2 g
T Fat 21 g
Chol 27 mg
Sod 1165 mg

**Dietary
Exchanges:**
Milk 0
Vegetable 1
Fruit 0
Bread/Starch 3
Meat 1; Fat 4

1 16-ounce package elbow macaroni
1 28-ounce can tomato sauce
1/2 cup margarine

8 slices American cheese
2 tablespoons oregano
Salt and pepper to taste

Cook macaroni using package directions; drain. Spoon 1/3 of the tomato sauce into greased 8x10-inch baking dish. Layer macaroni, margarine, cheese slices, remaining tomato sauce, oregano, salt and pepper 1/2 at a time over sauce. Bake at 350 degrees for 30 minutes.

Betty Myers, Graham

MACARONI AND CHEESE

Yield:
6 servings
Utensil:
baking dish
**Approx Per
Serving:**
Cal 198
Prot 8 g
Carbo 14 g
Fiber <1 g
T Fat 12 g
Chol 39 mg
Sod 339 mg

**Dietary
Exchanges:**
Milk 1/2
Vegetable 0
Fruit 0
Bread/Starch 1/2
Meat 1/2; Fat 2 1/2

1 cup uncooked macaroni
2 tablespoons butter
2 tablespoons flour
2 1/2 cups milk

3/4 cup shredded Cheddar cheese
1/2 teaspoon salt
Pepper and paprika to taste

Cook macaroni using package directions; drain. Melt butter in saucepan. Add flour; mix well. Stir in milk and cheese gradually, stirring well after each addition. Add salt and pepper; mix well. Cook over low heat until sauce thickens, stirring constantly. Pour macaroni into sauce, stirring to coat. Pour into lightly greased 8x10-inch baking dish; sprinkle with paprika. Bake at 350 degrees for 20 minutes or until golden brown. May also top with buttered bread crumbs.

Martha Tingen, Graham

HELEN'S MACARONI AND CHEESE

Yield:
8 servings
Utensil:
baking dish
Approx Per
Serving:
Cal 360
Prot 16 g
Carbo 22 g
Fiber 1 g
T Fat 24 g
Chol 59 mg
Sod 347 mg

Dietary
Exchanges:
Milk 1/2
Vegetable 0
Fruit 0
Bread/Starch 1
Meat 1 1/2; Fat 4

1/4 cup butter
1/4 cup flour
2 cups warm milk
Dash of pepper
1/2 teaspoon dry mustard
1 teaspoon Tabasco sauce

1/2 cup half and half
1 cup shredded
   Monterey Jack cheese
2 cups shredded sharp
   Cheddar cheese
3 cups cooked macaroni

Melt butter over low heat in heavy saucepan. Add flour. Stir with wooden spoon for 3 minutes or until roux is frothy. Add warm milk gradually, stirring well. Bring just to the boiling point; reduce heat. Simmer for 3 minutes, stirring constantly. Add pepper, mustard and Tabasco sauce; mix well. Stir in half and half. Simmer until flavors are blended, stirring constantly. Add Monterey Jack cheese and 1 cup Cheddar cheese, stirring well after each addition. Simmer until cheeses melt. Pour over cooked macaroni in greased 2-quart baking dish. Top with remaining 1 cup Cheddar cheese. Bake in preheated 350-degree oven for 30 minutes or until bubbly and golden brown.

Helen Grab, Bradenton, Florida

MACARONI CASSEROLE

Yield:
8 servings
Utensil:
baking dish
Approx Per
Serving:
Cal 420
Prot 8 g
Carbo 39 g
Fiber 2 g
T Fat 26 g
Chol 34 mg
Sod 888 mg

Dietary
Exchanges:
Milk 0
Vegetable 1/2
Fruit 0
Bread/Starch 3 1/2
Meat 1/2; Fat 6 1/2

1 8-ounce package
   macaroni
2 10-ounce cans
   cream of mushroom
   soup
1/2 cup mayonnaise
1/2 cup shredded sharp
   Cheddar cheese
1 green bell pepper,
   chopped

1 onion, chopped
1 2-ounce jar
   chopped pimento,
   drained
1 5-ounce can water
   chestnuts, drained,
   chopped
1 cup cracker crumbs
1/4 cup butter

Cook macaroni using package directions; drain. Combine with soup, mayonnaise, cheese, green pepper, onion, pimento and water chestnuts in large bowl; mix well. Pour into greased 2-quart baking dish. Sprinkle with cracker crumbs; dot with butter. Bake at 350 degrees for 30 minutes.

Joy Doub

CHILIES RELLEÑOS

1 22-ounce can whole green chilies, drained, split lengthwise
16 ounces Cheddar cheese, shredded
1 12-ounce can evaporated milk
4 eggs
4 tablespoons flour
16 ounces Monterey Jack cheese, shredded
2 6-ounce cans tomato sauce

Line lightly greased 9x13-inch baking pan with half the chilies. Sprinkle with Cheddar cheese to cover. Combine evaporated milk, eggs and flour in blender container. Process at medium speed for 2 to 3 minutes or until smooth. Pour over cheese layer. Bake at 375 degrees for 30 minutes. Layer with remaining chilies, Monterey Jack cheese and tomato sauce. Bake for 15 minutes longer.

Norma Hall, Mebane

MAKE-AHEAD STUFFING

1/2 cup chopped onion
1/2 cup chopped celery
1/4 cup margarine
1 17-ounce can cream-style corn
1/2 cup water
1 teaspoon poultry seasoning
1/2 teaspoon pepper
1 8-ounce package herb-seasoned stuffing mix
3 eggs, lightly beaten
1/2 cup melted margarine

Sauté onion and celery in 1/4 cup margarine in large saucepan until tender. Add corn, water, poultry seasoning and pepper. Bring to a boil. Pour over stuffing mix in bowl; stir well. Add eggs; mix well. Shape mixture into 8 balls. Arrange in 9-inch square baking pan. Drizzle with 1/2 cup melted margarine. Bake at 375 degrees for 25 minutes.

Imogene W. Carson

BROWN RICE CASSEROLE

1 cup uncooked rice
1 10-ounce can beef bouillon
1 10-ounce can beef consommé
1 onion, chopped
1/2 cup margarine

Combine rice, bouillon, consommé, onion and margarine in greased 1 1/2-quart baking dish; mix well. Bake, covered, at 325 degrees for 1 hour.

Thalia Shore, Boonville

CHINESE FRIED RICE

1/2 cup finely chopped cooked ham
2 tablespoons oil
1 4-ounce can mushrooms
4 cups cooked rice
1 green onion, chopped
2 tablespoons soy sauce
1 egg, well beaten

Stir-fry ham in hot oil in wok. Add mushrooms, rice, green onion and soy sauce. Stir-fry for 10 minutes. Add egg. Stir-fry for 5 minutes or until dry and fluffy. May add more soy sauce to taste.

Sarah L. Finley, Graham

RICE BALLS

Yield:
15 servings
Utensil:
deep-fryer
**Approx Per
Serving:**
Cal 387
Prot 17 g
Carbo 56 g
Fiber 1 g
T Fat 9 g
Chol 139 mg
Sod 290 mg

**Dietary
Exchanges:**
Milk 0
Vegetable 1/2
Fruit 0
Bread/Starch 3 1/2
Meat 1 1/2; Fat 1

32 ounces uncooked converted rice
6 egg yolks, slightly beaten
2 tablespoons Parmesan cheese
1 1/2 pounds ground beef
2 tablespoons chopped onion
1 15-ounce can tomato sauce
6 egg whites, slightly beaten
1 cup bread crumbs

Cook rice using package directions until just tender; drain. Place in bowl; let stand until cool. Add egg yolks to cooled rice; stir well. Add cheese; mix well. Brown ground beef with onion in skillet, stirring frequently; drain. Add tomato sauce; stir well. Form balls using 1 cup rice mixture mixed with 1/3 cup ground beef mixture. Dip in egg whites; coat with bread crumbs. Deep-fry until golden brown, turning once.

Mary Pickett, Winston-Salem

GREEN RICE CASSEROLE

Yield:
8 servings
Utensil:
baking dish
**Approx Per
Serving:**
Cal 314
Prot 16 g
Carbo 17 g
Fiber 2 g
T Fat 21 g
Chol 59 mg
Sod 1126 mg

**Dietary
Exchanges:**
Milk 0
Vegetable 1/2
Fruit 0
Bread/Starch 1
Meat 2; Fat 4

1 10-ounce package frozen chopped broccoli
1/2 cup chopped celery
1/2 cup chopped green bell pepper
1/2 cup chopped onion
1 tablespoon margarine
1 10-ounce can cream of celery soup
1 16-ounce jar Cheez Whiz
2 cups cooked rice

Cook broccoli using package directions; drain. Sauté celery, green pepper and onion in margarine in skillet until tender. Combine with broccoli and soup in bowl; mix well. Add Cheez Whiz and rice; stir well. Pour into lightly greased 2-quart baking dish. Bake at 375 degrees for 45 minutes.

Jean Creed May, Greensboro

MUSHROOM RICE CASSEROLE

Yield:
8 servings
Utensil:
baking dish
Approx Per Serving:
Cal 159
Prot 3 g
Carbo 21 g
Fiber 1 g
T Fat 7 g
Chol 15 mg
Sod 487 mg

Dietary Exchanges:
Milk 0
Vegetable 1/2
Fruit 0
Bread/Starch 1
Meat 0; Fat 1 1/2

1/4 cup butter
1 cup uncooked rice
1 10-ounce can beef broth
1 10-ounce can French onion soup
1 6-ounce can sliced mushrooms, drained

Melt butter in 8-inch square baking dish. Add rice, beef broth, French onion soup and mushrooms; mix well. Bake at 350 degrees for 40 minutes.

Sharon M. Fanelli, Gibsonville

STOVE-TOP MUSHROOM RICE

Yield:
8 servings
Utensil:
skillet
Approx Per Serving:
Cal 238
Prot 5 g
Carbo 42 g
Fiber 1 g
T Fat 5 g
Chol 5 mg
Sod 592 mg

Dietary Exchanges:
Milk 0
Vegetable 1/2
Fruit 0
Bread/Starch 3
Meat 0; Fat 1 1/2

2 cups uncooked quick-cooking rice
1 10-ounce can cream of mushroom soup
2 tablespoons dried minced onion
2 tablespoons Parmesan cheese
1 teaspoon garlic salt
1 teaspoon pepper
3 cups water
1 8-ounce can sliced mushrooms, drained
1 tablespoon butter

Combine rice, soup, onion, cheese, garlic salt and pepper in large skillet; mix well. Add water, mushrooms and butter; stir well. Cook over medium heat for 10 to 15 minutes or until rice is done.

Pat Anderton, Winston-Salem

CHEESE APPLES

Yield:
8 servings
Utensil:
baking dish
Approx Per Serving:
Cal 267
Prot 5 g
Carbo 41 g
Fiber 3 g
T Fat 11 g
Chol 15 mg
Sod 226 mg

Dietary Exchanges:
Milk 0
Vegetable 0
Fruit 1
Bread/Starch 1/2
Meat 1/2; Fat 2

3/4 cup sugar
1/2 cup flour
1/4 teaspoon salt
1/4 cup margarine
1 cup shredded sharp Cheddar cheese

6 tablespoons water
1 tablespoon lemon juice
7 medium tart apples, peeled, sliced

Combine sugar, flour and salt in medium bowl. Cut in margarine until crumbly. Add cheese; stir well. Mix water and lemon juice in small bowl; add apples. Spoon into lightly greased 5x9-inch baking dish. Sprinkle cheese mixture over apples. Bake at 350 degrees for 40 minutes.

Lyda H. Duvall, Kernersville

SPICED APPLE RINGS

Yield:
12 servings
Utensil:
baking dish
Approx Per Serving:
Cal 74
Prot <1 g
Carbo 19 g
Fiber 2 g
T Fat <1 g
Chol 0 mg
Sod 16 mg

Dietary Exchanges:
Milk 0
Vegetable 0
Fruit 1
Bread/Starch 0
Meat 0; Fat 0

6 medium apples
42 envelopes artificial sweetener
2 cinnamon sticks

2 or 3 whole cloves
1 1/2 cups unsweetened cranberry juice
1/4 cup lemon juice

Core apples; slice into thick rings. Arrange in 9x11-inch greased baking dish. Combine artificial sweetener, cinnamon, cloves, cranberry juice and lemon juice in saucepan. Bring to a boil. Cook for 5 minutes, stirring constantly; strain. Reserve 1/4 cup juice. Pour remaining juice over apple rings. Bake at 350 degrees for 45 minutes or until apple rings are transparent. Baste occasionally with reserved juice. Serve hot or cold. May substitute 1 1/2 cups sugar for artificial sweetener.

Janet Mills, Winston-Salem

APPLE-CRANBERRY CASSEROLE

Yield:
6 servings
Utensil:
glass baking dish
Approx Per
Serving:
Cal 506
Prot 4 g
Carbo 78 g
Fiber 4 g
T Fat 22 g
Chol 41 mg
Sod 162 mg

Dietary
Exchanges:
Milk 0
Vegetable 0
Fruit 1
Bread/Starch 1
Meat 0; Fat 5

3 cups sliced apples
2 cups fresh
    cranberries
1 cup sugar
1/2 cup butter
1 cup oats
1/3 cup flour
1/2 cup packed brown
    sugar
1/2 cup chopped pecans

Place apples and cranberries in lightly greased 9x11-inch glass baking dish; sprinkle with 1 cup sugar. Melt butter in saucepan. Add oats, flour, 1/2 cup brown sugar and pecans; stir well. Spread over apples. Bake at 350 degrees for 1 hour.

Jean H. Mahaffey, Winston-Salem

SPICY APPLE-CRANBERRY BAKE

Yield:
6 servings
Utensil:
baking dish
Approx Per
Serving:
Cal 481
Prot 3 g
Carbo 73 g
Fiber 4 g
T Fat 22 g
Chol 41 mg
Sod 161 mg

Dietary
Exchanges:
Milk 0
Vegetable 0
Fruit 1
Bread/Starch 1/2
Meat 0; Fat 5

2 cups fresh cranberries
3 cups sliced Granny
    Smith apples
1 cup sugar
1/2 cup packed brown
    sugar
1/2 cup chopped pecans
1/2 cup melted butter
1 cup uncooked quick-
    cooking spiced oats

Combine cranberries and apple slices in greased 9x11-inch baking dish; sprinkle with 1 cup sugar. Mix 1/2 cup brown sugar, pecans, melted butter and oats together in bowl. Spread over apples. Bake, covered, at 325 degrees for 55 minutes. Uncover and bake 5 minutes longer. Serve warm.

Nancy Garner, Burlington

APPLE DELIGHT

Yield:
6 servings
Utensil:
glass baking dish
Approx Per
Serving:
Cal 39
Prot <1 g
Carbo 10 g
Fiber 1 g
T Fat <1 g
Chol 0 mg
Sod 3 mg

Dietary
Exchanges:
Milk 0
Vegetable 0
Fruit 1/2
Bread/Starch 0
Meat 0; Fat 0

3 red Delicious apples, **4 envelopes artificial**
peeled, sliced **sweetener**
1 teaspoon cinnamon **6 tablespoons water**

Arrange apple slices in 8-inch square glass baking dish. Sprinkle with cinnamon and artificial sweetener. Add water. Microwave on High for 6 minutes. Serve immediately.

Judy C. Barr, Advance

CURRIED FRUIT

Yield:
24 servings
Utensil:
baking dish
Approx Per
Serving:
Cal 96
Prot <1 g
Carbo 13 g
Fiber <1 g
T Fat 5 g
Chol 0 mg
Sod 55 mg

Dietary
Exchanges:
Milk 0
Vegetable 0
Fruit 1/2
Bread/Starch 0
Meat 0; Fat 1

1 8-ounce can **1/2 cup margarine**
pineapple slices **1 cup packed brown**
1 8-ounce can peach **sugar**
halves **2 1/2 teaspoons curry**
1/2 cup pecan halves **powder**

Drain fruits. Layer fruits in 11x11-inch baking dish. Top with pecan halves. Combine margarine, brown sugar and curry powder in saucepan. Cook until heated through. Pour over fruit. Bake at 350 degrees for 30 minutes or until well-glazed. May use any combination of favorite fruits and nuts.

Lee P. Powell, Clemmons

CURRIED FRUIT BAKE

1 20-ounce can pineapple chunks, drained
1 16-ounce can pear halves, drained
1 16-ounce jar maraschino cherries, drained
1 17-ounce can apricot halves, drained
⅓ cup margarine
⅓ cup honey
1 teaspoon curry powder

Arrange pineapple, pear halves, cherries and apricot halves in 9x13-inch baking dish. Combine margarine, honey and curry powder in small saucepan. Heat until margarine is melted, stirring well. Pour over fruit. Bake at 325 degrees for 30 minutes or until bubbly.

Juanita Stone, Graham

PINEAPPLE-CHEESE CASSEROLE

2 20-ounce cans pineapple tidbits
¼ cup margarine
2 cups shredded Cheddar cheese
1 cup sugar
6 tablespoons flour
1 cup butter-flavored cracker crumbs
¼ cup melted margarine

Drain pineapple, reserving 6 tablespoons juice. Melt ¼ cup margarine in 2-quart baking dish; add pineapple and cheese. Combine sugar, flour and reserved pineapple juice in bowl; mix well. Spread over pineapple mixture. Toss crushed crackers with ¼ cup melted margarine. Sprinkle over top. Bake, covered, at 350 degrees for 45 minutes.

Martha M. Wheeler, Chapin, South Carolina

BAKED PINEAPPLE SLICES WITH CHEESE

Yield:
10 servings
Utensil:
baking dish
Approx Per
Serving:
Cal 356
Prot 7 g
Carbo 41 g
Fiber 1 g
T Fat 19 g
Chol 24 mg
Sod 354 mg

Dietary
Exchanges:
Milk 0
Vegetable 0
Fruit 1/2
Bread/Starch 1/2
Meat 1; Fat 3

2 15-ounce cans
    pineapple slices,
    drained
6 tablespoons flour
2 cups shredded
    Cheddar cheese

1 cup sugar
1 cup butter-flavored
    cracker crumbs
1/2 cup margarine,
    melted

Arrange pineapple slices in 9x13-inch baking dish. Combine flour, cheese and sugar in bowl; mix well. Spread over pineapple. Sprinkle with cracker crumbs. Drizzle with melted margarine. Bake at 325 degrees for 25 to 30 minutes or until golden brown.

Colleen Blackwood, Elon College

BARBECUE SAUCE FOR PORK

Yield:
18 servings
Utensil:
saucepan
Approx Per
Serving:
Cal 85
Prot <1 g
Carbo 8 g
Fiber <1 g
T Fat 6 g
Chol 0 mg
Sod 247 mg

Dietary
Exchanges:
Milk 0
Vegetable 0
Fruit 0
Bread/Starch 0
Meat 0; Fat 1

1/2 cup oil
1/2 cup vinegar
1/2 cup catsup
1/4 cup packed brown
    sugar
1/4 cup sugar
2 tablespoons
    Worcestershire sauce

Dash of Texas Pete
2 tablespoons
    (heaping) prepared
    mustard
1 teaspoon pepper
1/2 teaspoon onion salt
1/2 teaspoon garlic salt
1/4 teaspoon celery salt

Combine oil, vinegar and catsup in saucepan; stir well. Add 1/4 cup brown sugar, 1/4 cup sugar, Worcestershire sauce, Texas Pete, mustard and seasonings; mix well. Bring to a boil. Cook for 15 minutes, stirring constantly. Pour over pork. To use with chicken, increase catsup to 1 cup and add 1/2 cup chili sauce.

Catherine L. Mullis, Snow Camp

MILD BARBECUE SAUCE

Yield:
8 servings
Utensil:
saucepan
**Approx Per
Serving:**
Cal 31
Prot <1 g
Carbo 8 g
Fiber 0 g
T Fat 0 g
Chol 0 mg
Sod 316 mg

**Dietary
Exchanges:**
Milk 0
Vegetable 0
Fruit 0
Bread/Starch 0
Meat 0; Fat 0

½ cup catsup
2 tablespoons brown
  sugar
¼ cup vinegar
2 tablespoons
  Worcestershire sauce

½ teaspoon chili
  powder
½ teaspoon salt
Dash of pepper
2 to 3 drops of Tabasco
  sauce

Mix catsup, brown sugar and vinegar in saucepan. Add Worcestershire sauce, chili powder, salt, pepper and Tabasco sauce; stir well. Bring to a boil; reduce heat. Simmer for 10 to 15 minutes. May be used as a basting sauce or marinade for pork, chicken or beef.

Helen A. Howard, Pfafftown

SPICY BARBECUE SAUCE

Yield:
32 servings
Utensil:
saucepan
**Approx Per
Serving:**
Cal 17
Prot <1 g
Carbo 5 g
Fiber <1 g
T Fat <1 g
Chol 0 mg
Sod 158 mg

**Dietary
Exchanges:**
Milk 0
Vegetable 0
Fruit 0
Bread/Starch 0
Meat 0; Fat 0

2 cups vinegar
1   16-ounce bottle of
  catsup
1 tablespoon
  Worcestershire sauce
1 tablespoon Tabasco
  sauce
2 tablespoons paprika

1 tablespoon chili
  powder
3 tablespoons black
  pepper
¾ teaspoon prepared
  mustard
½ cup water
Red pepper to taste

Mix vinegar, catsup, Worcestershire sauce and Tabasco sauce in saucepan. Add paprika, chili powder, black pepper, mustard, water and red pepper to taste; stir well. Bring to a boil; reduce heat. Simmer for 15 minutes, stirring constantly. May store in refrigerator for 2 to 3 weeks.

Harriet Albright, Burlington

FAVORITE BARBECUE SAUCE

Yield:
24 servings
Utensil:
saucepan
Approx Per
Serving:
Cal 22
Prot <1 g
Carbo 2 g
Fiber <1 g
T Fat 2 g
Chol 0 mg
Sod 193 mg

Dietary
Exchanges:
Milk 0
Vegetable 0
Fruit 0
Bread/Starch 0
Meat 0; Fat 1/2

¹/₄ cup water
¹/₄ cup vinegar
3 tablespoons oil
¹/₂ cup catsup
3 tablespoons
  Worcestershire sauce

1 teaspoon dry mustard
1¹/₂ teaspoons salt
¹/₂ teaspoon pepper
2 tablespoons chopped
  onion

Mix water, vinegar, oil, catsup and Worcestershire sauce in small saucepan. Add mustard, salt, pepper and onion; stir well. Simmer for 5 to 10 minutes, stirring constantly. May store in refrigerator for 2 to 3 weeks.

Norma Hall, Mebane

HEALTHY CHICKEN GRAVY

Yield:
6 servings
Utensil:
saucepan
Approx Per
Serving:
Cal 89
Prot 4 g
Carbo 8 g
Fiber <1 g
T Fat 4 g
Chol 16 mg
Sod 444 mg

Dietary
Exchanges:
Milk 1/2
Vegetable 0
Fruit 0
Bread/Starch 0
Meat 0; Fat 1

1 12-ounce can
   evaporated milk
¹/₈ teaspoon pepper

2 teaspoons instant
  chicken bouillon
2 tablespoons flour

Combine 1¹/₄ cups evaporated milk, pepper and instant bouillon in small saucepan; stir well. Blend remaining evaporated milk with flour in bowl. Add to bouillon mixture, stirring well. Cook over medium heat until mixture is thick and bubbly, stirring constantly. Serve over chicken or vegetables.

Ruth Campbell, Pfafftown

CORN COB JELLY

Yield:
32 servings
Utensil:
saucepan
**Approx Per
Serving:**
Cal 132
Prot 1 g
Carbo 34 g
Fiber 3 g
T Fat <1 g
Chol 0 mg
Sod 7 mg

**Dietary
Exchanges:**
Milk 0
Vegetable 0
Fruit 0
Bread/Starch 1/2
Meat 0; Fat 0

16 red corn cobs   4 cups sugar
8 cups water
1 1³/4-ounce package
   fruit pectin

Slice corn cobs into 1/2-inch pieces. Bring 8 cups water to a boil in large saucepan. Add corn cobs. Boil for 30 minutes. Strain liquid into 4-cup measure; discard corn cobs. Add enough water to strained liquid to make 4 cups. Pour into saucepan. Stir in pectin. Boil for 1 minute. Add 4 cups sugar; stir well. Boil for 4 minutes, stirring frequently; remove from heat. Pour into hot sterilized jelly jars, leaving 1/4-inch headspace; seal with 2-piece lids. Looks and tastes like apple jelly.

W.C. and Mabel F. Lawson, Jr.

MICROWAVE JELLY

Yield:
80 servings
Utensil:
glass bowl
**Approx Per
Serving:**
Cal 35
Prot <1 g
Carbo 9 g
Fiber 0 g
T Fat <1 g
Chol 0 mg
Sod <1 mg

**Dietary
Exchanges:**
Milk 0
Vegetable 0
Fruit 0
Bread/Starch 0
Meat 0; Fat 0

2 cups grape juice   3¹/2 cups sugar
1 cup water
1 1³/4-ounce package
   fruit pectin

Pour juice and water into 2-quart glass bowl. Add pectin; stir well. Cover with plastic wrap. Microwave on High for 8 to 10 minutes or until bubbles appear at edge of bowl, stirring after 3 minutes. Add sugar gradually, mixing well. Microwave, covered, for 6 to 7 minutes or until mixture has boiled at least 1 minute. Skim off foam; stir well. Pour into hot sterilized jelly jars, leaving 1/4-inch headspace; seal with 2-piece lids. Cool; store in refrigerator. May substitute boysenberry, apple or blackberry juice for grape juice.

A Pioneer

FROZEN STRAWBERRY JAM

2 cups mashed
strawberries
4 cups sugar

1 cup water
1 1³/₄-ounce package
fruit pectin

Combine strawberries and sugar in bowl. Let stand for 20 minutes, stirring occasionally. Bring water to a boil in saucepan; add pectin. Boil for 1 minute, stirring constantly; remove from heat. Add strawberries; stir for 2 minutes. Pour into hot sterilized jelly jars, leaving ¼-inch headspace; seal with 2-piece lids. Let stand for 1 hour. Chill in refrigerator until firm. Store in freezer. Refrigerate after opening. May substitute peaches or cherries for strawberries.

Mary Pickett, Winston-Salem

DILLY BEANS

4 pounds green beans
4 teaspoons mustard
seed
4 teaspoons dillseed
4 cloves of garlic,
halved

2 teaspoons red pepper
5 cups vinegar
5 cups water
½ cup salt

Trim beans; pack lengthwise into sterilized 1-pint jars. Add ½ teaspoon mustard seed, ½ teaspoon dillseed, ¼ clove of garlic and ¼ teaspoon red pepper to each pint jar. Combine vinegar, water and salt in large saucepan. Bring to a boil. Pour over beans, leaving ½-inch headspace. Seal with 2-piece lids. Process in boiling water bath for 10 minutes. Remove jars; cool on wire rack. Store in cool location for 2 weeks to develop flavor.

Mabel F. Lawson

CUCUMBER APPLE RINGS

2 gallons large cucumbers, peeled
2 cups pickling lime
8½ quarts water
3 cups vinegar
1 tablespoon alum
2 cups water
10 cups sugar
1½ 9½-ounce packages red hot cinnamon candies
8 cinnamon sticks

Slice cucumbers ¼-inch thick; remove seed. Combine with mixture of lime and 8½ quarts water in crock. Let stand for 24 hours; drain and rinse. Soak cucumbers in ice water to cover for 3 hours; drain. Mix 1 cup vinegar and alum with enough water to cover cucumbers in large kettle. Simmer for 2 hours. Combine remaining 2 cups vinegar with remaining ingredients in saucepan. Bring to a boil. Pour over cucumbers. Add enough alum mixture to cover cucumbers. Let stand for 24 hours. Drain, reserving syrup. Bring reserved syrup to a boil. Pour over cucumbers. Repeat process 2 times. On third day, bring cucumbers and syrup to a boil. Ladle into pint jars, leaving ½-inch headspace; seal with 2-piece lids.

"Pete" Jones, Winston-Salem

PICKLED PEACHES

3 pounds sugar
2 cups water
1½ cups vinegar
2 to 3 cinnamon sticks
1 teaspoon whole cloves
5 pounds peaches

Mix sugar, water, vinegar and spices in large saucepan. Bring to a boil. Cook over high heat for 5 minutes. Add peaches. Cook for 5 to 10 minutes or until tender; drain, reserving syrup. Pack into hot sterilized jars. Fill with reserved syrup, leaving ½-inch headspace. Seal with 2-piece lids.

Connie Kelly, Mocksville

Bread and Butter Pickles

Yield:
150 servings
Utensil:
large saucepan
Approx Per Serving:
Cal 35
Prot <1 g
Carbo 9 g
Fiber 1 g
T Fat <1 g
Chol 0 mg
Sod 208 mg

Dietary Exchanges:
Milk 0
Vegetable 1/2
Fruit 0
Bread/Starch 0
Meat 0; Fat 0

25 to 30 cucumbers, thinly sliced
8 onions, chopped
2 green bell peppers, chopped
1/3 cup salt
5 cups cider vinegar
5 cups sugar
1 teaspoon turmeric
2 tablespoons white mustard seed
1/2 teaspoon whole cloves

Combine cucumbers, onions, green peppers and salt in large bowl. Cover with ice cubes; let stand for 3 hours. Drain. Combine vinegar, sugar, turmeric, mustard seed and cloves in large saucepan. Add cucumber mixture. Cook over medium heat until thoroughly heated; do not boil. Remove from heat. Pack into hot sterilized jars leaving 1/2-inch headspace; seal with 2-piece lids.

Mrs. Raymond Thorpe

Kosher Dill Pickles

Yield:
36 servings
Utensil:
two 1-quart jars
Approx Per Serving:
Cal 39
Prot 2 g
Carbo 10 g
Fiber 4 g
T Fat <1 g
Chol 0 mg
Sod 984 mg

Dietary Exchanges:
Milk 0
Vegetable 1 1/2
Fruit 0
Bread/Starch 0
Meat 0; Fat 0

3 cups vinegar
3 cups water
6 tablespoons salt
Fresh dill to taste
1 clove of garlic, halved
1 tablespoon mustard seed
36 small cucumbers, 3 to 4 inches long

Combine vinegar, water and salt in large saucepan. Bring to a boil. Place layer of dill, 1/2 clove of garlic and 1 1/2 teaspoons mustard seed in bottom of each 1-quart jar. Pack 1 layer cucumbers into jars. Sprinkle with dill. Pack jars with remaining cucumbers. Pour boiling brine over cucumbers, leaving 1/2-inch headspace. Seal with 2-piece lids. Process in boiling water bath for 5 minutes.

Mrs. Bobby G. Kye, Winston-Salem

GRAPE LEAF PICKLES

60 small cucumbers, 3 to 4 inches long
9 grape leaves
9 green Concord grapes
3 quarts water
1 cup cider vinegar
5 cups water
⅓ cup non-iodized pickling salt

Pack cucumbers into three 1-quart jars. Add 3 grape leaves and 3 grapes to each jar. Bring 3 quarts water to a boil in large saucepan. Pour over cucumbers; drain. Mix vinegar, 5 cups water and salt in saucepan. Bring to a boil; remove from heat. Pour over cucumbers, leaving ½-inch headspace. Seal with 2-piece lids. Chill before serving.

Faye G. Peddycord, Kernersville

ICICLE PICKLES

1 gallon cucumbers
2 teaspoons mustard seed
2 teaspoons celery seed
4 small onions
1 quart white vinegar
2½ cups sugar
¼ cup salt
1 cup water

Slice cucumbers lengthwise into eighths. Soak in ice water for 3 hours. Pack into 4 hot sterilized 1-quart jars, adding ½ teaspoon mustard seed, ½ teaspoon celery seed and 1 small onion to each jar. Mix vinegar, sugar, salt and water in large saucepan. Bring to a boil. Pour over cucumbers, leaving ½-inch headspace; seal with 2-piece lids. Process in boiling water bath for 10 minutes.

Bonne Cearley, Jefferson

Simple Simon Pickles

2 cups sugar
1/2 cup salt
1 quart vinegar

3 quarts small cucumbers

Combine sugar, salt and vinegar in bowl. Pack cucumbers into 3 sterilized 1-quart jars. Pour liquid over cucumbers, leaving 1/2-inch headspace. Seal with 2-piece lids.

Mrs. Athalene Burns

Squash Pickles

6 large yellow squash, sliced
4 large white onions, sliced
4 green bell peppers, sliced
1/2 cup salt
3 cups sugar
2 1/2 cups white vinegar
1 cup water
2 teaspoons turmeric
2 teaspoons celery seed

Place squash, onions and green peppers in large bowl; sprinkle with salt. Cover with ice cubes; let stand for 1 hour. Drain and rinse. Combine sugar, vinegar, water, turmeric and celery seed in large saucepan. Boil for 3 minutes. Add squash mixture. Cook over medium-high heat for 5 to 10 minutes. Pack into hot sterilized jars, leaving 1/2-inch headspace; seal with 2-piece lids.

Jessie Grandinetti

SWEET PICKLES

Yield:
56 servings
Utensil:
eight 1-quart jars
Approx Per
Serving:
Cal 159
Prot <1 g
Carbo 44 g
Fiber 1 g
T Fat <1 g
Chol 0 mg
Sod 37 mg

Dietary
Exchanges:
Milk 0
Vegetable ½
Fruit 0
Bread/Starch 0
Meat 0; Fat 0

7 pounds cucumbers,
  sliced
2 cups pickling lime
½ gallon vinegar

5 pounds sugar
½ cup pickling spice
1 teaspoon salt

Place cucumbers in crock. Add lime and enough water to cover cucumbers. Soak for 24 hours, stirring occasionally. Drain. Cover with water. Let stand for 1 hour; drain. Repeat process 3 times. Combine vinegar, sugar, pickling spice and salt in large saucepan. Bring to a boil. Pour over cucumbers. Soak overnight. Cook over medium heat for 1 hour. Pack cucumbers into hot sterilized jars. Pour in syrup, leaving ½-inch headspace; seal with 2-piece lids. Let stand until cool.

Connie Kelly, Mocksville

SWEET PEPPER RELISH

Yield:
128 servings
Utensil:
eight 1-pint jars
Approx Per
Serving:
Cal 21
Prot <1 g
Carbo 5 g
Fiber <1 g
T Fat <1 g
Chol 0 mg
Sod 32 mg

Dietary
Exchanges:
Milk 0
Vegetable ½
Fruit 0
Bread/Starch 0
Meat 0; Fat 0

12 sweet peppers,
  finely chopped
12 green bell peppers,
  finely chopped
2 hot green peppers,
  finely chopped
2 hot red peppers,
  finely chopped

12 medium onions,
  finely chopped
2 cups sugar
2 cups vinegar
2 teaspoons salt

Cover chopped peppers and onions with boiling water. Let stand for 10 minutes; drain. Combine 2 cups sugar, 2 cups vinegar and 2 teaspoons salt in saucepan. Add peppers and onions. Bring to a boil. Cook over medium heat for 20 minutes. Ladle into hot sterilized jars, leaving ½-inch headspace. Seal with 2-piece lids. May use food grinder or food processor to chop peppers and onions.

Connie Kelly, Mocksville

BREADS

ANGEL BISCUITS

Yield:
40 servings
Utensil:
baking sheet
Approx Per
Serving:
Cal 106
Prot 2 g
Carbo 14 g
Fiber <1 g
T Fat 5 g
Chol 2 mg
Sod 114 mg

Dietary
Exchanges:
Milk 0
Vegetable 0
Fruit 0
Bread/Starch 1
Meat 0; Fat 1

1 envelope dry yeast
1/2 cup warm water
5 cups flour
3 tablespoons sugar
1 tablespoon baking
  powder
1 teaspoon soda
1 teaspoon salt
3/4 cup shortening
2 cups buttermilk
2 tablespoons melted
  butter

Dissolve yeast in warm water. Mix flour, sugar, baking powder, soda and salt in bowl. Cut in shortening. Add yeast and buttermilk; mix well. Knead into ball. Store in refrigerator until needed. Roll on floured surface; cut as desired. Place on baking sheet. Let stand for 30 minutes. Brush with melted butter. Bake at 400 degrees for 10 to 20 minutes or until golden brown.

Ruth Kent Eslinger, Winston-Salem

BEER BISCUITS

Yield:
12 servings
Utensil:
muffin pan
Approx Per
Serving:
Cal 105
Prot 2 g
Carbo 17 g
Fiber 0 g
T Fat 3 g
Chol 0 mg
Sod 266 mg

Dietary
Exchanges:
Milk 0
Vegetable 0
Fruit 0
Bread/Starch 1
Meat 0; Fat 1/2

2 cups baking mix
2 tablespoons sugar
1 7-ounce bottle of
  beer

Combine baking mix, sugar and beer in bowl; mix well. Spoon into greased muffin cups. Bake at 450 degrees for 10 to 12 minutes or until golden brown.

Phyllis Lennon

CHEESE BISCUITS

Yield:
12 servings
Utensil:
baking sheet
Approx Per
Serving:
Cal 183
Prot 6 g
Carbo 8 g
Fiber <1 g
T Fat 14 g
Chol 20 mg
Sod 221 mg

Dietary
Exchanges:
Milk 0
Vegetable 0
Fruit 0
Bread/Starch ½
Meat ½; Fat 2½

8 ounces sharp Cheddar cheese, shredded, at room temperature

½ cup margarine, softened
1 cup packed flour

Combine cheese, margarine and flour in bowl; mix well. Shape into 2 rolls. Cut into ¼-inch slices. Place on greased baking sheet. Bake at 350 to 400 degrees for 10 minutes or until golden brown. May top each biscuit with pecan half before baking if desired.

Mary W. Allison, Hurdle Mills

EASY COFFEE CAKE

Yield:
12 servings
Utensil:
tube pan
Approx Per
Serving:
Cal 450
Prot 5 g
Carbo 58 g
Fiber <1 g
T Fat 22 g
Chol 114 mg
Sod 387 mg

Dietary
Exchanges:
Milk 0
Vegetable 0
Fruit 0
Bread/Starch 3
Meat ½; Fat 4½

1 2-layer package yellow cake mix
1 6-ounce package vanilla instant pudding mix
5 eggs
¾ cup oil

1 cup water
2 teaspoons vanilla extract
½ cup sugar
4 teaspoons cinnamon
½ cup chopped pecans

Combine cake mix, pudding mix, eggs, oil, water and vanilla in bowl; mix well. Mix sugar, cinnamon and pecans in small bowl. Spoon half the batter into greased and floured tube pan. Sprinkle with half the pecan mixture. Swirl with knife to mix lightly. Repeat layers; swirl again. Bake at 350 degrees for 50 to 55 minutes or until coffee cake tests done. Invert onto serving plate.

Fred Bowman, Burlington

CRANBERRY COFFEE CAKE

1/2 cup butter, softened
1 cup sugar
2 eggs
2 cups flour
1 teaspoon each baking powder and soda
1/4 teaspoon salt
8 ounces sour cream
1 teaspoon almond flavoring
1 16-ounce can whole cranberry sauce
1/2 cup chopped pecans
3/4 cup confectioners' sugar
1 tablespoon warm water
1/2 teaspoon almond flavoring

Cream butter and sugar in mixer bowl until light. Beat in eggs. Combine dry ingredients in bowl. Add to creamed mixture alternately with sour cream, mixing well after each addition. Stir in 1 teaspoon almond flavoring. Spoon 1/3 of the batter into 9x13-inch baking dish sprayed with nonstick cooking spray. Drop 1/3 of the cranberry sauce in spoonfuls over batter. Repeat layers twice. Sprinkle with pecans. Bake at 325 to 350 degrees for 25 minutes. Mix remaining ingredients in bowl. Drizzle over warm coffee cake.

Doris S. Icenhour, Winston-Salem

SOUR CREAM COFFEE CAKE

1 2-layer package yellow cake mix
1 4-ounce package vanilla instant pudding mix
1/2 cup oil
4 eggs
1 cup sour cream
1/2 cup sugar
1/2 cup pecans
2 tablespoons cinnamon
2¹/₄ cups confectioners' sugar
1/4 cup butter, softened
4 ounces cream cheese, softened
1¹/₂ teaspoons milk

Combine first 5 ingredients in mixer bowl. Beat for 10 minutes; do not underbeat. Combine sugar, pecans and cinnamon in small bowl. Layer batter and cinnamon mixture 1/2 at a time in greased and floured tube pan. Cut through layers with knife to marbleize. Bake at 350 degrees for 1 hour; do not underbake or open oven door during baking time. Invert onto serving plate. Combine confectioners' sugar, butter, cream cheese and milk in bowl; mix until smooth. Spread over coffee cake.

Zane Gerringer, Elon College

BROCCOLI CORN BREAD

Yield:
15 servings
Utensil:
baking pan
**Approx Per
Serving:**
Cal 130
Prot 5 g
Carbo 9 g
Fiber 2 g
T Fat 9 g
Chol 75 mg
Sod 226 mg

**Dietary
Exchanges:**
Milk 0
Vegetable 1/2
Fruit 0
Bread/Starch 1/2
Meat 1/2; Fat 11/2

2 10-ounce packages
   frozen chopped
   broccoli, thawed
4 eggs
2/3 cup cottage cheese

1 onion, chopped
1 8-ounce package
   corn bread mix
1/2 cup melted
   margarine

Press broccoli to remove moisture. Beat eggs in bowl. Add cottage cheese, onion, corn bread mix, broccoli and margarine; mix well. Spoon into greased 9x13-inch baking pan. Bake at 350 degrees for 45 minutes or until light brown.

Mary B. Marshall, Colfax

CALIFORNIA CORN BREAD

Yield:
6 servings
Utensil:
baking pan
**Approx Per
Serving:**
Cal 326
Prot 6 g
Carbo 33 g
Fiber <1 g
T Fat 20 g
Chol 108 mg
Sod 384 mg

**Dietary
Exchanges:**
Milk 0
Vegetable 0
Fruit 0
Bread/Starch 2
Meat 1/2; Fat 4

2 eggs
1 cup cream-style corn
1 cup sour cream
1/4 cup oil

1/4 cup minced onion
11/4 cups self-rising
   cornmeal mix
1/4 teaspoon salt

Beat eggs in medium mixer bowl. Add corn, sour cream, oil, onion, cornmeal mix and salt; mix well. Spoon into greased 8x8-inch baking pan. Bake at 425 degrees for 20 minutes or until brown. May prepare in advance, adding cornmeal mix just before baking.

Ruby W. Burrows, Winston-Salem

CORN BREAD

Yield:
9 servings
Utensil:
baking pan
**Approx Per
Serving:**
Cal 202
Prot 5 g
Carbo 26 g
Fiber 0 g
T Fat 9 g
Chol 65 mg
Sod 308 mg

**Dietary
Exchanges:**
Milk 0
Vegetable 0
Fruit 0
Bread/Starch 1½
Meat 0; Fat 1½

2 cups cornmeal
1 tablespoon baking
  powder
½ teaspoon soda
¾ teaspoon salt

2 eggs
1¼ cups milk
¼ cup melted
  shortening

Mix cornmeal, baking powder, soda and salt in bowl. Add eggs, milk and shortening; beat until smooth. Spoon into hot greased 9x9-inch baking pan. Bake at 425 degrees for 20 to 25 minutes or until brown. Serve with butter. May use self-rising cornmeal, omitting baking powder, soda and salt.

Sarah L. Tagert, Greensboro

NUMBER ONE CORN BREAD

Yield:
9 servings
Utensil:
baking pan
**Approx Per
Serving:**
Cal 103
Prot 3 g
Carbo 13 g
Fiber <1 g
T Fat 4 g
Chol 32 mg
Sod 202 mg

**Dietary
Exchanges:**
Milk 0
Vegetable 0
Fruit 0
Bread/Starch ½
Meat 0; Fat 1

¾ cup cornmeal
¼ cup flour
1 teaspoon baking
  powder
¼ teaspoon soda

½ teaspoon salt
¾ cup buttermilk
¼ cup milk
1 egg
2 tablespoons oil

Mix cornmeal, flour, baking powder, soda and salt in bowl. Add buttermilk, milk, egg and oil; mix well. Spoon into greased baking pan. Bake at 400 degrees for 20 to 30 minutes or until brown.

Doris Cope

GRANDMOTHER'S CORN BREAD

Yield:
8 servings
Utensil:
cast-iron skillet
Approx Per Serving:
Cal 275
Prot 7 g
Carbo 45 g
Fiber 0 g
T Fat 7 g
Chol 37 mg
Sod 216 mg

Dietary Exchanges:
Milk 1/2
Vegetable 0
Fruit 0
Bread/Starch 2 1/2
Meat 0; Fat 1 1/2

3 tablespoons oil
1 egg
2 1/2 cups buttermilk

3 cups self-rising
white cornmeal

Place oil in 8-inch cast-iron skillet. Heat in 450-degree oven. Break egg into small bowl. Add buttermilk and cornmeal; mix well. Sprinkle just enough additional cornmeal in hot skillet to barely cover bottom. Pour in batter. Bake at 450 degrees for 15 to 20 minutes or until brown.

Jean G. Tate, Haw River

MEXICAN CORN BREAD

Yield:
12 servings
Utensil:
baking pan
Approx Per Serving:
Cal 387
Prot 7 g
Carbo 41 g
Fiber 0 g
T Fat 22 g
Chol 11 mg
Sod 134 mg

Dietary Exchanges:
Milk 0
Vegetable 0
Fruit 0
Bread/Starch 2 1/2
Meat 1/2; Fat 4

4 cups cornmeal
1 cup shredded
   Cheddar cheese
1 cup oil

1 8-ounce can
   cream-style corn
1 cup buttermilk

Combine cornmeal, cheese, oil, corn and buttermilk in bowl; mix well. Spoon into greased baking pan. Bake at 360 degrees for 30 minutes or until dark brown.

Tommy Starr

NEVER-FAIL CORN BREAD

Yield:
12 servings
Utensil:
muffin pan
*Approx Per
Serving:*
Cal 109
Prot 3 g
Carbo 15 g
Fiber <1 g
T Fat 4 g
Chol 24 mg
Sod 112 mg

*Dietary
Exchanges:*
Milk 0
Vegetable 0
Fruit 0
Bread/Starch 1
Meat 0; Fat 1

1 cup self-rising
  cornmeal
1/2 cup self-rising flour
1 tablespoon sugar

1 egg
3 tablespoons oil
1 cup buttermilk

Mix cornmeal, flour and sugar in bowl. Add egg, oil and buttermilk; mix well. Spoon into greased muffin cups. Bake at 425 degrees for 25 minutes.

Polly Martin, Burlington

HUSH PUPPIES

Yield:
8 servings
Utensil:
skillet
*Approx Per
Serving:*
Cal 154
Prot 4 g
Carbo 30 g
Fiber <1 g
T Fat 1 g
Chol 34 mg
Sod 218 mg

*Dietary
Exchanges:*
Milk 0
Vegetable 0
Fruit 0
Bread/Starch 1 1/2
Meat 0; Fat 0

2 cups cornmeal
2 teaspoons baking
  powder
1 1/2 teaspoons sugar
1/2 teaspoon salt

1/2 cup finely chopped
  onion
1 egg
1 cup (about) beer
Shortening for frying

Combine cornmeal, baking powder, sugar, salt, onion and egg in bowl. Add enough beer to make of desired consistency; mix well. Drop into hot shortening in skillet. Fry until golden brown. Drain on paper towel.

Nutritional information does not include shortening for frying.

Carolyn Holt, Graham

FRY BREAD

2 cups sifted flour
2 teaspoons baking
    powder
½ teaspoon salt
¼ cup shortening
¾ cup milk
Shortening for
    deep-frying

Sift flour, baking powder and salt into bowl. Cut in shortening. Add milk; mix well. Roll on lightly floured surface. Cut into 3-inch strips. Slash centers of strips lengthwise. Deep-fry in hot shortening until brown. Drain on paper towel. Serve hot. Serve with soup; dip in honey or syrup and serve with bacon or ham for breakfast; dip in confectioners' sugar for dessert; or cut into circles for tacos.

Nutritional information does not include shortening for frying.

Edna Cassidy

BANANA BREAD

1¾ cups flour
1 teaspoon soda
1 teaspoon cream of
    tartar
½ teaspoon salt
⅓ cup shortening
⅔ cup sugar
2 eggs
1 cup mashed very
    ripe bananas
½ cup chopped pecans

Sift flour, soda, cream of tartar and salt into bowl. Cream shortening in mixer bowl until light. Add sugar, beating until fluffy. Beat in eggs. Add mixture of dry ingredients alternately with bananas, mixing well after each addition. Stir in pecans. Spoon into greased loaf pan. Bake at 350 degrees for 30 minutes. Reduce oven temperature to 325 degrees. Bake for 30 minutes longer. Remove to wire rack to cool.

Karen Kjaerbye Bailey

EASY BANANA NUT BREAD

Yield:
24 servings
Utensil:
2 loaf pans
**Approx Per
Serving:**
Cal 230
Prot 2 g
Carbo 24 g
Fiber <1 g
T Fat 14 g
Chol 46 mg
Sod 175 mg

**Dietary
Exchanges:**
Milk 0
Vegetable 0
Fruit 0
Bread/Starch 1½
Meat 0; Fat 3

1 2-layer package yellow cake mix
1 4-ounce package banana instant pudding mix
1 cup oil
¾ cup water
4 eggs
1 ripe banana, mashed
¾ cup chopped pecans

Combine cake mix, pudding mix, oil, water and eggs in mixer bowl; mix well. Add banana and pecans; mix well. Spoon into 2 greased and floured loaf pans. Bake at 325 degrees for 55 minutes. Remove to wire rack to cool.

Judy P. Sessoms, Greensboro

BANANA NUT BREAD

Yield:
12 servings
Utensil:
loaf pan
**Approx Per
Serving:**
Cal 288
Prot 4 g
Carbo 40 g
Fiber 2 g
T Fat 13 g
Chol 46 mg
Sod 178 mg

**Dietary
Exchanges:**
Milk 0
Vegetable 0
Fruit ½
Bread/Starch 1
Meat 0; Fat 3

½ cup oil
1 cup sugar
2 eggs, beaten
3 ripe bananas, mashed
2 cups flour
½ teaspoon baking powder
1 teaspoon soda
½ teaspoon salt
3 tablespoons milk
½ teaspoon each vanilla and almond extracts
½ cup chopped pecans

Combine oil and sugar in mixer bowl; beat until smooth. Add eggs and bananas; mix well. Sift flour, baking powder, soda and salt together. Add to batter alternately with milk and flavorings, mixing well after each addition. Stir in pecans. Spoon into greased and floured 5x9-inch loaf pan. Bake at 350 degrees for 1 hour. Remove to wire rack to cool. Store overnight to improve flavor.

Nora C. Shell, Burlington

BANANA AND PINEAPPLE BREAD

3 cups flour
1 teaspoon soda
2 cups sugar
1 teaspoon cinnamon
1 teaspoon salt
1 8-ounce can
    crushed pineapple
1½ cups oil
3 eggs
2 cups chopped
    bananas
1½ teaspoons vanilla
    extract
1½ cups chopped
    pecans

Sift flour, soda, sugar, cinnamon and salt into bowl. Add undrained pineapple, oil, eggs, bananas, vanilla and pecans; mix with wooden spoon just until moistened. Spoon into 2 greased and floured loaf pans or 9x13-inch baking pan. Bake at 350 degrees for 1 hour. Remove loaves to wire rack to cool.

Lettie A. Wilson, Graham

TOUCH-OF-LEMON BREAD

¾ cup margarine,
    softened
1½ cups sugar
3 eggs
2¼ cups sifted flour
¼ teaspoon soda
¼ teaspoon salt
¾ cup buttermilk
Grated rind of 1 lemon
¾ cup chopped pecans
½ cup sugar
Juice of 1 lemon

Cream margarine and 1½ cups sugar in mixer bowl until light and fluffy. Beat in eggs. Sift flour, soda and salt together. Add to batter alternately with buttermilk, mixing well after each addition. Stir in lemon rind and pecans. Spoon into greased and floured 5x9-inch loaf pan. Bake at 350 degrees for 1 hour or until loaf tests done. Cool in pan for 15 minutes. Remove to wire rack. Combine ½ cup sugar with lemon juice in bowl; mix well to dissolve sugar. Pierce loaf with fork. Spoon glaze over loaf. Cool completely.

Ellen M. Mercier, Greensboro

Irish Soda Bread

Yield:
12 servings
Utensil:
loaf pan
Approx Per
Serving:
Cal 246
Prot 6 g
Carbo 49 g
Fiber 2 g
T Fat 4 g
Chol 47 mg
Sod 362 mg

Dietary
Exchanges:
Milk 0
Vegetable 0
Fruit 1
Bread/Starch 1¹/2
Meat 0; Fat ¹/2

3 cups sifted flour
²/3 cups sugar
1 tablespoon baking powder
1 teaspoon soda
1¹/2 cups golden raisins
Caraway seed to taste
1 teaspoon salt
2 eggs, beaten
1¹/2 cups buttermilk
2 tablespoons oil

Mix flour, sugar, baking powder, soda, raisins, caraway seed and salt in bowl. Combine eggs, buttermilk and oil in blender container; process for 1 minute. Add all at once to flour mixture; mix just until moistened. Spoon into greased 4x8-inch loaf pan. Bake at 350 degrees for 1 hour and 10 minutes. Cool in pan for 10 minutes. Remove to wire rack to cool completely. May use dry buttermilk, adding 6 tablespoons powder with dry ingredients and 1¹/2 cups water with eggs.

Eileen M. Rindos, Burlington

Festive Pumpkin Bread

Yield:
12 servings
Utensil:
loaf pan
Approx Per
Serving:
Cal 297
Prot 3 g
Carbo 43 g
Fiber 1 g
T Fat 13 g
Chol 46 mg
Sod 199 mg

Dietary
Exchanges:
Milk 0
Vegetable 0
Fruit ¹/2
Bread/Starch 1
Meat 0; Fat 3

¹/2 cup oil
2 eggs
¹/3 cup water
1 cup cooked pumpkin
1²/3 cups self-rising flour
1¹/4 cups sugar
¹/2 teaspoon cinnamon
¹/2 teaspoon nutmeg
¹/2 cup chopped candied cherries
¹/2 cup chopped pecans

Combine oil, eggs, water and pumpkin in bowl; mix well. Sift flour, sugar, cinnamon and nutmeg together. Add to pumpkin mixture; beat until smooth. Fold in cherries and pecans. Spoon into greased and floured 5x9-inch loaf pan. Bake at 350 degrees for 1 hour. Remove to wire rack to cool. May add raisins, mixed fruit, dates or other nuts; may use spices of choice.

Ruth Kent Eslinger, Winston-Salem

MOIST PUMPKIN BREAD

Yield:
24 servings
Utensil:
2 loaf pans
Approx Per Serving:
Cal 246
Prot 4 g
Carbo 40 g
Fiber 1 g
T Fat 9 g
Chol 46 mg
Sod 212 mg

Dietary Exchanges:
Milk 0
Vegetable 0
Fruit 0
Bread/Starch 1
Meat 1/2; Fat 11/2

2/3 cup shortening
22/3 cups sugar
4 eggs
2 cups mashed cooked pumpkin
2/3 cup water
31/3 cups flour
2 teaspoons soda
1/2 teaspoon baking powder
1 teaspoon cinnamon
1 teaspoon cloves
11/2 teaspoons salt
2/3 cup ground walnuts
2/3 cup raisins

Cream shortening in mixer bowl until light. Add sugar gradually, beating until fluffy. Beat in eggs. Stir in pumpkin and water. Combine flour, soda, baking powder, cinnamon, cloves and salt in bowl. Add to pumpkin mixture; mix well. Fold in walnuts and raisins. Spoon into 2 greased and floured 5x9-inch loaf pans. Bake at 350 degrees for 1 hour and 10 minutes or until loaves test done. Remove to wire rack to cool.

Frances S. Marion, Kernersville

PUMPKIN BREAD

Yield:
24 servings
Utensil:
2 loaf pans
Approx Per Serving:
Cal 192
Prot 2 g
Carbo 27 g
Fiber <1 g
T Fat 9 g
Chol 34 mg
Sod 173 mg

Dietary Exchanges:
Milk 0
Vegetable 0
Fruit 0
Bread/Starch 11/2
Meat 1/2; Fat 2

1/3 cup sugar
1/3 cup oil
3 eggs
1 15-ounce can pumpkin
1 2-layer package butter-recipe cake mix
1 4-ounce package vanilla instant pudding mix
1 tablespoon pumpkin pie spice
1 cup chopped pecans

Combine sugar, oil, eggs and pumpkin in mixer bowl; beat at high speed for 1 minute. Add cake mix, pudding mix and pumpkin pie spice; beat for 2 minutes. Stir in pecans. Spoon into 2 greased and floured loaf pans. Bake at 350 degrees for 50 to 60 minutes or until loaves test done. Cool in pans.

Gaylene Fogleman, Graham

PUMPKIN-RAISIN BREAD

1½ cups sugar
2 eggs
1 cup pumpkin
½ cup oil
½ teaspoon salt
1⅓ cups flour
1 teaspoon soda

½ teaspoon baking
  powder
½ teaspoon cinnamon
½ teaspoon nutmeg
½ teaspoon cloves
½ cup raisins

Combine sugar, eggs, pumpkin, oil and salt in mixer bowl; mix well. Sift flour, soda, baking powder, cinnamon, nutmeg and cloves into bowl. Add to pumpkin mixture; mix well. Stir in raisins. Spoon into 2 greased miniature loaf pans. Bake at 325 degrees for 45 minutes or until top springs back when lightly touched. Remove to wire rack to cool.

Alison K. Mercier, Greensboro

POPPY SEED BREAD

1 cup margarine,
  softened
2 cups sugar
3 eggs
1½ cups milk
3 cups flour
1½ teaspoons baking
  powder
2 tablespoons poppy
  seed

1½ teaspoons vanilla
  extract
1½ teaspoons almond
  flavoring
¾ cup confectioners'
  sugar
½ teaspoon vanilla
  extract
2 tablespoons (about)
  milk

Cream margarine and sugar in mixer bowl until light and fluffy. Beat in eggs. Add 1½ cups milk, flour, baking powder, poppy seed, 1½ teaspoons vanilla and almond flavoring; mix well. Spoon into 2 greased and floured 5x9-inch loaf pans. Bake at 325 degrees for 50 minutes. Combine confectioners' sugar and ½ teaspoon vanilla with enough milk to make of spreading consistency in bowl; mix well. Spoon over hot loaves. Cool in pans.

Colon W. Farlow, Sophia

Coconut Poppy Seed Bread

Yield:
12 servings
Utensil:
loaf pan
Approx Per
Serving:
Cal 477
Prot 5 g
Carbo 47 g
Fiber 1 g
T Fat 31 g
Chol 91 mg
Sod 350 mg

Dietary
Exchanges:
Milk 0
Vegetable 0
Fruit 0
Bread/Starch 3
Meat 1/2; Fat 6 1/2

1 2-layer package butter-pecan cake mix
1 4-ounce package coconut creme instant pudding mix
3 tablespoons poppy seed
4 eggs
1 cup oil
1 cup chopped pecans
1 cup boiling water

Mix cake mix, pudding mix and poppy seed in bowl. Combine eggs and oil in mixer bowl; beat until smooth. Add dry ingredients and pecans; mix well. Stir in boiling water. Spoon into greased and floured loaf pan or 2 small loaf pans. Bake at 350 degrees for 30 minutes or until bread tests done. Remove to wire rack to cool.

Betty Scott

Pineapple Zucchini Bread

Yield:
24 servings
Utensil:
2 loaf pans
Approx Per
Serving:
Cal 270
Prot 4 g
Carbo 37 g
Fiber 1 g
T Fat 13 g
Chol 34 mg
Sod 168 mg

Dietary
Exchanges:
Milk 0
Vegetable 0
Fruit 1/2
Bread/Starch 1
Meat 1/2; Fat 2 1/2

3 eggs
1 cup oil
2 cups sugar
2 teaspoons vanilla extract
2 cups coarsely shredded zucchini
1 20-ounce can crushed pineapple
3 cups flour
1/2 teaspoon baking powder
2 teaspoons soda
1 1/2 teaspoons cinnamon
3/4 teaspoon nutmeg
1 teaspoon salt
1 cup finely chopped walnuts
1 cup currants

Beat eggs in mixer bowl. Add oil, sugar and vanilla; beat until thick and lemon-colored. Stir in zucchini and pineapple. Combine flour, baking powder, soda, cinnamon, nutmeg, salt, walnuts and currants in bowl. Add to zucchini mixture; stir with spoon to mix well. Spoon into 2 greased and floured 5x9-inch loaf pans. Bake at 350 degrees for 1 hour or until loaves test done. Cool in pans for 10 minutes. Remove to wire rack to cool completely.

Mary (Wilma) Gregory, Winston-Salem

ZUCCHINI BREAD

Yield:
12 servings
Utensil:
loaf pan
Approx Per
Serving:
Cal 260
Prot 3 g
Carbo 36 g
Fiber 2 g
T Fat 12 g
Chol 46 mg
Sod 170 mg

Dietary
Exchanges:
Milk 0
Vegetable 0
Fruit 1/2
Bread/Starch 1
Meat 0; Fat 2 1/2

1 1/2 cups flour
1/4 teaspoon baking powder
1 teaspoon soda
3/4 teaspoon cinnamon
1/2 teaspoon salt
1/3 cup chopped pecans
1/2 cup raisins
2 eggs
1 cup sugar
1/2 cup oil
1 teaspoon vanilla extract
1 cup chopped zucchini
1 8-ounce can crushed pineapple, drained

Mix flour, baking powder, soda, cinnamon, salt, pecans and raisins in bowl. Beat eggs slightly in large mixer bowl. Add sugar, oil and vanilla; beat until smooth. Add zucchini, pineapple and dry ingredients; mix just until moistened. Spoon into greased and floured 5x9-inch loaf pan. Bake at 350 degrees for 1 hour or until loaf tests done. Cool in pan for 10 minutes. Remove to wire rack to cool completely. May bake in 3 miniature loaf pans if preferred; bake for 45 to 50 minutes.

Nancy Garner, Burlington

APPLE MUFFINS

Yield:
12 servings
Utensil:
muffin pan
Approx Per
Serving:
Cal 212
Prot 3 g
Carbo 36 g
Fiber 1 g
T Fat 7 g
Chol 24 mg
Sod 121 mg

Dietary
Exchanges:
Milk 0
Vegetable 0
Fruit 0
Bread/Starch 1
Meat 0; Fat 1 1/2

1 1/2 cups flour
1 cup sugar
2 teaspoons baking powder
1/2 teaspoon cinnamon
1 egg
1/4 cup melted margarine
1/2 cup milk
1 cup grated tart apple with peeling
1/3 cup packed brown sugar
1/2 teaspoon cinnamon
1/3 cup chopped pecans

Sift flour, sugar, baking powder and 1/2 teaspoon cinnamon into bowl. Add egg, margarine, milk and apple; mix well. Spoon into paper-lined muffin cups. Mix brown sugar, 1/2 teaspoon cinnamon and pecans in small bowl. Sprinkle over batter. Bake at 400 degrees for 25 to 30 minutes or until muffins test done.

Ruth Angel, Greensboro

APPLESAUCE BREAKFAST MUFFINS

1½ cups unbleached
 flour
⅔ cup sugar
½ teaspoon baking
 powder
½ teaspoon soda
¾ teaspoon cinnamon
⅔ cup thin applesauce
1 egg
½ cup oil

Mix flour, sugar, baking powder, soda and cinnamon in bowl. Add applesauce, egg and oil; mix just until moistened. Spoon into greased muffin cups. Bake at 400 degrees for 20 minutes or until brown. Serve with jam or margarine.

Sherri Davis, Greensboro

BLUEBERRY MUFFINS

2 cups flour
½ cup sugar
1 tablespoon baking
 powder
½ teaspoon salt
1½ cups fresh or
 frozen blueberries
½ cup sour cream
1 egg, slightly beaten
½ cup milk
6 tablespoons melted
 butter
1 teaspoon grated
 lemon rind
2 teaspoons lemon
 juice

Sift flour, sugar, baking powder and salt onto waxed paper. Toss blueberries with 2 tablespoons flour mixture in bowl, coating well. Whisk sour cream in large bowl until smooth. Add egg, milk, butter, lemon rind and lemon juice, mixing well. Add remaining sifted dry ingredients; mix just until moistened. Fold in blueberries. Spoon by ⅓ cupfuls into paper-lined 2½-inch muffin cups. Bake at 400 degrees for 25 minutes or until wooden pick inserted in center comes out clean. Cool in pan for 5 minutes. Remove to wire rack.

Flora E. Cheshire, Efland

BLUEBERRY YOGURT MUFFINS

Yield:
15 servings
Utensil:
muffin pan
Approx Per
Serving:
Cal 114
Prot 2 g
Carbo 20 g
Fiber <1 g
T Fat 3 g
Chol 1 mg
Sod 229 mg

Dietary
Exchanges:
Milk 0
Vegetable 0
Fruit 0
Bread/Starch 1
Meat 0; Fat 1/2

2 cups no-cholesterol baking mix
1/2 cup sugar
1 cup low-fat plain yogurt
1 cup fresh blueberries
Egg substitute equal to 1 egg
2 teaspoons grated lemon rind
1 teaspoon lemon extract

Mix baking mix, sugar, yogurt, blueberries, egg substitute, lemon rind and lemon extract in order listed in bowl. Spoon into greased muffin cups. Bake at 400 degrees for 20 minutes or until muffins test done.

Erma T. Smart, Burlington

CHEDDAR MUFFINS

Yield:
12 muffins
Utensil:
muffin pan
Approx Per
Serving:
Cal 168
Prot 6 g
Carbo 17 g
Fiber 1 g
T Fat 8 g
Chol 46 mg
Sod 294 mg

Dietary
Exchanges:
Milk 0
Vegetable 0
Fruit 0
Bread/Starch 1
Meat 1/2; Fat 1 1/2

2 cups flour
3 1/2 teaspoons baking powder
1 cup shredded Cheddar cheese
1 teaspoon paprika
1/2 teaspoon salt
1 egg, beaten
1 cup milk
1/4 cup melted butter

Combine flour, baking powder, cheese, paprika and salt in large bowl; mix well. Make well in center. Combine egg, milk and butter in small bowl; mix well. Pour into well; mix just until moistened. Fill greased muffin cups 2/3 full. Bake at 425 degrees for 20 minutes. Remove immediately to wire rack.

S. M. Apple, Burlington

SIX-WEEK MUFFINS

Yield:
60 servings
Utensil:
muffin pan
Approx Per
Serving:
Cal 140
Prot 3 g
Carbo 24 g
Fiber 1 g
T Fat 4 g
Chol 19 mg
Sod 202 mg

Dietary
Exchanges:
Milk 0
Vegetable 0
Fruit 0
Bread/Starch 1
Meat 0; Fat 1

5 cups flour
5 teaspoons soda
2 teaspoons salt
1 15-ounce package
   Raisin Bran

3 cups sugar
4 eggs, beaten
4 cups buttermilk
1 cup oil

Sift flour, soda and salt into large bowl. Add cereal and sugar; mix well. Beat eggs, buttermilk and oil in small bowl until smooth. Add to cereal mixture; mix well. Store, covered, in refrigerator for up to 6 weeks. Spoon into desired number of greased muffin cups. Bake at 375 to 400 degrees for 25 minutes or until golden brown. Serve warm.

A Pioneer

RAISIN AND NUT BRAN MUFFINS

Yield:
12 servings
Utensil:
muffin pan
Approx Per
Serving:
Cal 211
Prot 5 g
Carbo 24 g
Fiber 2 g
T Fat 12 g
Chol 26 mg
Sod 222 mg

Dietary
Exchanges:
Milk 0
Vegetable 0
Fruit 1/2
Bread/Starch 1
Meat 1/2; Fat 2 1/2

1 cup whole bran
   cereal
1 cup flour
1 cup chopped walnuts
1/2 cup dark seedless
   raisins
1/4 cup sugar

1 tablespoon baking
   powder
1/2 teaspoon salt
1 egg
1 cup milk
1/4 cup oil

Combine cereal, flour, walnuts, raisins, sugar, baking powder and salt in medium bowl; mix well with fork. Beat egg slightly with fork in small bowl. Add milk and oil; mix well. Add to cereal mixture; mix just until moistened. Spoon into greased 2 1/2-inch muffin cups. Bake at 400 degrees for 25 minutes or until toothpick inserted in center comes out almost clean and tops are golden brown. Remove immediately from pan. May substitute water for milk if preferred.

Martha M. Wheeler, Chapin, South Carolina

CORN MUFFINS

Yield:
12 servings
Utensil:
muffin pan
Approx Per
Serving:
Cal 147
Prot 3 g
Carbo 22 g
Fiber <1 g
T Fat 5 g
Chol 26 mg
Sod 208 mg

Dietary
Exchanges:
Milk 0
Vegetable 0
Fruit 0
Bread/Starch 1
Meat 0; Fat 1

1 cup self-rising
  cornmeal
1 cup self-rising flour
¼ cup sugar

1 egg
1 cup milk
¼ cup melted
  margarine

Mix cornmeal, flour and sugar in bowl. Add egg, milk and margarine; mix just until moistened. Spoon into greased muffin cups. Bake at 400 degrees for 20 to 25 minutes or until muffins test done. May substitute buttermilk for milk.

Norma Hall, Mebane

LIGHT AND EASY MUFFINS

Yield:
12 servings
Utensil:
muffin pan
Approx Per
Serving:
Cal 133
Prot 6 g
Carbo 15 g
Fiber <1 g
T Fat 5 g
Chol 6 mg
Sod 215 mg

Dietary
Exchanges:
Milk 0
Vegetable 0
Fruit 0
Bread/Starch 1
Meat ½; Fat 1

1 cup flour
½ cup cornmeal
2 teaspoons baking
  powder
¼ teaspoon salt
2 ounces low-fat
  Cheddar cheese,
  shredded

2 ounces cooked lean
  ham, chopped
1 cup skim milk
½ cup instant grits
3 tablespoons oil
½ cup frozen egg
  substitute, thawed

Combine flour, cornmeal, baking powder, salt, cheese and ham in bowl; mix well. Make well in center. Heat milk to 120 to 130 degrees in saucepan, stirring constantly. Stir in grits. Combine oil and egg substitute in small bowl; mix well. Add grits and oil mixture to dry ingredients; mix just until moistened. Fill muffin cups sprayed with nonstick cooking spray ¾ full. Bake at 400 degrees for 20 to 25 minutes or until muffins are light brown.

Patricia A. Gibson, Ocracoke Island

MAYONNAISE MUFFINS

Yield:
6 servings
Utensil:
muffin pan
Approx Per
Serving:
Cal 102
Prot 3 g
Carbo 17 g
Fiber 1 g
T Fat 3 g
Chol 4 mg
Sod 248 mg

Dietary
Exchanges:
Milk 0
Vegetable 0
Fruit 0
Bread/Starch 1
Meat 0; Fat 1/2

1 cup self-rising flour   1 tablespoon
1/2 cup milk   mayonnaise

Combine flour, milk and mayonnaise in bowl; mix well. Spoon into greased muffin cups. Bake at 450 degrees for 8 minutes or until brown.

Gaylene Fogleman, Graham

MINUTE MUFFINS

Yield:
12 servings
Utensil:
muffin pan
Approx Per
Serving:
Cal 115
Prot 3 g
Carbo 17 g
Fiber 1 g
T Fat 4 g
Chol 3 mg
Sod 272 mg

Dietary
Exchanges:
Milk 0
Vegetable 0
Fruit 0
Bread/Starch 1
Meat 0; Fat 1

2 cups self-rising flour   1/4 cup mayonnaise
1 cup buttermilk

Combine flour, buttermilk and mayonnaise in mixer bowl; mix until smooth. Fill greased muffin cups 2/3 full. Bake at 400 degrees for 18 to 20 minutes or until golden brown.

Vicki Strickland, Greensboro

MORNING GLORY MUFFINS

Yield:
36 servings
Utensil:
muffin pan
Approx Per Serving:
Cal 275
Prot 3 g
Carbo 31 g
Fiber 2 g
T Fat 16 g
Chol 46 mg
Sod 160 mg

Dietary Exchanges:
Milk 0
Vegetable 0
Fruit 1/2
Bread/Starch 1/2
Meat 0; Fat 3 1/2

4 cups flour
2 1/2 cups sugar
4 teaspoons soda
4 teaspoons cinnamon
1 teaspoon salt
4 cups grated peeled apples
1 cup raisins
1 cup chopped pecans
1 cup coconut
1 cup grated carrot
6 eggs
2 cups oil
4 teaspoons vanilla extract

Sift flour, sugar, soda, cinnamon and salt into large bowl. Stir in apples, raisins, pecans, coconut and carrot. Combine eggs, oil and vanilla in blender container; process until smooth. Add to dry ingredients; mix just until moistened. Fill greased or paper-lined muffin cups 2/3 full. Bake at 350 degrees for 35 minutes or until muffins spring back when lightly touched. Cool in pan for 5 minutes. Remove to wire rack to cool completely. May use unbleached flour if preferred. May bake in 100 miniature muffin cups.

Edith Gerringer, Burlington

OAT AND BLUEBERRY MUFFINS

Yield:
12 servings
Utensil:
muffin pan
Approx Per Serving:
Cal 144
Prot 4 g
Carbo 23 g
Fiber 1 g
T Fat 5 g
Chol <1 mg
Sod 76 mg

Dietary Exchanges:
Milk 0
Vegetable 0
Fruit 0
Bread/Starch 1
Meat 0; Fat 1

2 1/2 cups oats
1/2 cup packed brown sugar
2 teaspoons baking powder
1/2 teaspoon cinnamon
Salt to taste
1 cup blueberries
2/3 cup skim milk
3 tablespoons oil
2 egg whites, slightly beaten

Process oats in blender for 1 minute, stopping occasionally to stir. Combine with brown sugar, baking powder, cinnamon and salt in bowl. Add blueberries, milk, oil and egg whites; mix just until moistened. Spoon into paper-lined muffin cups. Bake at 400 degrees for 20 to 22 minutes or until deep golden brown. May reheat frozen muffins in microwave on High for 30 seconds.

Mrs. Arthur H. Jones, Winston-Salem

OAT BRAN MUFFINS

2 cups oat bran
2 teaspoons baking powder
1/4 cup packed brown sugar
1/4 cup raisins
1/4 cup chopped walnuts
1 teaspoon cinnamon
1 cup skim milk
2 egg whites, slightly beaten
1/4 cup honey
2 tablespoons oil

Combine oat bran, baking powder, brown sugar, raisins, walnuts and cinnamon in bowl. Add milk, egg whites, honey and oil; mix just until moistened. Spoon into paper-lined muffin cups. Bake at 425 degrees for 15 minutes. May add 1/2 cup mashed banana, blueberries or chopped apple if desired.

A Pioneer

ZUCCHINI AND CARROT MUFFINS

1 1/3 cups all-purpose flour
1/3 cup whole wheat flour
2/3 cup packed light brown sugar
1/2 teaspoon soda
1 teaspoon cinnamon
1/4 teaspoon nutmeg
1/2 teaspoon salt
1/3 cup safflower oil
1/4 cup skim milk
3 egg whites
1 1/4 cups shredded carrots
2/3 cup shredded zucchini
1/2 cup chopped walnuts

Mix all-purpose flour, whole wheat flour, brown sugar, soda, cinnamon, nutmeg and salt in bowl. Combine oil, milk and egg whites in mixer bowl; mix well. Add to dry ingredients; mix just until moistened. Stir in carrots, zucchini and walnuts. Spoon into greased muffin cups. Bake at 425 degrees for 20 minutes.

A Pioneer

FRENCH TOAST

Yield:
6 servings
Utensil:
griddle
Approx Per
Serving:
Cal 147
Prot 5 g
Carbo 15 g
Fiber 1 g
T Fat 7 g
Chol 94 mg
Sod 376 mg

Dietary
Exchanges:
Milk 0
Vegetable 0
Fruit 0
Bread/Starch 1
Meat 1/2; Fat 1 1/2

2 eggs, slightly beaten   1/2 teaspoon salt
1 tablespoon sugar   6 slices bread
1/2 cup milk   2 tablespoons melted
1/4 teaspoon cinnamon   margarine

Combine eggs, sugar, milk, cinnamon and salt in shallow dish; mix well. Dip bread in egg mixture, turning to coat both sides. Cook in margarine on heated griddle for 4 minutes on each side or until golden brown. Garnish with confectioners' sugar. May use 6 to 8 slices diagonally sliced French bread if preferred.

Ruth Kent Eslinger, Winston-Salem

FAMOUS PANCAKES

Yield:
4 servings
Utensil:
griddle
Approx Per
Serving:
Cal 367
Prot 14 g
Carbo 54 g
Fiber 2 g
T Fat 10 g
Chol 156 mg
Sod 666 mg

Dietary
Exchanges:
Milk 1/2
Vegetable 0
Fruit 0
Bread/Starch 3
Meat 1/2; Fat 2

2 cups flour   2 cups buttermilk
1 teaspoon soda   2 tablespoons melted
1/2 teaspoon salt   butter
2 egg yolks   2 egg whites

Sift flour, soda and salt into bowl. Beat egg yolks in bowl. Add buttermilk. Add dry ingredients; mix just until moistened. Stir in butter. Beat egg whites in bowl until stiff but not dry. Fold into batter. Spoon onto griddle greased with bacon grease. Bake until golden brown on both sides. Serve with maple-flavored syrup. May add blueberries if desired.

Becky Lendford, Greensboro

CHEESE BREAD

Yield:
16 servings
Utensil:
2 round pans
Approx Per Serving:
Cal 310
Prot 12 g
Carbo 39 g
Fiber 1 g
T Fat 11 g
Chol 30 mg
Sod 430 mg

Dietary Exchanges:
Milk 0
Vegetable 0
Fruit 0
Bread/Starch 2
Meat 1; Fat 1½

1 package dry yeast
½ cup warm water
½ cup cornmeal
1¾ cups water
2 teaspoons salt
½ cup molasses
2 tablespoons shortening
4½ to 5 cups flour
1 pound sharp Cheddar cheese, cut into small cubes

Line 2 round pans with foil, allowing foil to extend over edge; grease foil. Dissolve yeast in ½ cup warm water. Combine cornmeal, 1¾ cups water and salt in saucepan. Cook over medium heat until thickened and bubbly, stirring constantly; remove from heat. Stir in molasses and shortening. Cool to room temperature. Mix with yeast and enough flour to make a stiff dough in bowl. Knead on floured surface for 5 minutes. Place in greased bowl, turning to coat surface. Let rise, covered, in warm place for 1 to 1½ hours. Divide into 2 portions. Knead half the cheese into each portion on surface sprinkled with additional cornmeal. Place in prepared pans. Let rise for 1 to 1¼ hours. Bake at 350 degrees for 45 to 55 minutes.

Frances Thompson, Winston-Salem

FRENCH HERB BREAD

Yield:
16 servings
Utensil:
baking pan
Approx Per Serving:
Cal 226
Prot 6 g
Carbo 38 g
Fiber 1 g
T Fat 5 g
Chol 18 mg
Sod 160 mg

Dietary Exchanges:
Milk 0
Vegetable 0
Fruit 0
Bread/Starch 2½
Meat 0; Fat 1

5 to 6 cups flour
2 packages dry yeast
1 envelope ranch salad dressing mix
1½ cups buttermilk
½ cup water
¼ cup shortening
1 egg
1 tablespoon melted margarine

Mix 2 cups flour, yeast and salad dressing mix in large bowl. Heat buttermilk, water and shortening in saucepan just until warm; shortening may not be completely melted. Add to flour mixture with egg. Beat for 3 minutes at medium speed, adding enough additional flour to make stiff dough. Knead on floured surface until smooth and elastic. Place in greased bowl, turning to coat surface. Let rise, covered, until doubled in bulk. Punch down and divide into 2 portions. Roll each portion into rectangle on floured surface. Roll up from wide side; place seam side down in greased baking pan. Let rise until doubled in bulk. Bake at 375 degrees for 25 minutes or until bread tests done. Brush with melted margarine. Remove to wire rack to cool.

Juanita Stone, Graham

HEALTH BREAD

2 envelopes dry yeast
½ cup warm water
1 cup quick-cooking
  oats
2 tablespoons shortening
1 cup raisins
2½ cups boiling water
1 cup All-Bran
¾ cup molasses
1 cup whole wheat flour
6 to 7 cups all-purpose
  flour

Dissolve yeast in ½ cup warm water. Mix next 5 ingredients in large bowl. Cool to lukewarm. Add yeast and molasses. Stir in whole wheat flour and 2 cups all-purpose flour; mix well. Add enough remaining all-purpose flour to make a soft dough. Knead on lightly floured surface until smooth and elastic. Place in greased bowl, turning to coat surface. Let rise, covered, in warm place for 1 hour or until doubled in bulk. Punch dough down and divide into 2 portions. Let rest, covered, in warm place for 10 minutes. Shape into 2 loaves; place in 2 greased 5x9-inch loaf pans. Let rise for 45 minutes or until doubled in bulk. Bake at 350 degrees for 55 minutes or until loaves test done. Remove to wire rack to cool.

Vi Munt, Winston-Salem

HONEY WHOLE WHEAT BREAD

3 cups whole wheat flour
½ cup nonfat dry milk
2 envelopes dry yeast
2 teaspoons salt
3 cups water
½ cup honey
2 tablespoons oil
1 cup whole wheat flour
4 to 4½ cups
  all-purpose flour

Mix first 4 ingredients in bowl. Heat water, honey and oil in saucepan just until warm. Pour over flour mixture. Beat at low speed for 1 minute. Beat at medium speed for 2 minutes. Stir in remaining 1 cup whole wheat flour and enough all-purpose flour to make a stiff dough. Knead on floured surface for 5 minutes. Place in greased bowl, turning to coat surface. Let rise, covered, in warm place for 45 minutes. Punch dough down and divide into 2 portions. Roll each portion into 7x14-inch rectangle on floured surface. Roll up and tuck ends under to form loaf. Place in 2 greased 5x9-inch loaf pans. Let rise until dough reaches tops of pans. Bake at 375 degrees for 40 minutes. Remove to wire rack to cool.

Connie Kelly, Mocksville

ZEPOLE (Italian Doughnuts)

1 envelope dry yeast
1 cup warm water
1/4 cup sugar
5 cups flour
1/2 teaspoon salt

1 1/2 cups water
2 cups oil for frying
1 cup confectioners'
sugar

Preheat oven to 100 degrees; turn off heat. Dissolve yeast in 1 cup warm water with pinch of sugar; let stand for 5 minutes. Mix remaining sugar with flour and salt in bowl. Add 1 1/2 cups water and yeast; mix by hand. Let rise, covered, in preheated oven for 2 hours. Drop by spoonfuls into hot oil in deep-fryer. Fry until golden brown. Drain on paper towel. Sprinkle cooled doughnuts with confectioners' sugar.

Nutritional information does not include oil for frying.

Antoinette Cerrito, Greensboro

OATMEAL BREAD

2 cups boiling water
1 cup oats
2 envelopes dry yeast
1/3 cup lukewarm water
1/2 cup molasses

2 tablespoons butter,
softened
2 1/2 teaspoons salt
6 to 6 1/2 cups flour

Pour boiling water over oats in large bowl. Let stand for 30 minutes. Dissolve yeast in lukewarm water. Let stand for 5 minutes; stir mixture. Add yeast, molasses, butter and salt to oats; mix well. Stir in 4 cups flour 1/2 at a time. Knead in enough remaining flour on floured surface to make an easily-handled dough. Place in greased bowl, turning to coat surface. Let rise, covered, in warm place for 3 hours or until doubled in bulk. Divide into 2 portions. Place in 2 greased 5x9-inch loaf pans, shaping dough to fill corners completely. Let rise, covered, for 1 to 2 hours or until risen as desired. Bake at 325 degrees on rack 4 inches from bottom of oven for 50 minutes. Remove to wire rack. May add raisins and nuts or substitute honey for molasses.

Raphnel Staples, Burlington

ORANGE BREAKFAST BREAD

Yield:
36 servings
Utensil:
3 loaf pans
Approx Per Serving:
Cal 111
Prot 3 g
Carbo 19 g
Fiber 1 g
T Fat 3 g
Chol <1 mg
Sod 83 mg

Dietary Exchanges:
Milk 0
Vegetable 0
Fruit 0
Bread/Starch 1
Meat 0; Fat 1/2

1½ cups bread flour
½ cup gluten flour
2 packages Rapid-Rise yeast
½ cup sugar
1½ teaspoons cinnamon
¾ teaspoon salt
4 teaspoons grated orange rind
1 cup low-fat milk
½ cup margarine
½ cup orange juice
3 egg whites, at room temperature
½ cup oat bran
½ cup whole wheat flour
3 cups bread flour

Mix 1½ cups bread flour, gluten flour, yeast, sugar, cinnamon, salt and orange rind in large bowl. Heat milk and margarine to 125 to 130 degrees in saucepan. Heat orange juice in small saucepan until warm. Add milk and orange juice to flour mixture. Beat until smooth. Add egg whites. Beat at medium speed for 3 minutes, scraping bowl occasionally. Add oat bran and whole wheat flour. Beat for 2 minutes. Stir in remaining 3 cups bread flour or enough to make a very stiff dough. Knead on floured surface for 6 to 8 minutes or until smooth and elastic. Place in greased bowl, turning to coat surface. Let rise, covered, in warm place for 20 minutes. Punch dough down and divide into 3 portions. Shape into loaves; place in three 5x9-inch loaf pans sprayed with nonstick cooking spray. Let rise until doubled in bulk. Bake at 350 degrees for 35 minutes. Remove to wire rack.

Rosa Richardson, Winston-Salem

SAUSAGE BREAD

| 1 16-ounce loaf frozen bread dough, thawed | 1 cup drained cooked sausage |
| 2 eggs | 4 ounces mozzarella cheese, shredded |

Place greased dough in greased loaf pan. Let rise, covered, in warm place overnight. Roll dough into large rectangle on lightly floured surface. Beat eggs in bowl. Spread on dough to within 1 inch of edges. Sprinkle sausage over egg. Sprinkle cheese over sausage. Roll up from long side, pinching ends to seal in filling. Return to loaf pan. Bake at 400 degrees for 30 minutes. Egg may bubble up through crust during baking time. May brown sausage the night before to reduce preparation time.

Lee P. Powell, Clemmons

MORAVIAN SUGAR CAKES

1 envelope dry yeast	1 teaspoon salt
1/2 cup lukewarm water	2 eggs, beaten
1 cup hot unseasoned mashed potatoes	4 to 5 cups flour
1 cup sugar	1/2 cup melted butter
1/4 cup butter	1/2 1-pound package brown sugar
1/2 cup shortening	Cinnamon to taste

Dissolve yeast in 1/2 cup lukewarm water. Combine potatoes, sugar, 1/4 cup butter, shortening and salt in bowl; mix well. Add yeast; mix well. Let rise in warm place until spongy. Add eggs and enough flour to make a soft dough. Let rise, covered, until doubled in bulk. Press evenly into 4 greased 8x8-inch pans, filling 3/4 full. Let rise until doubled in bulk. Make indentations close together in cakes with finger. Fill indentations with melted butter and brown sugar. Sprinkle with cinnamon. Bake at 375 degrees for 20 minutes or until golden brown. Remove to wire rack.

Dot Raker, Winston-Salem

THREE-GRAIN YEAST BREAD

<table>
<tr><td>

Yield:
24 *servings*
Utensil:
2 *loaf pans*
Approx Per
Serving:
Cal 180
Prot 6 g
Carbo 32 g
Fiber 3 g
T Fat 3 g
Chol 8 mg
Sod 301 mg

Dietary
Exchanges:
Milk 0
Vegetable 0
Fruit 0
Bread/Starch 2
Meat 0; Fat 1

</td></tr>
</table>

2 envelopes dry yeast
2 teaspoons sugar
1/2 cup warm water
1 1/2 cups oats
3 cups whole wheat flour
2 1/2 to 3 cups
  unbleached flour
1/3 cup butter
1/4 cup molasses
1/4 cup honey
1 tablespoon salt
2 1/2 cups buttermilk

Dissolve yeast and sugar in warm water. Process oats in blender until fine. Mix with whole wheat flour and unbleached flour in large bowl; make well in center. Heat butter, molasses, honey and salt in saucepan until warm. Heat buttermilk in small saucepan until warm. Add butter mixture, buttermilk and yeast to flour mixture; mix to form a stiff dough. Let rise, covered, in warm place for 1 hour. Punch dough down; divide into 2 portions. Shape into loaves in 2 greased loaf pans. Let rise for 45 minutes to 1 hour or until doubled in bulk. Bake at 375 degrees for 30 minutes or until loaves test done. Remove to wire rack.

Ethel W. Moore, Haw River

WHEAT BREAD

<table>
<tr><td>

Yield:
36 *servings*
Utensil:
3 *loaf pans*
Approx Per
Serving:
Cal 149
Prot 4 g
Carbo 28 g
Fiber 3 g
T Fat 3 g
Chol 0 mg
Sod 95 mg

Dietary
Exchanges:
Milk 0
Vegetable 0
Fruit 0
Bread/Starch 1 1/2
Meat 0; Fat 1/2

</td></tr>
</table>

2/3 cup (or less) honey
1/2 cup margarine
3 cups warm (105 to
  110-degree) water
1 teaspoon salt
4 cups all-purpose flour
2 tablespoons dry yeast
5 cups whole wheat
  flour

Combine honey, margarine, warm water and salt in bowl; stir to mix well. Add all-purpose flour gradually, mixing well. Add yeast gradually. Add whole wheat flour gradually, mixing to form dough and adding additional warm water if needed for desired consistency. Knead on floured surface for 10 minutes or until smooth and elastic. Place in greased bowl, turning to coat surface. Let rise, covered, in warm place for 1 hour or until doubled in bulk. Punch dough down. Let rest for 10 minutes. Shape dough into loaves in 3 greased loaf pans. Let rise until doubled in bulk. Bake at 350 degrees for 30 to 35 minutes or until loaves test done. Remove to wire rack.

Kathleen S. Yax, Mebane

NO-KNEAD CRUSTY ROLLS

Yield:
24 servings
Utensil:
muffin pan
Approx Per
Serving:
Cal 101
Prot 2 g
Carbo 15 g
Fiber 1 g
T Fat 3 g
Chol 14 mg
Sod 115 mg

Dietary
Exchanges:
Milk 0
Vegetable 0
Fruit 0
Bread/Starch 1
Meat 0; Fat 1/2

1 cake yeast, crumbled
1/4 cup lukewarm water
1/4 cup shortening
2 tablespoons sugar
11/4 teaspoons salt
1 cup boiling water
1 egg, beaten
31/2 cups flour
2 tablespoons melted
butter

Dissolve yeast in 1/4 cup lukewarm water. Combine shortening, sugar and salt in bowl. Add 1 cup boiling water; mix well. Cool to lukewarm. Add yeast and egg; mix well. Add enough flour to make a soft dough; mix well. Place in greased bowl, turning to coat surface. Place in refrigerator for 2 to 24 hours. Shape into rolls large enough to fill greased muffin cups 1/3 full. Brush tops with butter. Let rise, covered, in warm place for 2 hours or until doubled in bulk. Bake at 425 degrees for 20 minutes or until brown. Remove to wire rack.

Johnsie Estes, Winston-Salem

CHRISTMAS MORNING ROLLS

Yield:
24 servings
Utensil:
tube pan
Approx Per
Serving:
Cal 192
Prot 2 g
Carbo 26 g
Fiber <1 g
T Fat 9 g
Chol 0 mg
Sod 238 mg

Dietary
Exchanges:
Milk 0
Vegetable 0
Fruit 0
Bread/Starch 1
Meat 0; Fat 2

1 24-count package
frozen dinner roll
dough
1 4-ounce package
butterscotch
pudding and pie
filling mix
1/2 cup margarine
3/4 cup packed brown
sugar
3/4 teaspoon cinnamon
1 cup chopped pecans

Arrange frozen roll dough in greased tube pan. Sprinkle with pudding mix. Melt margarine in small saucepan over medium heat. Add brown sugar, cinnamon and pecans. Cook until bubbly, stirring constantly. Pour over rolls. Let stand, covered tightly with foil, overnight. Bake at 350 degrees for 30 minutes. Let cool in pan for 5 minutes. Invert onto serving plate.

Nell M. Yarbrough, Winston-Salem

POTATO ROLLS

Yield:
36 servings
Utensil:
baking pan
Approx Per
Serving:
Cal 127
Prot 3 g
Carbo 19 g
Fiber 1 g
T Fat 4 g
Chol 16 mg
Sod 134 mg

Dietary
Exchanges:
Milk 0
Vegetable 0
Fruit 0
Bread/Starch 1
Meat 0; Fat 1

2 envelopes dry yeast
1/2 cup lukewarm water
2/3 cup shortening
1/2 cup sugar
2 eggs, beaten
1 cup hot mashed
  potatoes
2 teaspoons salt
5 1/2 cups flour, sifted
1 cup milk, scalded

Dissolve yeast in lukewarm water. Combine shortening, sugar, eggs, potatoes and salt in bowl; mix well. Add flour alternately with milk, mixing well after each addition. Add yeast; mix well. Let rise, covered, at room temperature for 2 hours. Roll on floured surface; cut out as desired. Place in greased baking pan. Let rise for 2 hours. Bake at 400 degrees until brown.

A Pioneer

GARLIC BREAD

Yield:
12 servings
Utensil:
baking sheet
Approx Per
Serving:
Cal 262
Prot 4 g
Carbo 20 g
Fiber 1 g
T Fat 19 g
Chol 21 mg
Sod 373 mg

Dietary
Exchanges:
Milk 0
Vegetable 0
Fruit 0
Bread/Starch 1 1/2
Meat 0; Fat 4

1/2 cup butter, softened
1/2 cup margarine,
  softened
2 cloves of garlic,
  minced
1 1/2 tablespoons honey
1 loaf of French bread
Basil and paprika to
  taste
2 tablespoons olive oil

Combine butter, margarine, garlic and honey in bowl; mix well. Slice bread lengthwise. Spread butter mixture on cut sides of bread. Sprinkle lightly with basil and paprika. Place cut sides of loaf together. Brush loaf with olive oil. Wrap with foil; place on baking sheet. Bake at 350 degrees for 20 minutes or until heated through. May omit honey if preferred.

Joe Conti, Graham

DESSERTS

HOLIDAY AMBROSIA

1 20-ounce can pineapple chunks, drained
1½ cups seedless grapes
1 cup miniature marshmallows
1 11-ounce can mandarin orange segments, drained
1 cup flaked coconut
½ cup chopped pecans
¾ cup sour cream
1 tablespoon sugar

Combine pineapple, grapes, marshmallows, oranges, coconut and pecans in bowl; mix well. Stir in mixture of sour cream and sugar. Chill until serving time.

Roseleen Brandon, Winston-Salem

COUNTRY APPLE DESSERT

1 2-layer package yellow cake mix
⅓ cup butter, softened
1 egg
1 21-ounce can apple pie filling
½ cup packed brown sugar
½ cup chopped pecans
1 teaspoon cinnamon
8 ounces sour cream
1 egg
1 teaspoon vanilla extract

Combine cake mix, butter and 1 egg in bowl; mix well. Pat into 9x13-inch baking dish. Spread with pie filling. Combine brown sugar, pecans and cinnamon in bowl. Sprinkle over filling. Combine sour cream, remaining egg and vanilla in bowl; mix well. Spread over all. Bake at 350 degrees for 40 to 50 minutes. Chill until serving time. Cut into squares.

Teresa M. Crispino, High Point

CREAMY APPLE SQUARES

Yield:
15 servings
Utensil:
baking dish
Approx Per
Serving:
Cal 256
Prot 2 g
Carbo 34 g
Fiber <1 g
T Fat 12 g
Chol 25 mg
Sod 296 mg

Dietary
Exchanges:
Milk 0
Vegetable 0
Fruit 0
Bread/Starch 2
Meat 0; Fat 2½

1   2-layer package pudding-recipe yellow cake mix
½ cup margarine, softened
¼ cup packed brown sugar
½ teaspoon cinnamon
⅔ cup thinly sliced apples
1 cup sour cream
1 egg

Combine cake mix and margarine in bowl; mix until crumbly. Press ⅓ cup mixture into 9x13-inch baking dish. Stir brown sugar and cinnamon into remaining mixture. Arrange apples in prepared dish. Spread with mixture of sour cream and egg. Sprinkle with remaining crumbs. Bake at 350 degrees for 25 to 30 minutes.

Ellie Key, Graham

PENNSYLVANIA APPLE PAN DOWDY

Yield:
12 servings
Utensil:
baking dish
Approx Per
Serving:
Cal 251
Prot 3 g
Carbo 53 g
Fiber 02 g
T Fat 4 g
Chol 32 mg
Sod 235 mg

Dietary
Exchanges:
Milk 0
Vegetable 0
Fruit ½
Bread/Starch 1
Meat 0; Fat 1

2 cups water
1½ cups sugar
2 cups flour
4 teaspoons baking powder
½ teaspoon salt
2 tablespoons sugar
3 tablespoons butter
1 egg, slightly beaten
½ cup milk
6 apples, peeled, chopped
2 teaspoons sugar
1 teaspoon cinnamon

Combine water and 1½ cups sugar in saucepan; mix well. Bring to a slow boil. Cook until slightly thickened. Sift flour, baking powder, salt and 2 tablespoons sugar into bowl; mix well. Cut in butter until crumbly. Add egg and milk; mix well. Pat on lightly floured surface to ½-inch thickness. Arrange apples on dough. Sprinkle with remaining 2 teaspoons sugar and cinnamon. Roll up. Cut into slices. Place in 9x13-inch baking dish. Pour syrup over all. Bake at 350 degrees until lightly browned.

Lee P. Powell, Clemmons

STEWED APPLES AND RAISINS

2 apples
½ cup raisins
⅛ teaspoon salt

½ teaspoon cinnamon
¼ teaspoon nutmeg

Peel apples; cut into quarters. Combine with raisins, salt, cinnamon and nutmeg in 2-quart saucepan. Add enough water just to cover. Bring to a boil. Simmer for 8 to 10 minutes or until apples are tender. Turn off heat. Let stand until cool. Spoon into serving dish. Chill until serving time. May garnish with whipped topping and heart-shaped cinnamon candies.

Betty F. Lyon, Winston-Salem

APRICOT MARSHMALLOW DESSERT

1 tablespoon
   unflavored gelatin
½ cup cold water
1   20-ounce can
   apricots
20 marshmallows

1   8-ounce can
   crushed pineapple
1 envelope whipped
   topping mix
½ cup flaked coconut

Soften gelatin in cold water. Mash apricots in bowl. Place apricots and juice in saucepan. Add marshmallows and pineapple. Cook over low heat until marshmallows are melted, stirring frequently. Add gelatin; stir until dissolved. Chill until partially set. Prepared whipped topping using package directions. Stir in coconut. Fold into chilled mixture. Chill until serving time. Spoon into individual dessert dishes.

Mary Jane Daleiden, Greensboro

BANANA CREAM DREAM

Yield:
15 servings
Utensil:
baking dish
Approx Per Serving:
Cal 495
Prot 8 g
Carbo 50 g
Fiber 2 g
T Fat 31 g
Chol 25 mg
Sod 281 mg

Dietary Exchanges:
Milk 1/2
Vegetable 0
Fruit 1/2
Bread/Starch 1
Meat 0; Fat 7 1/2

1/2 cup margarine, softened
1 cup flour
1/2 cup chopped pecans
1 cup sifted confectioners' sugar
8 ounces cream cheese, softened
8 ounces whipped topping
1 3-ounce can flaked coconut
2 4-ounce packages vanilla instant pudding mix
3 cups cold milk
3 bananas, sliced
4 ounces whipped topping
1/2 cup chopped pecans

Cut margarine into flour in bowl until crumbly. Stir in 1/2 cup pecans. Press into 9x13-inch baking dish. Bake at 350 degrees for 20 minutes. Cream confectioners' sugar and cream cheese in mixer bowl until light and fluffy. Stir in 8 ounces whipped topping. Spread over cooled crust. Sprinkle with coconut. Combine pudding mix and milk in mixer bowl. Beat at medium speed for 2 minutes. Spread over coconut. Top with banana slices. Spread with 4 ounces whipped topping. Sprinkle with 1/2 cup pecans. Chill for 8 hours.

Peggy Welborn, King

BANANA SPLIT DESSERT

Yield:
24 servings
Utensil:
serving dish
Approx Per Serving:
Cal 312
Prot 4 g
Carbo 32 g
Fiber 1 g
T Fat 20 g
Chol 54 mg
Sod 187 mg

Dietary Exchanges:
Milk 0
Vegetable 0
Fruit 1/2
Bread/Starch 1/2
Meat 0; Fat 4

2 cups graham cracker crumbs
1/2 cup melted butter
2 cups confectioners' sugar
2 eggs
1 cup butter, softened
5 bananas, sliced
1 20-ounce can crushed pineapple, drained
12 ounces whipped topping
1 cup chopped walnuts

Combine crumbs and melted butter in bowl; mix well. Pat into 9x13-inch serving dish. Combine confectioners' sugar, eggs and softened butter in mixer bowl. Beat at high speed for 15 minutes; do not underbeat. Spread over crumb mixture. Top with banana slices. Cover with pineapple. Spread with whipped topping. Sprinkle with walnuts. Chill for 3 hours. Cut into squares.

Pat L. Burke, Burlington

BLUEBERRY DELIGHT

1 cup self-rising flour
1 cup finely chopped
  walnuts
½ cup margarine,
  softened
¼ cup packed light
  brown sugar

8 ounces cream cheese,
  softened
1 cup sugar
8 ounces whipped
  topping
1 16-ounce can
  blueberry pie filling

Combine flour, walnuts, margarine and brown sugar in bowl; mix well. Shape into soft ball. Pat into 9x13-inch baking dish; spread to edges. Bake at 375 degrees for 20 minutes or until lightly browned. Combine cream cheese and sugar in bowl; mix well. Stir in whipped topping. Spread over cooled crust. Top with pie filling. Chill for 10 hours. Cut into 2-inch squares.

Ken Gonzalez, Graham

BLUEBERRY NUT CRUNCH

1 20-ounce can
  crushed pineapple
2 cups blueberries
¾ cup sugar
1 2-layer package
  yellow cake mix

½ cup melted butter
1 cup chopped pecans
¼ cup sugar

Pour pineapple with juice into lightly greased 9x13-inch baking dish. Arrange blueberries over pineapple. Sprinkle with ¾ cup sugar. Spread cake mix over all. Drizzle with melted butter. Top with pecans. Sprinkle with remaining ¼ cup sugar. Bake at 350 degrees for 25 minutes. Make slice to bottom of pan to allow juices to rise. Return to oven. Bake for 15 minutes longer.

Lou Bullard, Winston-Salem

STRAWBERRY COBBLER

1/2 cup margarine
1 cup sugar
1 cup self-rising flour

1 cup milk
1 quart fresh or frozen
  strawberries

Melt margarine in deep baking dish. Add sugar, flour, milk and strawberries; mix well. Bake at 325 degrees for 1 hour or until golden brown.

Ruby Hudspeth, Yadkinville

YANKEE COBBLER

1/2 cup margarine
1 cup sugar
11/4 teaspoons baking
  powder

1/8 teaspoon salt
1 cup flour
3/4 cup milk
2 cups cherries

Melt margarine in 9x13-inch baking dish. Combine sugar, baking powder, salt, flour and milk in bowl; mix well. Pour over melted margarine; do not stir. Spoon in cherries. Bake at 350 degrees for 1 hour.

Mary Pickett, Winston-Salem

CHEESECAKE

Yield:
12 servings
Utensil:
springform pan
Approx Per
Serving:
Cal 407
Prot 7 g
Carbo 33 g
Fiber 1 g
T Fat 28 g
Chol 138 mg
Sod 281 mg

Dietary
Exchanges:
Milk 0
Vegetable 0
Fruit 0
Bread/Starch 1
Meat 1/2; Fat 6 1/2

1 1/4 cups graham cracker crumbs
1/4 cup melted butter
1/4 cup sugar
16 ounces cream cheese, softened
1/2 cup sugar
3 eggs
3/4 teaspoon vanilla extract
2 cups sour cream
1 teaspoon vanilla extract
1/4 cup sugar

Combine cracker crumbs, melted butter and 1/4 cup sugar in bowl; mix until moistened. Press to within 1 inch of top of greased springform pan. Chill until needed. Combine cream cheese, 1/2 cup sugar, eggs and 3/4 teaspoon vanilla in mixer bowl. Beat for 3 minutes. Spread over chilled crumb mixture. Bake at 375 degrees for 20 minutes. Let stand for 15 minutes. Combine sour cream, remaining 1 teaspoon vanilla and 1/4 cup sugar in bowl; mix by hand. Pour over cooled filling. Bake at 450 degrees for 10 minutes. Let stand for 6 hours. Chill until serving time.

Dorothy J. Faircloth, Clemmons

CHOCOLATE CHEESECAKE

Yield:
12 servings
Utensil:
springform pan
Approx Per
Serving:
Cal 210
Prot 8 g
Carbo 15 g
Fiber 1 g
T Fat 14 g
Chol 65 mg
Sod 154 mg

Dietary
Exchanges:
Milk 0
Vegetable 0
Fruit 0
Bread/Starch 1/2
Meat 1/2; Fat 3

15 ounces low-fat ricotta cheese
12 ounces cream cheese, softened
1 egg
3 egg whites
1 cup unsweetened apple juice concentrate
3 tablespoons baking cocoa
1 tablespoon cornstarch
1 tablespoon sugar
1 teaspoon vanilla extract
2 teaspoons baking cocoa

Grease bottom and side of 9-inch springform pan lightly. Wrap outside of pan with aluminum foil. Combine first 9 ingredients in blender container. Make 2 batches if necessary. Process until smooth. Spoon into prepared pan. Place on baking sheet. Bake at 350 degrees for 45 minutes. Turn off oven. Let stand with door closed for 1 hour. Chill until serving time. Let stand for 10 minutes. Sprinkle with remaining 2 teaspoons cocoa. Loosen and unmold cheesecake. Slice with knife dipped in hot water.

Mary Allison, Hurdle Mills

MINT-CHOCOLATE CHIP CHEESECAKE

Yield:
12 servings
Utensil:
springform pan
Approx Per Serving:
Cal 485
Prot 10 g
Carbo 37 g
Fiber <1 g
T Fat 34 g
Chol 143 mg
Sod 341 mg

Dietary Exchanges:
Milk 1
Vegetable 0
Fruit 0
Bread/Starch 1
Meat 1/2; Fat 8

1½ cups fine Hydrox cookie crumbs
2 tablespoons melted margarine
24 ounces cream cheese, softened
1 14-ounce can sweetened condensed milk
3 eggs
2 teaspoons vanilla extract
½ cup mint chocolate chips
1 teaspoon flour
½ cup mint chocolate chips

Mix crumbs and melted margarine in bowl. Press onto bottom of 9-inch springform pan. Beat cream cheese in mixer bowl until light and fluffy. Add condensed milk gradually, beating until smooth. Beat in eggs and vanilla. Toss ½ cup chocolate chips with flour. Stir into batter. Spoon into prepared pan. Top with ½ cup chocolate chips. Bake at 300 degrees for 55 minutes or until center is set. Let stand until cool. Chill until serving time.

Juanita Stone, Graham

MINI CHEESECAKES

Yield:
24 servings
Utensil:
muffin pan
Approx Per Serving:
Cal 296
Prot 6 g
Carbo 31 g
Fiber <1 g
T Fat 17 g
Chol 73 mg
Sod 247 mg

Dietary Exchanges:
Milk 1/2
Vegetable 0
Fruit 1
Bread/Starch 1
Meat 0; Fat 3½

1½ cups graham cracker crumbs
¼ cup sugar
¼ cup melted margarine
24 ounces cream cheese, softened
1 14-ounce can sweetened condensed milk
3 eggs
2 teaspoons vanilla extract
1 21-ounce can cherry pie filling, chilled

Mix crumbs, sugar and margarine in bowl. Press into lightly greased muffin cups. Beat cream cheese in mixer bowl until light and fluffy. Add condensed milk gradually, beating until smooth. Beat in eggs and vanilla. Spoon into prepared muffin cups. Bake at 300 degrees for 20 minutes or until set. Let stand until cool. Chill until serving time. Top with pie filling. May add 1 cup melted semisweet chocolate chips to batter.

Mary Allison, Hurdle Mills

PETITE CHERRY CHEESECAKES

24 vanilla wafers
16 ounces cream
 cheese, softened
2 eggs
1/4 cup lemon juice

1 tablespoon vanilla
 extract
3/4 cup sugar
1 21-ounce can cherry
 pie filling

Place 1 vanilla wafer in each paper-lined muffin cup. Combine cream cheese, eggs, lemon juice, vanilla and sugar in bowl; mix well. Spoon onto vanilla wafers. Bake at 350 degrees for 15 to 20 minutes or until set. Let stand until cool. Top with pie filling.

Vicki Strickland, Greensboro

CHERRY YUM-YUM

3 cups graham cracker
 crumbs
3/4 cup melted
 margarine
8 ounces cream cheese,
 softened

3/4 cup sugar
1 cup cold milk
2 envelopes whipped
 topping mix
2 21-ounce cans
 cherry pie filling

Combine crumbs and melted margarine in bowl; mix well. Spread half the mixture in 9x13-inch serving dish. Beat cream cheese and sugar in mixer bowl until light and fluffy. Add milk and whipped topping mix. Beat until stiff. Spoon into prepared dish. Spread with pie filling. Top with remaining crumb mixture. Chill for 24 hours.

Sarah L. Finley, Graham

DUMP CAKE

1 2-layer package yellow cake mix
1 8-ounce can crushed pineapple
1 21-ounce can cherry pie filling
1 cup chopped pecans
1 cup coconut
3/4 cup melted margarine

Layer cake mix, pineapple and pie filling in 9x13-inch baking dish. Sprinkle with pecans and coconut. Pour melted margarine over all. Bake at 350 degrees for 30 to 40 minutes or until golden brown.

Dot Fesperman, Winston-Salem

CHOCOLATE DREAM DESSERT

1 cup flour
1/2 cup margarine, softened
1 cup chopped pecans
1 cup confectioners' sugar
8 ounces cream cheese, softened
1 cup whipped topping
1 4-ounce package vanilla instant pudding mix
1 4-ounce package chocolate instant pudding mix
2 cups milk
1 8-ounce English toffee candy bar, grated

Combine flour, margarine and pecans in bowl; mix well. Press into 9x13-inch baking dish with fork. Bake at 350 degrees for 20 minutes. Cream confectioners' sugar, cream cheese and whipped topping in mixer bowl until light and fluffy. Spread over cooled crust. Combine pudding mixes and milk in bowl; mix well. Spread over cream cheese mixture. Sprinkle with grated candy. May substitute butterscotch pudding mix for either vanilla or chocolate pudding mix.

Kathy Southern, Winston-Salem

CHOCOLATE ÉCLAIR CAKE

Yield:
15 servings
Utensil:
serving dish
Approx Per
Serving:
Cal 484
Prot 9 g
Carbo 72 g
Fiber 1 g
T Fat 19 g
Chol 8 mg
Sod 415 mg

Dietary
Exchanges:
Milk 1/2
Vegetable 0
Fruit 0
Bread/Starch 2
Meat 0; Fat 3

1 16-ounce package graham crackers
2 4-ounce packages vanilla instant pudding mix
3 cups milk
16 ounces whipped topping
1 16-ounce can chocolate frosting

Line 9x13-inch serving dish with part of the graham crackers. Combine pudding mix, milk and whipped topping in bowl; mix well. Spread in prepared dish. Frost remaining graham crackers individually and arrange over pudding mixture. Mound any remaining frosting over top.

Ruth B. Settle, Winston-Salem

DOUBLE CHOCOLATE MINT DESSERT

Yield:
15 servings
Utensil:
baking dish
Approx Per
Serving:
Cal 434
Prot 4 g
Carbo 60 g
Fiber 1 g
T Fat 23 g
Chol 73 mg
Sod 261 mg

Dietary
Exchanges:
Milk 0
Vegetable 0
Fruit 0
Bread/Starch 1
Meat 1/2; Fat 4 1/2

1 cup flour
1 cup sugar
1/2 cup margarine, softened
4 eggs
1 1/2 cups chocolate syrup
2 cups confectioners' sugar
1 tablespoon water
1/2 cup margarine, softened
1/2 teaspoon mint extract
3 drops of green food coloring
6 tablespoons margarine
1 cup mint chocolate chips

Combine flour, sugar, 1/2 cup margarine, eggs and chocolate syrup in bowl; mix well. Pour into 9x13-inch baking dish. Bake at 350 degrees for 25 to 30 minutes. Combine confectioners' sugar, water, 1/2 cup margarine, mint extract and food coloring in bowl; mix well. Spread over cooled crust. Chill for 30 minutes. Combine remaining 6 tablespoons margarine and chocolate chips in glass bowl. Microwave on High for 1 to 1 1/2 minutes or until melted, stirring frequently. Spread over chilled layer. Chill for 45 minutes to 1 hour or until firm.

Laurie Tarnowsky, Greensboro

CHOCOLATE HOT FUDGE SYRUP

1 cup butter
5 ounces unsweetened
   chocolate
3 cups confectioners'
   sugar

1 12-ounce can
   evaporated milk

Combine butter and chocolate in saucepan. Cook over low heat until melted, stirring frequently. Add confectioners' sugar and evaporated milk alternately, stirring well. Bring to a boil, stirring constantly. Store in covered container in refrigerator. Serve hot over ice cream, cake or fruit.

Ramona P. Cheek, Graham

DIRT CAKE

2 4-ounce packages
   French vanilla
   instant pudding mix
4 cups milk
8 ounces whipped
   topping
¹/₂ cup confectioners'
   sugar

8 ounces cream cheese,
   softened
¹/₂ cup margarine,
   softened
2 16-ounce packages
   Oreo cookies,
   crushed

Combine pudding mix and milk in bowl; mix well. Fold in whipped topping. Cream confectioners' sugar, cream cheese and margarine in mixer bowl until light and fluffy. Stir into pudding mixture. Alternate layers of cookie crumbs and pudding mixture in plastic flowerpot, ending with crumbs. Insert artificial flowers. Serve with clean plastic trowel.

Dot Fesperman, Winston-Salem

FROZEN FRUIT CUPS

Yield:
18 servings
Utensil:
muffin pan
Approx Per
Serving:
Cal 123
Prot 1 g
Carbo 17 g
Fiber 1 g
T Fat 6 g
Chol 11 mg
Sod 28 mg

Dietary
Exchanges:
Milk 0
Vegetable 0
Fruit 1/2
Bread/Starch 0
Meat 0; Fat 1 1/2

2 cups sour cream
2 tablespoons lemon
  juice
3/4 cup sugar
1/8 teaspoon salt
1 8-ounce can
   crushed pineapple
1/4 cup chopped
  maraschino cherries
3 bananas, peeled,
  chopped
1/4 cup chopped pecans

Combine sour cream, lemon juice, sugar, salt, pineapple with juice, cherries, bananas and pecans in bowl; mix well. Spoon into muffin cups. Freeze until firm. Store in plastic bag.

Sue Loy, Graham

HOMEMADE ICE CREAM

Yield:
32 servings
Utensil:
ice cream freezer
Approx Per
Serving:
Cal 115
Prot 4 g
Carbo 17 g
Fiber 0 g
T Fat 4 g
Chol 39 mg
Sod 55 mg

Dietary
Exchanges:
Milk 1/2
Vegetable 0
Fruit 0
Bread/Starch 0
Meat 0; Fat 1

3 eggs
1 12-ounce can
   evaporated milk
2 cups sugar
10 cups milk
1 tablespoon vanilla
  extract

Combine eggs, evaporated milk and sugar in bowl; mix well. Stir in milk. Pour into ice cream freezer container. Freeze according to manufacturer's instructions. May add favorite fruit.

Zane G. Gerringer, Elon College

OREO ICE CREAM

3 egg yolks
1 14-ounce can sweetened condensed milk
2 cups whipping cream, whipped
4 teaspoons vanilla extract
1 cup Oreo cookie crumbs

Beat egg yolks in large bowl. Stir in condensed milk and whipped cream. Add vanilla and crumbs; mix well. Spoon into 2-quart freezer container. Freeze, covered, for 6 hours or until firm.

Sarah L. Tagert, Greensboro

HOT PORT SAUCE

1 1/2 teaspoons cornstarch
1/4 cup sugar
1/2 cup boiling water
1/2 cup Port
1/4 cup chopped pecans

Combine cornstarch and sugar in saucepan; mix well. Add boiling water. Cook until thickened and clear, stirring constantly. Add half the Port gradually, stirring until smooth. Add remaining Port and pecans; mix well. Cook until heated through; do not boil. Serve hot over vanilla ice cream.

Leonora H. Stoddard, Ponte Vedra Beach, Florida

PINEAPPLE-ORANGE PARFAITS

Yield:
8 servings
Utensil:
8 parfait glasses
Approx Per
Serving:
Cal 212
Prot 3 g
Carbo 25 g
Fiber <1 g
T Fat 12 g
Chol 44 mg
Sod 55 mg

Dietary
Exchanges:
Milk 0
Vegetable 0
Fruit 1/2
Bread/Starch 1
Meat 0; Fat 2 1/2

1 6-ounce can frozen orange juice concentrate, thawed

1/4 cup crushed pineapple
4 cups vanilla ice cream

Combine orange juice concentrate and pineapple in bowl; mix well. Alternate layers of ice cream and pineapple mixture in 8 parfait glasses. Store, covered, in freezer. Remove from freezer a few minutes before serving.

Flora Efland Cheshire, Efland

YUMMY DELICIOUS FROZEN DESSERT

Yield:
15 servings
Utensil:
9x13-inch pan
Approx Per
Serving:
Cal 392
Prot 7 g
Carbo 40 g
Fiber 0 g
T Fat 21 g
Chol 2 mg
Sod 108 mg

Dietary
Exchanges:
Milk 1/2
Vegetable 0
Fruit 0
Bread/Starch 1 1/2
Meat 0; Fat 4

4 8-ounce packages ice cream sandwiches

3/4 cup Kahlua
16 ounces whipped topping

Line 9x13-inch pan with ice cream sandwiches, cutting to fit. Prick with fork. Pour Kahlua over ice cream. Spread with whipped topping. Freeze, covered, until firm. Remove from freezer. Let stand for 15 minutes. Cut into slices.

Deloris L. Peterson, Greensboro

NUTTY FRUIT CASSEROLE

3 cups chopped, peeled tart apples
2 cups fresh cranberries
¾ cup sugar
½ cup margarine
1 cup oats
⅓ cup flour
½ cup packed brown sugar
¾ cup chopped pecans

Combine chopped apples and cranberries in greased 9x13-inch baking dish. Sprinkle with ¾ cup sugar. Melt margarine in saucepan. Add oats, flour and ½ cup brown sugar, stirring well after each addition. Spread over apples and cranberries. Top with pecans. Bake at 350 degrees for 1 hour.

Mrs. C.H. Love, Winston-Salem

FRUIT COMPOTE

1 16-ounce can pineapple chunks
1 11-ounce can mandarin orange slices
1 4-ounce package vanilla instant pudding mix
1 banana, sliced
2 tablespoons maraschino cherries

Drain pineapple and mandarin oranges, reserving juices. Place fruit in compote. Combine reserved juices and pudding mix in bowl; mix well. Pour over fruit. Chill for 4 hours. Fold in bananas and cherries before serving.

Kathleen Oakley

Fruit Dessert

3 bananas, sliced
1 tablespoon lemon
  juice
1 8-ounce can
  pineapple chunks
1 16-ounce can fruit
  cocktail, drained
1 11-ounce can
  mandarin orange
  slices, drained
1 4-ounce package
  lemon instant
  pudding mix

Dip bananas into lemon juice in bowl. Combine with pineapple, fruit cocktail, mandarin oranges and pudding mix in bowl; mix well. Spoon into 9x13-inch serving dish. Chill until serving time. May substitute or add 1 cup maraschino cherries, 1/2 cup raisins, 1/2 cup pecans, 1/2 cup coconut or 1 cup miniature marshmallows.

Jean Jarrett, Thomasville

Fruit Parfait

1 4-ounce package
  vanilla instant
  pudding mix
1/2 cup sour cream
1 1/2 cups milk
1/2 teaspoon almond
  extract
1 21-ounce can cherry
  pie filling

Combine pudding mix, sour cream, milk and almond extract in bowl. Whip for 2 minutes or until well blended. Alternate layers of pudding mixture and pie filling in 4 parfait glasses. Garnish with toasted almonds or whipped cream. Serve with sugar cookies. May substitute favorite pie filling or preserves for cherry pie filling.

Gay King, Advance

FAYE'S FRUIT SAUCE

Yield:
32 servings
Utensil:
saucepan
**Approx Per
Serving:**
Cal 17
Prot <1 g
Carbo 4 g
Fiber <1 g
T Fat <1 g
Chol 9 mg
Sod 3 mg

**Dietary
Exchanges:**
Milk 0
Vegetable 0
Fruit 0
Bread/Starch 0
Meat 0; Fat 0

⅓ cup sugar
¼ cup lemon juice
1 tablespoon flour
1 egg, beaten
1 cup miniature
  marshmallows

Combine sugar, lemon juice, flour, egg and marshmallows in saucepan. Cook over medium heat until thickened, stirring frequently. Cool. Use as dip or spread for chunks of fresh fruit. May roll fruit in finely chopped toasted pecans.

Norma Hall, Mebane

HAWAIIAN PUDDING DESSERT

Yield:
10 servings
Utensil:
9x13-inch dish
**Approx Per
Serving:**
Cal 620
Prot 10 g
Carbo 73 g
Fiber 3 g
T Fat 34 g
Chol 26 mg
Sod 276 mg

**Dietary
Exchanges:**
Milk 1½
Vegetable 0
Fruit 1
Bread/Starch 1
Meat 0; Fat 7½

2 cups vanilla wafer
  crumbs
½ cup melted
  margarine
1 14-ounce can
  sweetened
  condensed milk
⅓ cup lemon juice
4 bananas, sliced
1 15-ounce can
  crushed pineapple
12 ounces whipped
  topping
1 cup coconut
½ cup chopped pecans
1 4-ounce jar
  maraschino cherries

Combine vanilla wafer crumbs and melted margarine in bowl; mix well. Press into 9x13-inch dish. Mix condensed milk and lemon juice together in bowl. Layer bananas, condensed milk mixture, crushed pineapple, whipped topping, coconut and pecans over crumb crust. Garnish with maraschino cherries.

Dot Fesperman, Winston-Salem

IDIOT'S DELIGHT

Yield:
12 servings
Utensil:
parfait glasses
**Approx Per
Serving:**
Cal 301
Prot 3 g
Carbo 46 g
Fiber 2 g
T Fat 14 g
Chol 27 mg
Sod 53 mg

**Dietary
Exchanges:**
Milk 0
Vegetable 0
Fruit 1
Bread/Starch 1
Meat 0; Fat 3½

1 3-ounce package
   strawberry gelatin
1 3-ounce package
   orange gelatin
1 8-ounce can
   crushed pineapple
Sections of 2 oranges

2 tart apples, finely
   chopped
1 cup sugar
3 bananas, chopped
1 cup chopped pecans
1 cup whipping cream,
   whipped

Prepare strawberry gelatin and orange gelatin using package directions. Pour each into shallow round pan. Chill overnight. Combine pineapple, oranges, apples and sugar in large bowl; mix well. Chill for 24 hours. Drain fruit 1 hour before serving. Cut gelatin into cubes. Add gelatin cubes, bananas and pecans to fruit mixture; mix well. Fold in whipped cream. Spoon into parfait glasses. Chill until serving time.

Meg Webster, Winston-Salem

COCONUT AND RAISIN IGLOOS

Yield:
48 servings
Utensil:
9x13-inch dish
**Approx Per
Serving:**
Cal 235
Prot 3 g
Carbo 28 g
Fiber 1 g
T Fat 13 g
Chol 5 mg
Sod 149 mg

**Dietary
Exchanges:**
Milk 0
Vegetable 0
Fruit 0
Bread/Starch 1
Meat 0; Fat 3

½ cup butter
1 cup sugar
1 cup ground raisins
1 16-ounce can
   crushed pineapple,
   drained
1 cup chopped pecans
3 12-ounce packages
   butter cookies

12 ounces whipped
   topping
1 12-ounce package
   coconut
1 8-ounce jar
   maraschino cherries

Cream butter and sugar in mixer bowl until light and fluffy. Stir in raisins, pineapple and pecans. Arrange cookies in stacks of 3, spreading mixture between layers. Place in 9x13-inch dish. Chill for 4 hours to overnight to soften. Spread each igloo with whipped topping just before serving; sprinkle with coconut. Top each with maraschino cherry.

Patsye Forbes, Graham

DATE IGLOOS

Yield:
15 servings
Utensil:
9x13-inch dish
**Approx Per
Serving:**
Cal 328
Prot 6 g
Carbo 36 g
Fiber 1 g
T Fat 19 g
Chol 2 mg
Sod 161 mg

**Dietary
Exchanges:**
Milk 1/2
Vegetable 0
Fruit 1/2
Bread/Starch 1 1/2
Meat 0; Fat 5

1/4 cup melted margarine
1 16-ounces can crushed pineapple, drained
4 ounces chopped dates
1/2 cup chopped pecans
45 butter-flavored cookies
16 ounces whipped topping
1 4-ounce jar maraschino cherries

Combine margarine, pineapple, dates and pecans in bowl; mix well. Arrange cookies in stacks of 3, spreading date mixture between cookies. Place in 9x13-inch dish. Chill overnight. Cover each igloo with whipped topping just before serving; top with cherry.

Angela White, Greensboro

LEMON BISQUE

Yield:
10 servings
Utensil:
10x13-inch dish
**Approx Per
Serving:**
Cal 159
Prot 4 g
Carbo 29 g
Fiber <1 g
T Fat 3 g
Chol 10 mg
Sod 141 mg

**Dietary
Exchanges:**
Milk 1/2
Vegetable 0
Fruit 0
Bread/Starch 1
Meat 0; Fat 1/2

1 3-ounce package lime or lemon gelatin
1 cup boiling water
1/8 teaspoon salt
Grated rind and juice of 2 lemons
1/2 cup sugar
1 12-ounce can evaporated milk, chilled
16 graham crackers, crushed

Dissolve gelatin in boiling water in bowl. Add salt, lemon rind, lemon juice and sugar; mix well. Chill until partially congealed. Beat evaporated milk in mixer bowl until stiff. Add partially congealed gelatin mixture; beat until well blended. Line 10x13-inch dish with foil. Sprinkle half the graham cracker crumbs into dish. Pour gelatin mixture over crumbs; top with remaining crumbs. Chill for 6 hours or longer before serving. Keeps well in refrigerator.

Minta Coeyman, Greensboro

LEMON FLUFF

Yield:
8 servings
Utensil:
baking dish
**Approx Per
Serving:**
Cal 719
Prot 15 g
Carbo 70 g
Fiber 1 g
T Fat 44 g
Chol 46 mg
Sod 410 mg

**Dietary
Exchanges:**
Milk 1/2
Vegetable 0
Fruit 0
Bread/Starch 2
Meat 0; Fat 10

1 cup flour
1/2 cup margarine,
  softened
1/2 cup chopped pecans
1 tablespoon sugar
8 ounces cream cheese,
  softened
1 cup confectioners'
  sugar
1 cup whipped topping
1 6-ounce package
  lemon instant
  pudding mix
3 cups milk
1 1/2 cups whipped
  topping
1/4 cup chopped pecans

Mix flour and margarine in bowl. Add 1/2 cup pecans and sugar; mix well. Press into 12x12-inch baking dish. Bake at 300 degrees for 15 minutes or until light brown. Cool. Combine cream cheese, confectioners' sugar and 1 cup whipped topping in bowl; mix well. Spread over cooled crust. Combine lemon pudding mix and milk in bowl; mix well. Spread over cream cheese layer. Top with remaining 1 1/2 cups whipped topping; sprinkle with remaining 1/4 cup pecans. Chill for several hours.

Mrs. Carlton Tuttle, Germanton

PASTEL MINT REFRIGERATOR DESSERT

Yield:
6 servings
Utensil:
9x12-inch dish
**Approx Per
Serving:**
Cal 668
Prot 5 g
Carbo 72 g
Fiber 0 g
T Fat 42 g
Chol 109 mg
Sod 412 mg

**Dietary
Exchanges:**
Milk 0
Vegetable 0
Fruit 0
Bread/Starch 3 1/2
Meat 0; Fat 9

32 Hydrox cookies,
  crushed
1 cup crushed pastel
  after dinner mints
2 cups whipping
  cream, whipped
2 cups miniature
  marshmallows

Spread half the cookie crumbs in 9x12-inch dish. Combine mints, whipped cream and marshmallows in bowl. Spread over cookie layer; top with remaining cookie crumbs. Chill for 2 days before serving.

Ellen M. Mercier, Greensboro

MOLASSES CREAM SOUFFLÉ

2 envelopes
  unflavored gelatin
2 cups cold water
1 1/2 cups milk
1 cup sugar
2 tablespoons instant
  coffee

1/2 cup molasses
4 egg yolks, beaten
4 egg whites
2 teaspoons vanilla
  extract
1 cup whipping cream,
  whipped

Soften gelatin in cold water. Combine with milk, 3/4 cup sugar, coffee granules and molasses in double boiler. Heat until gelatin is dissolved, stirring frequently. Stir a small amount of hot mixture into egg yolks; stir eggs into hot mixture. Cook for 15 minutes or until thickened, stirring frequently. Chill until partially congealed, stirring occasionally. Add foil collar to top of large soufflé dish. Beat egg whites in bowl until soft peaks form. Add remaining 1/4 cup sugar and vanilla gradually, beating until stiff peaks form. Fold whipped cream and stiffy beaten egg whites into gelatin mixture. Spoon into soufflé dish.

Gale Owens, Greensboro

DELICIOUS OATMEAL BAKE

1 cup raw cashews
1 quart water
1/4 teaspoon salt
6 dates
3/4 cup chopped pecans
3 cups chopped
  unsweetened peaches

3 cups oats
1/2 cup unsweetened
  coconut
1 teaspoon salt
1 teaspoon vanilla
  extract

Purée cashews, 2 cups water, 1/4 teaspoon salt and dates in blender. Pour into container with cover. Add remaining water; cover. Shake well before using. Combine pecans, peaches, oats, coconut, 1 teaspoon salt, vanilla and 3 1/2 cups cashew mixture in bowl; mix well. Pour into casserole. Bake at 375 degrees for 40 minutes or until top is golden brown.

Nutritional information includes entire amount of cashew mixture.

Kathleen S. Yax, Mebane

PEACH CRISP

Yield:
6 servings
Utensil:
baking dish
Approx Per Serving:
Cal 167
Prot 2 g
Carbo 37 g
Fiber 2 g
T Fat 2 g
Chol 0 mg
Sod 70 mg

Dietary Exchanges:
Milk 0
Vegetable 0
Fruit 1½
Bread/Starch 1
Meat 0; Fat 0

½ cup unsweetened peach juice
⅓ cup chopped dates
½ teaspoon coriander
½ banana, chopped

4 cups drained unsweetened peach slices
1 cup granola

Combine peach juice, dates, coriander, banana and peach slices in bowl; mix well. Pour into 9x13-inch baking dish. Bake at 350 degrees for 30 minutes. Sprinkle with granola just before serving.

Kathleen S. Yax, Mebane

LAYERED PEACH DELIGHT

Yield:
6 servings
Utensil:
baking dish
Approx Per Serving:
Cal 1226
Prot 11 g
Carbo 152 g
Fiber 4 g
T Fat 67 g
Chol 41 mg
Sod 960 mg

Dietary Exchanges:
Milk ½
Vegetable 0
Fruit 1
Bread/Starch 3
Meat 0; Fat 15½

2 cups self-rising flour
1 cup margarine, softened
1 cup chopped pecans
8 ounces cream cheese, softened
8 ounces whipped topping

2½ cups confectioners' sugar
4 cups fresh peach slices
¼ cup peach gelatin
¼ cup all-purpose flour
1 cup sugar
1 cup water

Combine 2 cups self-rising flour and margarine in mixer bowl; mix well. Add pecans; mix well. Press into 9x13-inch baking dish. Bake at 350 degrees for 20 minutes. Cool. Combine cream cheese, whipped topping and confectioners' sugar in bowl. Spread over cooled crust. Arrange peach slices over top. Chill in refrigerator. Combine peach gelatin, ¼ cup all-purpose flour and sugar in saucepan; mix well. Add water; mix well. Cook over medium heat until thickened, stirring constantly. Cool. Spread over peaches. Chill until serving time.

Doris Cope

PINEAPPLE REFRIGERATOR DESSERT

1 cup milk
1/3 cup sugar
2 teaspoons flour
1/8 teaspoon salt
4 egg yolks, beaten
1 cup confectioners'
  sugar
1/2 cup margarine,
  softened

1 16-ounce can
  crushed pineapple,
  drained
4 egg whites, stiffly
  beaten
40 vanilla wafers
1 cup whipping cream,
  whipped

Scald milk in saucepan. Beat sugar, flour, salt and egg yolks. Stir in half the hot milk; stir mixture into hot milk. Cook until mixture is thickened and coats a spoon, stirring constantly. Cool. Cream confectioners' sugar and margarine in mixer bowl until light and fluffy. Add pineapple and cooled custard; mix well. Fold in egg whites. Line bottom of 5x9-inch dish with vanilla wafers. Layer custard mixture and remaining vanilla wafers 1/3 at a time in prepared dish. Chill overnight. Serve with whipped cream.

Vi Munt, Winston-Salem

CREAM CHEESE PINEAPPLE DESSERT

1 1/2 cups graham
  cracker crumbs,
  toasted
6 tablespoons melted
  margarine
1 14-ounce can
  sweetened
  condensed milk

8 ounces cream cheese,
  softened
1/4 cup lemon juice
8 ounces whipped
  topping
1 16-ounce can
  crushed pineapple,
  drained

Combine toasted graham cracker crumbs and melted margarine in bowl; mix well. Press 2/3 of the mixture into 9x13-inch dish. Combine condensed milk, cream cheese and lemon juice in bowl; mix well. Add whipped topping; mix well. Fold in pineapple. Pour over graham cracker crumbs in dish. Sprinkle with remaining 1/3 of the crumbs. Chill until serving time.

Carlene Clinton, Pfafftown

BANANA PUDDING

Yield:
6 servings
Utensil:
large dish
Approx Per
Serving:
Cal 896
Prot 10 g
Carbo 122 g
Fiber 3 g
T Fat 44 g
Chol 75 mg
Sod 484 mg

Dietary
Exchanges:
Milk 1
Vegetable 0
Fruit 2
Bread/Starch 4½
Meat 0; Fat 10

1 4-ounce package
   vanilla instant
   pudding mix
2 cups milk
8 ounces sour cream

16 ounces whipped
   topping
1 16-ounce package
   vanilla wafers
6 bananas, sliced

Combine pudding mix and milk in mixer bowl; mix well. Add sour cream and half the whipped topping; mix well. Alternate layers of vanilla wafers, banana slices and pudding in large dish until all are used. Top with remaining whipped topping. Chill until serving time.

Sarah L. Finley, Graham

DELICIOUS BANANA PUDDING

Yield:
8 servings
Utensil:
6x8-inch dish
Approx Per
Serving:
Cal 493
Prot 9 g
Carbo 78 g
Fiber 1 g
T Fat 17 g
Chol 30 mg
Sod 251 mg

Dietary
Exchanges:
Milk 2
Vegetable 0
Fruit 1
Bread/Starch 1½
Meat 0; Fat 3½

1 14-ounce can
   sweetened
   condensed milk
1½ cups cold water
1 4-ounce package
   vanilla instant
   pudding mix

2 cups whipped
   topping
3 medium bananas,
   sliced
½ cup lemon juice
36 vanilla wafers

Combine condensed milk, cold water and pudding mix in mixer bowl; mix well. Chill in freezer for 5 minutes. Fold in whipped topping. Combine bananas and lemon juice in bowl, stirring gently to coat bananas; drain. Alternate layers of 1 cup pudding, vanilla wafers and ⅓ of the banana slices in 6x8-inch dish until all are used, ending with pudding. Chill until serving time.

Mildred M. Crowder, Burlington

GLORIA'S BANANA PUDDING

2 cups vanilla instant pudding
1 cup milk
½ cup whipped cream
1 cup sour cream
4 medium bananas, sliced

1 10-ounce package vanilla wafers
3 egg whites
1½ cups sugar

Combine vanilla pudding and milk in bowl; mix well. Add whipped cream and sour cream; mix well. Alternate layers of pudding, bananas and vanilla wafers in 9x13-inch baking dish. Beat egg whites in bowl until soft peaks form. Add sugar gradually, beating until stiff peaks form. Spread over banana pudding. Bake at 350 degrees for 5 minutes or until brown.

Gloria Stinson, Winston-Salem

LOW-CALORIE BANANA PUDDING

1 6-ounce package sugar-free vanilla instant pudding mix
3½ cups low-fat milk
4 bananas, sliced

1 16-ounce package vanilla wafers
3 egg whites
6 tablespoons sugar

Prepare pudding mix with milk using package directions. Alternate layers of bananas, vanilla wafers and pudding in 3-quart casserole. Beat egg whites in bowl until soft peaks form. Add sugar gradually, beating until stiff peaks form. Spread over layers. Bake at 400 degrees for 10 minutes or until brown. Chill, covered, until serving time.

Bobby Lewis Thompson, Burlington

MAMA'S VERY RICH BANANA PUDDING

2½ cups sugar
½ cup flour
Salt to taste
2 12-ounce cans
   evaporated milk
2 cups milk
5 egg yolks, beaten
1½ teaspoons vanilla
   extract
6 bananas, sliced
1 16-ounce package
   vanilla wafers
5 egg whites
¾ cup sugar
1¼ teaspoons vanilla
   extract

Combine first 5 ingredients in 3-quart saucepan; mix well. Cook over medium low heat until mixture coats a spoon, stirring constantly. Stir a small amount of mixture into egg yolks; stir egg yolks into hot mixture. Cook until thickened, stirring constantly. Stir in 1½ teaspoons vanilla. Cool. Alternate layers of cooled pudding, bananas and vanilla wafers in 9x13-inch baking dish. Beat egg whites in bowl until soft peaks form. Add ¾ cup sugar and 1¼ teaspoons vanilla gradually, beating until stiff. Spread over layers. Bake at 400 degrees for 4 minutes.

Maxine Franklin, Burlington

BEST-EVER CHOCOLATE PUDDING DESSERT

1 3-ounce package
   vanilla instant
   pudding mix
2 cups milk
1 3-ounce package
   chocolate instant
   pudding mix
2 cups milk
1 12-ounce package
   chocolate chip
   cookies
1½ cups milk
8 ounces whipped
   topping
1 1½-ounce bar
   chocolate candy

Prepare vanilla pudding mix with 2 cups milk using package directions. Prepare chocolate pudding mix with 2 cups milk using package directions. Dip cookies in remaining 1½ cups milk 1 at a time, arranging in bottom of 9x13-inch dish. Layer vanilla pudding, half the whipped topping, cookies dipped in milk, chocolate pudding and remaining whipped topping in prepared dish. Shave chocolate candy bar over top. Chill for several hours.

Ina Livingston, Winston-Salem

CRANBERRY PUDDING WITH BUTTER SAUCE

2 cups sifted flour
1 cup sugar
3 teaspoons baking powder
½ teaspoon salt
1 cup milk
3 tablespoons melted butter
2 cups whole fresh cranberries
½ cup butter
1 cup packed brown sugar
¾ cup whipping cream

Sift flour, sugar, baking powder and salt together in mixer bowl. Add milk and 3 tablespoons butter; mix well. Stir in cranberries. Pour into well greased 10-inch baking dish. Bake at 375 degrees for 45 minutes or until firm. Combine remaining ½ cup butter, brown sugar and cream in saucepan. Bring to a rolling boil, stirring frequently. Turn off heat. Cook for 10 minutes, stirring frequently. Serve pudding warm with sauce.

Juanita Walker, Winston-Salem

FRUIT COCKTAIL PUDDING

1 cup flour
1 cup (scant) sugar
1 teaspoon soda
½ teaspoon salt
2 tablespoons oil
1 egg, beaten
1 16-ounce can fruit cocktail, drained
½ cup packed brown sugar
½ cup chopped pecans

Combine flour, sugar, soda and salt in mixer bowl. Add oil and egg; mix well. Stir in fruit cocktail. Pour into well greased baking dish. Sprinkle brown sugar and pecans over top. Bake at 350 degrees for 35 minutes. Serve hot with brandy sauce or cold with whipped cream.

Karen Kjaerbye Bailey

OZARK PUDDING

1 egg
¾ cup sugar
3 tablespoons flour
1¼ teaspoons baking
   powder
1 teaspoon vanilla
   extract
1 cup pecans
1 cup chopped apple
½ cup chopped dates

Beat egg in mixer bowl. Add sugar gradually, beating until smooth. Mix flour and baking powder together. Add to mixture; beat well. Stir in vanilla, pecans, apple and dates. Pour into greased 9x9-inch baking dish. Bake at 350 degrees for 30 minutes or until brown. Pudding will be crunchy and will fall. Serve with ice cream or whipped cream.

Mary H. Harden, Graham

PERSIMMON PUDDING

1½ cups sugar
½ cup butter
4 eggs
1 cup buttermilk
1 cup (or less) flour
⅛ teaspoon soda
1 teaspoon vanilla
   extract
2 cups persimmon
   purée

Combine sugar and butter in mixer bowl. Add eggs and buttermilk; mix well. Add mixture of flour and soda, vanilla and persimmon purée; mix well. Pour into greased 9x9-inch baking dish. Bake at 300 degrees for 1 hour.

Nancy W. Bradley, Greensboro

TASTY PERSIMMON PUDDING

Yield:
12 servings
Utensil:
baking dish
Approx Per Serving:
Cal 539
Prot 10 g
Carbo 110 g
Fiber 1 g
T Fat 9 g
Chol 91 mg
Sod 390 mg

Dietary Exchanges:
Milk 1/2
Vegetable 0
Fruit 2
Bread/Starch 2
Meat 1/2; Fat 1 1/2

3 cups sugar
4 cups flour
2 teaspoons baking powder
1 teaspoon soda
1 teaspoon salt
1/4 cup butter, softened
3 eggs
4 cups persimmon purée
4 1/2 cups milk
Vanilla extract to taste

Combine sugar, flour, baking powder, soda and salt in mixer bowl. Add butter; mix well. Add eggs and persimmon purée; mix well. Stir in milk and vanilla. Pour into greased baking dish. Bake at 325 degrees for 1 hour or until pudding tests done.

Maude Murray, Snow Camp

RICE AND APPLE PUDDING

Yield:
6 servings
Utensil:
baking dish
Approx Per Serving:
Cal 307
Prot 1 g
Carbo 61 g
Fiber 4 g
T Fat 8 g
Chol 20 mg
Sod 164 mg

Dietary Exchanges:
Milk 0
Vegetable 0
Fruit 1 1/2
Bread/Starch 1/2
Meat 0; Fat 1 1/2

6 tart apples
2/3 cup water
1/4 cup butter
1/3 cup sugar
1/4 teaspoon salt
1 1/2 cups cooked rice
1/2 cup orange marmalade

Peel apples; slice. Combine apple slices, water, butter, sugar and salt in saucepan. Simmer over medium heat until apples are tender, stirring occasionally. Layer half the rice, apple slices, marmalade and remaining rice in greased baking dish. Bake at 350 degrees for 15 to 20 minutes or until pudding tests done. Let stand until cold. Unmold onto serving plate. Serve with desired pudding sauce. May substitute apricots or other fruit for apples.

Lillie B. Allison, Burlington

LEMON CUSTARD RICE PUDDING

Yield:
6 servings
Utensil:
baking dish
**Approx Per
Serving:**
Cal 232
Prot 6 g
Carbo 30 g
Fiber 1 g
T Fat 10 g
Chol 117 mg
Sod 120 mg

**Dietary
Exchanges:**
Milk 1/2
Vegetable 0
Fruit 0
Bread/Starch 1/2
Meat 1/2; Fat 2 1/2

1 cup cooked brown rice
2 egg yolks, beaten
1/4 cup packed brown sugar
Grated rind and juice of 1 lemon
2 cups milk, scalded
3 tablespoons melted butter
Salt to taste
2 egg whites
1/4 cup sugar
2 teaspoons lemon juice

Combine rice, egg yolks, brown sugar, rind and juice of 1 lemon, milk, butter and salt in bowl; mix well. Pour into greased baking dish. Bake at 325 degrees for 25 minutes or until thickened. Beat egg whites in bowl until soft peaks form. Add sugar and remaining 2 teaspoons lemon juice gradually, beating until stiff peaks form. Spread over pudding. Bake at 350 degrees for 8 minutes or until brown.

Louise Faulkner

LOW-FAT AND LOW-CALORIE RICE PUDDING

Yield:
6 servings
Utensil:
6 ramekins
**Approx Per
Serving:**
Cal 243
Prot 8 g
Carbo 52 g
Fiber 1 g
T Fat 1 g
Chol 3 mg
Sod 680 mg

**Dietary
Exchanges:**
Milk 1
Vegetable 0
Fruit 1/2
Bread/Starch 2
Meat 0; Fat 0

1 6-ounce package sugar-free vanilla pudding and pie filling mix
4 1/2 cups skim milk
3/4 cup minute rice
1/2 cup raisins
1/4 teaspoon cinnamon

Combine pudding and pie filling mix with skim milk in saucepan; mix well. Add rice, raisins and cinnamon. Bring to a boil over medium heat, stirring constantly. Cook until thickened, stirring constantly. Pour into 6 ramekins. May serve warm or chill for 30 minutes.

Mary Ann Gerhard, Greensboro

Sailor Duff

2 tablespoons butter, softened
1/2 cup sugar
1 teaspoon soda
1/2 teaspoon salt
1 1/2 cups flour
1/2 cup hot water

2 tablespoons molasses
1/2 cup raisins
1 egg white
3/4 cup sugar
1 cup whipping cream, whipped

Cream butter and 1/2 cup sugar in mixer bowl. Mix soda, salt and flour together. Add to creamed mixture; mix well. Add hot water and molasses; mix well. Stir in raisins. Spoon into 6 greased custard cups. Cook in steamer for 15 to 20 minutes or until pudding is firm. Beat egg whites in bowl until soft peaks form. Add 3/4 cup sugar gradually, beating until stiff peaks form. Fold into whipped cream. Unmold pudding onto serving plates. Break into 2 pieces. Spoon whipped cream sauce over warm pudding.

Margaret Schell, Hendersonville

Steamed Suet Pudding

1 cup raisins
3 cups sifted flour
1 teaspoon soda
1 teaspoon cinnamon
1 teaspoon cloves
1 teaspoon salt

1/2 teaspoon grated nutmeg
1 cup ground suet
1 cup sour milk
1 cup molasses

Mix raisins with 1/2 cup flour in bowl. Sift remaining flour, soda, cinnamon, cloves, salt and nutmeg together into mixer bowl. Mix suet, sour milk and molasses in bowl. Add to dry ingredients; mix well. Stir in raisins. Fill greased pudding mold 2/3 full. Steam, covered tightly, for 3 hours. Unmold onto serving plate. Serve with hard sauce.

Lillie B. Allison, Burlington

GRATED SWEET POTATO PUDDING

Yield:
6 servings
Utensil:
baking dish
**Approx Per
Serving:**
Cal 591
Prot 8 g
Carbo 85 g
Fiber 2 g
T Fat 26 g
Chol 143 mg
Sod 311 mg

**Dietary
Exchanges:**
Milk 1/2
Vegetable 0
Fruit 0
Bread/Starch 1 1/2
Meat 1/2; Fat 6

1/2 cup butter
4 cups grated sweet
   potatoes
1 1/2 cups packed
   brown sugar
2 cups milk

1/2 cup chopped pecans
1/2 teaspoon soda
1/2 cup flour
1 teaspoon nutmeg
2 eggs, beaten

Place butter in baking dish. Bake at 325 degrees until butter is melted. Combine sweet potatoes, brown sugar, milk and pecans in mixer bowl; mix well. Mix soda, flour and nutmeg together. Add to sweet potato mixture; mix well. Add melted butter and eggs; mix well. Pour into hot baking dish. Bake at 325 degrees for 40 minutes, stirring crusted edges into pudding 1 time.

Eileen Rindos, Burlington

MOM'S SWEET POTATO PUDDING

Yield:
6 servings
Utensil:
baking dish
**Approx Per
Serving:**
Cal 245
Prot 6 g
Carbo 28 g
Fiber 1 g
T Fat 12 g
Chol 166 mg
Sod 146 mg

**Dietary
Exchanges:**
Milk 1/2
Vegetable 0
Fruit 0
Bread/Starch 1/2
Meat 1/2; Fat 2 1/2

2 medium sweet
   potatoes, peeled,
   grated
3 eggs, beaten
1/2 cup sugar

1 teaspoon vanilla
   extract
1 1/2 cups milk
1/4 cup butter

Combine sweet potatoes, eggs, sugar, vanilla and milk in mixer bowl; mix well. Melt butter in 1-quart baking dish. Add sweet potato mixture; mix well. Bake at 350 degrees for 30 to 45 minutes or until pudding is set and brown.

Ellie Key, Graham

PUMPKIN DESSERT

1 16-ounce can pumpkin
½ teaspoon cinnamon
¼ teaspoon salt
¼ teaspoon ginger
40 large marshmallows
⅓ cup melted butter
20 graham crackers, finely crushed
¼ cup packed brown sugar
1 pint whipping cream, whipped

Combine pumpkin, cinnamon, salt, ginger and marshmallows in double boiler. Cook until marshmallows are melted, stirring frequently. Cool. Combine butter, graham cracker crumbs and brown sugar in bowl; mix well. Press half the mixture into 7x11-inch baking dish. Add whipped cream to cooled pumpkin mixture. Pour over graham cracker crust. Top with remaining graham cracker crumbs. Chill for 8 hours to overnight.

Ellen M. Mercier, Greensboro

RITZ CRACKER DESSERT

4 egg whites
1 cup sugar
1 teaspoon vanilla extract
40 Ritz crackers, crushed
1 cup chopped pecans
1 pint whipping cream, whipped
2 cups miniature marshmallows
½ cup coconut

Beat egg whites in bowl until soft peaks form. Add sugar gradually, beating until stiff peaks form. Add vanilla, cracker crumbs and pecans; mix well. Spoon into greased 9x13-inch baking dish. Bake at 325 degrees for 25 minutes. Cool. Spread whipped cream over cooled dessert. Sprinkle with marshmallows and coconut. Chill until serving time. May store for several days in refrigerator.

Ellen M. Mercier, Greensboro

STRAWBERRY DELIGHT

Yield:
12 servings
Utensil:
9x13-inch dish
**Approx Per
Serving:**
Cal 588
Prot 13 g
Carbo 102 g
Fiber 2 g
T Fat 16 g
Chol 10 mg
Sod 383 mg

**Dietary
Exchanges:**
Milk ½
Vegetable 0
Fruit 1½
Bread/Starch 4
Meat 0; Fat 3

1 package angel food cake mix
1 6-ounce package strawberry gelatin
½ cup boiling water
1 quart sweetened strawberries
1½ cups strawberry juice
1 6-ounce package vanilla instant pudding mix
3 cups milk
16 ounces whipped topping

Prepare angel food cake using package directions. Dissolve gelatin in boiling water in bowl. Chill for 10 to 15 minutes or until partially congealed. Add strawberries with juice. Break half the cooled cake into bite-sized pieces. Place in 9x13-inch dish. Pour gelatin over cake pieces. Prepare pudding with milk using package directions. Break remaining cake into bite-sized pieces. Arrange cake over strawberries. Spoon pudding over layers. Top with whipped topping. Chill until serving time.

Mrs. Coy M. Vance, Raleigh

STRAWBERRY PUDDING DESSERT

Yield:
12 servings
Utensil:
9x13-inch dish
**Approx Per
Serving:**
Cal 654
Prot 11 g
Carbo 99 g
Fiber 2 g
T Fat 25 g
Chol 42 mg
Sod 348 mg

**Dietary
Exchanges:**
Milk ½
Vegetable 0
Fruit 1½
Bread/Starch 3
Meat 0; Fat 5

1 quart strawberries
½ cup sugar
1 3-ounce package strawberry gelatin
2 4-ounce packages vanilla instant pudding mix
3 cups cold milk
1 cup sour cream
16 ounces whipped topping
1 16-ounce package vanilla wafers

Combine strawberries, sugar and gelatin in saucepan. Heat until gelatin is dissolved, stirring constantly. Cool. Combine pudding mix and milk in bowl; mix well. Add sour cream; mix well. Fold ¾ of the whipped topping into pudding. Alternate layers of vanilla wafers, pudding and strawberry mixture in 9x13-inch dish. Top with remaining whipped topping. Garnish additional with strawberries. Chill until serving time.

Kathleen Oakley

STRAWBERRY PIZZA

1 cup self-rising flour
1/4 cup confectioners' sugar
1/2 cup margarine
8 ounces cream cheese, softened
1 14-ounce can sweetened condensed milk
1/3 cup lemon juice
1 teaspoon vanilla extract
2 tablespoons cornstarch
1/2 cup water
1/2 cup sugar
Red food coloring to taste
1 quart strawberries
8 ounces whipped topping

Combine first 3 ingredients in bowl; mix well. Press into 12-inch pizza pan. Bake at 350 degrees for 10 minutes. Cool. Spread mixture of cream cheese, condensed milk, lemon juice and vanilla in bowl over cooled crust. Chill in refrigerator. Combine cornstarch, water and sugar in saucepan; mix well. Cook until thickened, stirring constantly. Add food coloring. Stir in strawberries. Spoon over pizza. Top with whipped topping. Garnish with additional strawberries. Chill until serving time.

Doris D. Burnette, Graham

EASY STRAWBERRY OR CHERRY PIZZA

1 cup sifted flour
10 tablespoons melted margarine
2 tablespoons sugar
1 cup confectioners' sugar
8 ounces cream cheese, softened
1/2 teaspoon vanilla extract
2 cups whipped topping
1 21-ounce can strawberry or cherry pie filling

Combine first 3 ingredients in bowl; mix well. Press into pizza pan. Bake at 350 degrees for 10 minutes. Let stand until cool. Cream confectioners' sugar, cream cheese and vanilla in bowl until light and fluffy. Spread over crust. Top with pie filling.

Ruth L. Brown, Hamptonville

STRAWBERRY SHORTCAKE

Yield:
6 servings
Utensil:
baking pan
Approx Per
Serving:
Cal 493
Prot 6 g
Carbo 77 g
Fiber 3 g
T Fat 19 g
Chol 4 mg
Sod 701 mg

Dietary
Exchanges:
Milk 0
Vegetable 0
Fruit ½
Bread/Starch 2
Meat 0; Fat 4

1 quart fresh
  strawberries
1 cup sugar
2 cups self-rising flour
3 tablespoons sugar

⅓ cup margarine
⅔ cup (about) milk
¼ cup margarine,
  softened

Slice strawberries. Sprinkle with 1 cup sugar. Let stand for 1 hour. Combine flour and 3 tablespoons sugar in bowl. Cut in ⅓ cup margarine until crumbly. Add just enough milk to form soft, puffy, easy to roll dough. Shape dough into ball. Knead on lightly floured surface 20 to 25 times or until smooth. Place dough in ungreased 9-inch round baking pan. Press to fit pan. Bake at 450 degrees for 10 to 12 minutes or until brown. Split shortcake while warm. Spread with remaining ¼ cup margarine. Fill and top with prepared strawberries. Serve with ice cream, whipped topping or whipped cream. May substitute peaches or blueberries for strawberries.

Ruth Kent Eslinger, Winston-Salem

FRUITY YUM-YUM

Yield:
12 servings
Utensil:
9x13-inch dish
Approx Per
Serving:
Cal 612
Prot 6 g
Carbo 83 g
Fiber 1 g
T Fat 30 g
Chol 24 mg
Sod 564 mg

Dietary
Exchanges:
Milk 0
Vegetable 0
Fruit 3½
Bread/Starch 3
Meat 0; Fat 5

2½ cups graham
  cracker crumbs
¾ cup melted
  margarine
1½ cups sugar
1 cup milk

8 ounces cream cheese,
  softened
4 envelopes whipped
  topping mix
2 21-ounce cans
  cherry pie filling

Combine graham cracker crumbs, margarine and ½ cup sugar in bowl; mix well. Spread half the crumb mixture in 9x13-inch dish. Combine milk and cream cheese in mixer bowl; beat well. Add remaining 1 cup sugar and whipped topping mix; mix well. Layer half the cream cheese mixture, all the pie filling, remaining cream cheese mixture and remaining crumb mixture in prepared dish. Chill for several hours before serving.

Beulah T. White, Greensboro

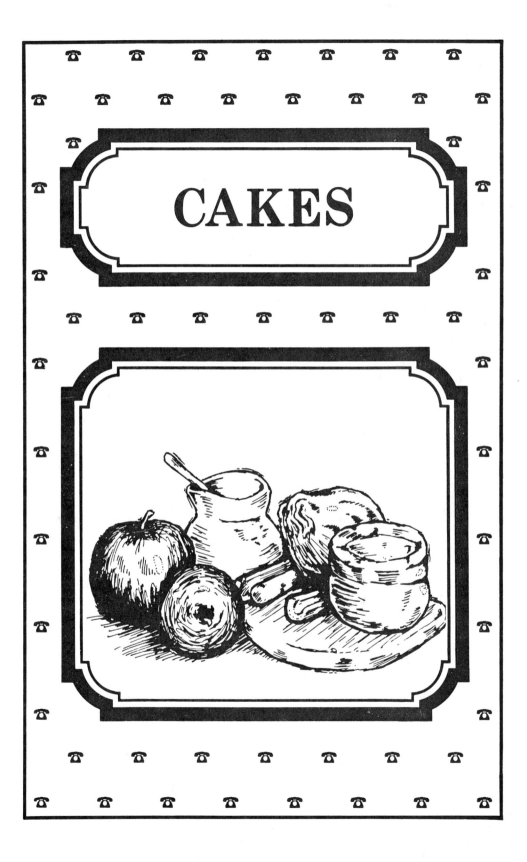

CAKES

FRESH APPLE CAKE

Yield:
16 servings
Utensil:
tube pan
Approx Per
Serving:
Cal 444
Prot 5 g
Carbo 54 g
Fiber 3 g
T Fat 25 g
Chol 51 mg
Sod 128 mg

Dietary
Exchanges:
Milk 0
Vegetable 0
Fruit 1/2
Bread/Starch 1
Meat 0; Fat 5 1/2

2 cups sugar
3 cups flour
1 teaspoon cinnamon
1/2 teaspoon salt
1 teaspoon soda
1 1/4 cups oil
3 eggs, beaten

2 teaspoons vanilla
 extract
3 cups chopped apples
1 cup coconut
1 cup chopped pecans
1 cup raisins

Sift sugar, flour, cinnamon, salt and soda into large bowl; mix well. Stir in mixture of oil, eggs and vanilla. Add apples, coconut, pecans and raisins; mix well. Pour into greased tube pan. Bake at 350 degrees for 1 hour and 30 minutes. Cool in pan for 10 minutes. Invert onto serving plate.

Lillie B. Allison, Burlington

UGLY APPLE CAKE

Yield:
15 servings
Utensil:
cake pan
Approx Per
Serving:
Cal 424
Prot 4 g
Carbo 53 g
Fiber 2 g
T Fat 23 g
Chol 37 mg
Sod 381 mg

Dietary
Exchanges:
Milk 0
Vegetable 0
Fruit 1/2
Bread/Starch 1
Meat 0; Fat 4 1/2

2 cups sugar
3 cups flour
2 teaspoons soda
2 teaspoons salt
2 teaspoons cinnamon
1 1/2 cups oil

2 eggs
2 teaspoons vanilla
 extract
4 cups chopped apples
1/2 cup raisins

Combine sugar, flour, soda, salt and cinnamon in bowl; mix well. Stir in oil, eggs and vanilla. Add apples and raisins; mix well. Pour into greased 9x13-inch cake pan. Bake at 325 degrees for 1 hour and 30 minutes.

Norma Hauser, Winston-Salem

APPLE TORTE

Yield:
8 servings
Utensil:
cake pan
Approx Per
Serving:
Cal 405
Prot 4 g
Carbo 54 g
Fiber 3 g
T Fat 21 g
Chol 34 mg
Sod 176 mg

Dietary
Exchanges:
Milk 0
Vegetable 0
Fruit 1
Bread/Starch 1
Meat 0; Fat 5

1 cup sugar
1/2 cup shortening
1 egg
1 1/4 cups flour
1 teaspoon cinnamon
1 teaspoon nutmeg
1 teaspoon soda
1/4 teaspoon salt
4 cups thinly sliced
apples
1/2 cup chopped pecans
1/4 cup raisins
1 cup whipped cream

Cream sugar and shortening in mixer bowl until light and fluffy. Add egg; beat well. Stir in flour, cinnamon, nutmeg, soda and salt. Add apples, pecans and raisins; mix well. Pour into greased 9-inch square cake pan. Bake at 350 degrees for 45 minutes. Serve warm topped with whipped cream. May substitute orange glaze for whipped cream.

Connie Kelly, Mocksville

APPLE-BUTTERSCOTCH CAKE

Yield:
20 servings
Utensil:
cake pan
Approx Per
Serving:
Cal 303
Prot 4 g
Carbo 32 g
Fiber 2 g
T Fat 19 g
Chol 41 mg
Sod 130 mg

Dietary
Exchanges:
Milk 0
Vegetable 0
Fruit 0
Bread/Starch 1 1/2
Meat 0; Fat 4

1 cup oil
3 eggs
1 cup sugar
3 cups flour
1 teaspoon salt
1/2 teaspoon soda
2 teaspoons vanilla
extract
1 1/2 teaspoons
cinnamon
3 cups chopped
Granny Smith
apples
1 cup chopped pecans
6 ounces butterscotch
morsels

Combine oil, eggs and sugar in bowl; mix well. Stir in flour, salt, soda, vanilla and cinnamon. Add apples and pecans; mix well. Pour into lightly greased and floured 9x13-inch cake pan. Sprinkle with butterscotch morsels. Bake at 350 degrees for 1 hour.

Boyd S. Blackburn, Kernersville

APPLE-WALNUT CAKE

2 cups flour
1 teaspoon cinnamon
1 teaspoon nutmeg
½ teaspoon cloves
1 teaspoon salt
2 teaspoons soda
2 cups sugar
½ cup oil
2 eggs
1 21-ounce can apple
   pie filling
1½ teaspoons vanilla
   extract
1 cup chopped black
   walnuts
1 cup butter, softened
8 ounces cream cheese,
   softened
1 teaspoon vanilla
   extract
1 1-pound package
   confectioners' sugar

Sift dry ingredients together. Mix sugar and oil in large bowl. Beat in eggs. Stir in flour mixture. Add pie filling and 1½ teaspoons vanilla; mix well. Stir in walnuts. Pour into greased tube pan. Bake at 350 degrees for 55 minutes or until cake tests done. Cool in pan for 10 minutes. Invert onto serving plate. Cream next 3 ingredients in mixer bowl until light and fluffy. Stir in confectioners' sugar gradually until of spreading consistency. Spread over cooled cake.

Jane Vannoy, Winston-Salem

BANANA-WALNUT CAKE

2¼ cups flour
1⅔ cups sugar
1¼ teaspoons baking
   powder
1 teaspoon salt
1 teaspoon soda
1¼ cups mashed ripe
   bananas
⅔ cup margarine,
   softened
⅔ cup buttermilk
2 eggs
⅔ cup chopped walnuts
⅓ cup margarine,
   softened
4 cups confectioners'
   sugar
¼ teaspoon salt
2 to 3 tablespoons milk
1 teaspoon vanilla extract

Beat first 8 ingredients at low speed in mixer bowl just until moistened. Beat at medium speed for 2 minutes. Add eggs. Beat for 2 minutes. Stir in walnuts. Pour into lightly greased and floured 9x13-inch cake pan. Bake at 350 degrees for 35 minutes or until cake tests done. Cream ⅓ cup margarine in mixer bowl until light and fluffy. Beat in confectioners' sugar and salt. Add milk gradually, stirring until of spreading consistency. Beat in vanilla. Spread over cooled cake.

Ruth Kent Eslinger, Winston-Salem

GLAZED BANANA CAKE

2 cups flour
1 tablespoon baking powder
1/2 teaspoon salt
1/4 cup oil
2 eggs
1 teaspoon vanilla extract
1/2 cup skim milk
1 cup mashed ripe bananas
1/4 teaspoon cinnamon
16 envelopes artificial sweetener
3 tablespoons boiling water
Yogurt Cream Cheese Frosting

Sift flour, baking powder and salt together in bowl. Mix next 4 ingredients in bowl. Stir in bananas. Add to flour mixture, stirring just until moistened. Pour into 8-inch round cake pans sprayed with nonstick cooking spray. Bake at 350 degrees for 20 minutes or until layers test done. Pierce layers at 1-inch intervals with kitchen fork. Combine cinnamon and artificial sweetener in bowl; mix well. Add boiling water gradually, stirring until of glaze consistency. Drizzle over warm layers. Cool in pans for 10 minutes. Remove to wire racks to cool completely. Frost with Yogurt Cream Cheese Frosting.

Yogurt Cream Cheese Frosting

8 ounces low-calorie cream cheese, softened
1/2 cup plain low-fat yogurt
14 envelopes artificial sweetener
1 teaspoon grated lemon rind
1 teaspoon vanilla extract

Blend cream cheese and yogurt in bowl. Stir in artificial sweetener, lemon rind and vanilla. Chill slightly. May use on banana, carrot, lemon or spice cake.

Janet Mills, Winston-Salem

BLACKBERRY WINE CAKE

Yield:
16 servings
Utensil:
bundt pan
Approx Per
Serving:
Cal 405
Prot 4 g
Carbo 55 g
Fiber 0 g
T Fat 18 g
Chol 69 mg
Sod 263 mg

Dietary
Exchanges:
Milk 0
Vegetable 0
Fruit 0
Bread/Starch 2½
Meat ½; Fat 3½

1 2-layer package yellow cake mix
4 eggs
1 cup oil
1 cup blackberry wine
1 6-ounce package blackberry gelatin
2½ cups confectioners' sugar
½ cup blackberry wine

Combine cake mix, eggs, oil, 1 cup wine and gelatin in bowl; mix well. Pour into greased bundt pan. Bake at 350 degrees for 45 minutes. Combine confectioners' sugar and remaining ½ cup wine in bowl; mix well. Drizzle a small amount over warm cake in pan. Cool in pan for several minutes. Invert onto serving plate. Drizzle with remaining glaze.

Ree Hayes, Hillsborough

BROWN SUGAR CAKE

Yield:
16 servings
Utensil:
tube pan
Approx Per
Serving:
Cal 450
Prot 5 g
Carbo 53 g
Fiber 1 g
T Fat 25 g
Chol 118 mg
Sod 226 mg

Dietary
Exchanges:
Milk 0
Vegetable 0
Fruit 0
Bread/Starch 1
Meat ½; Fat 5½

1 cup butter, softened
½ cup shortening
1 1-pound package light brown sugar
½ cup sugar
5 eggs
3 cups flour
½ teaspoon salt
½ teaspoon baking powder
1 cup milk
1 teaspoon vanilla extract
1 cup chopped pecans

Cream butter, shortening and brown sugar in mixer bowl until light and fluffy. Add sugar; mix well. Add eggs 1 at a time, beating well after each addition. Beat for 3 minutes longer. Sift flour, salt and baking powder together. Add to creamed mixture alternately with milk. Stir in vanilla and pecans. Pour into greased tube pan. Bake at 325 degrees for 1 hour and 30 minutes. Cool in pan for 10 minutes. Invert onto serving plate.

Mary Lou Ziglar, Winston-Salem

Yield:
12 servings
Utensil:
cake pans
*Approx Per
Serving:*
Cal 773
Prot 13 g
Carbo 95 g
Fiber 1 g
T Fat 40 g
Chol 93 mg
Sod 486 mg

*Dietary
Exchanges:*
Milk 1/2
Vegetable 0
Fruit 1 1/2
Bread/Starch 1 1/2
Meat 1/2; Fat 8

2 cups cake flour
1/3 cup baking cocoa
1 teaspoon soda
1/2 teaspoon salt
1/2 cup butter, softened
1 1/4 cups sugar
2 eggs
1 cup water
1 teaspoon almond
  extract
Cream Cheese Filling
2 cups cherry pie
  filling
1/4 cup sliced toasted
  almonds

Sift cake flour, cocoa, soda and salt together. Cream butter and sugar in mixer bowl until light and fluffy. Add eggs 1 at a time, beating well after each addition. Add cake flour mixture and water alternately to creamed mixture. Stir in almond extract. Pour into 2 greased 8-inch cake pans. Bake at 350 degrees for 20 to 25 minutes or until cake tests done. Cool in pans for 10 minutes. Remove to wire racks to cool completely. Slice each cake layer horizontally to make 4 layers. Place 1 layer on cake plate. Spread with 1 cup Cream Cheese Filling. Place second layer on top. Spread with half the pie filling. Add third layer. Spread with 1 cup Cream Cheese Filling. Add fourth layer. Spread with remaining pie filling. Spoon remaining Cream Cheese Filling into decorator tube fitted with number-5 tip. Decorate sides of cake. Sprinkle almonds over top.

Cream Cheese Filling

*Nutritional
information for
Cream Cheese
Filling is
included above.*

2 cups sifted
  confectioners' sugar
9 ounces cream cheese,
  softened
24 ounces whipped
  topping

Cream confectioners' sugar and cream cheese in mixer bowl until light and fluffy. Fold in whipped topping.

Judy B. Allen, Burlington

CHOCOLATE CHERRY CAKE

1 2-layer package devil's food cake mix
½ cup oil
2 eggs, beaten
1 tablespoon almond extract
1 21-ounce can cherry pie filling
1 cup sugar
5 tablespoons margarine
⅓ cup milk
1 tablespoon almond extract
1 cup chocolate chips

Combine cake mix, oil, eggs and 1 tablespoon almond extract in bowl; mix well by hand. Stir in pie filling. Spoon into greased and floured 10x15-inch cake roll pan. Bake at 350 degrees for 20 minutes or until cake tests done. Combine sugar, margarine, milk and remaining 1 tablespoon almond extract in saucepan; mix well. Bring to a boil. Cook for 2 minutes, stirring constantly. Remove from heat. Add chocolate chips, stirring until blended. Pour over warm cake.

Mrs. Garland Bryant, Archdale

BROWNSTONE FRONT CAKE

4 ounces semisweet chocolate
1 cup hot water
1 cup butter, softened
2 cups sugar
3 eggs
3 cups flour
1 cup buttermilk
1 teaspoon soda
1 teaspoon vanilla extract
1 cup butter
1 5-ounce can evaporated milk
2⅔ cups sugar
1 tablespoon vanilla extract

Melt chocolate in hot water. Cream 1 cup butter and 2 cups sugar in mixer bowl until light and fluffy. Beat in eggs. Beat flour and mixture of buttermilk and soda alternately into creamed mixture. Stir in cooled chocolate mixture and 1 teaspoon vanilla. Pour into 2 greased and floured cake pans. Bake at 350 degrees for 30 minutes. Cool in pans for several minutes. Remove to wire rack to cool. Combine remaining ingredients in saucepan. Cook over low heat until sugar is dissolved, stirring constantly. Cook over medium heat to 280 degrees on candy thermometer, soft-ball stage. Beat until of spreading consistency. Frost cake.

Peggy P. Brooks, Burlington

Brown Sugar Fudge Cake

2¹/4 cups sifted cake flour
1 teaspoon soda
¹/2 teaspoon salt
¹/2 cup shortening
2 cups firmly packed brown sugar
3 eggs
2 ounces melted unsweetened chocolate
1 cup buttermilk
1 teaspoon vanilla extract
Fudge Frosting
¹/4 cup grated semisweet chocolate

Sift cake flour, soda and ¹/2 teaspoon salt together. Cream shortening in mixer bowl until light and fluffy. Add brown sugar gradually, beating at medium speed. Add eggs 1 at a time, beating well after each addition. Stir in melted chocolate. Add flour mixture and buttermilk alternately to creamed mixture, mixing well after each addition. Stir in 1 teaspoon vanilla. Pour into 3 greased and floured 8-inch round cake pans. Bake at 350 degrees for 25 to 30 minutes or until layers test done. Cool in pans for 10 minutes. Remove to wire racks to cool completely. Spread Fudge Frosting between layers and over top and side of cooled cake. Sprinkle with grated chocolate.

Fudge Frosting

³/4 cup margarine
³/4 cup baking cocoa
¹/2 cup milk
¹/4 teaspoon salt
2¹/4 teaspoons vanilla extract
6³/4 cups sifted confectioners' sugar

Combine margarine, cocoa and milk in saucepan. Cook over low heat until margarine is melted, stirring constantly. Remove from heat. Add ¹/4 teaspoon salt, 2¹/4 teaspoons vanilla and confectioners' sugar. Beat at high speed until of spreading consistency, adding additional milk if necessary.

Ruth Kent Eslinger, Winston-Salem

CHOCOLATE CAKE WITH MOCHA FROSTING

Yield:
12 servings
Utensil:
cake pans
Approx Per
Serving:
Cal 572
Prot 5 g
Carbo 97 g
Fiber 2 g
T Fat 21 g
Chol 49 mg
Sod 353 mg

Dietary
Exchanges:
Milk 0
Vegetable 0
Fruit 0
Bread/Starch 1
Meat 1/2; Fat 4

2 cups self-rising flour
5 tablespoons baking
  cocoa
2 cups sugar
1/2 cup shortening
2 eggs
1¼ cups milk
1 teaspoon vanilla
  extract
1/4 cup chopped walnuts
Mocha Frosting

Sift flour and 5 tablespoons cocoa together. Cream sugar and shortening in mixer bowl until light and fluffy. Add eggs 1 at a time, beating well after each addition. Add flour mixture to creamed mixture alternately with milk. Stir in 1 teaspoon vanilla and walnuts. Pour into 2 well greased 9-inch cake pans. Bake at 350 degrees for 25 to 30 minutes or until layers test done. Cool in pans for several minutes. Remove to wire racks to cool completely. Spread Mocha Frosting between layers and over top and side of cooled cake.

Nutritional
information for
Mocha Frosting
is included
above.

Mocha Frosting

1/2 cup margarine,
  softened
5 tablespoons baking
  cocoa
1 1-pound package
  confectioners' sugar
2 teaspoons vanilla
  extract
3/4 cup hot black coffee

Cream margarine, 5 tablespoons cocoa and confectioners' sugar in mixer bowl until light and fluffy. Add 2 teaspoons vanilla and coffee, beating until of spreading consistency. May add milk to coffee if desired.

Eileen Rindos, Burlington

CHOCOLATE CHIP CAKE

Yield:
16 servings
Utensil:
bundt pan
Approx Per
Serving:
Cal 331
Prot 4 g
Carbo 40 g
Fiber <1 g
T Fat 18 g
Chol 75 mg
Sod 271 mg

Dietary
Exchanges:
Milk 0
Vegetable 0
Fruit 0
Bread/Starch 2¹/₂
Meat ¹/₂; Fat 3¹/₂

1 2-layer package yellow cake mix
1 4-ounce package chocolate instant pudding mix
1 cup sour cream
¹/₂ cup oil
1 tablespoon vanilla extract
4 eggs
1 cup chocolate chips

Combine cake mix, pudding mix, sour cream, oil and vanilla in bowl; mix well. Add eggs 1 at a time, beating well after each addition. Stir in chocolate chips. Pour into greased bundt pan. Bake at 350 degrees for 45 to 50 minutes or until cake is done but still moist. Cool in pan for several minutes. Invert onto serving plate.

Lillian Buie, Winston-Salem

CHOCOLATE ICE CREAM CAKE

Yield:
16 servings
Utensil:
bundt pan
Approx Per
Serving:
Cal 186
Prot 3 g
Carbo 31 g
Fiber 0 g
T Fat 5 g
Chol 59 mg
Sod 225 mg

Dietary
Exchanges:
Milk 0
Vegetable 0
Fruit 0
Bread/Starch 2
Meat 0; Fat 1

1 2-layer package chocolate cake mix
1 pint chocolate ice cream, softened
3 eggs
1 cup water

Combine cake mix, ice cream, eggs and water in bowl; mix well. Pour into greased bundt pan. Bake at 350 degrees for 45 minutes. Cool in pan for several minutes. Invert onto serving plate.

Ronald Belcher, Advance

CANDY BAR CAKE

Yield:
12 servings
Utensil:
cake pans
Approx Per
Serving:
Cal 800
Prot 11 g
Carbo 88 g
Fiber 1 g
T Fat 47 g
Chol 95 mg
Sod 463 mg

Dietary
Exchanges:
Milk 1/2
Vegetable 0
Fruit 0
Bread/Starch 3
Meat 1/2; Fat 12

1 2-layer package devil's food cake mix
1½ cups milk
3 eggs
¾ cup oil
1 4-ounce package vanilla instant pudding mix
½ cup sugar
1 cup confectioners' sugar
8 ounces cream cheese, softened
12 ounces whipped topping
1 cup chopped pecans
4 chocolate candy bars, frozen, chopped

Combine cake mix, milk, eggs, oil and pudding mix in bowl; mix well. Pour into 3 greased 9-inch round cake pans. Bake at 325 degrees for 30 minutes. Cool in pan for several minutes. Remove to wire rack to cool completely. Cream sugar, confectioners' sugar and cream cheese in mixer bowl until light and fluffy. Add whipped topping, pecans and candy; mix well. Spread between layers and over top and side of cooled cake.

Polly Y. Simpson, Greensboro

HERSHEY BAR CAKE

Yield:
16 servings
Utensil:
tube pan
Approx Per
Serving:
Cal 551
Prot 6 g
Carbo 80 g
Fiber 1 g
T Fat 26 g
Chol 72 mg
Sod 254 mg

Dietary
Exchanges:
Milk 0
Vegetable 0
Fruit 0
Bread/Starch 1
Meat 1/2; Fat 7½

1 cup margarine, softened
2 cups sugar
4 eggs
¼ teaspoon soda
1 cup buttermilk
2½ cups flour
⅛ teaspoon salt
1 cup chocolate syrup
1 tablespoon vanilla extract
6 Hershey bars, melted
1 cup chopped pecans
1 5-ounce can evaporated milk
1½ cups sugar
6 small Hershey bars
2 tablespoons margarine

Cream first 2 ingredients in mixer bowl until light and fluffy. Beat in eggs 1 at a time. Dissolve soda in buttermilk. Add to creamed mixture alternately with flour and salt. Mix in next 4 ingredients. Pour into greased and floured tube pan. Bake at 300 degrees for 1½ hours or until cake tests done. Cool in pan for several minutes. Invert onto serving plate. Bring evaporated milk and 1½ cups sugar to a boil in saucepan. Cook for 10 minutes, stirring frequently. Add remaining candy and margarine; beat until of spreading consistency. Spread over cooled cake.

Jeanie Sams

Chocolate Sour Cream Cake

1 2-layer package devil's food cake mix
1/2 cup water
1 cup sour cream
3 eggs
1/4 cup sugar
1/2 teaspoon cinnamon
1/2 cup semisweet chocolate chips

Combine cake mix, water, sour cream and eggs in mixer bowl. Beat at low speed just until moistened. Beat at high speed for 2 minutes. Pour into greased and floured 9x13-inch cake pan. Combine sugar, cinnamon and chocolate chips in bowl; mix well. Sprinkle over cake batter. Bake at 350 degrees for 30 to 40 minutes or until cake tests done.

Dot Ashby, Winston-Salem

Chocolate Syrup Cake

1 cup cake flour
1/8 teaspoon salt
1 teaspoon baking powder
1/2 cup margarine, softened
1 cup sugar
4 eggs
1 teaspoon vanilla extract
1 16-ounce can chocolate syrup
3/4 cup margarine
2 cups sugar
2/3 cup evaporated milk
6 ounces chocolate chips
1 teaspoon vanilla extract

Sift cake flour, salt and baking powder together. Cream 1/2 cup margarine and 1 cup sugar in mixer bowl until light and fluffy. Beat in eggs 1 at a time. Stir in 1 teaspoon vanilla and syrup. Add cake flour mixture to creamed mixture gradually; mix well. Pour into greased 9x13-inch cake pan. Bake at 350 degrees for 30 minutes or until cake tests done. Combine 3/4 cup margarine, 2 cups sugar and evaporated milk in saucepan. Simmer for 4 minutes, stirring frequently. Add chocolate chips, stirring until melted. Stir in 1 teaspoon vanilla. Pour over cooled cake.

Hilda C. Stockard

Coca-Cola Cake

Yield:
15 servings
Utensil:
cake pan
Approx Per Serving:
Cal 555
Prot 4 g
Carbo 84 g
Fiber 2 g
T Fat 24 g
Chol 37 mg
Sod 322 mg

Dietary Exchanges:
Milk 0
Vegetable 0
Fruit 0
Bread/Starch 1
Meat 0; Fat 5

2 cups flour
2 cups sugar
1 cup Coca-Cola
2 tablespoons baking cocoa
1 cup margarine
1/2 cup buttermilk
1 teaspoon soda
2 eggs
1 teaspoon vanilla extract
1 1/2 cups miniature marshmallows
1/2 cup margarine
1/2 cup Coca-Cola
3 tablespoons baking cocoa
1   1-pound package confectioners' sugar
1 cup chopped pecans

Combine flour and sugar in large bowl; mix well. Combine 1 cup Coca-Cola, 2 tablespoons cocoa and 1 cup margarine in saucepan. Bring to a boil. Stir into flour mixture. Combine next 5 ingredients in medium bowl; mix well. Stir into flour mixture. Pour into greased 9x13-inch cake pan. Bake at 350 degrees for 45 minutes or until cake tests done. Combine next 3 ingredients in saucepan. Bring to a boil. Remove from heat. Stir in confectioners' sugar. Add pecans; mix well. Pour over hot cake.

Phyllis Lennon

Hot Fudge Pudding Cake

Yield:
8 servings
Utensil:
cake pan
Approx Per Serving:
Cal 312
Prot 3 g
Carbo 58 g
Fiber 2 g
T Fat 9 g
Chol 22 mg
Sod 236 mg

Dietary Exchanges:
Milk 0
Vegetable 0
Fruit 0
Bread/Starch 1
Meat 0; Fat 2

3/4 cup sugar
1 cup flour
3 tablespoons baking cocoa
2 teaspoons baking powder
1/4 teaspoon salt
1/2 cup milk
1/3 cup melted butter
1 1/2 teaspoons vanilla extract
1/2 cup sugar
1/2 cup packed light brown sugar
1/4 cup baking cocoa
1 1/4 cups hot water

Combine 3/4 cup sugar, flour, 3 tablespoons cocoa, baking powder and salt in bowl; mix well. Add milk, melted butter and vanilla; mix well. Pour into greased 8-inch square cake pan. Combine remaining 1/2 cup sugar, brown sugar and remaining 1/4 cup cocoa in bowl; mix well. Sprinkle over cake batter. Pour hot water over all; do not stir. Bake at 350 degrees for 40 minutes or until center is almost set. Let stand for 15 minutes. Spoon into serving bowls. Drizzle with liquid from pan.

Marion S. Haerle, Greensboro

MISSISSIPPI MUD CAKE

1 1/2 cups self-rising
  flour
1/3 cup baking cocoa
1/4 teaspoon salt
2 cups sugar
1 cup oil
4 eggs
1 tablespoon vanilla
  extract
1 cup chopped pecans

1 6-ounce package
  miniature
  marshmallows
1/2 cup margarine
3 cups confectioners'
  sugar
1/4 cup baking cocoa
1/3 cup evaporated milk
1 teaspoon vanilla extract
1 cup chopped pecans

Sift flour, 1/3 cup cocoa and salt together. Cream sugar and oil in mixer bowl until light. Beat in eggs 1 at a time. Add flour mixture to creamed mixture; mix well. Stir in 1 tablespoon vanilla and 1 cup pecans. Spoon into greased 9x13-inch cake pan. Bake at 350 degrees for 30 to 40 minutes. Spread marshmallows over cake. Bake until marshmallows are lightly browned. Melt margarine in saucepan. Add next 4 ingredients; mix well. Stir in 1 cup pecans. Pour over warm cake. Cool in pan.

Ann Wallace, Winston-Salem

MYSTERY MOCHA CAKE

3/4 cup sugar
1 cup sifted flour
2 teaspoons baking
  powder
1/8 teaspoon salt
1 ounce chocolate
2 tablespoons butter
1/2 cup milk

1 teaspoon vanilla
  extract
1/2 cup packed brown
  sugar
1/2 cup sugar
1/4 cup baking cocoa
1 cup cold coffee

Sift 3/4 cup sugar, flour, baking powder and salt together. Place chocolate and butter in double boiler. Cook over boiling water until melted, stirring frequently. Stir into flour mixture. Add milk and vanilla; mix well. Pour into greased 8-inch square cake pan. Combine brown sugar, remaining 1/2 cup sugar and cocoa in bowl; mix well. Sprinkle over batter. Pour coffee over all. Bake at 350 degrees for 40 minutes or until cake tests done. Serve warm or cold. May serve with whipped cream or ice cream.

Helen J. Sawyer, Winston-Salem

RED VELVET CAKE

Yield:
12 servings
Utensil:
cake pans
**Approx Per
Serving:**
Cal 727
Prot 6 g
Carbo 96 g
Fiber 1 g
T Fat 37 g
Chol 131 mg
Sod 537 mg

**Dietary
Exchanges:**
Milk 0
Vegetable 0
Fruit 0
Bread/Starch 1
Meat 1/2; Fat 8 1/2

*Nutritional
information for
Cream Cheese
Frosting is
included above.*

2 1/2 cups cake flour
1 1/2 teaspoons soda
1/2 teaspoon salt
1 cup butter, softened
2 cups sugar
3 eggs
1 tablespoon baking
  cocoa
1 tablespoon vinegar
2 ounces red food
  coloring
1 cup buttermilk
1 teaspoon vanilla extract
Cream Cheese Frosting
1 cup chopped pecans
  (optional)

Sift cake flour, soda and salt together. Cream butter and sugar in mixer bowl until light and fluffy. Add eggs 1 at a time, beating well after each addition. Add cocoa, vinegar and food coloring; mix well. Add flour mixture and buttermilk alternately to creamed mixture, beating well after each addition. Stir in 1 teaspoon vanilla. Pour into 2 greased and floured 9-inch round cake pans. Bake at 350 degrees for 25 minutes. Cool in pan for several minutes. Remove to wire racks to cool completely. Spread Cream Cheese Frosting between layers and over top and side of cooled cake. Sprinkle with pecans.

Cream Cheese Frosting

1/2 cup margarine,
  softened
8 ounces cream cheese,
  softened
1 1-pound package
  confectioners'
  sugar, sifted
1 teaspoon vanilla extract

Cream margarine and cream cheese in mixer bowl until light and fluffy. Stir in confectioners' sugar. Add vanilla; mix well.

Elizabeth Ann B. Smith, Burlington

OOEY GOOEY CHOCOLATE CAKE

Yield:
12 servings
Utensil:
cake pans
**Approx Per
Serving:**
Cal 857
Prot 12 g
Carbo 88 g
Fiber 1 g
T Fat 53 g
Chol 96 mg
Sod 485 mg

**Dietary
Exchanges:**
Milk 1/2
Vegetable 0
Fruit 0
Bread/Starch 3
Meat 1/2; Fat 12

1 2-layer package chocolate cake mix
3 eggs
1 4-ounce package vanilla instant pudding mix
1 1/2 cups milk
1 cup oil
1 cup confectioners' sugar
8 ounces cream cheese, softened
1/2 cup sugar
1 cup chopped pecans
2 Hershey bars, chopped
16 ounces whipped topping

Combine cake mix, eggs, pudding mix, milk and oil in bowl; mix well. Pour into 3 greased 9-inch round cake pans. Bake at 350 degrees for 15 minutes; do not overbake. Cool in pans for several minutes. Remove to wire racks to cool completely. Cream confectioners' sugar, cream cheese and sugar in mixer bowl until light and fluffy. Stir in pecans and candy. Fold in whipped topping. Spread between layers and over top and side of cooled cake.

Caren Bryant, Burlington

SPAGHETTI SQUASH CAKES FOR CHOCOLATE LOVERS

Yield:
16 servings
Utensil:
loaf pans
**Approx Per
Serving:**
Cal 363
Prot 4 g
Carbo 45 g
Fiber 1 g
T Fat 20 g
Chol 51 mg
Sod 138 mg

**Dietary
Exchanges:**
Milk 0
Vegetable 0
Fruit 0
Bread/Starch 1 1/2
Meat 0; Fat 4

2 cups cooked spaghetti squash
2 1/2 cups flour
1/4 cup baking cocoa
1/2 teaspoon baking powder
1 teaspoon soda
1/2 teaspoon cinnamon
1/2 teaspoon cloves
1/2 cup butter, softened
1/2 cup oil
1 3/4 cups sugar
2 eggs
1 teaspoon vanilla extract
1/2 cup buttermilk
1 cup chocolate chips
1/2 cup chopped walnuts

Purée squash in blender. Sift flour, cocoa, baking powder, soda, cinnamon and cloves together. Combine butter, oil and sugar in mixer bowl; mix well. Add eggs, vanilla and buttermilk; mix well. Stir in flour mixture. Add squash, chocolate chips and walnuts; mix well. Pour into 2 greased and floured loaf pans. Bake at 325 degrees for 50 minutes or until loaves spring back when lightly touched. May spread with your favorite fudge frosting for a real taste binge.

Vicki Strickland, Greensboro

Texas Chocolate Cake

2 1/2 cups sifted flour
1/4 teaspoon salt
1 teaspoon soda
1 cup margarine, softened
2 cups sugar
4 egg yolks
6 ounces German's chocolate, melted
1 cup buttermilk
1 teaspoon vanilla extract
4 egg whites, stiffly beaten
Whipped Cream Frosting

Sift flour, salt and soda together. Cream margarine and 2 cups sugar in mixer bowl until light and fluffy. Stir in 4 egg yolks and melted chocolate. Add flour mixture and buttermilk alternately to creamed mixture. Stir in vanilla. Fold in egg whites. Pour into 3 greased 9-inch cake pans. Bake at 350 degrees for 30 minutes or until layers test done. Cool in pans for several minutes. Remove to wire racks to cool completely. Spread Whipped Cream Frosting between layers and over top and side of cooled cake.

Whipped Cream Frosting

2 cups whipping cream
1/2 cup butter
3 egg yolks
1 cup sugar
1 cup chopped pecans
1 cup flaked coconut

Combine whipping cream, butter, 3 egg yolks and 1 cup sugar in saucepan. Cook for 12 minutes or until mixture begins to thicken, stirring frequently. Remove from heat. Stir in pecans and coconut. Let stand until cool.

A Pioneer

TURTLE CAKE

Yield:
15 servings
Utensil:
cake pan
Approx Per
Serving:
Cal 446
Prot 4 g
Carbo 58 g
Fiber 1 g
T Fat 24 g
Chol 26 mg
Sod 379 mg

Dietary
Exchanges:
Milk 0
Vegetable 0
Fruit 0
Bread/Starch 2½
Meat 0; Fat 9½

1 2-layer package German chocolate cake mix
¾ cup melted butter
¼ cup evaporated milk
1 14-ounce package caramels
1 cup chocolate chips
1 cup chopped pecans

Prepare cake mix using package directions. Pour half the batter into greased 9x13-inch cake pan. Bake at 350 degrees for 15 minutes. Combine melted butter, evaporated milk and caramels in saucepan. Cook over low heat until caramels are melted, stirring frequently. Pour over cake. Sprinkle with chocolate chips and half the pecans. Top with remaining batter. Sprinkle with remaining pecans. Bake for 20 minutes.

Jewel Smith, Clemmons

COCONUT CAKE

Yield:
15 servings
Utensil:
cake pan
Approx Per
Serving:
Cal 333
Prot 5 g
Carbo 43 g
Fiber 3 g
T Fat 16 g
Chol 4 mg
Sod 250 mg

Dietary
Exchanges:
Milk 0
Vegetable 0
Fruit 0
Bread/Starch 2
Meat 0; Fat 4

1 2-layer package pudding-recipe cake mix
2 6-ounce packages frozen coconut, thawed
½ teaspoon vanilla extract
1 5-ounce can evaporated milk
⅓ cup confectioners' sugar
8 ounces whipped topping

Prepare and bake cake mix using package directions adding ½ cup coconut and ½ teaspoon vanilla for 9x13-inch cake pan. Add enough water to evaporated milk to measure 1½ cups. Combine with sugar in saucepan. Heat over medium heat, stirring frequently. Do not boil. Pierce holes in hot cake with fork. Pour hot evaporated milk mixture over cake. Cool. Cover with whipped topping. Sprinkle with remaining coconut.

Elwood and Patsy Mann

GOLDEN COCONUT CAKE

Yield:
15 servings
Utensil:
cake pan
Approx Per Serving:
Cal 396
Prot 6 g
Carbo 51 g
Fiber 3 g
T Fat 20 g
Chol 6 mg
Sod 269 mg

Dietary Exchanges:
Milk ½
Vegetable 0
Fruit 0
Bread/Starch 2
Meat 0; Fat 5

2 6-ounce packages frozen coconut, thawed
1 2-layer package golden cake mix
2 cups milk
½ cup sugar
1 teaspoon vanilla extract
12 ounces whipped topping

Spread 1 package coconut in 9x13-inch cake pan. Prepare cake mix using package directions. Pour batter over coconut. Bake using package directions. Combine milk, sugar and vanilla in saucepan. Bring to the boiling point. Do not boil. Pierce holes in hot cake with fork. Pour hot milk over cake slowly until all is absorbed. Cool. Spread whipped topping over cake. Sprinkle with remaining package coconut. Chill in refrigerator.

Norma Hall, Mebane

RAYMOND'S FOUR-DAY COCONUT CAKE

Yield:
12 servings
Utensil:
cake pans
Approx Per Serving:
Cal 487
Prot 4 g
Carbo 74 g
Fiber 3 g
T Fat 21 g
Chol 17 mg
Sod 290 mg

Dietary Exchanges:
Milk 0
Vegetable 0
Fruit 0
Bread/Starch 2½
Meat 0; Fat 6

2 cups sugar
2 cups sour cream
2 6-ounce packages frozen coconut, thawed
1 2-layer package butter-recipe cake mix
1 teaspoon vanilla extract
½ teaspoon lemon extract

Combine sugar, sour cream and coconut in bowl; mix well. Chill overnight. Prepare and bake cake using package directions for two 9-inch cake pans, adding vanilla and lemon extract. Cool in pans for several minutes. Invert onto wire rack to cool completely. Split layers into halves horizontally. Spread icing between layers and over top and side of cooled cake. Store in refrigerator for at least 4 days before serving.

Raymond Porter, Winston-Salem

FRESH COCONUT SOUR CREAM CAKE

1 cup butter
2 cups sugar
4 eggs
2¾ cups sifted flour
2 teaspoons baking
   powder
½ teaspoon salt
1 cup sour cream
¼ cup milk
2 teaspoons lemon
   flavoring
2 6-ounce packages
   frozen coconut,
   thawed
Five-Minute Frosting

Cream butter and 2 cups sugar in mixer bowl until light and fluffy. Add eggs 1 at a time, beating well after each addition. Mix flour, baking powder and ½ teaspoon salt together. Mix sour cream and milk together. Add flour mixture to batter alternately with sour cream mixture, mixing well after each addition. Add lemon flavoring; mix well. Pour into 3 greased and floured 9-inch cake pans. Bake at 350 degrees for 35 minutes or until layers test done. Cool in pans for several minutes. Invert onto wire rack to cool completely. Spread Five-Minute Frosting between layers and over top and side of cooled cake. Sprinkle coconut over frosting.

Five-Minute Frosting

1 cup sugar
3 tablespoons water
¼ teaspoon salt
2 tablespoons light
   corn syrup
2 egg whites
1½ cups sifted
   confectioners' sugar
1 teaspoon vanilla
   extract

Combine 1 cup sugar, water, ¼ teaspoon salt, corn syrup and egg whites in double boiler over hot water. Beat well for 5 minutes or until soft peaks form. Remove from heat. Add confectioners' sugar and vanilla, beating until smooth.

Pauline B. Hart, Clemmons

STATELY COCONUT LAYER CAKE

1 cup shortening
2 cups sugar
4 eggs
3 cups sifted cake flour
2½ teaspoons baking powder
½ teaspoon salt
1 cup milk
1 teaspoon almond extract
1 teaspoon vanilla extract
½ cup sifted cake flour
1 cup sugar
¼ teaspoon salt
¼ cup water
2 tablespoons grated orange rind
1 tablespoon grated lemon rind
1¼ cups orange juice
2 tablespoons lemon juice
4 egg yolks, beaten
1½ cups sugar
½ teaspoon cream of tartar
⅛ teaspoon salt
½ cup hot water
4 egg whites
½ teaspoon almond extract
½ teaspoon coconut extract
1 small fresh coconut, grated

Cream shortening and 2 cups sugar in mixer bowl until light and fluffy. Add eggs 1 at a time, beating well after each addition. Mix 3 cups cake flour, baking powder and ½ teaspoon salt together. Add to batter alternately with milk, beating well after each addition. Add almond and vanilla extracts; beat well. Pour into 3 greased and floured 9-inch round cake pans. Bake at 375 degrees for 20 to 25 minutes or until layers test done. Cool in pans for 10 minutes. Invert onto wire rack to cool completely. Combine remaining ½ cup cake flour, 1 cup sugar, ¼ teaspoon salt and water in heavy saucepan; mix well. Stir in fruit rinds and juices. Cook over medium heat until thickened, stirring constantly. Stir a small amount of hot mixture into beaten egg yolks; stir egg yolks into hot mixture. Cook for 1 to 2 minutes or until thickened, stirring constantly. Cool completely. Combine 1½ cups sugar, cream of tartar, ⅛ teaspoon salt and water in heavy saucepan. Cook over medium heat until clear, stirring constantly. Cook to 240 degrees on candy thermometer, soft-ball stage; do not stir. Beat egg whites in mixer bowl until soft peaks form. Add syrup and flavorings gradually, beating until stiff peaks form. Spread filling between layers. Spread frosting over top and side of cake. Sprinkle with coconut.

Roseleen Brandon, Winston-Salem

TOASTED COCONUT CAKE

1　2-layer package white cake mix
1　3-ounce package vanilla instant pudding mix
1⅓ cups water
¼ cup oil
4 eggs
1⅓ cups coconut
1 cup chopped pecans
Toasted Coconut Cream Cheese Frosting

Combine cake mix, pudding mix, water, oil and eggs in mixer bowl. Beat at medium speed for 4 minutes. Stir in 1⅓ cups coconut and pecans. Pour into 3 greased and floured 9-inch cake pans. Bake at 350 degrees for 20 to 25 minutes or until layers test done. Cool in pans for 10 minutes. Invert onto wire rack to cool completely. Spread Toasted Coconut Cream Cheese Frosting between layers and over top and side of cake. Sprinkle with reserved toasted coconut.

Toasted Coconut Cream Cheese Frosting

2 tablespoons butter
2½ cups coconut
2 tablespoons butter, softened
8 ounces cream cheese, softened
3½ cups sifted confectioners' sugar
2 teaspoons milk
½ teaspoon vanilla extract

Melt 2 tablespoons butter in large skillet. Stir in remaining 2½ cups coconut. Cook over medium heat until golden brown, stirring constantly. Cool. Combine remaining 2 tablespoons butter and cream cheese in bowl; beat until light and fluffy. Add confectioners' sugar, milk and vanilla; beat until smooth. Reserve ½ cup toasted coconut. Stir remaining toasted coconut into frosting.

Anna E. Myers, Hillsville, Virginia

DATE RAISIN CAKE

Yield:
12 servings
Utensil:
cake pans
Approx Per
Serving:
Cal 891
Prot 7 g
Carbo 173 g
Fiber 7 g
T Fat 23 g
Chol 56 mg
Sod 259 mg

Dietary
Exchanges:
Milk 0
Vegetable 0
Fruit 3
Bread/Starch 1/2
Meat 0; Fat 51/2

Nutritional
information for
Coffee Frosting
is included
above.

1 teaspoon soda
1 cup hot water
1 cup chopped pecans
1 8-ounce package
   chopped dates
1 15-ounce package
   raisins
3/4 cup butter, softened
1 cup sugar
1 egg
1 cup milk
23/4 cups flour
1 teaspoon vanilla
   extract
Coffee Frosting

Stir soda into water in bowl until dissolved. Add pecans, dates and raisins. Let stand for several minutes. Cream 3/4 cup butter and sugar in mixer bowl until light and fluffy. Add egg and milk; mix well. Add flour and vanilla; mix well. Stir in fruit mixture. Pour into 3 greased and floured cake pans. Bake at 350 degrees for 45 minutes or until layers test done. Cool in pans for several minutes. Invert onto wire rack to cool completely. Spread Coffee Frosting between layers and over top and side of cooled cake.

Coffee Frosting

1 2-pound package
   confectioners' sugar
1/4 cup baking cocoa
1/4 cup margarine,
   softened
1 to 11/2 cups strong
   black coffee

Combine confectioners' sugar, cocoa and margarine in mixer bowl; mix well. Add coffee until of spreading consistency.

Clifton Loy, Graham

FRENCH CREAM CAKE

Yield:
12 servings
Utensil:
cake pans
Approx Per Serving:
Cal 483
Prot 5 g
Carbo 69 g
Fiber 1 g
T Fat 22 g
Chol 74 mg
Sod 505 mg

Dietary Exchanges:
Milk 0
Vegetable 0
Fruit 1/2
Bread/Starch 2 1/2
Meat 1/2; Fat 4 1/2

1 2-layer package yellow cake mix
1 1/2 cups sugar
2 cups milk
5 tablespoons flour
3 eggs
1 cup margarine
2 bananas, sliced

Prepare and bake cake using package directions for 2-layer cake. Cool in pans for several minutes. Invert onto wire racks to cool completely. Combine sugar, milk, flour and eggs in saucepan; mix well. Cook over medium heat until very thick, stirring constantly. Add margarine; beat until smooth. Place 1 cake layer on cake plate. Spread with frosting. Arrange banana slices over top. Add second cake layer. Spread remaining frosting over top and side of cake. May substitute pineapple for bananas.

Mary Kiser

CUPCAKE FRUITCAKE

Yield:
35 servings
Utensil:
muffin pan
Approx Per Serving:
Cal 167
Prot 2 g
Carbo 28 g
Fiber 2 g
T Fat 6 g
Chol 4 mg
Sod 29 mg

Dietary Exchanges:
Milk 1/2
Vegetable 0
Fruit 1 1/2
Bread/Starch 0
Meat 0; Fat 1 1/2

8 ounces candied cherries, chopped
1 pound dates, chopped
8 ounces candied pineapple, chopped
1 4-ounce package coconut
2 cups chopped pecans
1/4 teaspoon salt
1/2 teaspoon vanilla extract
1 14-ounce can sweetened condensed milk

Combine cherries, dates, pineapple, coconut and pecans in bowl; mix well. Mix salt, vanilla and condensed milk together in bowl. Add to fruit; mix well. Fill miniature muffin cups 2/3 full. Bake at 325 degrees for 25 to 30 minutes or until cupcakes test done. Cool in pan for several minutes. Invert onto wire rack to cool completely. Store in tightly covered container for 2 weeks before serving.

Virginia Ward, Graham

HAWAIIAN FRUITCAKE

Yield:
12 servings
Utensil:
loaf pan
Approx Per Serving:
Cal 456
Prot 7 g
Carbo 58 g
Fiber 4 g
T Fat 24 g
Chol 69 mg
Sod 109 mg

Dietary Exchanges:
Milk 0
Vegetable 0
Fruit 2
Bread/Starch 1
Meat 1; Fat 5½

¾ cup self-rising flour
¾ cup sugar
3 eggs, beaten
1½ teaspoons vanilla extract
1 6-ounce package frozen coconut, thawed
1 7-ounce jar whole macadamia nuts
1 cup whole almonds
16 ounces candied pineapple
2 tablespoons light corn syrup
1 tablespoon water

Line 5x9-inch loaf pan with foil; grease well. Combine flour, sugar, eggs and vanilla in bowl; mix well. Stir in coconut, macadamia nuts, almonds and pineapple. Press into prepared pan. Bake at 300 degrees for 1 hour and 15 minutes. Cover cake with foil to prevent excess browning. Bake for 30 minutes longer. Cool in pan for several minutes. Invert onto wire rack to cool. Combine corn syrup and water in saucepan. Bring to a rolling boil. Cool to lukewarm. Pour over cake. Cool. Store, wrapped in plastic wrap, in cool place.

Karen S. Watterson, Greensboro

REFRIGERATOR FRUITCAKE

Yield:
32 servings
Utensil:
container
Approx Per Serving:
Cal 462
Prot 7 g
Carbo 58 g
Fiber 4 g
T Fat 25 g
Chol 4 mg
Sod 94 mg

Dietary Exchanges:
Milk ½
Vegetable 0
Fruit 1½
Bread/Starch 1
Meat ½; Fat 6½

1 16-ounce package graham crackers
1 16-ounce package miniature marshmallows
1 pound pecans
1 16-ounce package candied cherries
1 pound walnuts
1 16-ounce package coconut
1 15-ounce package raisins
1 14-ounce can sweetened condensed milk

Roll graham crackers with rolling pin until very fine crumbs. Combine crumbs, marshmallows, pecans, cherries, walnuts, coconut and raisins in large bowl; mix well. Add condensed milk; mix well. Line refrigerator container with waxed paper. Press mixture into container. Chill, covered, for several days.

Peggy Mitchell, Burlington

PECAN BOURBON CAKE

3 cups sifted flour
1 pound pecans, coarsely chopped
1 16-ounce package golden raisins
1 4-ounce package mixed candied fruit, finely chopped
2 teaspoons nutmeg
2 teaspoons baking powder
1 cup butter
2 cups sugar
6 egg yolks
1 cup bourbon
6 egg whites, stiffly beaten

Grease 10-inch tube pan; line with waxed paper. Grease waxed paper. Combine 2 tablespoons flour, pecans, raisins and candied fruit in bowl; toss to coat pecans and fruit. Sift remaining flour, nutmeg and baking powder together. Cream butter and sugar in mixer bowl until light and fluffy. Add egg yolks 1 at a time, beating well after each addition. Add flour mixture alternately with bourbon, beating well after each addition. Stir in pecans and fruit. Fold in stiffly beaten egg whites. Spoon into prepared pan. Place shallow pan of water on top shelf of oven. Bake cake at 250 degrees for 2 hours. Remove pan of water. Bake cake for 2 hours longer or until cake tests done. Cool in pan for 30 minutes. Invert onto wire rack; remove waxed paper. Cool completely. Dip cheesecloth in additional bourbon; wrap cooled cake. Wrap cake in plastic wrap. Store in airtight container.

Kathryn Howerton

WHITE FRUITCAKE

Yield:
20 servings
Utensil:
tube pan
Approx Per
Serving:
Cal 467
Prot 5 g
Carbo 59 g
Fiber 2 g
T Fat 25 g
Chol 93 mg
Sod 119 mg

Dietary
Exchanges:
Milk 0
Vegetable 0
Fruit 2½
Bread/Starch 1½
Meat ½; Fat 6

1 cup butter
1 cup sugar
5 eggs
2 teaspoons each
   vanilla extract and
   lemon extract
1 cup cake flour
½ teaspoon baking
   powder
¾ cup flour
4 cups pecans,
   coarsely chopped
1 pound candied red
   and green cherries,
   chopped
1 pound mixed
   candied fruit,
   chopped

Cream butter and sugar in mixer bowl until light and fluffy. Beat in eggs 1 at a time. Stir in flavorings. Sift 1 cup cake flour and baking powder together. Add to batter; mix well. Combine ¾ cup flour and pecans in bowl; toss to coat pecans. Stir pecans and fruit into batter. Pour into greased and floured 10-inch tube pan. Bake at 250 degrees for 2½ hours or until cake tests done. Cool in pan for 15 minutes. Invert onto wire rack to cool. Store, wrapped in plastic wrap, in covered container for several days before serving.

Zora P. Hemrick, Kernersville

ORANGE COCONUT FRUITCAKE

Yield:
20 servings
Utensil:
tube pan
Approx Per
Serving:
Cal 446
Prot 5 g
Carbo 60 g
Fiber 3 g
T Fat 23 g
Chol 82 mg
Sod 193 mg

Dietary
Exchanges:
Milk 0
Vegetable 0
Fruit 2
Bread/Starch 1
Meat ½; Fat 5½

8 ounces candied
   cherries, chopped
8 ounces candied
   pineapple, chopped
8 ounces pecans,
   chopped
4 ounces citron, finely
   chopped
1 cup golden raisins
½ cup orange juice
1 cup margarine
1½ cups sugar
6 egg yolks, beaten
3 cups sifted cake flour
½ teaspoon salt
½ cup orange juice
8 ounces coconut
6 egg whites, stiffly
   beaten

Combine first 5 ingredients in bowl; mix well. Add ½ cup orange juice. Cream margarine and sugar in mixer bowl until light and fluffy. Beat in egg yolks 1 at a time. Add mixture of cake flour and salt alternately with ½ cup orange juice, beating well after each addition. Stir in coconut and fruit mixture. Fold in egg whites. Pour into greased and floured 10-inch tube pan. Bake at 275 degrees for 3 to 3½ hours or until cake tests done. Cool in pan for several minutes. Invert onto wire rack to cool.

Ruth Kent Eslinger, Winston-Salem

Fruit Cocktail Cake

Yield:
15 servings
Utensil:
cake pan
Approx Per
Serving:
Cal 368
Prot 4 g
Carbo 60 g
Fiber 2 g
T Fat 14 g
Chol 56 mg
Sod 264 mg

Dietary
Exchanges:
Milk 0
Vegetable 0
Fruit 1/2
Bread/Starch 1
Meat 0; Fat 3 1/2

2 eggs
2 cups sugar
2 cups self-rising flour
1 16-ounce can fruit
  cocktail
1/2 cup butter
1 cup sugar
1 5-ounce can
  evaporated milk
1 cup chopped pecans
1 cup coconut

Beat eggs in mixer bowl until light and fluffy. Add 2 cups sugar; beat well. Add flour gradually, beating well after each addition. Stir in fruit cocktail and juice. Spoon into greased and floured 9x13-inch cake pan. Bake at 350 degrees for 30 minutes. Combine butter, 1 cup sugar and evaporated milk in saucepan; mix well. Bring to a boil, stirring frequently. Stir in pecans and coconut. Pour hot topping over hot cake.

Dot Ellerbe, Burlington

Honey Bun Cake

Yield:
15 servings
Utensil:
cake pan
Approx Per
Serving:
Cal 370
Prot 4 g
Carbo 51 g
Fiber 0 g
T Fat 17 g
Chol 80 mg
Sod 241 mg

Dietary
Exchanges:
Milk 0
Vegetable 0
Fruit 0
Bread/Starch 2
Meat 1/2; Fat 3 1/2

1 2-layer package
  yellow cake mix
1/2 cup sugar
2/3 cup oil
4 eggs
1 cup sour cream
1/2 cup packed brown
  sugar
2 teaspoons cinnamon
1 cup confectioners'
  sugar
1/4 cup milk

Combine cake mix, sugar, oil, eggs and sour cream in mixer bowl; mix well. Combine brown sugar and cinnamon in small bowl; mix well. Pour half the batter in greased 9x13-inch cake pan. Sprinkle half the cinnamon mixture over batter. Add remaining batter; sprinkle with remaining cinnamon mixture. Swirl back and forth with knife. Bake at 350 degrees for 35 minutes. Combine confectioners' sugar and milk in bowl; mix well. Pour over warm cake.

Lee P. Powell, Clemmons

ITALIAN CREAM CAKE

Yield:
12 servings
Utensil:
cake pans
Approx Per
Serving:
Cal 844
Prot 11 g
Carbo 100 g
Fiber 4 g
T Fat 47 g
Chol 135 mg
Sod 329 mg

Dietary
Exchanges:
Milk 0
Vegetable 0
Fruit 0
Bread/Starch 1
Meat 1; Fat 10½

½ cup margarine
½ cup shortening
2 cups sugar
5 egg yolks
2 cups flour
1 teaspoon soda
1 cup buttermilk
1 teaspoon vanilla
  extract

1 7-ounce can coconut
1 cup finely chopped
  black walnuts
5 egg whites, stiffly
  beaten
Creamy Confectioners'
  Sugar Frosting
1 cup chopped black
  walnuts

Cream ½ cup margarine, shortening and sugar in mixer bowl until light and fluffy. Add egg yolks, 1 at a time, beating well after each addition. Add mixture of flour and soda alternately with buttermilk. Add vanilla. Stir in coconut and 1 cup walnuts. Fold in stiffly beaten egg whites. Pour into 2 greased and floured 9-inch cake pans. Bake at 350 degrees for 25 minutes. Cool in pans for several minutes. Invert onto wire rack to cool completely. Spread Creamy Confectioners' Sugar Frosting between layers and over top and side of cake. Sprinkle walnuts over top.

Creamy Confectioners' Sugar Frosting

Nutritional
information for
Creamy
Confectioners'
Sugar Frosting
is included
above.

8 ounces cream cheese,
  softened
¼ cup margarine,
  softened

1 16-ounce package
  confectioners' sugar
1 teaspoon vanilla
  extract

Combine cream cheese and ¼ cup margarine in mixer bowl; mix well. Add confectioners' sugar and vanilla; beat until smooth.

Ethel W. Chrisco, Greensboro

OATMEAL CAKE

Yield:
15 servings
Utensil:
cake pan
Approx Per
Serving:
Cal 409
Prot 4 g
Carbo 57 g
Fiber 2 g
T Fat 20 g
Chol 39 mg
Sod 230 mg

Dietary
Exchanges:
Milk 0
Vegetable 0
Fruit 0
Bread/Starch 1
Meat 0; Fat 4

1½ cups boiling water
1 cup oats
½ cup oil
1 cup packed brown sugar
1 cup sugar
1½ cups flour
1 teaspoon soda
½ teaspoon salt
1 teaspoon cinnamon
2 eggs
½ cup margarine
1 cup packed brown sugar
½ cup evaporated milk
1 teaspoon vanilla extract
1 3-ounce can coconut
½ cup chopped pecans

Pour water over oats in bowl. Let stand for several minutes. Cream oil, 1 cup brown sugar and sugar in mixer bowl until light. Sift dry ingredients together. Add to creamed mixture alternately with eggs, beating well after each addition. Stir in oats. Pour into greased 9x13-inch cake pan. Bake at 350 degrees for 35 to 40 minutes. Combine next 3 ingredients in saucepan. Cook over medium heat until thickened, stirring constantly. Remove from heat. Stir in vanilla and remaining ingredients. Pour over hot cake.

Gradie Vaden, Winston-Salem

ORANGE DATE CAKE

Yield:
12 servings
Utensil:
tube pan
Approx Per
Serving:
Cal 371
Prot 5 g
Carbo 55 g
Fiber 3 g
T Fat 16 g
Chol 46 mg
Sod 260 mg

Dietary
Exchanges:
Milk 0
Vegetable 0
Fruit 1
Bread/Starch 1
Meat 0; Fat 3½

½ cup shortening
1 cup sugar
2 eggs
¾ cup buttermilk
2 cups cake flour
1 teaspoon soda
1 teaspoon salt
Grated rind of 1 orange
Juice of 2 oranges
1 teaspoon vanilla extract
1 cup chopped pecans
1 cup chopped dates
Grated rind of 1 orange
½ cup sugar
¼ cup orange juice

Cream shortening and 1 cup sugar in mixer bowl until light and fluffy. Beat in eggs 1 at a time. Add buttermilk; mix well. Mix cake flour, soda and salt together. Add to batter; mix well. Add orange rind, orange juice, vanilla, pecans and dates; mix well. Pour into greased and floured tube pan. Bake at 350 degrees for 1 hour and 10 minutes or until cake tests done. Cool in pan for several minutes. Invert onto serving plate. Combine remaining orange rind, ½ cup sugar and ¼ cup orange juice in bowl; mix well. Pour over hot cake.

Wilma Hiatt, Tobaccoville

ORANGE NUT CAKE

<table>
<tr><td>

Yield:
9 servings
Utensil:
cake pan
Approx Per
Serving:
Cal 490
Prot 5 g
Carbo 80 g
Fiber 2 g
T Fat 18 g
Chol 66 mg
Sod 358 mg

Dietary
Exchanges:
Milk 0
Vegetable 0
Fruit ½
Bread/Starch 1
Meat 0; Fat 4

</td></tr>
</table>

½ cup butter, softened
1 cup packed brown
  sugar
1 egg
1 cup buttermilk
2 cups sifted flour
1 teaspoon soda
1 teaspoon baking
  powder
¼ teaspoon salt

Rind of 1 orange, ground
½ cup raisins, ground
½ cup chopped
  pecans, ground
⅓ cup orange juice
2 tablespoons melted
  butter
2 cups confectioners'
  sugar
⅓ cup orange juice

Cream ½ cup butter and brown sugar in mixer bowl. Beat in egg and buttermilk. Add mixture of dry ingredients; mix well. Stir in half the orange rind, raisins and pecans. Pour into greased 9x9-inch cake pan. Bake at 350 degrees for 40 minutes or until cake tests done. Cool in pan for several minutes. Invert onto serving plate. Pour ⅓ cup orange juice over hot cake. Combine butter, confectioners' sugar and enough orange juice to make of spreading consistency. Stir in remaining orange rind, raisins and pecans. Spread over cake.

Betty Gregory, Greensboro

ORANGE PINEAPPLE CAKE

<table>
<tr><td>

Yield:
12 servings
Utensil:
cake pans
Approx Per
Serving:
Cal 616
Prot 4 g
Carbo 77 g
Fiber 1 g
T Fat 34 g
Chol 91 mg
Sod 456 mg

Dietary
Exchanges:
Milk 0
Vegetable 0
Fruit 0
Bread/Starch 3
Meat ½; Fat 7

</td></tr>
</table>

1 2-layer package
   orange supreme
   cake mix
1 4-ounce package
   coconut creme
   pudding and pie
   filling mix
4 eggs
1 cup oil

1 12-ounce can lemon-
   lime beverage
1 8-ounce can
   crushed pineapple
1½ cups sugar
½ cup margarine
3 tablespoons flour
1 3-ounce can coconut

Combine first 3 ingredients in bowl; mix well. Add oil and lemon-lime beverage; mix well. Pour into 3 greased and floured 9-inch cake pans. Bake at 350 degrees for 30 minutes. Cool in pans for several minutes. Invert onto wire rack to cool completely. Combine pineapple, sugar, margarine and flour in saucepan; mix well. Cook until thickened, stirring constantly. Add coconut; mix well. Cool. Spread between layers and over top and side of cooled cake.

Pauline B. Hart, Clemmons

PEA PICKING CAKE

1/2 cup margarine, softened
4 eggs
1 11-ounce can mandarin oranges
1 2-layer package yellow cake mix
12 ounces whipped topping
1 4-ounce package vanilla instant pudding mix
1 16-ounce can crushed pineapple, drained

Cream margarine in mixer bowl until light and fluffy. Add eggs 1 at a time, beating well after each addition. Add mandarin oranges and juice; beat well. Add cake mix; mix well. Pour into 2 greased and floured cake pans. Bake at 350 degrees for 25 to 30 minutes or until cake tests done. Cool in pans for several minutes. Invert onto wire rack to cool completely. Let whipped topping stand at room temperature for 15 minutes. Combine whipped topping and pudding mix in bowl; mix well. Add crushed pineapple; mix well. Spread between layers and over top and side of cooled cake.

Mabel F. Lawson

PIÑA COLADA CAKE

1 2-layer package pudding-recipe cake mix
1 14-ounce can sweetened condensed milk
1 8-ounce can cream of coconut
2 6-ounce packages frozen coconut, thawed
2 8-ounce cans crushed pineapple
8 ounces whipped topping

Prepare and bake cake using package directions for 9x13-inch cake pan. Pierce top of hot cake with handle of wooden spoon. Mix condensed milk, cream of coconut and 1 package coconut in bowl. Pour over hot cake. Cool. Spread undrained pineapple over cake. Combine whipped topping and remaining coconut in bowl; mix well. Spread over cake. Chill for several hours before serving.

Kathryn Loy, Gibsonville

GRAHAM CRACKER PINEAPPLE CAKE

3/4 cup oil
1 1/2 cups sugar
3 egg yolks
1 1/2 cups milk
1 teaspoon salt
1 tablespoon baking powder
1 16-ounce package graham crackers, crushed

3 egg whites, stiffly beaten
1 20-ounce can crushed pineapple
1/2 cup melted margarine
1 16-ounce package confectioners' sugar
1/2 3-ounce can coconut

Combine oil, sugar, egg yolks, milk, salt and baking powder in mixer bowl; mix well. Add graham cracker crumbs; mix well. Fold in stiffly beaten egg whites. Pour into greased 9x13-inch cake pan. Bake at 350 degrees for 30 to 35 minutes. Drain pineapple, reserving juice. Pour reserved juice over hot cake. Combine margarine and confectioners' sugar in mixer bowl; beat well. Add coconut and pineapple; mix well. Spread over cake.

Jean Jarrett, Thomasville

GRAHAM CRACKER PINEAPPLE LAYER CAKE

1 16-ounce package graham crackers, crushed
2 teaspoons baking powder
2 cups sugar
1/4 teaspoon salt
1 cup shortening
1 cup milk

5 eggs
1 3-ounce can coconut
1 teaspoon vanilla extract
1/3 cup shortening
2 16-ounce packages confectioners' sugar
1 8-ounce can crushed pineapple

Mix graham crackers, baking powder, sugar and salt in mixer bowl. Add 1 cup shortening; mix well. Add milk and eggs; mix well. Stir in coconut and vanilla. Pour into 3 greased and floured 9-inch round cake pans. Bake at 350 degrees for 25 minutes. Cool in pans for 5 minutes. Invert onto wire rack to cool. Beat 1/3 cup shortening in mixer bowl until light and fluffy. Add confectioners' sugar alternately with drained pineapple, beating well after each addition. Spread between layers and over top and side of cake.

Lillie B. Allison, Burlington

PINEAPPLE UPSIDE-DOWN CAKE

1½ cups packed light brown sugar
2 tablespoons butter
1 16-ounce can sliced pineapple, drained
20 maraschino cherry halves
1½ cups sugar
3 eggs
½ cup water
1½ cups flour
1½ teaspoons baking powder
1 teaspoon vanilla extract
Salt to taste

Spread brown sugar in 8-inch skillet. Dot with butter. Dry pineapple slices with paper towels. Arrange over butter. Cut remaining slices into wedges. Place around pineapple slices. Dry maraschino cherries with paper towels. Place in holes of pineapple slices and around edges seed side up. Beat sugar and 1 egg in mixer bowl. Beat in remaining eggs 1 at a time. Add water and flour alternately, beating well. Add baking powder, vanilla and salt; mix well. Pour over pineapple. Bake at 350 degrees for 35 minutes. Reduce temperature to 300 degrees. Bake for 10 minutes or until cake tests done. Invert immediately onto serving plate.

Mrs. Paul Schneeloch, Clemmons

POPPY SEED CAKE

1 2-layer package yellow cake mix
1 6-ounce package vanilla instant pudding mix
4 eggs
½ cup oil
1 cup hot water
2 tablespoons poppy seed
2 teaspoons almond extract

Combine cake mix and pudding mix in mixer bowl. Add eggs 1 at a time, beating well after each addition. Add oil, water, poppy seed and almond extract. Beat for 4 minutes. Pour into 2 greased and floured cake pans. Bake at 350 degrees for 45 minutes or until layers test done. Cool in cake pans for several minutes. Invert onto wire rack to cool completely.

Wenona Baker, Kernersville

AUNT JESSIE'S POUND CAKE

3 cups sifted flour
1/4 teaspoon salt
1/2 teaspoon baking powder
1 cup butter, softened
1/2 cup shortening
3 cups sugar
1 teaspoon vanilla extract
6 eggs
1 cup milk
1/2 cup baking cocoa
11/2 cups confectioners' sugar
Dash of salt
3 tablespoons hot water
1/3 cup melted butter
1/2 teaspoon vanilla

Sift flour with salt and baking powder. Cream butter, shortening and sugar in mixer bowl until light and fluffy. Stir in 1 teaspoon vanilla. Add eggs 1 at a time, beating well after each addition. Add sifted dry ingredients and milk alternately, mixing well after each addition. Pour into greased and floured tube pan. Bake at 325 degrees for 11/2 to 13/4 hours or until cake tests done. Cool on wire rack for 10 minutes. Turn onto cake plate. Combine cocoa, confectioners' sugar and salt in bowl. Add remaining ingredients; mix well. Spread over warm cake.

Jessie Grandinetti

AUNT LULA'S POUND CAKE

3 cups sifted flour
1/2 teaspoon baking powder
11/2 cups shortening
3 cups sugar
6 eggs
1 cup evaporated milk
1 teaspoon vanilla extract
1 teaspoon lemon extract

Sift flour with baking powder. Cream shortening and sugar in mixer bowl until light and fluffy. Add eggs 1 at a time, beating well after each addition. Add sifted dry ingredients and evaporated milk alternately, mixing well after each addition. Add vanilla and lemon extracts; mix well. Pour into greased and floured tube pan. Bake at 350 degrees for 11/2 hours or until cake tests done. Cool in pan for 10 minutes. Remove to wire rack to cool completely. Invert onto cake plate.

Nancy Boner Parnell, Winston-Salem

EASY POUND CAKE

Yield:
16 servings
Utensil:
tube pan
Approx Per
Serving:
Cal 418
Prot 5 g
Carbo 55 g
Fiber 1 g
T Fat 21 g
Chol 136 mg
Sod 161 mg

Dietary
Exchanges:
Milk 0
Vegetable 0
Fruit 0
Bread/Starch 1
Meat 1/2; Fat 4

½ cup shortening
3 cups sugar
6 eggs
3 cups cake flour
½ teaspoon baking
  powder
1 cup milk
2 teaspoons vanilla
  extract
2 teaspoons lemon
  extract
1 cup butter, melted

Combine shortening, sugar, eggs, cake flour, baking powder, milk and flavorings in mixer bowl; beat until smooth. Add melted butter; beat well. Pour into greased and floured tube pan. Bake at 325 degrees for 1 hour and 10 minutes. Cool in pan for 10 minutes. Remove to wire rack to cool completely. Invert onto cake plate.

Ruth H. Highsmith, Winston-Salem

LOW-CHOLESTEROL AND LOW-FAT POUND CAKE

Yield:
18 servings
Utensil:
tube pan
Approx Per
Serving:
Cal 345
Prot 4 g
Carbo 49 g
Fiber 1 g
T Fat 16 g
Chol 2 mg
Sod 247 mg

Dietary
Exchanges:
Milk 0
Vegetable 0
Fruit 0
Bread/Starch 1
Meat 0; Fat 3½

1½ cups corn oil
  margarine, softened
3 cups sugar
6 extra large egg
  whites
3 cups flour
1 teaspoon baking
  powder
1 cup milk
1 tablespoon lemon
  extract

Cream margarine and sugar in mixer bowl until light and fluffy. Add egg whites 1 at a time, beating well after each addition. Stir in dry ingredients alternately with milk and lemon extract; mix well. Pour into greased and floured tube pan. Bake at 325 degrees for 1 hour and 10 minutes. Cool on wire rack for 10 minutes. Turn onto cake plate.

Peggy S. Smith, Burlington

My Favorite Pound Cake

3 cups flour
1 teaspoon baking
  powder
1/2 teaspoon salt
1 cup margarine,
  softened
1/2 cup shortening

3 cups sugar
6 eggs
1 cup milk
1 teaspoon vanilla
  extract
2 teaspoons lemon
  extract

Sift flour with baking powder and salt. Cream margarine, shortening and sugar in bowl until light and fluffy. Beat in eggs 1 at a time. Add sifted dry ingredients and milk alternately, stirring well after each addition. Stir in vanilla and lemon extracts. Pour into greased and floured tube pan. Bake at 325 degrees for 30 minutes. Increase temperature to 350 degrees. Bake for 30 minutes longer. Reduce temperature to 325 degrees. Bake for 30 minutes longer or until cake tests done. Cool on wire rack for 10 minutes. Turn onto cake plate.

Nancy K. Southern, Clemmons

Black Walnut Pound Cake

3 cups sugar
1 cup margarine,
  softened
1/2 cup shortening
5 eggs
3 cups flour
1/2 teaspoon baking
  powder

1 cup evaporated milk
1/2 teaspoon walnut
  extract
1 7-ounce can black
   walnuts, finely
   chopped

Cream sugar, margarine and shortening in mixer bowl until light and fluffy. Add eggs, flour, baking powder, milk and walnut extract; beat well. Stir in walnuts. Pour into greased and floured tube pan. Bake at 350 degrees for 1 hour or until cake tests done. Cool on wire rack for 10 minutes. Turn onto cake plate.

Bob Webster, Elon College

BLUEBERRY POUND CAKE

2³/₄ cups flour
1 teaspoon baking powder
1 cup butter, softened
2 cups sugar
4 eggs
1¹/₂ teaspoons vanilla extract
1 pint blueberries
¹/₄ cup flour

Sift 2³/₄ cups flour with baking powder. Cream butter and sugar in bowl until light and fluffy. Add eggs 1 at a time, beating well after each addition. Add dry ingredients; mix well. Stir in vanilla. Toss blueberries with ¹/₄ cup flour to coat. Fold into mixture gently. Pour into greased and floured bundt pan. Bake at 325 degrees for 1¹/₄ hours or until cake tests done. Cool on wire rack for 10 minutes. Turn onto cake plate.

Becky Lankford, Greensboro

BROWN SUGAR POUND CAKE

3¹/₂ cups flour
1 teaspoon baking powder
1¹/₂ cups butter
3¹/₄ cups packed light brown sugar
5 eggs
1 teaspoon vanilla extract
1 cup milk
1 cup water
1 cup sugar
1 teaspoon vanilla extract

Sift flour with baking powder. Cream butter and brown sugar in mixer bowl until light and fluffy. Add eggs 1 at a time, beating well on high speed after each addition. Add 1 teaspoon vanilla; stir well. Add sifted dry ingredients alternately with milk, beating on low speed until blended. Pour into greased and floured tube pan. Bake at 325 degrees for 1¹/₄ to 1¹/₂ hours or until cake tests done. Cool on wire rack for 10 minutes. Turn onto cake plate. Combine water, sugar and remaining 1 teaspoon vanilla in saucepan. Bring to a boil. Pour over cooled cake. May sprinkle cake with toasted pecans.

Dovie Smith, King

LEMON-ORANGE BUTTERMILK POUND CAKE

3½ cups flour
½ teaspoon soda
½ teaspoon salt
1 cup shortening
½ cup butter, softened
2½ cups sugar
4 eggs
1 cup buttermilk

2 teaspoons lemon
  extract
2 teaspoons orange
  extract
½ cup sugar
½ cup water
Juice of 1 lemon
Grated rind of 1 lemon

Sift flour with soda and salt. Cream shortening, butter and 2½ cups sugar in bowl until light and fluffy. Add eggs 1 at a time, beating well after each addition. Add sifted dry ingredients alternately with buttermilk, mixing well after each addition. Add lemon and orange extracts; blend well. Pour into greased and floured tube pan. Bake at 325 degrees for 1¼ hours or until cake tests done. Turn onto cake plate. Combine ½ cup sugar, water, lemon juice and lemon rind in saucepan. Cook over medium heat, stirring constantly until syrupy. Prick cake with toothpick. Drizzle syrup over hot cake.

A Pioneer

CHOCOLATE POUND CAKE

1 cup butter, softened
3 cups sugar
5 eggs
3 cups flour
½ cup baking cocoa
½ teaspoon salt

1 teaspoon baking
  powder
1 cup milk
1 teaspoon vanilla
  extract

Cream butter and sugar in large bowl until light and fluffy. Add eggs 1 at a time, beating well after each addition. Combine flour, cocoa, salt and baking powder together in medium bowl. Add alternately with milk to creamed mixture, beginning and ending with dry ingredients. Stir in vanilla. Pour into greased and floured tube pan. Bake at 325 degrees for 1 hour and 20 minutes or until cake tests done.

Mary Rudisill, Hendersonville

CHOCOLATE SYRUP POUND CAKE

1 cup butter, softened
½ cup shortening
3 cups sugar
5 eggs
3 cups flour
½ teaspoon baking
  powder
1 cup milk
1 teaspoon vanilla
  extract

1 16-ounce can
   chocolate syrup
1 1-pound package
   confectioners' sugar
½ cup butter, softened
3 ounces cream cheese,
   softened
1 teaspoon vanilla extract
¼ cup milk
½ cup baking cocoa

Cream 1 cup butter, shortening and 3 cups sugar in bowl until light. Beat in eggs 1 at a time. Beat in mixture of flour and baking powder alternately with milk, beginning and ending with flour. Stir in mixture of vanilla and chocolate syrup. Pour into greased and floured tube pan. Bake at 325 degrees for 1½ hours or until cake tests done. Cool on wire rack for 10 minutes. Invert onto cake plate. Cream confectioners' sugar, ½ cup butter and cream cheese in bowl. Add remaining ingredients; mix well. Spread frosting over cake.

Thelma S. Horton, Winston-Salem

PLAIN POUND CAKE

3 cups flour
½ teaspoon baking
  powder
¼ teaspoon salt
½ cup margarine,
  softened

1 cup shortening
6 eggs
3 cups sugar
1 cup milk
1½ teaspoons lemon
   extract

Sift together flour, baking powder and salt. Cream margarine and shortening in mixer bowl until light and fluffy. Add eggs 1 at a time alternately with sugar, mixing well after each addition. Add mixture of dry ingredients alternately with milk, beating well after each addition. Add lemon extract. Beat for 1 minute. Pour into greased and floured tube pan. Bake at 325 degrees for 1½ hours or until golden brown. Cool in pan for 15 minutes. Invert onto cake plate. Cover with waxed paper to retain moisture.

Peggy Cassada, Clemmons

RED VELVET POUND CAKE

1 1/2 cups shortening
3 cups sugar
1/4 teaspoon salt
3 cups flour
1 teaspoon baking
  powder
7 ounces milk
7 eggs
2 1-ounce bottles of
  red food coloring
2 teaspoons vanilla
  extract
1/2 cup margarine,
  softened
8 ounces cream cheese,
  softened
1 1-pound package
  confectioners' sugar
2 teaspoons vanilla
  extract

Cream shortening, sugar and salt in large bowl until light. Sift flour and baking powder together. Add dry ingredients alternately with milk to creamed mixture, mixing well. Beat in eggs 1 at a time. Stir in food coloring and 2 teaspoons vanilla. Pour into greased and floured tube pan. Bake at 325 degrees for 1 1/2 hours or until cake tests done. Cool in pan for 10 minutes. Remove to wire rack to cool completely. Invert onto cake plate. Cream margarine and remaining ingredients in bowl until light. Spread over cake.

Lois L. Bennett, Winston-Salem

SOUR CREAM POUND CAKE

1 cup margarine,
  softened
1/2 cup oil
3 cups sugar
5 eggs
3 1/2 cups flour
1 teaspoon baking
  powder
1/2 teaspoon salt
1 cup sour cream
1 teaspoon vanilla
  extract
1 teaspoon lemon
  extract

Cream margarine, oil and sugar in bowl until light and fluffy. Add eggs 1 at a time, beating well after each addition. Sift flour, baking powder and salt together. Add to creamed mixture alternately with sour cream, beating well after each addition. Stir in flavorings; mix well. Pour into greased and floured tube pan. Bake at 325 degrees for 1 1/2 hours or until cake tests done. Cool on wire rack for 10 minutes. Turn onto cake plate.

Mavis Peterson, Elon College

COLD OVEN POUND CAKE

1 cup butter, softened
1/2 cup shortening
3 cups sugar
4 eggs
3 cups cake flour
1 cup milk
2 teaspoons vanilla extract
1 teaspoon almond extract

Cream butter, shortening and sugar in bowl until light and fluffy. Add eggs 1 at a time, beating well after each addition. Add cake flour and milk alternately, beating well after each addition. Stir in vanilla and almond extracts. Pour into greased and floured tube pan. Place in cold oven. Bake at 325 degrees for 1 1/4 to 1 1/2 hours or until cake tests done. Cool in pan for 10 minutes. Remove to wire rack to cool completely. Turn onto cake plate.

Elizabeth Ann B. Smith, Burlington

COCONUT-CREAM CHEESE POUND CAKE

1/2 cup butter, softened
1/2 cup shortening
8 ounces cream cheese, softened
3 cups sugar
6 eggs
3 cups flour
1/4 teaspoon soda
1/4 teaspoon salt
1 6-ounce package frozen shredded coconut, thawed
1 teaspoon vanilla extract
1 teaspoon coconut extract

Cream butter, shortening and cream cheese in mixer bowl. Add sugar gradually, beating at medium speed until mixture is light and fluffy. Add eggs 1 at a time, beating well after each addition. Sift flour, soda and salt together. Add to creamed mixture, beating well. Add shredded coconut and flavorings; mix well. Pour into greased and floured tube pan. Bake at 300 degrees for 1 1/4 hours or until cake tests done. Cool in pan for 10 to 15 minutes. Remove to wire rack to cool completely. Turn onto cake plate.

Doris D. Burnette, Graham

ELVIS' FAVORITE POUND CAKE

1 cup butter-flavored margarine
3 cups sugar
7 eggs
3 cups flour
1 cup whipping cream
2 teaspoons vanilla extract
2 teaspoons lemon extract

Cream margarine and sugar in bowl until light and fluffy. Add eggs 1 at a time, beating well after each addition. Add flour and whipping cream alternately to creamed mixture, beating well after each addition. Stir in vanilla and lemon extracts. Pour into greased and floured tube pan. Bake at 325 degrees for 1 to 1¼ hours or until cake tests done. Cool on wire rack for 10 minutes. Turn onto cake plate.

Reba S. Holt, Cooleemee

LEMON-CREAM CHEESE POUND CAKE

½ cup margarine, softened
8 ounces cream cheese, softened
1 cup sugar
1 cup flour
1 2-layer package butter cake mix
5 eggs
1 cup milk
2 teaspoons lemon extract

Cream margarine, cream cheese and sugar in bowl until light and fluffy. Add flour, cake mix, eggs and milk alternately to creamed mixture, beating well after each addition. Stir in lemon extract. Pour into greased and floured tube pan. Bake at 325 degrees for 1 hour and 20 minutes or until cake tests done. Cool on wire rack for 10 minutes. Turn onto cake plate. May make a chocolate pound cake by substituting chocolate cake mix and chocolate flavoring for butter cake mix and lemon extract.

Pat Jones, Kernersville

EASY LEMON POUND CAKE

Yield:
16 servings
Utensil:
tube pan
**Approx Per
Serving:**
Cal 272
Prot 3 g
Carbo 32 g
Fiber <1 g
T Fat 15 g
Chol 86 mg
Sod 254 mg

**Dietary
Exchanges:**
Milk 0
Vegetable 0
Fruit 0
Bread/Starch 2
Meat 1/2; Fat 3

1 2-layer package yellow cake mix
1 3-ounce package lemon instant pudding mix
3/4 cup water
3/4 cup canola oil
1 tablespoon lemon extract
5 eggs, beaten

Combine cake mix, pudding mix, water, oil, lemon extract and eggs in large bowl; beat well. Pour into greased and floured tube pan. Bake at 325 degrees for 1 to 1 1/4 hours or until cake tests done. Cool on wire rack for 10 minutes. Turn onto cake plate.

Judy C. Barr, Advance

FRESH LEMON POUND CAKE

Yield:
16 servings
Utensil:
tube pan
**Approx Per
Serving:**
Cal 459
Prot 5 g
Carbo 64 g
Fiber 1 g
T Fat 22 g
Chol 122 mg
Sod 182 mg

**Dietary
Exchanges:**
Milk 0
Vegetable 0
Fruit 0
Bread/Starch 1
Meat 1/2; Fat 4 1/2

1 cup butter
1/2 cup shortening
3 cups sugar
2 tablespoons boiling water
5 eggs
3 cups flour
1 teaspoon baking powder
1 cup milk
2 teaspoons fresh lemon juice
1 teaspoon vanilla extract
3/4 cup sugar
2 tablespoons butter
3 tablespoons fresh lemon juice

Cream 1 cup butter, shortening and 3 cups sugar in mixer bowl until light and fluffy. Add boiling water; beat well. Beat in eggs 1 at a time. Sift in flour and baking powder alternately with milk, beating well after each addition. Stir in 2 teaspoons lemon juice and vanilla; mix well. Pour into greased and floured tube pan. Place in cold oven. Bake at 325 degrees for 1 1/2 hours or until cake tests done. Cool in pan for 10 minutes. Remove to wire rack. Bring 3/4 cup sugar, 2 tablespoons butter, and 3 tablespoons lemon juice to a boil in saucepan, stirring constantly. Brush over cake.

Eileen Rindos, Burlington

LEMON POUND CAKE

3 cups flour
1/2 teaspoon salt
1/2 teaspoon baking
    powder
1 cup butter, softened
1/2 cup shortening
3 cups sugar

5 eggs
1 cup milk
1 teaspoon vanilla
    extract
1 teaspoon lemon
    extract

Sift flour, salt and baking powder together. Cream butter, shortening and sugar in bowl until light and fluffy. Add eggs 1 at a time, beating well after each addition. Add sifted dry ingredients and milk alternately, beginning and ending with flour, beating well after each addition. Stir in flavorings; mix well. Pour into greased and floured tube pan. Bake at 325 degrees for 1 hour and 20 minutes or until cake tests done. Cool in pan 10 minutes. Turn onto cake plate. Wrap with foil while warm. Best served after cooling overnight. Cake stays fresh for 1 week.

A Pioneer

ORANGE CRUSH POUND CAKE

1 cup shortening
1/4 cup margarine,
    softened
2 3/4 cups sugar
5 eggs
3 cups cake flour
1/2 teaspoon salt
1 cup Orange Crush
    soft drink

1 teaspoon each vanilla
    and orange extract
1 cup confectioners'
    sugar
3 ounces cream cheese,
    softened
1/2 teaspoon each
    vanilla and orange
    extract

Cream shortening, margarine and sugar in bowl until light and fluffy. Beat in eggs 1 at a time. Add sifted cake flour and salt alternately with orange drink, beating well after each addition. Stir in 1 teaspoon vanilla and orange extracts. Pour into greased and floured tube pan. Bake at 325 degrees for 1 hour and 10 minutes or until cake tests done. Cool in pan for 5 minutes. Turn onto cake plate. Cream confectioners' sugar and cream cheese in small bowl until light and fluffy. Stir in 1/2 teaspoon vanilla and orange extracts. Spread over warm cake.

Pat L. Burke, Burlington

PINEAPPLE POUND CAKE

1/2 cup butter, softened
1/2 cup shortening
2 3/4 cups sugar
6 eggs
3 cups sifted cake flour
1 teaspoon baking
  powder
1/4 cup milk
1 teaspoon vanilla extract
3/4 cup crushed
  pineapple with juice
1/4 cup margarine
1 1/2 cups sifted
  confectioners' sugar
1 cup crushed
  pineapple, drained

Cream butter, shortening and sugar in bowl. Beat in eggs 1 at a time. Add sifted cake flour and baking powder alternately with milk, mixing well after each addition. Stir in vanilla. Add pineapple with juice; mix well. Pour into greased and floured tube pan. Place in cold oven. Bake at 325 degrees for 1 1/2 hours or until cake tests done. Cool in pan for 5 minutes. Turn onto cake plate. Cream margarine and confectioners' sugar in bowl until light and fluffy. Stir in drained pineapple. Spread over warm cake.

Elizabeth Ann B. Smith, Burlington

RUM POUND CAKE

1 cup chopped pecans
1 cup margarine,
  softened
1/2 cup shortening
2 1/2 cups sugar
5 eggs
3 1/2 cups flour
1/2 teaspoon baking
  powder
1/2 teaspoon salt
1 cup milk
1 tablespoon rum
  extract
1 cup packed brown
  sugar
1/3 cup water
1/2 cup margarine
2 teaspoons rum extract

Sprinkle greased tube pan with pecans; flour lightly. Cream 1 cup margarine with shortening and sugar in bowl. Beat in eggs 1 at a time. Add sifted flour, baking powder and salt to creamed mixture alternately with milk, beating well after each addition. Stir in 1 table-spoon rum extract. Pour into prepared pan. Bake at 225 degrees for 1 hour. Bake at 300 degrees for 45 minutes or until cake tests done. Cool in pan for 5 minutes. Turn onto cake plate. Bring brown sugar, water and 1/2 cup margarine to a boil in saucepan, stirring constantly. Stir in 2 teaspoons rum extract. Spoon over cake.

Ruth Settle

PRUNE CAKE

Yield:
15 servings
Utensil:
cake pan
Approx Per
Serving:
Cal 415
Prot 4 g
Carbo 49 g
Fiber 1 g
T Fat 24 g
Chol 64 mg
Sod 100 mg

Dietary
Exchanges:
Milk 0
Vegetable 0
Fruit 1/2
Bread/Starch 1/2
Meat 0; Fat 5

1 cup oil
1½ cups sugar
3 eggs
1½ cups flour
1 teaspoon cinnamon
1 teaspoon allspice
1 teaspoon nutmeg
1 teaspoon soda
1 cup buttermilk
1 teaspoon vanilla extract

1 cup chopped pecans
1 cup chopped cooked
  prunes
1 cup sugar
1/2 cup buttermilk
1/2 teaspoon soda
1 tablespoon corn syrup
1/4 cup butter
1/2 teaspoon vanilla
  extract

Blend oil and sugar in mixer bowl. Beat in eggs 1 at a time. Add mixture of next 5 ingredients to batter alternately with buttermilk and vanilla, beating well. Stir in pecans and prunes. Pour into greased and floured 9x13-inch cake pan. Bake at 300 degrees for 45 minutes or until cake tests done. Combine remaining ingredients in saucepan. Cook to 234 to 240 degrees on candy thermometer, soft-ball stage; do not stir. Pour over hot cake.

Jean W. Burnette, Winston-Salem

PUMPKIN CAKE ROLL

Yield:
8 servings
Utensil:
cake pan
Approx Per
Serving:
Cal 460
Prot 6 g
Carbo 57 g
Fiber 1 g
T Fat 25 g
Chol 142 mg
Sod 349 mg

Dietary
Exchanges:
Milk 0
Vegetable 0
Fruit 0
Bread/Starch 1
Meat 1/2; Fat 6

3 eggs
1 cup sugar
2/3 cup pumpkin pie
  filling
1 teaspoon lemon juice
3/4 teaspoon baking
  powder
2 teaspoons cinnamon
1 teaspoon ginger
3/4 cup flour

1/2 teaspoon nutmeg
1/2 teaspoon salt
1 cup chopped pecans
1 cup confectioners'
  sugar
6 ounces cream cheese,
  softened
1/4 cup butter, softened
1/2 teaspoon vanilla
  extract

Beat eggs in mixer bowl at high speed for 5 minutes. Add 1 cup sugar gradually, beating well. Stir in pie filling and lemon juice. Add dry ingredients; mix well. Spread in greased and floured 10x15-inch cake pan. Top with pecans. Bake at 375 degrees for 15 minutes. Turn onto towel sprinkled with confectioners' sugar. Roll cake in towel from narrow end. Cool on wire rack. Cream confectioners' sugar, cream cheese, butter and vanilla in bowl until light and fluffy. Unroll cake. Spread with filling; reroll. Chill in refrigerator.

Mary B. Kolischak, Winston-Salem

GRAM'S BOILED RAISIN CAKE

1½ cups golden raisins
1 cup water
⅓ cup flour
2½ cups flour
2½ teaspoons baking powder
1½ teaspoons soda
3 teaspoons cinnamon
2 teaspoons nutmeg
1 teaspoon allspice
1 teaspoon cloves
½ teaspoon ginger
1 teaspoon salt
¾ cup shortening
1½ cups sugar
3 eggs
1½ cups milk

Combine raisins and water in saucepan. Bring to a boil. Drain, reserving ½ cup liquid. Spread raisins to cool. Combine raisins with ⅓ cup flour; toss to coat. Sift dry ingredients together. Cream shortening and sugar in mixer bowl until light and fluffy. Add eggs 1 at a time, beating well after each addition. Add flour mixture alternately with milk and reserved raisin liquid, beating well after each addition. Fold in raisins. Pour into greased tube pan. Bake at 350 degrees for 45 to 50 minutes or until cake tests done. Garnish with confectioners' sugar.

Lucille H. Kurre, Winston-Salem

RUM CAKE

1 cup chopped walnuts
1 2-layer package yellow cake mix
1 4-ounce package vanilla instant pudding mix
4 eggs
½ cup cold water
½ cup oil
½ cup rum
½ cup butter
¼ cup water
1 cup sugar
½ cup rum

Sprinkle walnuts in greased and floured 10-inch tube pan. Combine cake mix, pudding mix, eggs, cold water, oil and ½ cup rum in mixer bowl. Beat at medium speed for 2 minutes. Pour over walnuts. Bake at 325 degrees for 50 to 60 minutes or until cake tests done. Combine butter, ¼ cup water, sugar and ½ cup rum in saucepan. Bring to a boil. Cook for 5 minutes, stirring frequently. Pour over hot cake. Let stand for 30 minutes. Invert onto serving plate.

Ruby Hudspeth, Yadkinville

SPICE CAKE

Yield:
16 servings
Utensil:
4 round cake pans
Approx Per Serving:
Cal 357
Prot 5 g
Carbo 68 g
Fiber 3 g
T Fat 9 g
Chol 1 mg
Sod 139 mg

Dietary Exchanges:
Milk 0
Vegetable 0
Fruit 1½
Bread/Starch 1
Meat 0; Fat 2

2 cups sugar
2 teaspoons soda
1 teaspoon nutmeg
1 teaspoon allspice
1 teaspoon cloves
1 teaspoon cinnamon
¼ cup baking cocoa
⅔ cup shortening
3 cups flour
2 cups buttermilk
1   15-ounce package raisins, finely chopped
¼ cup sugar
1 cup warm water
2 recipes Brown Sugar Frosting (see page 390)

Combine 2 cups sugar, soda, spices and cocoa in large mixer bowl; mix well. Cut in shortening until crumbly. Beat in flour alternately with buttermilk. Beat for 3 to 4 minutes. Mix in raisins. Pour into 4 greased 9-inch cake pans. Bake at 350 degrees for 35 minutes. Layers will be about ⅝ inch thick. Cool in pans for 15 minutes. Remove to wire rack to cool completely. Dissolve ¼ cup sugar in warm water. Spoon syrup over each layer before adding frosting. Spread Brown Sugar Frosting between layers and over top and side of cake.

Peggy Cassada, Clemmons

STRAWBERRY CAKE

Yield:
12 servings
Utensil:
8-inch cake pans
Approx Per Serving:
Cal 801
Prot 6 g
Carbo 100 g
Fiber 3 g
T Fat 44 g
Chol 93 mg
Sod 419 mg

Dietary Exchanges:
Milk 0
Vegetable 0
Fruit ½
Bread/Starch 2½
Meat ½; Fat 10

1   2-layer package white cake mix
1   3-ounce package strawberry gelatin
½ cup milk
4 eggs, beaten
1 cup oil
1 cup frozen strawberries, thawed
1 cup flaked coconut
1 cup chopped pecans
1   1-pound package confectioners' sugar
½ cup margarine
½ cup frozen strawberries, thawed
½ cup pecans
½ cup flaked coconut

Combine first 5 ingredients in large bowl, stirring until smooth. Stir in 1 cup strawberries, 1 cup coconut and 1 cup pecans; mix well. Pour into 3 greased and floured 8-inch cake pans. Bake at 350 degrees for 25 to 30 minutes or until layers test done. Cool in pans for 10 minutes. Remove to wire rack to cool completely. Cream confectioners' sugar with margarine in bowl until light and fluffy. Stir in remaining ingredients; mix well. Spread frosting between layers and over top and side of cooled cake.

Earline Goin, Hamptonville

YAM CAKE

1½ cups oil
2 cups sugar
4 egg yolks
¼ cup hot water
2½ cups flour
3 teaspoons baking
  powder
¼ teaspoon salt
1½ cups grated yams
1 cup chopped pecans
1 teaspoon cinnamon
1 teaspoon nutmeg
1 teaspoon vanilla
  extract
4 egg whites
Coconut Frosting

Grease and flour three 8-inch round cake pans; line with greased and floured brown paper. Combine oil and sugar in mixer bowl; beat until light and fluffy. Add egg yolks; beat well. Stir in hot water. Sift in flour, baking powder and salt; beat well. Stir in yams, pecans, cinnamon, nutmeg and vanilla. Beat egg whites bowl at high speed in mixer bowl until stiff peaks form. Fold into batter. Spoon into prepared pans. Bake at 350 degrees for 25 to 30 minutes or until layers test done. Cool in pans for 10 minutes. Remove to wire rack to cool completely. Invert onto serving plate. Spread between layers and over top and side of cake with Coconut Frosting.

Coconut Frosting

1 5-ounce can
   evaporated milk
1 cup sugar
½ cup margarine
3 egg yolks
1 teaspoon vanilla
  extract
1⅓ cups flaked
   coconut

Combine evaporated milk, 1 cup sugar, margarine and 3 egg yolks in saucepan; mix well. Cook over medium heat for 12 minutes or until mixture thickens, stirring constantly. Remove from heat. Add 1 teaspoon vanilla and 1⅓ cups coconut. Beat until of spreading consistency.

Shelba E. Patraw, Greensboro

WATERGATE CAKE

1 2-layer package white cake mix
1 cup oil
3 eggs, beaten
1 cup club soda
1 4-ounce package pistachio instant pudding mix
½ cup chopped pecans
1 cup milk
1 cup confectioners' sugar
16 ounces whipped topping
1 cup sour cream
1 4-ounce package pistachio instant pudding mix
½ cup chopped pecans

Combine cake mix, oil and eggs in mixer bowl; mix well. Add next 3 ingredients. Beat for 4 minutes. Pour into 2 greased and floured 8-inch cake pans. Bake at 325 degrees for 30 minutes or until layers test done. Cool in pans for 10 minutes. Remove to wire rack to cool completely. Turn onto cake plate. Combine milk and next 3 ingredients in mixer bowl. Beat until mixture is smooth. Add 1 package pistachio pudding mix; beat until stiff peaks form. Fold in pecans. Frost cooled cake with mixture. Store cake in refrigerator.

Dorothy S. Best, Winston-Salem

BROWN SUGAR FROSTING

⅓ cup margarine
1½ cups packed brown sugar
¼ cup milk
Salt to taste
2 cups confectioners' sugar
1 teaspoon vanilla extract

Melt margarine in saucepan over medium heat. Add brown sugar, milk and salt; mix well. Bring to a boil, stirring constantly. Boil for 3 minutes. Let stand until cool. Beat until fluffy. Add confectioners' sugar gradually, beating constantly at low speed. Add vanilla. Beat until of spreading consistency, adding additional milk ¼ teaspoonful at a time if necessary. This recipe makes enough for a 2-layer cake. Do not double recipe.

Peggy Cassada, Clemmons

FLUFFY CHOCOLATE-BUTTER FROSTING

Yield:
12 servings
Utensil:
bowl
Approx Per Serving:
Cal 202
Prot 1 g
Carbo 27 g
Fiber 0 g
T Fat 11 g
Chol 0 mg
Sod 103 mg

Dietary Exchanges:
Milk 0
Vegetable 0
Fruit 0
Bread/Starch 0
Meat 0; Fat 3

1/2 cup margarine, softened
3 ounces melted unsweetened chocolate, cooled
2 1/2 cups confectioners' sugar
1/4 cup hot water
1 teaspoon vanilla extract

Blend margarine and chocolate in mixer bowl. Add confectioners' sugar alternately with hot water, beating well after each addition. Place bowl in ice water; beat until fluffy. Stir in vanilla.

Gradie Vaden, Winston-Salem

FLUFFY FROSTING FOR COCONUT CAKE

Yield:
12 servings
Utensil:
double boiler
Approx Per Serving:
Cal 120
Prot 1 g
Carbo 26 g
Fiber 1 g
T Fat 2 g
Chol 0 mg
Sod 11 mg

Dietary Exchanges:
Milk 0
Vegetable 0
Fruit 0
Bread/Starch 0
Meat 0; Fat 1

2 egg whites
1 1/2 cups sugar
1 1/2 teaspoons light corn syrup
1/3 cup cold water
1/8 teaspoon vanilla extract
1 3-ounce can coconut

Combine egg whites, sugar, corn syrup and cold water in top of double boiler. Cook over rapidly boiling water for 7 minutes or until soft peaks form, beating constantly with mixer. Remove from heat. Add vanilla. Beat for 2 minutes or until of spreading consistency. Spread icing between layers and over top and side of cooled cake, sprinkling coconut over icing.

Barbara Johnson, Graham

GERMAN CHOCOLATE CAKE ICING

½ cup melted
   margarine
1 cup evaporated milk
1 cup sugar
¼ teaspoon cream of
   tartar

3 egg yolks, beaten
¾ cup chopped pecans
1 teaspoon vanilla
   extract
1¼ cups coconut

Combine melted margarine, evaporated milk, sugar, cream of tartar and egg yolks in saucepan; mix well. Cook over low heat for 12 minutes or until thickened, stirring constantly. Stir in pecans, vanilla and coconut. Cool completely.

Helen A. Howard, Pfafftown

COCONUT CREAM CHEESE FROSTING

¾ cup butter, softened
8 ounces cream cheese,
   softened
1 1-pound package
   confectioners' sugar

1½ teaspoons vanilla
   extract
1 7-ounce can coconut

Cream butter and cream cheese in mixer bowl. Add confectioners' sugar gradually, beating until light and fluffy. Stir in vanilla and coconut. May substitute nuts, strawberries, pineapple or chocolate bits for coconut.

Ruth McCoy

COOKIES
and CANDIES

CHOCOLATE CHIP BROWNIES

½ cup butter
1 cup packed light
  brown sugar
1 teaspoon vanilla
  extract
1 egg
1 cup flour
½ teaspoon salt
1 cup semisweet
  chocolate chips

Melt butter in saucepan; stir in brown sugar. Pour into mixer bowl; cool. Add vanilla and egg; beat until fluffy. Add flour and salt; mix well. Fold in chocolate chips. Spoon into greased 9x9-inch baking pan. Bake at 350 degrees for 25 minutes or until edges pull away from sides of pan. Cool on wire rack. Cut into 16 squares.

Janice Albright, Mebane

BROWNIES

2 cups sugar
4 eggs
1 cup oil
1 teaspoon vanilla extract
1 cup chopped pecans
2 cups flour
¾ teaspoon salt
1½ teaspoons baking
  powder
¾ cup baking cocoa
1½ cups miniature
  marshmallows
½ cup evaporated milk
¼ cup margarine
4 cups confectioners'
  sugar
2 teaspoons vanilla
  extract

Combine first 5 ingredients in bowl; mix well. Sift in flour, salt, baking powder and ¼ cup cocoa; mix well. Pour into 2 greased and floured 9x9-inch baking pans. Bake at 350 degrees for 25 minutes. Turn off oven. Sprinkle marshmallows over top of warm brownies. Return to oven for 4 minutes. Combine evaporated milk and margarine in saucepan. Cook over medium heat until margarine is melted. Sift in confectioners' sugar and ½ cup cocoa; mix well. Stir in vanilla. Spread over top. Cool on wire rack.

Pat L. Burke, Burlington

DELICIOUS BROWNIES

Yield:
24 servings
Utensil:
baking pan
**Approx Per
Serving:**
*Cal 243
Prot 3 g
Carbo 33 g
Fiber <1 g
T Fat 11 g
Chol 78 mg
Sod 173 mg*

**Dietary
Exchanges:**
*Milk 0
Vegetable 0
Fruit 0
Bread/Starch 1½
Meat 0; Fat 2½*

1 22-ounce package
   brownie mix
3 eggs, beaten
2 tablespoons water
8 ounces cream cheese,
   softened
5 tablespoons butter,
   softened
2 eggs
1 teaspoon vanilla
   extract
½ cup sugar
2 tablespoons flour
Cocoa Frosting

Prepare brownie mix using package directions using 3 eggs and 2 tablespoons water. Spread ½ of the batter over bottom of well greased 9x12-inch baking pan. Beat cream cheese and 5 tablespoons butter in small bowl until light and fluffy. Add eggs, 1 teaspoon vanilla, sugar and flour; mix well. Pour over batter in pan. Dot remaining batter over cream cheese mixture. Swirl top two layers together. Bake at 350 degrees for 35 minutes. Cool on wire rack; place on serving plate. Spread Cocoa Frosting over cooled brownies. Cut into 24 bars.

Cocoa Frosting

*Nutritional
information for
Cocoa Frosting
is included
above.*

3 tablespoons melted
   butter
2 tablespoons baking
   cocoa
1½ cups (about)
   confectioners' sugar
2 tablespoons (about)
   milk
1 teaspoon vanilla
   extract

Melt butter in saucepan. Stir in cocoa. Add enough confectioners' sugar and milk to make of desired spreading consistency. Stir in remaining 1 teaspoon vanilla.

Jacob Stutts, Snow Camp

Butterscotch Brownies

1 cup butterscotch chips
1/4 cup margarine
1 cup packed light brown sugar
1/2 teaspoon vanilla extract
2 eggs, beaten
1 cup flour
1 teaspoon baking powder
3/4 teaspoon salt
1/2 cup chopped pecans

Melt butterscotch chips with margarine in top of double boiler, stirring frequently. Remove from heat. Stir in brown sugar; cool. Add vanilla and eggs; mix well. Sift flour, baking powder and salt together into butterscotch mixture; mix well. Stir in pecans. Spread into greased and floured 9x13-inch baking pan. Bake at 350 degrees for 20 to 25 minutes or until edges pull away from sides of pan. Cool on wire rack. Cut into 24 bars.

Sarah L. Finley, Graham

Brown Sugar Tea Cakes

2 cups packed brown sugar
1 cup butter, softened
2 eggs, beaten
1 1/2 teaspoons soda
1 tablespoon milk
1 tablespoon butter, melted
1 cup (about) flour

Cream brown sugar and butter in bowl until fluffy. Add eggs; mix well. Dissolve soda in milk and 1 tablespoon melted butter. Add to creamed mixture; stir well. Add enough flour to make soft dough. Roll out on floured surface; cut into 24 circles. Place on cookie sheet. Bake at 375 degrees for 8 minutes. Cool on wire rack.

Mary Pickett, Winston-Salem

Butterscotch-Cream Cheese Bars

Yield:
36 servings
Utensil:
baking pan
Approx Per
Serving:
Cal 174
Prot 3 g
Carbo 16 g
Fiber 1 g
T Fat 12 g
Chol 18 mg
Sod 98 mg

Dietary
Exchanges:
Milk ½
Vegetable 0
Fruit 0
Bread/Starch ½
Meat 0; Fat 2½

½ cup margarine
2 cups butterscotch chips
2 cups graham cracker crumbs
1 cup chopped pecans
8 ounces cream cheese, softened
1 14-ounce can sweetened condensed milk
1 teaspoon vanilla extract
1 egg

Melt margarine and butterscotch chips in saucepan over low heat, stirring frequently. Stir in graham cracker crumbs and pecans. Press half the mixture into greased 9x13-inch baking pan. Beat cream cheese in mixer bowl until fluffy. Add condensed milk, vanilla and egg; beat well. Pour over butterscotch crust. Top with remaining butterscotch mixture. Bake at 350 degrees for 20 minutes. Chill in refrigerator until firm. Cut into 36 bars. Do not use glass baking dish.

Mary Gilliam, Burlington

Cheesecake Squares

Yield:
36 servings
Utensil:
baking pan
Approx Per
Serving:
Cal 78
Prot 1 g
Carbo 5 g
Fiber <1 g
T Fat 6 g
Chol 21 mg
Sod 56 mg

Dietary
Exchanges:
Milk 0
Vegetable 0
Fruit 0
Bread/Starch 0
Meat 0; Fat 1½

⅔ cup graham cracker crumbs
¼ cup sugar
½ cup chopped pecans
¼ cup flour
½ cup butter, melted
¼ cup sugar
8 ounces cream cheese, softened
1 egg, beaten

Combine graham cracker crumbs, sugar, pecans and flour in bowl; mix well. Stir in melted butter. Press mixture in 8x8-inch baking pan. Bake at 350 degrees for 12 minutes. Cream sugar and cream cheese in small bowl. Add egg; beat until creamy. Pour over prepared crust. Bake at 350 degrees for 20 to 25 minutes or until firm. Cool on wire rack. Cut into 36 squares.

Nettie M. Blankenship, Fairview

CHESS SQUARES

½ cup margarine,
melted
1 egg
1 2-layer package
yellow cake mix

8 ounces cream cheese,
softened
2 eggs, beaten
1 1-pound package
confectioners' sugar

Mix cooled, melted margarine and 1 egg in bowl. Add cake mix; mix well. Press mixture into greased and floured 9x13-inch baking pan. Beat cream cheese with 2 eggs in small bowl. Add confectioners' sugar; stir well. Pour over cake mix mixture. Bake at 350 degrees for 35 to 40 minutes or until golden brown. Cool on wire rack. Cut into 24 pieces.

Doris Whitesell

CHEW BREAD

½ cup margarine,
melted
1 1-pound package
light brown sugar
3 eggs, beaten

2 cups self-rising flour
1 teaspoon vanilla
extract
1 cup chopped pecans

Combine melted margarine, brown sugar, eggs, flour, vanilla and pecans in large bowl; mix well. Pour into greased and floured 9x13-inch baking pan. Bake at 350 degrees for 25 minutes. Cool on wire rack. Cut into 36 bars.

Laverne Albright, Burlington

CHOCOLATE KISS COOKIES

Yield:
36 servings
Utensil:
cookie sheet
Approx Per Serving:
Cal 125
Prot 1 g
Carbo 11 g
Fiber <1 g
T Fat 9 g
Chol 0 mg
Sod 69 mg

Dietary Exchanges:
Milk 0
Vegetable 0
Fruit 0
Bread/Starch 1/2
Meat 0; Fat 2

1 cup margarine, softened
1/2 cup confectioners' sugar
1 teaspoon vanilla extract
2 cups flour
1 cup finely chopped walnuts
1 5-ounce package chocolate kisses
1/2 cup (about) confectioners' sugar

Cream margarine, 1/2 cup confectioners' sugar and vanilla in mixer bowl until light and fluffy. Add flour and walnuts; mix well. Shape dough around chocolate kisses to form a ball. Arrange on ungreased cookie sheet. Bake at 325 degrees for 12 minutes. Roll warm cookies in 1/2 cup confectioners' sugar to coat. Cool on wire rack.

John P. Kelly, Greensboro

PEANUT BUTTER CHOCOLATE KISS COOKIES

Yield:
48 servings
Utensil:
cookie sheet
Approx Per Serving:
Cal 98
Prot 2 g
Carbo 12 g
Fiber 1 g
T Fat 5 g
Chol 6 mg
Sod 33 mg

Dietary Exchanges:
Milk 0
Vegetable 0
Fruit 0
Bread/Starch 1/2
Meat 0; Fat 1

1/2 cup sugar
1/2 cup packed light brown sugar
1/2 cup shortening
1/2 cup peanut butter
1 egg, beaten
1 teaspoon vanilla extract
2 tablespoons milk
1 3/4 cups flour
1 teaspoon soda
1/2 teaspoon salt
1/2 cup (about) confectioners' sugar
48 chocolate kisses

Mix sugars, shortening and peanut butter in bowl until creamy. Add egg, vanilla and milk, stirring well. Stir in flour, soda and salt. Shape dough into 1-inch balls; roll in confectioners' sugar to coat. Arrange on ungreased cookie sheet. Bake at 375 degrees for 10 to 12 minutes or until golden brown. Press chocolate kiss in center of each warm cookie. Cool on wire rack.

Emmaline Lindsay, Greensboro

CHOCOLATE COOKIES

Yield:
48 servings
Utensil:
cookie sheet
Approx Per
Serving:
Cal 59
Prot 1 g
Carbo 7 g
Fiber <1 g
T Fat 4 g
Chol 11 mg
Sod 50 mg

Dietary
Exchanges:
Milk 0
Vegetable 0
Fruit 0
Bread/Starch 0
Meat 0; Fat 1

½ cup butter
½ cup sugar
¼ cup packed brown
   sugar
1 egg, beaten
1 teaspoon vanilla
   extract
1 cup flour
½ teaspoon soda
½ teaspoon salt
4 ounces German's
   sweet chocolate, cut
   into quarters
½ cup chopped pecans

Cream butter and sugars in bowl until light and fluffy. Add egg and vanilla; beat well. Add flour, soda and salt; mix well. Stir in chocolate and pecans. Drop by teaspoonfuls 2 inches apart onto ungreased cookie sheet. Bake at 375 degrees for 8 to 10 minutes or until lightly browned. Cool on wire rack.

John P. Kelly, Greensboro

CHOCOLATE-PEANUT BUDDY BARS

Yield:
48 servings
Utensil:
baking pan
Approx Per
Serving:
Cal 114
Prot 2 g
Carbo 12 g
Fiber 1 g
T Fat 7 g
Chol 17 mg
Sod 60 mg

Dietary
Exchanges:
Milk 0
Vegetable 0
Fruit 0
Bread/Starch ½
Meat ½; Fat 1½

1 cup peanut butter
6 tablespoons
   margarine, softened
1¼ cups sugar
3 eggs
1 teaspoon vanilla
   extract
1 cup flour
¼ teaspoon salt
2 cups chocolate chips

Beat peanut butter and margarine in mixer bowl until smooth. Add sugar, eggs and vanilla; beat until creamy. Stir in flour and salt. Fold in 1 cup chocolate chips. Spread mixture in ungreased 9x13-inch baking pan. Bake at 350 degrees for 25 to 30 minutes or until edges begin to brown. Sprinkle with remaining 1 cup chocolate chips. Let stand 15 minutes or until chocolate chips melt. Smooth chocolate evenly over top. Cool on wire rack. Cut into 48 bars.

Grace Moody, Burlington

DOUBLE CHOCOLATE CHIP TREASURES

1 cup plus 1
   tablespoon flour
1/2 teaspoon salt
1/2 teaspoon soda
1/2 cup butter, softened
1/2 cup packed brown
   sugar
1/2 cup sugar
1/2 teaspoon vanilla
   extract
1 egg
1 10-ounce package
   large chocolate
   morsels

Sift flour, salt and soda together. Cream butter and sugars in large bowl until light and fluffy. Add vanilla and egg; beat until creamy. Add sifted dry ingredients gradually, beating well after each addition. Stir in chocolate morsels. Drop by rounded teaspoonfuls onto ungreased cookie sheet. Bake at 375 degrees for 8 to 10 minutes or until golden brown. Cool on wire rack.

Dave Wilson, Kernersville

KRISPIE CHOCOLATE CHIP COOKIES

1 cup margarine,
   softened
2 cups sugar
2 teaspoons vanilla
   extract
2 eggs
2 1/2 cups flour
1 teaspoon salt
1 teaspoon baking
   powder
1 teaspoon soda
2 cups chocolate chips
4 cups crisp rice cereal

Cream margarine and sugar in mixer bowl until light and fluffy. Add vanilla and eggs. Beat for 5 minutes. Sift flour, salt, baking powder and soda into mixture; mix well. Stir in chocolate chips and cereal. Drop by teaspoonfuls onto nonstick cookie sheet. Bake at 375 degrees for 9 to 10 minutes or until golden brown. Cool on wire rack.

Deloris Peterson, Greensboro

CREAM CHEESE BARS

Yield:
36 servings
Utensil:
baking pan
Approx Per
Serving:
Cal 164
Prot 2 g
Carbo 25 g
Fiber 0 g
T Fat 6 g
Chol 30 mg
Sod 146 mg

Dietary
Exchanges:
Milk 0
Vegetable 0
Fruit 0
Bread/Starch 1
Meat 0; Fat 1½

1 2-layer package yellow cake mix
½ cup margarine, softened
1 egg, beaten
3¾ cups confectioners' sugar
8 ounces cream cheese, softened
2 eggs
1 teaspoon vanilla extract
¼ cup confectioners' sugar

Mix cake mix, margarine and 1 egg together in bowl. Press into greased 9x13-inch baking pan. Beat 3¾ cups confectioners' sugar, cream cheese, 2 eggs and vanilla in medium bowl until creamy. Pour over cake mix mixture. Bake at 350 degrees for 35 minutes. Sift remaining ¼ cup confectioners' sugar over top. Cool for 30 minutes. Cut into bars. Store in refrigerator or freezer. May add chopped nuts to cream cheese filling. May spread jelly on crust before adding cream cheese filling.

Jean Andrews

CHRISTMAS BUTTER COOKIES

Yield:
108 servings
Utensil:
cookie sheet
Approx Per
Serving:
Cal 35
Prot <1 g
Carbo 4 g
Fiber <1 g
T Fat 2 g
Chol 7 mg
Sod 22 mg

Dietary
Exchanges:
Milk 0
Vegetable 0
Fruit 0
Bread/Starch 0
Meat 0; Fat ½

1 cup butter, softened
1 cup sugar
1 egg
2 teaspoons vanilla extract
3 cups flour
½ teaspoon baking powder
⅛ teaspoon salt

Cream butter and sugar in bowl until light and fluffy. Add egg and vanilla; beat well. Add flour, baking powder and salt gradually, beating well after each addition. Spoon mixture into cookie press fitted with star tip. Press onto baking sheet. Bake at 350 degrees for 10 to 12 minutes or until lightly browned. Decorate with sprinkles or colored sugar.

Jessie Grandinetti

CHRISTMAS FRUITCAKE COOKIES

Yield:
72 servings
Utensil:
cookie sheet
Approx Per
Serving:
Cal 172
Prot 2 g
Carbo 21 g
Fiber 2 g
T Fat 10 g
Chol 11 mg
Sod 50 mg

Dietary
Exchanges:
Milk 0
Vegetable 0
Fruit 1
Bread/Starch 1/2
Meat 0; Fat 2 1/2

1 cup margarine,
softened
1 cup packed light
brown sugar
3 eggs, beaten
3 cups flour
1 teaspoon vanilla
extract

1 teaspoon soda
3/4 pound white raisins
2 cups chopped dates
1 1/2 cups chopped
candied pineapple
2 cups chopped
candied cherries
7 cups chopped pecans

Cream margarine and brown sugar in bowl until light and fluffy. Add eggs, flour, vanilla and soda; mix well. Stir in raisins, dates, pineapple, cherries and pecans. Drop by teaspoonfuls onto nonstick cookie sheet. Bake at 350 degrees for 15 to 20 minutes or until golden brown. Cool on wire rack.

Teresa Crispino, High Point

SPICY FRUITCAKE COOKIES

Yield:
60 servings
Utensil:
cookie sheet
Approx Per
Serving:
Cal 192
Prot 2 g
Carbo 26 g
Fiber 2 g
T Fat 10 g
Chol 22 mg
Sod 36 mg

Dietary
Exchanges:
Milk 0
Vegetable 0
Fruit 1
Bread/Starch 1/2
Meat 0; Fat 2 1/2

1 cup packed brown
sugar
1/2 cup butter, softened
4 eggs, beaten
2 1/2 cups flour
1 teaspoon soda
1/2 teaspoon nutmeg
1 teaspoon vanilla
extract

3/4 cup apple juice
1 pound candied
pineapple, chopped
1/2 pound candied
cherries, chopped
1 pound raisins
1 1/2 pounds pecans,
chopped
1/2 cup flour

Beat brown sugar, butter and eggs in bowl until creamy. Sift in 2 1/2 cups flour, soda and nutmeg; mix well. Add vanilla and juice; stir well. Toss candied pineapple, cherries, raisins and pecans with 1/2 cup flour to coat. Add to batter, stirring well. Chill dough until firm. Drop by teaspoonfuls onto non-stick cookie sheet. Bake at 325 degrees for 15 to 20 minutes or until lightly browned. Cool on wire rack.

Kathryn Smith, Burlington

MERRY CHRISTMAS COOKIES

Yield:
36 servings
Utensil:
cookie sheet
Approx Per
Serving:
Cal 98
Prot 1 g
Carbo 12 g
Fiber <1 g
T Fat 5 g
Chol 21 mg
Sod 76 mg

Dietary
Exchanges:
Milk 0
Vegetable 0
Fruit 0
Bread/Starch 1/2
Meat 0; Fat 1

1 cup butter, softened
1 1/2 cups confectioners' sugar
1 1/2 teaspoons vanilla extract
1 egg
2 1/2 cups flour
1 teaspoon soda
1 teaspoon cream of tartar

Cream butter and confectioners' sugar in bowl until light and fluffy. Add vanilla and egg; mix well. Sift flour, soda and cream of tartar into mixture; stir well. Chill dough until firm. Roll out on lightly floured surface. Cut with cookie cutter; arrange on lightly greased cookie sheet. Bake at 375 degrees for 7 to 8 minutes or until lightly browned. Cool on wire rack.

Mary H. Pitts, Winston-Salem

CINNAMON CRISPIES

Yield:
24 servings
Utensil:
cookie sheet
Approx Per
Serving:
Cal 128
Prot 2 g
Carbo 13 g
Fiber <1 g
T Fat 8 g
Chol 33 mg
Sod 138 mg

Dietary
Exchanges:
Milk 0
Vegetable 0
Fruit 0
Bread/Starch 1/2
Meat 0; Fat 1 1/2

2 cups flour
1 teaspoon baking powder
1/2 teaspoon salt
1 tablespoon sugar
1/2 cup butter, softened
1 egg, beaten
1/2 cup (about) milk
3 tablespoons butter, melted
1/2 cup sugar
1 tablespoon cinnamon
5 tablespoons butter, melted

Sift first 4 ingredients into bowl. Cut in 1 cup butter until crumbly. Mix egg with enough milk to yield 3/4 cup liquid. Add to flour mixture; stir well. Turn out onto floured surface; knead 25 times. Roll out to 1/4-inch thickness. Brush with 3 tablespoons melted butter. Combine 1/2 cup sugar with cinnamon in bowl; mix well. Sprinkle 1/4 cup of cinnamon-sugar mixture over dough. Roll up as for jelly roll. Wrap in waxed paper; chill overnight. Slice dough 1/4 inch thick. Dip into 5 tablespoons melted butter; coat with remaining cinnamon-sugar mixture. Place on lightly greased cookie sheet. Bake at 425 degrees for 7 to 10 minutes. Cool on wire rack.

Nettie M. Blankenship

CONGO SQUARES

Yield:
24 servings
Utensil:
baking pan
Approx Per
Serving:
Cal 253
Prot 3 g
Carbo 36 g
Fiber 1 g
T Fat 12 g
Chol 34 mg
Sod 86 mg

Dietary
Exchanges:
Milk 0
Vegetable 0
Fruit 0
Bread/Starch 1
Meat 0; Fat 2½

2½ cups brown sugar
⅔ cup shortening,
  melted
3 eggs
2¾ cups cake flour

½ teaspoon salt
2½ teaspoons baking
  powder
1 cup chocolate chips
1 cup chopped pecans

Stir sugar into melted shortening in bowl. Add eggs 1 at a time, beating well after each addition. Add cake flour, salt and baking powder; mix well. Stir in chocolate chips and pecans. Spoon into nonstick 9x13-inch baking pan. Bake at 350 degrees for 25 minutes. Cool on wire rack. Cut into 24 squares.

Ileen M. Brooks, Greensboro

CURIOUS CAKE SQUARES

Yield:
24 servings
Utensil:
baking pan
Approx Per
Serving:
Cal 283
Prot 3 g
Carbo 36 g
Fiber 1 g
T Fat 15 g
Chol 17 mg
Sod 241 mg

Dietary
Exchanges:
Milk 0
Vegetable 0
Fruit 0
Bread/Starch 1½
Meat 0; Fat 6

¾ cup butter, melted
1 2-layer package
  German chocolate
  cake mix
1 5-ounce can
  evaporated milk

1 14-ounce package
  caramels
1 cup chocolate chips
1 cup chopped pecans

Stir melted butter into cake mix in bowl. Add ⅓ cup evaporated milk; mix well. Spread half the mixture into lightly greased 9x13-inch baking pan. Bake at 350 degrees for 5 minutes. Combine caramels and remaining evaporated milk in saucepan. Cook over low heat until caramels are melted. Sprinkle baked cake with chocolate chips and pecans. Spoon caramel mixture over top. Sprinkle remaining half of cake mixture over caramels. Bake at 350 degrees for 20 minutes. Cool on wire rack. Cut into squares.

Laura Anderson, Winston-Salem

DAD'S COOKIES

Yield:
50 servings
Utensil:
cookie sheet
Approx Per
Serving:
Cal 104
Prot 1 g
Carbo 15 g
Fiber 1 g
T Fat 5 g
Chol 21 mg
Sod 59 mg

Dietary
Exchanges:
Milk 0
Vegetable 0
Fruit 0
Bread/Starch 1/2
Meat 0; Fat 1

1 cup butter, softened
2 cups packed brown
  sugar
2 eggs
1 teaspoon soda
1 tablespoon boiling
  water
1 cup coconut
2 cups oats
2 cups flour

Cream butter and brown sugar together in bowl until light and fluffy. Add eggs, beating well. Mix soda with 1 tablespoon boiling water; stir into creamed mixture. Add coconut, oats and flour; mix well. Shape dough into 1-inch balls. Press onto non-stick cookie sheet. Bake at 350 degrees for 9 to 10 minutes or until golden brown. Cool on wire rack.

W.B. (Bill) Piper, Greensboro

FIVE-WAY COOKIES

Yield:
30 servings
Utensil:
cookie sheet
Approx Per
Serving:
Cal 97
Prot 3 g
Carbo 16 g
Fiber 1 g
T Fat 3 g
Chol 4 mg
Sod 38 mg

Dietary
Exchanges:
Milk 1/2
Vegetable 0
Fruit 1/2
Bread/Starch 0
Meat 0; Fat 1/2

1 14-ounce can
  sweetened
  condensed milk
1/2 cup peanut butter
2 cups raisins

Combine condensed milk, peanut butter and raisins in bowl; mix well. Drop by teaspoonfuls onto greased cookie sheet. Bake at 375 degrees for 15 minutes or until golden brown. Cool on wire rack. May substitute one of the following for 2 cups raisins, 2 cups cornflakes, 2 cups bran flakes, 3 cups shredded coconut or 1 cup chopped nuts.

Mary Pickett, Winston-Salem

Fruit Cookies

Yield:
48 servings
Utensil:
cookie sheet
Approx Per
Serving:
Cal 117
Prot 1 g
Carbo 16 g
Fiber 1 g
T Fat 6 g
Chol 17 mg
Sod 67 mg

Dietary
Exchanges:
Milk 0
Vegetable 0
Fruit 1/2
Bread/Starch 1/2
Meat 0; Fat 1

1 cup margarine, softened
1 1/2 cups packed brown sugar
3 eggs, beaten
2 1/2 cups flour
1/2 teaspoon soda
1/2 teaspoon nutmeg
1 teaspoon ground cloves
1 1/2 teaspoons cinnamon
1 1/2 cups raisins
1 cup chopped pecans

Cream margarine and brown sugar in bowl until light and fluffy. Add eggs; beat well. Sift flour, soda, nutmeg, cloves and cinnamon together. Add to creamed mixture, mixing well. Stir in raisins and pecans. Drop by teaspoonfuls onto greased cookie sheet. Bake at 325 degrees for 8 to 10 minutes or until golden brown. Cool on wire rack.

Virginia Cope, Mocksville

Ginger Cookies

Yield:
24 servings
Utensil:
cookie sheet
Approx Per
Serving:
Cal 129
Prot 1 g
Carbo 18 g
Fiber <1 g
T Fat 6 g
Chol 27 mg
Sod 153 mg

Dietary
Exchanges:
Milk 0
Vegetable 0
Fruit 0
Bread/Starch 1/2
Meat 0; Fat 1 1/2

3/4 cup shortening
1 cup sugar
1 egg
1/4 cup molasses
2 cups flour
2 teaspoons soda
1/4 teaspoon salt
1 1/4 teaspoons cinnamon
3/4 teaspoon ground cloves
1 1/4 teaspoons ginger

Cream shortening and sugar in large bowl until light and fluffy. Add egg and molasses; mix well. Sift flour, soda, salt, cinnamon, cloves and ginger together. Add to creamed mixture; mix well. Shape dough into 1-inch balls. Place on ungreased cookie sheet. Bake at 350 degrees for 10 to 12 minutes or until golden brown. Cool on wire rack. May add chopped nuts or raisins.

Bobbi C. Campbell, High Point

GINGERSNAPS

Yield:
72 servings
Utensil:
cookie sheet
Approx Per
Serving:
Cal 50
Prot <1 g
Carbo 7 g
Fiber <1 g
T Fat 2 g
Chol 4 mg
Sod 25 mg

Dietary
Exchanges:
Milk 0
Vegetable 0
Fruit 0
Bread/Starch 0
Meat 0; Fat 1/2

³/₄ cup shortening
1 cup sugar
¹/₄ cup molasses
1 egg
2 cups flour
2 teaspoons soda

1 teaspoon cinnamon
1 teaspoon ground
    cloves
1 teaspoon ginger
¹/₂ cup sugar

Cream shortening and 1 cup sugar in bowl until light and fluffy. Add molasses and egg; beat well. Sift flour and soda into mixture; stir well. Add cinnamon, cloves and ginger; mix well. Shape dough into 1-inch balls. Roll in ¹/₂ cup sugar to coat. Arrange on nonstick cookie sheet. Bake at 350 degrees for 10 to 12 minutes or until golden brown. Cool on wire rack.

Jessie Grandinetti

GRANDMA WILSON'S COOKIES

Yield:
48 servings
Utensil:
cookie sheet
Approx Per
Serving:
Cal 115
Prot 1 g
Carbo 15 g
Fiber <1 g
T Fat 6 g
Chol 11 mg
Sod 74 mg

Dietary
Exchanges:
Milk 0
Vegetable 0
Fruit 0
Bread/Starch 1/2
Meat 0; Fat 1

1 cup margarine,
    softened
2 cups packed brown
    sugar
2 eggs, beaten
3 cups flour
Pinch of salt

1 teaspoon soda
1 teaspoon cream of
    tartar
1 teaspoon vanilla
    extract
1 cup chopped pecans

Cream margarine and brown sugar in bowl until light and fluffy. Add eggs; beat well. Sift flour, salt, soda and cream of tartar together. Add to creamed mixture; stir well. Add vanilla and pecans; mix well. Drop by teaspoonfuls onto nonstick cookie sheet. Bake at 350 degrees for 10 minutes. Do not overbake. Place cookies on wire rack to cool.

Betty Gregory, Greensboro

HELLO DOLLIES

½ cup margarine
1 cup graham cracker crumbs
1 cup chocolate chips
1 6-ounce package frozen coconut, thawed

1 cup pecans
1 14-ounce can sweetened condensed milk

Melt margarine in 9x13-inch baking pan. Press graham cracker crumbs over bottom of pan. Layer chocolate chips, coconut and pecans over crumbs. Pour condensed milk over all. Bake at 350 degrees for 10 minutes or until bubbly. Cool; cut into 36 bars.

Sara M. Jones, Greensboro

LOUISE'S ICEBOX COOKIES

1 cup butter, softened
2 cups packed brown sugar
2 eggs, beaten
2 teaspoons vanilla extract

3½ cups flour
¾ teaspoon salt
1 teaspoon soda
1 cup chopped pecans

Cream butter and brown sugar in bowl until light and fluffy. Add eggs and vanilla; beat well. Add flour, salt, soda and pecans, stirring well after each addition. Shape dough into log. Chill, tightly wrapped, in refrigerator until firm. Cut into ¼-inch slices. Place on nonstick cookie sheet. Bake at 350 degrees for 12 to 15 minutes or until golden brown. Cool on wire rack.

Nancy McGinnis, Greensboro

LADYFINGERS

Yield:
24 servings
Utensil:
cookie sheet
Approx Per Serving:
Cal 76
Prot 1 g
Carbo 7 g
Fiber <1 g
T Fat 5 g
Chol 10 mg
Sod 39 mg

Dietary Exchanges:
Milk 0
Vegetable 0
Fruit 0
Bread/Starch ½
Meat 0; Fat 1½

½ cup butter, softened
1 tablespoon sugar
1½ teaspoons vanilla
1 cup flour

½ cup finely chopped pecans
⅓ cup confectioners' sugar

Cream butter and sugar in bowl. Add vanilla; mix well. Combine flour and pecans. Add to creamed mixture; stir well. Shape into thumb-sized bars. Place on nonstick cookie sheet. Bake at 350 degrees for 15 minutes. Roll warm cookies in confectioners' sugar to coat. Cool on wire rack.

Doris S. Simpson, Burlington

LEMON BARS

Yield:
36 servings
Utensil:
baking pan
Approx Per Serving:
Cal 171
Prot 2 g
Carbo 27 g
Fiber <1 g
T Fat 6 g
Chol 37 mg
Sod 138 mg

Dietary Exchanges:
Milk 0
Vegetable 0
Fruit 0
Bread/Starch 1
Meat 0; Fat 1½

1 2-layer package yellow cake mix
½ cup butter, softened
1 egg, beaten
1 teaspoon lemon juice
1 1-pound package confectioners' sugar

8 ounces cream cheese, softened
1 teaspoon lemon juice
2 eggs, beaten

Combine cake mix, butter, egg and 1 teaspoon lemon juice in large bowl; mix well. Spread mixture in greased 9x13-inch baking pan. Cream confectioners' sugar with cream cheese in bowl until light and fluffy. Add 1 teaspoon lemon juice; stir well. Add eggs, beating until mixture is creamy. Spread over cake mix mixture. Bake at 300 degrees for 20 to 25 minutes or until firm. Cool in pan; cut into 36 bars.

Zane G. Gerringer, Elon College

LEMON CRUMB BARS

Yield:
36 servings
Utensil:
baking pan
Approx Per Serving:
Cal 147
Prot 2 g
Carbo 21 g
Fiber <1 g
T Fat 6 g
Chol 35 mg
Sod 196 mg

Dietary Exchanges:
Milk ½
Vegetable 0
Fruit 0
Bread/Starch 1
Meat 0; Fat 1

1 2-layer package yellow cake mix
½ cup margarine, softened
1 egg, beaten
2 cups saltine cracker crumbs
3 egg yolks
1 14-ounce can sweetened condensed milk
½ cup lemon juice

Combine cake mix, margarine and egg in large bowl; mix well. Stir in cracker crumbs. Reserve 2 cups of crumb mixture for topping. Press remaining crumb mixture into greased 9x13-inch baking pan. Bake in preheated 350-degree oven for 15 minutes. Blend egg yolks, condensed milk and lemon juice together in small bowl. Spread evenly over prepared crust. Top with reserved crumb mixture. Bake for 15 to 20 minutes or until firm. Cool on wire rack. Cut into bars.

Juanita Stone, Graham

FORGOTTEN COOKIES

Yield:
40 servings
Utensil:
cookie sheet
Approx Per Serving:
Cal 54
Prot 1 g
Carbo 7 g
Fiber <1 g
T Fat 3 g
Chol 0 mg
Sod 3 mg

Dietary Exchanges:
Milk 0
Vegetable 0
Fruit 0
Bread/Starch 0
Meat 0; Fat 1

2 jumbo egg whites
¾ cup sugar
1 teaspoon vanilla extract
1 cup butterscotch chips
1 cup chopped pecans

Beat egg whites in bowl until stiff peaks form. Add sugar, 3 tablespoons at a time, beating well after each addition. Add vanilla; beat well. Fold in butterscotch chips and pecans gently. Drop by teaspoonfuls onto greased cookie sheet. Place cookies in preheated 400-degree oven. Turn off oven. Let stand in closed oven overnight. May substitute peanut butter chips or chocolate chips for butterscotch chips.

Elaine Ruth Morrison, Hobe Sound, Florida

PASTEL MERINGUE KISSES

Yield:
40 servings
Utensil:
cookie sheet
Approx Per Serving:
Cal 10
Prot <1 g
Carbo 2 g
Fiber 0 g
T Fat 0 g
Chol 0 mg
Sod 3 mg

Dietary Exchanges:
Milk 0
Vegetable 0
Fruit 0
Bread/Starch 0
Meat 0; Fat 0

2 egg whites
1/2 cup sugar

Green food coloring
Red food coloring

Beat egg whites in bowl until stiff peaks form. Add sugar, 1 teaspoonful at a time, beating until sugar is dissolved. Divide meringue into 3 portions in bowls. Tint 1 portion pale green and 1 portion pale rose. Drop by teaspoonfuls onto foil-lined cookie sheet. Bake at 275 degrees for 1 hour. Cool on wire rack. Store in airtight containers.

Adeline Schneeloch, Clemmons

SURPRISE COOKIES

Yield:
40 servings
Utensil:
cookie sheet
Approx Per Serving:
Cal 45
Prot <1 g
Carbo 6 g
Fiber <1 g
T Fat 2 g
Chol 0 mg
Sod 3 mg

Dietary Exchanges:
Milk 0
Vegetable 0
Fruit 0
Bread/Starch 0
Meat 0; Fat 1/2

2 egg whites
Pinch of salt
1/2 teaspoon cream of tartar
3/4 cup sugar

1 teaspoon vanilla extract
1 cup chocolate chips
1/2 cup chopped pecans

Beat egg whites in bowl until stiff peaks form. Add salt, cream of tartar, sugar and vanilla gradually, beating well after each addition. Fold in chocolate chips and pecans gently. Drop by teaspoonfuls onto cookie sheet sprayed with nonstick cooking spray. Place in preheated 375-degree oven. Turn off oven. Let stand in closed oven overnight.

Mrs. V.B. Williamson, Graham

SPICE MOLASSES COOKIES

Yield:
50 servings
Utensil:
cookie sheet
**Approx Per
Serving:**
Cal 69
Prot 1 g
Carbo 11 g
Fiber <1 g
T Fat 3 g
Chol 13 mg
Sod 63 mg

**Dietary
Exchanges:**
Milk 0
Vegetable 0
Fruit 0
Bread/Starch 0
Meat 0; Fat 1/2

¾ cup butter, softened
1 cup sugar
1 egg
¼ cup molasses
2 cups flour
1 teaspoon soda
1 teaspoon baking
  powder
¼ teaspoon salt
1 teaspoon ginger
1 teaspoon cinnamon
½ teaspoon nutmeg
¼ teaspoon ground
  cloves
¼ teaspoon allspice
½ cup sugar

Cream butter and 1 cup sugar at medium speed in mixer bowl until light and fluffy. Add egg and molasses; mix well. Combine flour, soda, baking powder, salt, ginger, cinnamon, nutmeg, cloves and allspice in bowl; mix well. Add to creamed mixture gradually, beating well after each addition. Chill dough for 1 hour. Shape into 1-inch balls; roll in remaining ½ cup sugar. Place 2 inches apart onto ungreased cookie sheet. Bake at 350 degrees for 8 to 10 minutes or until surface of cookie cracks. Cool on wire rack.

W. B. (Bill) Piper, Greensboro

MUD HENS

Yield:
24 servings
Utensil:
baking pan
**Approx Per
Serving:**
Cal 166
Prot 2 g
Carbo 24 g
Fiber 1 g
T Fat 8 g
Chol 34 mg
Sod 147 mg

**Dietary
Exchanges:**
Milk 0
Vegetable 0
Fruit 0
Bread/Starch 1/2
Meat 0; Fat 11/2

½ cup margarine,
  softened
1 cup sugar
1½ cups self-rising
  flour
½ teaspoon vanilla
  extract
3 egg yolks
1 egg white
1 cup chopped pecans
1 cup packed brown
  sugar
2 egg whites

Cream margarine and sugar in bowl until light and fluffy. Add flour, vanilla, egg yolks and 1 egg white; mix well. Spread mixture into lightly greased 9x13-inch baking pan; sprinkle with pecans. Combine brown sugar and remaining 2 egg whites in bowl; spread over pecans. Bake at 325 degrees for 20 minutes. Cool; cut into 24 pieces.

Jane Dalton, Winston-Salem

NUT BALLS

1 cup margarine,
  softened
1/3 cup packed brown
  sugar
2 cups flour
1/2 teaspoon salt

1/2 teaspoon vanilla
  extract
1 cup chopped pecans
1/2 cup confectioners'
  sugar

Cream margarine and brown sugar in bowl until light and fluffy. Add flour, salt and vanilla; mix well. Stir in pecans. Shape into small balls; place on cookie sheet. Bake at 375 degrees for 10 to 12 minutes. Cool on wire rack. Roll cookies in confectioners' sugar.

Phil and Glenda Epperson

NUT DROPS

1/2 cup butter, softened
2 tablespoons sugar
11/4 cups cake flour

1 cup chopped pecans
1/4 cup confectioners'
  sugar

Cream butter and sugar in bowl until light and fluffy. Add cake flour and pecans; mix well. Shape into small balls; place on cookie sheet. Bake at 350 degrees for 16 minutes. Cool on wire rack. Roll cooled cookies in confectioners' sugar. Store in airtight container.

Gaylene Fogleman, Graham

BOILED COOKIES

2 cups sugar
½ cup milk
½ cup butter
3 tablespoons baking cocoa

1 cup chopped pecans
½ cup oats
2 tablespoons vanilla extract

Boil sugar, milk, butter and cocoa in saucepan for 2 minutes. Remove from heat; add pecans, oats and vanilla. Beat until well mixed. Cool for 2 minutes. Drop by spoonfuls onto waxed paper; cool.

Pernie Gough, Yadkinville

CHOCOLATE OATMEAL COOKIES

½ cup butter, softened
1 cup sugar
1 egg, lightly beaten
2 ounces melted baking chocolate

1 teaspoon vanilla extract
1 cup self-rising flour, sifted
1½ cups oats

Cream butter and sugar in large bowl. Add egg, chocolate and vanilla; mix well. Mix flour and oats in bowl. Add to creamed mixture; mix well. Shape into balls. Place on greased cookie sheet; flatten with fork. Bake at 350 degrees for 8 to 10 minutes or until firm. Cool on wire rack.

Pat Anderton, Winston-Salem

Oatmeal Coconut Macaroons

Yield:
60 cookies
Utensil:
cookie sheet
Approx Per
Serving:
Cal 100
Prot 1 g
Carbo 13 g
Fiber 1 g
T Fat 5 g
Chol 9 mg
Sod 40 mg

Dietary
Exchanges:
Milk 0
Vegetable 0
Fruit 0
Bread/Starch 1/2
Meat 0; Fat 1

1 cup packed brown sugar
1 cup sugar
1 cup shortening
2 eggs
2 cups flour
1/2 teaspoon salt
1 teaspoon soda
1 teaspoon baking powder
1 teaspoon vanilla extract
1 cup coconut
3 cups oats
1/2 cup chopped pecans

Cream brown sugar, sugar, shortening and eggs in mixer bowl until light and fluffy. Sift in flour, salt, soda and baking powder; mix well. Stir in vanilla, coconut, oats and pecans. Drop by teaspoonfuls onto greased cookie sheet. Flatten with glass. Bake at 350 degrees for 8 to 10 minutes. Cool on wire rack. May add 1 cup chocolate chips to batter.

Connie Kelly, Mocksville

Soft Oatmeal Cookies

Yield:
36 servings
Utensil:
cookie sheet
Approx Per
Serving:
Cal 134
Prot 2 g
Carbo 17 g
Fiber 1 g
T Fat 7 g
Chol 15 mg
Sod 95 mg

Dietary
Exchanges:
Milk 0
Vegetable 0
Fruit 0
Bread/Starch 1/2
Meat 0; Fat 1 1/2

2 eggs
1 cup sugar
1 cup margarine, softened
2 cups flour
2 cups oats
1 cup raisins
1/2 cup water
1 teaspoon soda
1/2 cup chopped pecans

Cream eggs, sugar and margarine in bowl until smooth. Add flour and oats; mix well. Cook raisins in 1/2 cup water in saucepan for 2 to 3 minutes. Drain, reserving 1/2 cup liquid. Combine reserved liquid and soda in bowl; stir into batter immediately. Add raisins and pecans. Drop by teaspoonfuls onto cookie sheet. Bake at 350 degrees for 10 to 12 minutes or until light brown. Cool on wire rack.

Mary Anne Hopper, Greensboro

OATMEAL ICEBOX COOKIES

Yield:
60 servings
Utensil:
cookie sheet
Approx Per
Serving:
Cal 102
Prot 1 g
Carbo 12 g
Fiber 1 g
T Fat 5 g
Chol 9 mg
Sod 50 mg

Dietary
Exchanges:
Milk 0
Vegetable 0
Fruit 0
Bread/Starch ½
Meat 0; Fat 1

1 cup shortening
1 cup sugar
1 cup packed brown
  sugar
2 eggs, beaten
1 teaspoon vanilla
  extract
1½ cups flour

1 teaspoon soda
1 teaspoon salt
3 cups quick-cooking
  oats
½ cup chopped pecans
1 6-ounce package
  frozen shredded
  coconut, thawed

Cream shortening, sugar and brown sugar in large bowl until light and fluffy. Blend in eggs and vanilla. Sift flour, soda and salt together. Add to creamed mixture. Stir in oats, pecans and coconut. Shape into 2 or 3 rolls. Chill, wrapped, in refrigerator. Cut into slices. Place on greased cookie sheet. Bake at 375 degrees for 10 minutes. Do not overbake.

Edith Gerringer, Burlington

OATMEAL-BRAN COOKIES

Yield:
48 servings
Utensil:
cookie sheet
Approx Per
Serving:
Cal 105
Prot 1 g
Carbo 13 g
Fiber 1 g
T Fat 5 g
Chol 0 mg
Sod 15 mg

Dietary
Exchanges:
Milk 0
Vegetable 0
Fruit 0
Bread/Starch ½
Meat 0; Fat 1

1 cup canola oil
1 cup sugar
½ cup packed brown
  sugar
3 egg whites
¼ cup water
1 teaspoon vanilla
  extract

2 cups flour
1½ teaspoons soda
1 teaspoon cinnamon
1 teaspoon nutmeg
½ cup pecan pieces
½ cup raisins
1 cup oats
½ cup oat bran

Cream oil, sugar and brown sugar in mixer bowl until light and fluffy. Blend in egg whites. Add water and vanilla; mix well. Sift in flour, soda, cinnamon and nutmeg; mix well. Stir in pecans, raisins, oats and oat bran. Drop by teaspoonfuls onto cookie sheet coated with nonstick cooking spray. Bake at 350 degrees for 10 minutes or until brown.

Jane Walters, Winston-Salem

OATMEAL COOKIES

1 egg
1 cup melted margarine
1/2 cup packed light brown sugar
1 cup sugar
1 1/2 cups flour
1 teaspoon soda
1 teaspoon cinnamon
1 1/2 cups oats
3/4 cup raisins
1 teaspoon vanilla extract

Combine egg, margarine, brown sugar and sugar in mixer bowl; beat until smooth. Sift in flour, soda and cinnamon; mix well. Stir in oats, raisins and vanilla. Place mixture in small bowl. Refrigerate for at least 1 hour. Drop by teaspoonfuls onto greased cookie sheet; flatten. Bake at 350 degrees for 10 minutes.

Dorothy L. Clapp, Burlington

CREAM-FILLED OATMEAL COOKIES

1 cup margarine, softened
2 cups packed brown sugar
3 cups flour
2 eggs
1/2 teaspoon salt
1 cup oats
1 teaspoon vanilla extract
1 teaspoon soda
3 cups confectioners' sugar
1/2 cup shortening
2 tablespoons powdered whipped topping mix
1 teaspoon vanilla extract
1/2 cup (about) milk

Combine margarine, brown sugar, flour, eggs, salt, oats, 1 teaspoon vanilla and soda in large bowl; mix well. Shape into balls; place on greased cookie sheet. Flatten slightly. Bake at 350 degrees for 10 minutes or until golden brown. Cool on wire rack. Combine confectioners' sugar, shortening, whipped topping powder and remaining 1 teaspoon vanilla in bowl. Stir in enough milk to make of filling consistency. Spread on half the cookies; top with remaining cookies. Store in airtight container.

Earline Goin, Hamptonville

OATIES

Yield:
12 servings
Utensil:
round baking pan
Approx Per
Serving:
Cal 252
Prot 4 g
Carbo 28 g
Fiber 2 g
T Fat 15 g
Chol 0 mg
Sod 140 mg

Dietary
Exchanges:
Milk 0
Vegetable 0
Fruit 1/2
Bread/Starch 1
Meat 0; Fat 31/2

1/2 cup melted margarine
1/2 cup packed brown sugar
1 teaspoon vanilla extract
2 cups quick-cooking oats
1/2 cup flour
1/2 teaspoon soda
1 cup chopped pecans
1/2 cup raisins

Combine margarine, brown sugar, vanilla, oats, flour, soda and pecans in bowl; mix well. Reserve 3/4 cup of oat mixture for topping. Stir raisins into remaining oat mixture. Press into greased 9-inch round baking pan. Top with reserved oat mixture, pressing onto bottom layer. Bake at 350 degrees for 25 minutes. Press lightly while warm; cut into wedges. Serve warm or cool and break into pieces.

Barbara Joyce, Burlington

OATMEAL CRUNCHIES

Yield:
42 servings
Utensil:
cookie sheet
Approx Per
Serving:
Cal 67
Prot 1 g
Carbo 9 g
Fiber <1 g
T Fat 3 g
Chol 7 mg
Sod 28 mg

Dietary
Exchanges:
Milk 0
Vegetable 0
Fruit 0
Bread/Starch 0
Meat 0; Fat 1/2

1 cup flour
1/2 cup sugar
1/2 teaspoon baking powder
1/2 teaspoon soda
1/4 teaspoon salt
1/2 cup packed brown sugar
1/2 cup shortening
1 egg
1/4 teaspoon vanilla extract
3/4 cup quick-cooking oats
1/4 cup chopped walnuts
1/4 cup (about) sugar

Sift flour, 1/2 cup sugar, baking powder, soda and salt into mixer bowl. Add brown sugar, shortening, egg and vanilla; beat well. Stir in oats and walnuts. Shape into small balls; dip tops into remaining 1/4 cup sugar. Place on ungreased cookie sheet. Bake at 375 degrees for 10 to 12 minutes or until golden brown. Cool on wire rack.

Grace M. Roth, Burlington

OATMEAL-RAISIN COOKIES

Yield:
60 servings
Utensil:
cookie sheet
Approx Per
Serving:
Cal 72
Prot 1 g
Carbo 13 g
Fiber 1 g
T Fat 2 g
Chol 9 mg
Sod 72 mg

Dietary
Exchanges:
Milk 0
Vegetable 0
Fruit 0
Bread/Starch ¹/₂
Meat 0; Fat ¹/₂

¹/₂ cup margarine,
  softened
1¹/₄ cups sugar
¹/₂ cup North Carolina
  molasses
2 eggs

1³/₄ cups flour
1 teaspoon salt
1 teaspoon soda
1 teaspoon cinnamon
2 cups oats
1¹/₂ cups raisins

Combine margarine, sugar, molasses and eggs in bowl; mix well. Add flour, salt, soda, cinnamon, oats and raisins; mix well. Shape by teaspoonfuls onto greased cookie sheet. Bake at 350 degrees for 10 minutes or until lightly browned. Cool on wire rack.

Jesse Meredith, Thomasville

CHOCOLATE OATMEAL COOKIES

Yield:
36 servings
Utensil:
saucepan
Approx Per
Serving:
Cal 113
Prot 2 g
Carbo 16 g
Fiber 1 g
T Fat 5 g
Chol <1 mg
Sod 36 mg

Dietary
Exchanges:
Milk 0
Vegetable 0
Fruit 0
Bread/Starch ¹/₂
Meat 0; Fat 1

2 cups sugar
6 tablespoons baking
  cocoa
¹/₂ cup margarine
¹/₂ cup milk

3 cups oats
1 teaspoon vanilla
  extract
1 cup chopped pecans

Combine sugar, cocoa, margarine and milk in saucepan. Bring to a boil, stirring constantly. Remove from heat. Add oats, vanilla and pecans; mix well. Drop by teaspoonfuls onto waxed paper. Let stand until cool; store in covered container.

Kate Brothers, Liberty

No-Bake Quaker Oats Cookies

2 cups sugar
½ cup milk
½ cup margarine
¼ cup baking cocoa
½ cup peanut butter

2 teaspoons vanilla extract
¼ teaspoon salt
2½ cups oats
1 cup chopped pecans

Combine sugar, milk, margarine and cocoa in heavy saucepan. Bring to a boil. Boil for 1½ minutes, stirring constantly. Add peanut butter, vanilla and salt; mix well. Pour over mixture of oats and pecans in bowl; mix well. Drop by teaspoonfuls onto waxed paper-lined cookie sheet. Cool; store in covered container.

Ruth Kent Eslinger, Winston-Salem

Orange Bars

1 orange
2 tablespoons margarine, softened
1 cup packed brown sugar
2 eggs
½ teaspoon salt
1¼ cups flour

1¼ cups pecans
1 8-ounce package orange slice candy, chopped
2 tablespoons flour
½ cup sugar
1 cup confectioners' sugar

Extract juice from orange; grate orange rind. Mix orange juice and grated rind in bowl. Cream margarine and brown sugar in mixer bowl until light. Beat in eggs. Add 2 tablespoons orange mixture, salt, 1¼ cups flour and pecans; mix well. Dust candy with remaining 2 tablespoons flour. Stir into batter. Spoon into greased 7x10-inch baking pan. Bake at 350 degrees for 30 minutes. Pour mixture of remaining orange mixture and sugar over baked layer. Bake for 1 minute. Let stand until cool. Cut into bars; dust with confectioners' sugar.

Vi Munt, Winston-Salem

ORANGE FINGERS

2 cups flour
18 gumdrop orange slices, cut into pieces
1/2 cup pecan pieces
4 eggs, beaten
2 1/2 cups packed brown sugar
1/4 cup confectioners' sugar

Combine flour, gumdrop pieces and pecans in bowl; mix well. Add eggs and brown sugar; mix well. Spread 1/2-inch thick into buttered 9x13-inch baking pan. Bake at 350 degrees for 30 to 40 minutes. Cool. Cut into strips; roll in confectioners' sugar.

Ronald J. Belcher, Advance

PEACHES AND CREAM COOKIES

4 eggs
1 cup sugar
1 cup oil
4 cups flour
3 teaspoons baking powder
1 3-ounce package vanilla instant pudding mix
1/2 cup sweet vermouth
1/4 teaspoon red food coloring
1 tube green decorator icing
1 3-ounce package peach gelatin

Beat eggs in mixer bowl. Add sugar, oil, flour and baking powder; mix well. Chill overnight. Shape into 2-inch balls; place on lightly greased cookie sheet. Bake at 325 degrees for 15 to 18 minutes or until lightly browned. Scoop out center of flat side with melon baller. Cook pudding using package directions. Fill center of cookies with pudding. Place flat sides of cookies together. Combine vermouth and red food coloring in small bowl. Dip 1/3 of cookie into colored mixture. Roll cookies in dry peach gelatin. Pipe green stem on one end.

Meg Webster

ITALIAN PIZZELLE

3 eggs
¾ cup sugar
¾ cup melted butter
2 teaspoons anise extract
1 teaspoon vanilla extract
1½ cups flour
1 teaspoon baking powder

Combine eggs and sugar in mixer bowl; mix well. Stir in butter and flavorings. Add flour and baking powder; mix well. Drop by rounded tablespoonfuls onto center of hot pizzelle iron; cover. Cook for 30 to 60 seconds. Cool.

Vicki Strickland, Greensboro

I CAN'T BELIEVE IT'S A COOKIE

1 cup sugar
1 cup peanut butter
1 egg
48 chocolate star candies

Combine sugar, peanut butter and egg in bowl; mix well. Shape into 1-inch balls. Place on cookie sheet; press chocolate star into center of each cookie. Bake at 350 degrees for 6 minutes. Cool on wire rack.

Sarah L. Tagert, Greensboro

Pumpkin Bars

Yield:
24 servings
Utensil:
baking pan
Approx Per Serving:
Cal 343
Prot 3 g
Carbo 46 g
Fiber <1 g
T Fat 17 g
Chol 66 mg
Sod 128 mg

Dietary Exchanges:
Milk 0
Vegetable 0
Fruit 0
Bread/Starch ½
Meat 0; Fat 3½

4 eggs
1⅔ cups sugar
1 cup oil
2 cups cooked pumpkin
2 cups flour
1 teaspoon soda
2 teaspoons pumpkin pie spice
1 teaspoon baking powder
½ cup butter, softened
8 ounces cream cheese, softened
1 teaspoon vanilla extract
1 1-pound package confectioners' sugar

Beat eggs, sugar and oil in mixer bowl. Add pumpkin; beat until light and fluffy. Add mixture of flour, soda, pumpkin pie spice and baking powder; mix well. Spread batter into ungreased 10x15-inch baking pan. Bake at 350 degrees for 25 minutes. Cool in pan. Cream butter, cream cheese and vanilla in bowl until light and fluffy. Add confectioners' sugar, beating until smooth. Spread over baked layer. Cut into bars.

Inez McPherson, Mebane

Pumpkin Cookies

Yield:
36 servings
Utensil:
cookie sheet
Approx Per Serving:
Cal 125
Prot 1 g
Carbo 16 g
Fiber 1 g
T Fat 7 g
Chol 0 mg
Sod 52 mg

Dietary Exchanges:
Milk 0
Vegetable 0
Fruit 0
Bread/Starch ½
Meat 0; Fat 1½

1 cup sugar
¾ cup oil
1½ cups cooked pumpkin
2¼ cups flour
4 teaspoons baking powder
1 teaspoon cinnamon
¼ teaspoon ginger
¼ teaspoon nutmeg
½ teaspoon vanilla extract
¼ teaspoon salt
1 cup raisins
1 cup pecans

Combine sugar and oil in bowl; mix well. Add pumpkin, flour, baking powder, cinnamon, ginger, nutmeg, vanilla and salt; mix well. Stir in raisins and pecans. Drop by tablespoonfuls onto cookie sheet. Bake at 350 degrees for 10 minutes or until golden brown.

Mary B. Marshall, Colfax

REFRIGERATOR COOKIES

1   16-ounce package graham crackers
1 cup margarine
1 cup sugar
1/2 cup evaporated milk
1 egg, beaten
1 cup chopped pecans
1 cup graham cracker crumbs
1 1/4 cups coconut
1 teaspoon vanilla extract
2 1/2 cups confectioners' sugar
1 teaspoon vanilla extract
1/2 cup (about) evaporated milk

Line bottom of 9x13-inch pan with whole graham crackers. Bring margarine, sugar, 1/2 cup evaporated milk and egg to a boil in saucepan. Remove from heat. Stir in chopped pecans, graham cracker crumbs, coconut and 1 teaspoon vanilla. Pour over whole graham crackers in pan. Top with another layer of whole graham crackers. Combine confectioners' sugar, remaining 1 teaspoon vanilla and enough remaining evaporated milk to moisten. Spread over top layer. Chill for several hours to overnight. Cut into bars.

Patricia R. Little, Gibsonville

RICE CHEX COOKIES

1 cup sugar
1 cup packed brown sugar
1 cup shortening
2 eggs
2 cups flour
1/2 teaspoon salt
1/2 teaspoon soda
1/2 teaspoon baking powder
1/2 teaspoon almond extract
1/2 teaspoon vanilla extract
4 cups Rice Chex cereal, crushed
3/4 cup chopped pecans
1 cup coconut

Cream sugar, brown sugar and shortening in mixer bowl until light and fluffy. Add eggs, flour, salt, soda, baking powder, almond extract and vanilla, stirring after each addition. Stir in cereal, pecans and coconut. Shape into 1-inch balls on cookie sheet; flatten with fork. Bake at 375 degrees for 4 minutes. Cool on wire rack.

Helen A. Howard, Pfafftown

EMERY'S SAND BARS

Yield:
180 servings
Utensil:
cookie sheet
Approx Per
Serving:
Cal 41
Prot 1 g
Carbo 4 g
Fiber <1 g
T Fat 2 g
Chol 2 mg
Sod 34 mg

Dietary
Exchanges:
Milk 0
Vegetable 0
Fruit 0
Bread/Starch 0
Meat 0; Fat ¹/₂

1¹/₂ cups margarine, softened
¹/₂ cup sugar
1 teaspoon vanilla extract
1¹/₄ teaspoons salt
1 egg
6 cups flour
¹/₄ to ¹/₂ cup water
2 cups finely chopped pecans
¹/₂ cup confectioners' sugar

Cream margarine in mixer bowl. Add sugar, vanilla, salt and egg; mix well. Add flour and water alternately to creamed mixture, mixing constantly. Stir in pecans. Dough will be stiff. Roll very thin on floured surface; cut into strips. Place strips on cookie sheet. Bake at 375 degrees for 8 to 10 minutes or until brown around the edges. Roll warm strips in confectioners' sugar.

Lynn Kiger, Rural Hall

DUBLIN SHORTBREAD

Yield:
8 servings
Utensil:
springform pan
Approx Per
Serving:
Cal 232
Prot 2 g
Carbo 30 g
Fiber 1 g
T Fat 12 g
Chol 31 mg
Sod 117 mg

Dietary
Exchanges:
Milk 0
Vegetable 0
Fruit 0
Bread/Starch 1
Meat 0; Fat 2¹/₂

1¹/₄ cups flour
¹/₄ cup sugar
3 tablespoons cornstarch
¹/₂ cup butter, cubed
¹/₄ cup orange marmalade

Combine flour, sugar, cornstarch and butter in food processor container. Pulse until finely crumbled. Press dough into 9-inch springform pan with removable bottom. Bake at 375 degrees for 25 minutes. Cool for 5 minutes; remove rim. Spread with marmalade; cut into 8 wedges. May substitute raspberry preserves for orange marmalade.

Peggy Glosek, Burlington

Scottish Shortbread

1 cup butter, softened
1 cup margarine,
  softened
1 cup sugar
¾ cup cornstarch
4½ cups flour
½ teaspoon baking
  powder

Mix butter, margarine and sugar in bowl with a fork. Add cornstarch, flour and baking powder. Mix with wooden spoon until mixture forms ball. Flatten into 9x13-inch baking pan; prick with fork. Bake at 250 degrees for 2 hours. Cut into bars while warm.

Emmaline Lindsay, Greensboro

Sugar Cookies

1 cup butter, softened
1 cup corn oil
1 cup sugar
1 cup confectioners'
  sugar
2 eggs
4 cups flour
1 teaspoon soda
1 teaspoon cream of
  tartar
1 teaspoon vanilla
  extract

Cream butter, oil, and sugars in bowl until light and fluffy. Add eggs; mix well. Sift in flour, soda and cream of tartar. Add vanilla; mix well. Drop by teaspoonfuls onto ungreased cookie sheet. Bake at 350 degrees for about 10 minutes or until golden brown. May sprinkle with red and green sugar before baking for holiday cookies.

Leola M. Vaughn, Stokesdale

MOLASSES SUGAR COOKIES

3/4 cup shortening
1 cup sugar
1/4 cup molasses
1 egg
2 cups flour
2 teaspoons soda

1/2 teaspoon ground
    cloves
1/2 teaspoon ginger
1 teaspoon cinnamon
1/2 teaspoon salt

Combine shortening, sugar, molasses and egg in mixer bowl; mix well. Sift in flour soda, ground cloves, ginger, cinnamon and salt; mix well. Chill dough. Shape chilled dough into 1-inch balls. Place 2 inches apart on greased cookie sheet. Bake at 375 degrees for 8 to 10 minutes or until golden brown.

Mrs. N. O. Vestal, Lexington

TEXAS RANGERS

1 cup margarine,
    softened
1 cup sugar
1 cup packed brown
    sugar
2 eggs
2 cups flour
1/2 teaspoon salt

2 teaspoons soda
1 teaspoon baking
    powder
1 teaspoon vanilla
    extract
2 cups oats
1 cup coconut
1 cup chopped pecans

Cream margarine, sugar and brown sugar in bowl until light and fluffy. Add eggs 1 at a time, beating well after each addition. Add flour, salt, soda, baking powder and vanilla; mix well. Stir in oats, coconut and pecans. Drop by rounded teaspoonfuls onto cookie sheet. Bake at 375 degrees for 10 minutes or until golden brown.

Cheryl Hodge, Burlington

TOFFEE BARS

Yield:
60 servings
Utensil:
baking pan
Approx Per
Serving:
Cal 91
Prot 1 g
Carbo 9 g
Fiber <1 g
T Fat 6 g
Chol 13 mg
Sod 37 mg

Dietary
Exchanges:
Milk 0
Vegetable 0
Fruit 0
Bread/Starch 0
Meat 0; Fat 2

1 cup butter, softened
1 cup packed light
  brown sugar
1 egg yolk
1 teaspoon vanilla
  extract

2 cups flour
6 1¹/₂-ounce bars
  chocolate
¹/₂ to 1 cup chopped
  pecans

Combine butter, brown sugar, egg yolk, vanilla and flour in bowl; mix well. Spread into 10x15-inch baking pan. Bake at 350 degrees for 20 minutes. Place chocolate bars on baked layer while hot. Spread melted chocolate evenly; sprinkle with pecans. Cool; cut into bars.

Jessie Grandinetti

VACUUM CLEANER COOKIES

Yield:
48 servings
Utensil:
baking pan
Approx Per
Serving:
Cal 139
Prot 1 g
Carbo 21 g
Fiber <1 g
T Fat 6 g
Chol 22 mg
Sod 110 mg

Dietary
Exchanges:
Milk 0
Vegetable 0
Fruit 0
Bread/Starch ¹/₂
Meat 0; Fat 1¹/₂

¹/₂ cup melted
  margarine
1 18-ounce package
  yellow cake mix
3 eggs
8 ounces cream cheese,
  softened

1 1-pound package
  confectioners' sugar
¹/₂ cup flaked coconut
¹/₂ cup chopped pecans

Combine margarine, cake mix and 1 egg in bowl; stir just until moistened. Pat mixture into well greased 10x15-inch baking pan. Beat remaining 2 eggs in mixer bowl. Add cream cheese and confectioners' sugar, beating until smooth. Stir in coconut and pecans. Pour over mixture in jelly roll pan, spreading evenly. Bake at 325 degrees for 45 to 50 minutes or until golden brown. Cool in pan on wire rack. Cut into bars. These cookies were originally named Neiman-Marcus Squares, but they disappeared so quickly that a family renamed the recipe Vacuum Cleaner Cookies.

Mary Kiser

ALMOND BRITTLE

Yield:
20 servings
Utensil:
saucepan
Approx Per
Serving:
Cal 153
Prot 3 g
Carbo 19 g
Fiber 1 g
T Fat 9 g
Chol 3 mg
Sod 85 mg

Dietary
Exchanges:
Milk 0
Vegetable 0
Fruit 0
Bread/Starch 0
Meat 1/2; Fat 1 1/2

1 cup sugar
1/2 cup light corn syrup
1/4 teaspoon salt
1 10-ounce package
   blanched almonds

2 tablespoons butter
1 teaspoon soda

Combine sugar, corn syrup and salt in saucepan. Heat until sugar dissolves, stirring constantly. Stir in almonds. Cook to 300 to 310 degrees on candy thermometer, hard-crack stage. Remove from heat. Stir in butter and soda. Pour onto greased tray or baking sheet; spread into thin rectangle with 2 forks. Let stand until cool; break into small pieces. Store in airtight container.

John P. Kelly, Greensboro

WALNUT BOURBON BALLS

Yield:
42 servings
Utensil:
bowl
Approx Per
Serving:
Cal 67
Prot 1 g
Carbo 10 g
Fiber <1 g
T Fat 3 g
Chol 3 mg
Sod 15 mg

Dietary
Exchanges:
Milk 0
Vegetable 0
Fruit 0
Bread/Starch 1/2
Meat 0; Fat 1/2

2 1/2 cups finely
   crushed vanilla
   wafers
1 cup confectioners'
   sugar
2 tablespoons baking
   cocoa

3 tablespoons corn
   syrup
1/4 cup Bourbon
1 cup finely chopped
   walnuts
1/2 cup confectioners'
   sugar

Combine cookie crumbs, 1 cup confectioners' sugar, cocoa, corn syrup, Bourbon and walnuts in bowl; mix well. Shape into 1-inch balls. Roll in 1/2 cup confectioners' sugar. Store in airtight container. May substitute coconut for part of the walnuts if desired.

Jerry Jarrell, Jamestown

BOURBON BALLS

½ cup chopped raisins
¼ cup Bourbon
2 cups crushed
  chocolate wafer
  crumbs
½ cup finely chopped
  pecans

½ cup packed dark
  brown sugar
¼ cup molasses
½ teaspoon cinnamon
½ teaspoon ginger
¼ teaspoon cloves
1 cup chopped pecans

Soak raisins in Bourbon in small bowl for 15 minutes. Combine cookie crumbs, ½ cup pecans, brown sugar, molasses, cinnamon, ginger and cloves in large bowl. Add raisins and Bourbon; mix well. Shape into 1-inch balls. Roll in 1 cup pecans, coating well. Store in airtight container for 1 week before serving. May substitute vanilla wafers for chocolate wafers, walnuts for pecans and Kahlua for half the Bourbon. May coat with confectioners' sugar if preferred.

Elaine Ruth Morrison, Hobe Sound, Florida

EASY BOURBON BALLS

1 cup crushed vanilla
  wafers
1 cup confectioners'
  sugar
½ cup chopped pecans

2 ounces (about)
  Bourbon
½ cup confectioners'
  sugar

Combine cookie crumbs, 1 cup confectioners' sugar, pecans and Bourbon in bowl; mix well. Shape into 1-inch balls. Roll in ½ cup confectioners' sugar, coating well. Store in airtight container.

Angela White, Greensboro

CHOCOLATE BOURBON BALLS

1 cup graham cracker crumbs
1 cup finely chopped pecans
1 cup confectioners' sugar
2 tablespoons baking cocoa
1 1/2 teaspoons light corn syrup
1/4 cup Bourbon

Combine cracker crumbs, pecans, confectioners' sugar, cocoa, corn syrup and Bourbon in bowl; mix well. Shape into 1-inch balls. Wrap each ball in foil. Store in airtight container for several weeks.

Vicki Strickland, Greensboro

CHEERIO BARS

1/2 cup butter
32 large marshmallows
1/2 cup peanut butter
1/2 cup nonfat dry milk
1/4 cup orange breakfast drink mix
1 cup raisins
4 cups Cheerios

Melt butter and marshmallows in large saucepan over low heat, stirring to mix well. Stir in peanut butter, milk powder and drink mix. Fold in raisins and cereal. Pack into buttered 9x9-inch pan. Let stand until cool. Cut into bars.

Connie Kelly, Mocksville

CHOCOLATE SCOTCHEROONS

1 cup sugar
1 cup light corn syrup
1 cup peanut butter
6 cups crisp rice cereal
1 cup semisweet
  chocolate chips
1 cup butterscotch
  chips

Combine sugar and corn syrup in 3-quart saucepan. Cook over medium heat until bubbly; remove from heat. Stir in peanut butter. Add cereal; mix well. Press into buttered 9x13-inch dish. Melt chocolate chips and butterscotch chips over very low heat or in double boiler, stirring to mix well. Spread evenly over cereal mixture. Cool until firm. Cut into bars.

Frankie H. Hubbard, Elon College

CHRISTMAS CANDY

2 1-pound packages
   brown sugar
1/2 cup butter
1 cup evaporated milk
1 7-ounce jar
   marshmallow creme
2 6-ounce packages
   butterscotch chips
2 1/2 cups coarsely
   chopped peanuts
1 teaspoon vanilla
   extract

Combine brown sugar, butter and evaporated milk in saucepan. Cook to 234 to 240 degrees on candy thermometer, soft-ball stage; remove from heat. Add marshmallow creme, beating for 8 minutes or until thick and creamy. Add butterscotch chips, peanuts and vanilla; mix well. Spoon into buttered 9x13-inch dish. Let stand until firm. Cut into bite-sized pieces with warm sharp knife.

Patricia R. Little, Gibsonville

Coconut Balls

Yield:
36 servings
Utensil:
bowl
Approx Per
Serving:
Cal 79
Prot 2 g
Carbo 5 g
Fiber 1 g
T Fat 6 g
Chol 0 mg
Sod 42 mg

Dietary
Exchanges:
Milk 0
Vegetable 0
Fruit 0
Bread/Starch 0
Meat 1/2; Fat 1 1/2

1 cup creamy peanut butter
1 cup sifted confectioners' sugar
2 tablespoons melted margarine
1/2 cup chopped pecans
1 cup coconut

Combine peanut butter, confectioners' sugar, margarine and pecans in bowl; mix well. Shape into 1/2-inch balls. Roll in coconut, coating well. Chill in refrigerator.

Ruby A. Welborn, Ronda

Coconut Mounds

Yield:
40 servings
Utensil:
bowl
Approx Per
Serving:
Cal 168
Prot 2 g
Carbo 25 g
Fiber 2 g
T Fat 8 g
Chol 3 mg
Sod 16 mg

Dietary
Exchanges:
Milk 1/2
Vegetable 0
Fruit 0
Bread/Starch 1/2
Meat 0; Fat 2

16 ounces coconut
1 14-ounce can sweetened condensed milk
1 1-pound package confectioners' sugar
1 teaspoon vanilla extract
1 12-ounce package semisweet chocolate chips
1/2 square paraffin

Combine coconut, condensed milk, confectioners' sugar and vanilla in bowl; mix well. Shape into balls; place on tray. Chill for several hours. Melt chocolate chips with paraffin in saucepan, mixing well. Dip balls into chocolate; place on waxed paper. Let stand until firm.

Kathryn Loy, Gibsonville

FUDGE

Yield:
96 servings
Utensil:
saucepan
Approx Per
Serving:
Cal 78
Prot 1 g
Carbo 11 g
Fiber <1 g
T Fat 4 g
Chol 6 mg
Sod 25 mg

Dietary
Exchanges:
Milk 0
Vegetable 0
Fruit 0
Bread/Starch 0
Meat 0; Fat 1

4 cups sugar
1   15-ounce can
    evaporated milk
2 cups chocolate chips
1 cup butter, chopped
1 cup chopped pecans
1 teaspoon vanilla
    extract

Bring sugar and evaporated milk to a boil in deep saucepan, stirring constantly; reduce heat. Cook for 12 to 15 minutes or to 234 to 240 degrees on candy thermometer, soft-ball stage; remove from heat. Add chocolate chips, butter, pecans and vanilla. Beat until thick and creamy. Pour into lightly buttered dish. Chill in refrigerator. Cut into small squares.

Candace K. Bryan, Elon College

CHOCOLATE CREAM FUDGE

Yield:
36 servings
Utensil:
shallow pan
Approx Per
Serving:
Cal 52
Prot <1 g
Carbo 7 g
Fiber <1 g
T Fat 3 g
Chol 3 mg
Sod 7 mg

Dietary
Exchanges:
Milk 0
Vegetable 0
Fruit 0
Bread/Starch 0
Meat 0; Fat 1

3 ounces cream cheese,
    softened
2 cups sifted
    confectioners' sugar
2 ounces baking
    chocolate, melted
1/2 cup chopped pecans
1/4 teaspoon vanilla
    extract
Salt to taste

Beat cream cheese in mixer bowl until smooth. Add confectioners' sugar gradually, beating until fluffy. Add melted chocolate; mix well. Stir in pecans, vanilla and salt. Press into buttered shallow pan. Chill until firm. Cut into squares. Store, tightly wrapped, in refrigerator.

Pat Anderton, Winston-Salem

Chocolate Fudge

Yield:
96 servings
Utensil:
saucepan
Approx Per
Serving:
Cal 101
Prot 1 g
Carbo 14 g
Fiber <1 g
T Fat 6 g
Chol 1 mg
Sod 31 mg

Dietary
Exchanges:
Milk 0
Vegetable 0
Fruit 0
Bread/Starch 0
Meat 0; Fat 1½

4½ cups sugar
1 12-ounce can
  evaporated milk
1 cup margarine

2 cups chopped pecans
2 cups miniature
  marshmallows
3 cups chocolate chips

Bring sugar, evaporated milk and margarine to a boil in large saucepan, stirring constantly. Cook for 11 minutes. Add pecans, marshmallows and chocolate chips, stirring until chocolate and marshmallows dissolve. Pour immediately into buttered pan. Cool for 15 minutes. Cut into small pieces. Store in refrigerator.

Judy C. Barr, Advance

Chocolate Marshmallow Fudge

Yield:
96 servings
Utensil:
saucepan
Approx Per
Serving:
Cal 100
Prot 1 g
Carbo 15 g
Fiber <1 g
T Fat 5 g
Chol 1 mg
Sod 32 mg

Dietary
Exchanges:
Milk 0
Vegetable 0
Fruit 0
Bread/Starch 0
Meat 0; Fat 1

5 cups sugar
1 cup margarine
1 15-ounce can
  evaporated milk
1 teaspoon vanilla
  extract

2 cups semisweet
  chocolate chips
1 7-ounce jar
  marshmallow creme
2 cups chopped pecans

Bring sugar, margarine and evaporated milk to a boil in heavy saucepan over medium-high heat. Cook for 8 minutes, stirring constantly; remove from heat. Add vanilla, chocolate chips, marshmallow creme and pecans; mix well. Pour into buttered 10x15-inch pan. Let stand until cool. Cut into squares. May substitute grated 12-ounce vanilla bar and walnuts or peanut butter chips and peanuts for chocolate and pecans if preferred.

Ruth Kent Eslinger, Winston-Salem

MICROWAVE DOUBLE CHOCOLATE FUDGE

Yield:
64 servings
Utensil:
glass dish
Approx Per
Serving:
Cal 66
Prot 1 g
Carbo 7 g
Fiber <1 g
T Fat 4 g
Chol 2 mg
Sod 9 mg

Dietary
Exchanges:
Milk 0
Vegetable 0
Fruit 0
Bread/Starch 0
Meat 0; Fat 1

1 14-ounce can sweetened condensed milk
2 cups semisweet chocolate chips
1 ounce unsweetened chocolate
1½ cups chopped pecans
1 teaspoon vanilla extract

Combine condensed milk, chocolate chips and chocolate in 2-quart glass dish. Microwave, uncovered, on High for 3 minutes or until chocolate melts, stirring after 1 minute. Stir in pecans and vanilla. Spread in buttered 8x8-inch pan. Chill until firm. Cut into 1-inch squares.

Melanie Vance, Kernersville

QUICK MICROWAVE CHOCOLATE FUDGE

Yield:
64 servings
Utensil:
glass dish
Approx Per
Serving:
Cal 113
Prot 1 g
Carbo 18 g
Fiber 1 g
T Fat 5 g
Chol 8 mg
Sod 30 mg

Dietary
Exchanges:
Milk 0
Vegetable 0
Fruit 0
Bread/Starch 0
Meat 0; Fat 1

2 1-pound packages confectioners' sugar
1 cup baking cocoa
½ cup milk
1 cup butter
1½ cups chopped pecans
2 tablespoons vanilla extract

Mix confectioners' sugar and cocoa in glass dish. Add milk and butter; do not mix. Microwave on High for 4½ to 6 minutes or until butter melts; mix well. Add pecans and vanilla; mix well. Spoon into buttered square dish. Chill until firm. Cut into small squares. May chop pecans coarsely and add 1 cup miniature marshmallows with pecans for Rocky Road Fudge.

Wendy Needham, Winston-Salem

HEAVENLY FUDGE

Yield:
96 servings
Utensil:
saucepan
Approx Per
Serving:
Cal 63
Prot <1 g
Carbo 10 g
Fiber <1 g
T Fat 3 g
Chol 1 mg
Sod 10 mg

Dietary
Exchanges:
Milk 0
Vegetable 0
Fruit 0
Bread/Starch 0
Meat 0; Fat ½

3 cups sugar
¼ cup margarine
⅔ cup evaporated milk
1 ounce chocolate, chopped
2 cups chocolate chips

1 7-ounce jar marshmallow creme
1 teaspoon vanilla extract
1 cup chopped pecans

Combine sugar, margarine, evaporated milk and chocolate in heavy 2½-quart saucepan. Bring to a rolling boil, stirring constantly. Cook for exactly 5 minutes, stirring constantly; remove from heat. Stir in chocolate chips until melted. Beat in marshmallow creme and vanilla. Stir in pecans. Pour into lightly buttered 9x13-inch dish. Cool to room temperature. Cut fudge into squares. Store in airtight container.

Jane Walters

COCOA FUDGE

Yield:
36 servings
Utensil:
saucepan
Approx Per
Serving:
Cal 82
Prot 1 g
Carbo 17 g
Fiber <1 g
T Fat 2 g
Chol 5 mg
Sod 25 mg

Dietary
Exchanges:
Milk 0
Vegetable 0
Fruit 0
Bread/Starch 0
Meat 0; Fat ½

⅔ cup baking cocoa
3 cups sugar
⅛ teaspoon salt
1½ cups milk

¼ cup butter
1 teaspoon vanilla extract

Mix cocoa, sugar and salt in heavy 4-quart saucepan. Stir in milk. Bring to a boil, stirring constantly. Cook to 234 to 240 degrees on candy thermometer, soft-ball stage; do not stir. Remove from heat. Add butter and vanilla; do not stir. Let stand at room temperature until 110 degrees. Beat until mixture thickens and loses its luster. Spread immediately in buttered 8x8 or 9x9-inch dish; cool completely. Cut into squares.

A Pioneer

NEVER-FAIL FUDGE

Yield:
96 servings
Utensil:
saucepan
Approx Per
Serving:
Cal 84
Prot 1 g
Carbo 12 g
Fiber <1 g
T Fat 4 g
Chol 1 mg
Sod 31 mg

Dietary
Exchanges:
Milk 0
Vegetable 0
Fruit 0
Bread/Starch 0
Meat 0; Fat 1

4½ cups sugar
1 15-ounce can
   evaporated milk
1 cup margarine
1 teaspoon vanilla
   extract
3 cups chocolate chips

Combine sugar, evaporated milk, margarine and vanilla in saucepan. Cook for 6 minutes, stirring constantly; remove from heat. Stir in chocolate chips until melted. Spoon into buttered dish. Let stand until cool. Cut into small squares.

Barbara Johnson, Graham

NO-FAIL FUDGE

Yield:
96 servings
Utensil:
saucepan
Approx Per
Serving:
Cal 86
Prot 1 g
Carbo 13 g
Fiber <1 g
T Fat 4 g
Chol 1 mg
Sod 31 mg

Dietary
Exchanges:
Milk 0
Vegetable 0
Fruit 0
Bread/Starch 0
Meat 0; Fat 1

2 cups semisweet
   chocolate chips
1 cup chopped pecans
1 cup margarine
1 tablespoon vanilla
   extract
1 15-ounce can
   evaporated milk
5 cups sugar

Mix chocolate chips, pecans, margarine and vanilla in large mixer bowl. Combine evaporated milk and sugar in saucepan. Cook to 234 to 240 degrees on candy thermometer, soft-ball stage. Pour over chocolate chip mixture; beat until well mixed. Pour into buttered 9x13-inch dish. Chill overnight. Cut into squares.

Laverne Albright, Burlington

OLD-FASHIONED FUDGE

2 cups milk chocolate chips
2 cups marshmallow creme
2 cups chopped pecans
4 1/2 cups sugar
2 tablespoons butter
1 15-ounce can evaporated milk
Salt to taste

Combine chocolate chips, marshmallow creme and pecans in bowl; mix well. Combine sugar, butter, evaporated milk and salt in saucepan. Cook over low heat until sugar dissolves, stirring constantly. Bring to a boil. Boil gently for 8 minutes. Pour over chocolate chip mixture; mix until chocolate melts. Pour into buttered 8x11-inch dish. Let stand until cool and firm. Cut into small squares.

Ina Livingston, Winston-Salem

PEANUT BUTTER FUDGE

1 1/2 pounds white chocolate
16 ounces chunky peanut butter

Microwave white chocolate on High in large glass bowl until melted. Stir in peanut butter, mixing well. Pour into buttered dish. Cool to room temperature. Cut into squares.

Edith Gerringer, Burlington

STAINED GLASS FUDGE

Yield:
64 servings
Utensil:
saucepan
Approx Per
Serving:
Cal 93
Prot 1 g
Carbo 14 g
Fiber <1 g
T Fat 4 g
Chol 2 mg
Sod 15 mg

Dietary
Exchanges:
Milk 0
Vegetable 0
Fruit 0
Bread/Starch 1/2
Meat 0; Fat 1

1½ pounds vanilla candy coating
1 14-ounce can sweetened condensed milk
⅛ teaspoon salt
1½ cups chopped mixed gumdrops
1½ teaspoons vanilla extract

Melt candy coating and condensed milk with salt in heavy saucepan, stirring to mix well. Stir in gumdrops and vanilla. Spread in 9x9-inch dish lined with waxed paper. Chill for 2 hours or until firm. Invert onto cutting board; remove waxed paper. Cut into squares. Store at room temperature in airtight container. May substitute chocolate candy coating for vanilla and pecans for gumdrops.

Juanita Stone, Graham

GRAHAM CRACKER CRISPS

Yield:
24 servings
Utensil:
baking pan
Approx Per
Serving:
Cal 125
Prot 1 g
Carbo 10 g
Fiber 1 g
T Fat 9 g
Chol 10 mg
Sod 110 mg

Dietary
Exchanges:
Milk 0
Vegetable 0
Fruit 0
Bread/Starch 1/2
Meat 0; Fat 2

24 honey graham crackers
6 tablespoons margarine
½ cup butter
½ cup sugar
3 ounces sliced blanched almonds

Break graham crackers apart. Arrange in single layer in 10x15-inch baking pan. Combine margarine, butter and sugar in saucepan. Bring to a boil, stirring until margarine and butter melts and sugar dissolves. Boil for 2 minutes. Pour over graham crackers. Sprinkle with almonds. Bake at 325 degrees for 10 minutes. Remove immediately to wire rack over waxed paper; let stand until cool. Store in airtight container.

Ruth C. Cline, Winston-Salem

GRAHAM CRACKER GOODIES

Yield:
24 servings
Utensil:
baking sheet
Approx Per Serving:
Cal 140
Prot 1 g
Carbo 10 g
Fiber 1 g
T Fat 11 g
Chol 20 mg
Sod 110 mg

Dietary Exchanges:
Milk 0
Vegetable 0
Fruit 0
Bread/Starch ½
Meat 0; Fat 2½

24 graham crackers
1 cup broken pecans
1 cup butter
½ cup sugar
½ teaspoon vanilla extract

Arrange single layer of graham crackers on baking sheet lined with foil. Sprinkle with pecans. Bring butter and sugar to a boil in saucepan. Boil for 2 minutes; remove from heat. Stir in vanilla. Spoon over graham crackers. Bake at 350 degrees for 7 minutes. Cool completely. Break into pieces.

Jean Jarrett, Thomasville

PRALINE CONFECTIONS

Yield:
80 servings
Utensil:
baking pan
Approx Per Serving:
Cal 48
Prot <1 g
Carbo 4 g
Fiber <1 g
T Fat 3 g
Chol 6 mg
Sod 34 mg

Dietary Exchanges:
Milk 0
Vegetable 0
Fruit 0
Bread/Starch 0
Meat 0; Fat 1

24 whole graham crackers
1 cup packed light brown sugar
1 cup butter
1 cup chopped pecans

Line 10x15-inch baking pan with graham crackers. Bring brown sugar and butter to a rolling boil in heavy saucepan. Boil for 2 minutes, stirring constantly; remove from heat. Cool slightly. Stir in pecans. Spoon over graham crackers. Bake at 350 degrees for 10 minutes. Cool in pan for several minutes. Cut into small squares.

Lillie Haywood, Burlington

Goochies

Yield:
24 servings
Utensil:
baking sheet
Approx Per
Serving:
Cal 136
Prot 1 g
Carbo 10 g
Fiber <1 g
T Fat 11 g
Chol 11 mg
Sod 127 mg

Dietary
Exchanges:
Milk 0
Vegetable 0
Fruit 0
Bread/Starch ½
Meat 0; Fat 2½

24 graham crackers   ½ cup margarine
¾ cup chopped pecans   ½ cup sugar
½ cup butter

Arrange graham crackers on baking sheet lined with foil; sprinkle with pecans. Melt butter and margarine in saucepan. Add sugar; mix well. Bring to a boil. Boil for 2 minutes. Spoon over graham crackers. Bake at 325 degrees for 10 minutes. Cool to room temperature. Store in airtight container.

Ron Watkins, Winston-Salem

Mint Candy

Yield:
60 servings
Utensil:
candy molds
Approx Per
Serving:
Cal 42
Prot <1 g
Carbo 9 g
Fiber 0 g
T Fat 1 g
Chol 0 mg
Sod 5 mg

Dietary
Exchanges:
Milk 0
Vegetable 0
Fruit 0
Bread/Starch 0
Meat 0; Fat 0

1   1-pound package   2 tablespoons hot
    confectioners' sugar   water
2 tablespoons   Mint extract or other
    shortening   flavoring to taste
2 tablespoons
    margarine, softened

Combine confectioners' sugar, shortening, margarine, hot water and flavoring in bowl; knead until smooth. Press into candy molds. Invert onto waxed paper. Store in airtight container.

B. S. Cuthrell, Winston-Salem

PEANUT BUTTER BARS

1 cup melted butter
1 cup graham cracker
crumbs
1 1-pound package
confectioners' sugar
1 cup chunky peanut
butter
2 cups chocolate chips,
melted

Combine butter, graham cracker crumbs, confectioners' sugar and peanut butter in bowl; mix well. Press into buttered 10x15-inch dish. Spread chocolate over top. Chill until firm. Cut into bars.

Jerry Jarrell, Jamestown

PEANUT BUTTER BALLS

1 12-ounce jar peanut
butter
1/2 cup butter, softened
1 1-pound package
confectioners' sugar
1 teaspoon vanilla
extract
1 cup chocolate chips
2 tablespoons
shortening

Combine peanut butter, butter, confectioners' sugar and vanilla in mixer bowl; mix until smooth. Shape into small balls. Chill, covered, for 2 hours to overnight. Melt chocolate chips and shortening in saucepan, mixing well. Dip balls into chocolate, coating well. Place on waxed paper. Let stand until firm. Store in refrigerator.

Jessie Grandinetti

REESE SQUARES

1 **18-ounce jar chunky peanut butter**
1/2 cup melted butter
1/2 cup packed brown sugar
21/2 cups confectioners' sugar
1 teaspoon vanilla extract
1 cup milk chocolate chips
1/3 cup butter

Combine peanut butter, 1/2 cup melted butter, brown sugar, confectioners' sugar and vanilla in bowl; mix well. Press into buttered shallow pan. Melt chocolate chips with 1/3 cup butter in saucepan. Spread over peanut butter mixture. Chill until firm. Cut into squares.

Polly Y. Simpson, Greensboro

RITZ MINT PATTIES

8 ounces green candy coating
Peppermint oil to taste
24 Ritz crackers
8 ounces dark chocolate

Melt green candy coating in saucepan. Flavor as desired with peppermint oil. Dip crackers into coating. Chill in refrigerator. Melt dark chocolate in saucepan. Dip chilled patties into dark chocolate, coating well. Let stand until firm. Use peppermint oil very sparingly; it has a much stronger flavor than peppermint extract.

B. S. Cuthrell, Winston-Salem

SHIRLEY'S PEANUT BRITTLE

Yield:
20 servings
Utensil:
saucepan
Approx Per Serving:
Cal 144
Prot 4 g
Carbo 18 g
Fiber 1 g
T Fat 7 g
Chol 0 mg
Sod 89 mg

Dietary Exchanges:
Milk 0
Vegetable 0
Fruit 0
Bread/Starch 0
Meat 1/2; Fat 1

½ cup corn syrup
1 cup sugar
2 cups blanched peanuts

2 teaspoons (heaping) soda

Bring corn syrup, sugar and peanuts to a boil in saucepan. Cook for 12 to 15 minutes or to 300 degrees on candy thermometer, hard-crack stage, stirring constantly; remove from heat. Add soda; mix well. Pour immediately into buttered dish. Let stand until cool. Break into pieces.

Ruth C. Cline, Winston-Salem

CHOCOLATE AND PEANUT CLUSTERS

Yield:
48 servings
Utensil:
saucepan
Approx Per Serving:
Cal 75
Prot 2 g
Carbo 5 g
Fiber 1 g
T Fat 6 g
Chol 0 mg
Sod 30 mg

Dietary Exchanges:
Milk 0
Vegetable 0
Fruit 0
Bread/Starch 1/2
Meat 1/2; Fat 1 1/2

2 tablespoons peanut butter
1 cup semisweet chocolate chips

1 cup butterscotch chips
2 cups salted Spanish peanuts

Combine peanut butter, chocolate chips and butterscotch chips in saucepan. Cook over low heat until melted, stirring to mix well. Stir in peanuts. Drop by teaspoonfuls onto waxed paper. Chill until firm. Store in refrigerator.

Sue Loy, Graham

Swedish Nuts

1½ cups almonds
2 cups walnuts
½ cup pecans
2 egg whites

1 cup sugar
⅛ teaspoon salt
½ cup melted butter

Spread almonds, walnuts and pecans on baking sheet. Bake at 275 degrees until toasted. Beat egg whites in bowl until foamy. Add sugar 1 tablespoonful at a time, beating constantly until stiff peaks form. Beat in salt. Stir in toasted nuts, coating well. Spoon into melted butter in 10x15-inch baking pan. Bake at 300 degrees for 30 minutes, stirring several times. May turn entire baked layer after 15 minutes or bake without turning if preferred.

Joanne G. DeWolf, Winston-Salem

Zesty Pecans

1 tablespoon melted
  butter
1 pound pecans
Salt to taste

3 tablespoons
  Worcestershire sauce
Tabasco sauce to taste

Mix butter and pecans in large baking pan. Bake at 300 degrees for 5 minutes. Add salt; mix well. Bake for 10 minutes. Mix Worcestershire sauce and Tabasco sauce in small bowl. Pour over pecans; mix well. Bake for 15 to 20 minutes longer or until done to taste.

Jerry Jarrell, Jamestown

WHITE BRITTLE

1 pound white   1 cup broken pretzel
  chocolate   sticks
1 cup Spanish peanuts

Melt white chocolate in saucepan. Stir in peanuts
and pretzels. Spread in thin layer on large tray. Chill
in freezer until firm. Break into pieces.

B. S. Cuthrell, Winston-Salem

WHITE CHOCOLATE CANDY

2 pounds white   1 24-ounce jar
  chocolate   dry-roasted peanuts
1 cup peanut butter   1 10-ounce package
3 cups crisp rice cereal   marshmallows

Melt white chocolate and peanut butter in saucepan, stirring to mix well. Combine with cereal,
peanuts and marshmallows in large bowl; mix well.
Drop by spoonfuls onto waxed paper. Let stand
until firm. Store in airtight container.

Jean Jarrett, Thomasville

PIES

Yield:
8 servings
Utensil:
pie plate
**Approx Per
Serving:**
*Cal 284
Prot 3 g
Carbo 39 g
Fiber <1 g
T Fat 14 g
Chol 177 mg
Sod 93 mg*

**Dietary
Exchanges:**
*Milk 0
Vegetable 0
Fruit 0
Bread/Starch 0
Meat 1/2; Fat 3*

*Nutritional
information for
Lemon Filling
is included
above.*

1/2 teaspoon vinegar
1/2 teaspoon water
1/2 teaspoon vanilla
    extract
3 egg whites
1/2 teaspoon baking
    powder
1/8 teaspoon salt
1 cup sugar
Lemon Filling

Combine vinegar, water and vanilla in small bowl. Beat egg whites with baking powder and salt in mixer bowl until soft peaks form. Add 1 cup sugar 1 tablespoon at a time, alternating with vinegar mixture, beating constantly until stiff peaks form. Spoon into greased 10-inch pie plate, building up edge. Bake at 275 degrees for 1 hour. Cool to room temperature. Spoon in Lemon Filling. Store in refrigerator.

Lemon Filling

1/2 teaspoon vinegar
1/2 teaspoon water
1/2 teaspoon vanilla
    extract
4 egg yolks
1 tablespoon flour
1/2 cup water
1/2 cup sugar
3 tablespoons lemon
    juice
Grated rind of 1 lemon
1 cup whipping cream
1/2 teaspoon vanilla
    extract

Combine vinegar, 1/2 teaspoon water, 1/2 teaspoon vanilla, egg yolks, flour, 1/2 cup water, sugar, lemon juice and lemon rind in double boiler. Cook until thickened, stirring constantly. Let cool to room temperature. Beat whipping cream with 1/2 teaspoon vanilla in mixer bowl until soft peaks form. Fold into cooled lemon mixture.

Mrs. Paul Schneeloch, Clemmons

Brown Sugar Apple Pie

6 cooking apples, peeled, sliced
2/3 cup sugar
Cinnamon to taste
2 tablespoons butter
1/2 cup packed brown sugar
1/2 cup butter, softened
1 cup flour
Salt to taste

Spread apples in buttered 9-inch pie plate. Sprinkle with sugar and cinnamon; dot with 2 tablespoons butter. Cream brown sugar and 1/2 cup butter in mixer bowl until light and fluffy. Add flour and salt; mix well. Sprinkle over apples, pressing down firmly. Bake at 325 degrees for 45 minutes or until apples are tender. Serve with whipped cream. May substitute peaches for apples.

Geraldine Crane Waterhouse, Greensboro

Apple and Cranberry Pie

2 cups sugar
1/4 cup cornstarch
1/2 teaspoon cinnamon
6 apples, peeled, sliced
2 cups fresh cranberries
1/4 lemon, finely chopped
1 recipe 2-crust pie pastry
1 tablespoon milk
1 tablespoon sugar

Mix 2 cups sugar, cornstarch and cinnamon in bowl. Add apples, cranberries and lemon; toss to coat well. Spoon into pastry-lined 10-inch pie plate. Top with remaining pastry. Trim and seal edges; cut vents. Brush with milk. Sprinkle with 1 tablespoon sugar. Bake at 350 degrees for 1 hour or until crust is brown. Serve warm with vanilla ice cream. May substitute flour for cornstarch.

Flora Efland Cheshire, Efland

DUTCH APPLE PIE

6 cups sliced tart
  apples
½ cup sugar
1 tablespoon lemon
  juice
1 teaspoon cinnamon

1 unbaked 9-inch pie
  shell
1 cup flour
¾ cup sugar
½ cup butter

Combine apples, ½ cup sugar, lemon juice and cinnamon in large bowl; mix well. Spread in pie shell. Mix flour and ¾ cup sugar in bowl. Cut in butter until crumbly. Sprinkle over apples. Bake at 400 degrees for 50 to 60 minutes or until apples are tender.

Caron C. Hairston, Walkertown

BUTTERSCOTCH PIES

2 cups packed light
  brown sugar
6 tablespoons butter
½ cup cream
4 egg yolks, beaten
½ cup flour

4 cups milk
2 baked 9-inch pie
  shells
4 egg whites
½ cup sugar

Combine brown sugar, butter and cream in heavy saucepan. Cook over medium heat for 15 minutes or to desired butterscotch color. Combine egg yolks, flour and milk in bowl; mix well. Combine with cooked mixture in double boiler. Cook until slightly thickened, stirring constantly. Spoon into pie shells. Beat egg whites in bowl until soft peaks form. Add sugar, beating until stiff peaks form. Spoon onto pies, sealing to edges. Bake at 350 degrees for 15 minutes or until golden brown. Cool for 2 hours before serving.

Dovie Smith, Kino

CHESS PIE

1/2 cup butter, softened
3 cups sugar
4 eggs
1 1/4 teaspoons vanilla
  extract
2 tablespoons cornmeal
Salt to taste
1 cup milk
1 unbaked 9-inch pie
  shell

Cream butter and sugar in mixer bowl until light and fluffy. Beat in eggs, vanilla, cornmeal, salt and milk. Pour into pie shell. Bake at 350 degrees until set and brown; center will sink as pie cools. May bake in 2 smaller pie shells if preferred.

Mary Rudisill, Hendersonville

BUTTERMILK CHESS PIE

3 tablespoons melted
  butter
1 1/2 cups packed light
  brown sugar
3 eggs
3 tablespoons buttermilk
1 teaspoon vanilla
  extract
1 unbaked 9-inch pie
  shell

Combine butter and brown sugar in mixer bowl; mix well. Beat in eggs at medium speed. Add buttermilk, beating constantly at medium speed. Add vanilla; beat at high speed for 1 minute. Pour into pie shell. Bake at 375 degrees for 25 to 30 minutes or until set.

Thelma M. Kimball, Winston-Salem

CHOCOLATE CHESS PIE

¼ cup melted margarine
1½ cups sugar
3 tablespoons baking cocoa
2 eggs
1 5-ounce can evaporated milk
1 teaspoon vanilla extract
1 unbaked 9-inch pie shell

Combine margarine, sugar, cocoa, eggs, evaporated milk and vanilla in bowl; mix well. Spoon into pie shell. Bake at 325 degrees for 45 minutes.

Sarah L. Finley, Graham

GRANDMA'S LEMON CHESS PIE

¼ cup butter, softened
1½ cups sugar
4 eggs
Juice of 2 lemons
1 tablespoon cornmeal
1 unbaked pie shell

Cream butter and sugar in mixer bowl until light and fluffy. Stir in eggs; do not beat. Stir in lemon juice and cornmeal. Spoon into pie shell. Bake at 350 degrees for 45 minutes to 1 hour.

Nancy Garner, Burlington

PINEAPPLE CHESS PIES

1/2 cup margarine, softened
1 1-pound package brown sugar
2 tablespoons flour
3 eggs
1 8-ounce can crushed pineapple
1/2 teaspoon vanilla extract
2 unbaked pie shells

Preheat oven to 375 degrees. Cream margarine, brown sugar and flour in mixer bowl until light and fluffy. Beat in eggs. Add pineapple and vanilla; mix well. Spoon into pie shells. Reduce oven temperature to 350 degrees. Bake pies until set and light brown.

Gradie Vaden

CHESS TARTS

1/2 cup butter, softened
4 cups packed brown sugar
5 eggs, beaten
3 tablespoons milk
1 1/2 teaspoons vanilla extract
36 unbaked tart shells

Cream butter and brown sugar in mixer bowl until light and fluffy. Beat in eggs, milk and vanilla. Spoon into tart shells. Bake at 350 degrees for 10 to 15 minutes. May reduce recipe by half, reducing eggs from 5 to 3.

Lillian Buie, Winston-Salem

CHOCOLATE CHIP PIE

1 cup sugar
1/2 cup flour
2 eggs, beaten
1/2 cup melted margarine
1 cup chocolate chips
1 cup chopped pecans
1 teaspoon vanilla extract
1 unbaked 9-inch pie shell

Mix sugar and flour in bowl. Beat in eggs. Add margarine, chocolate chips, pecans and vanilla; mix well. Spoon into pie shell. Bake at 350 degrees for 30 to 40 minutes or until set.

Sarah L. Finley, Graham

CHOCOLATETOWN PIE

1/2 cup butter, softened
1 cup sugar
2 eggs, beaten
2 teaspoons vanilla extract
1/2 cup flour
1 cup semisweet chocolate chips
1 cup chopped pecans
1 unbaked 9-inch deep-dish pie shell
1/2 cup whipping cream, chilled
2 tablespoons confectioners' sugar
1 teaspoon Bourbon

Cream butter and sugar in mixer bowl until light. Beat in eggs and vanilla. Add flour; mix well. Stir in chocolate chips and pecans. Spoon into pie shell. Bake at 350 degrees for 45 to 50 minutes or until golden brown. Cool for 1 hour. Combine whipping cream, confectioners' sugar and Bourbon in mixer bowl; beat until soft peaks form. Serve with pie.

Nancy Garner, Burlington

CHOCOLATE DELIGHT PIE

Yield:
8 servings
Utensil:
pie plate
Approx Per
Serving:
Cal 739
Prot 13 g
Carbo 74 g
Fiber 1 g
T Fat 45 g
Chol 44 mg
Sod 489 mg

Dietary
Exchanges:
Milk 1/2
Vegetable 0
Fruit 0
Bread/Starch 2
Meat 0; Fat 10

1/2 cup melted margarine
1 cup flour
2 tablespoons
  confectioners' sugar
1/2 cup crushed pecans
8 ounces cream cheese,
  softened
1 cup confectioners'
  sugar
1 cup whipped topping
1 6-ounce package
  chocolate instant
  pudding mix
2 1/2 cups cold milk
2 cups whipped
  topping
2 tablespoons chopped
  pecans

Combine margarine, flour and 2 tablespoons confectioners' sugar in bowl; mix well. Stir in 1/2 cup pecans. Spread in buttered 9-inch pie plate. Bake at 350 degrees for 20 minutes. Cool to room temperature. Blend cream cheese, 1 cup confectioners' sugar and 1 cup whipped topping in bowl until smooth. Spread in pie crust. Combine pudding mix and milk in bowl; mix until thickened and smooth. Chill in refrigerator. Spread over cream cheese layer. Top with 2 cups whipped topping and 2 tablespoons pecans. Chill until serving time.

A Pioneer

FRENCH SILK CHIFFON PIE

Yield:
8 servings
Utensil:
pie plate
Approx Per
Serving:
Cal 496
Prot 6 g
Carbo 40 g
Fiber 1 g
T Fat 34 g
Chol 150 mg
Sod 192 mg

Dietary
Exchanges:
Milk 0
Vegetable 0
Fruit 0
Bread/Starch 1/2
Meat 1; Fat 7 1/2

3/4 cup lightly salted
  butter
1 cup plus 2
  tablespoons sugar
1 teaspoon vanilla
  extract
1 1/2 squares
  unsweetened
  chocolate, melted
3 eggs
1 baked 10-inch pie
  shell
3/4 cup thinly sliced
  almonds

Cream butter, sugar and vanilla in mixer bowl until light and fluffy. Beat in chocolate. Add eggs 1 at a time, beating at high speed for 3 minutes after each addition. Spoon into pie shell; smooth top. Sprinkle with almonds. Chill for 3 hours or longer.

Barbara N. Grieser, Greensboro

FROZEN CHOCOLATE PIES

1 envelope unflavored
    gelatin
2 tablespoons water
2 4-ounce bars sweet
    baking chocolate
4 egg yolks
4 egg whites
1 teaspoon vanilla
    extract
Salt to taste
1 cup sugar
16 ounces whipped
    topping
1 cup chopped pecans
2 9-inch chocolate
    wafer pie shells
2 tablespoons chopped
    pecans

Dissolve gelatin in water in bowl. Melt chocolate in double boiler over simmering water. Stir a small amount of chocolate into egg yolks; stir egg yolks into chocolate. Add gelatin. Cook until gelatin is dissolved, stirring constantly. Cool to room temperature. Beat egg whites with vanilla and salt in mixer bowl for 1 minute. Add sugar gradually, beating until stiff. Fold egg whites, whipped topping and 1 cup pecans gently into chocolate mixture. Spoon into pie shells; sprinkle with 2 tablespoons pecans. Freeze for 3 hours. Let stand at room temperature for 10 minutes before serving.

Martha M. Wheeler, Chapin, South Carolina

GERMAN CHOCOLATE PIES

3 cups sugar
5 tablespoons baking
    cocoa
Salt to taste
4 eggs, beaten
1 15-ounce can
    evaporated milk
6 tablespoons melted
    margarine
2 cups coconut
1 cup chopped pecans
1 teaspoon vanilla
    extract
3 unbaked pie shells

Mix sugar, cocoa and salt in bowl. Add eggs; mix well. Stir in evaporated milk, margarine, coconut, pecans and vanilla. Spoon into pie shells. Bake at 350 degrees for 40 minutes or until set.

Earline Goin, Hamptonville

HERSHEY PIE

Yield:
8 servings
Utensil:
pie plate
Approx Per
Serving:
Cal 610
Prot 11 g
Carbo 62 g
Fiber 0 g
T Fat 37 g
Chol 2 mg
Sod 336 mg

Dietary
Exchanges:
Milk 1/2
Vegetable 0
Fruit 0
Bread/Starch 2
Meat 0; Fat 11 1/2

6 1½-ounce chocolate bars with almonds
12 ounces whipped topping
1 9-inch chocolate wafer pie shell

Place chocolate bars in glass dish. Microwave on High for 1 to 1½ minutes or until melted. Blend in whipped topping. Spoon into pie shell. Freeze until serving time. Garnish with shaved chocolate.

Sharon M. Fanelli, Gibsonville

JOY'S CHOCOLATE MERINGUE PIE

Yield:
8 servings
Utensil:
pie plate
Approx Per
Serving:
Cal 302
Prot 8 g
Carbo 42 g
Fiber 1 g
T Fat 12 g
Chol 118 mg
Sod 245 mg

Dietary
Exchanges:
Milk 1/2
Vegetable 0
Fruit 0
Bread/Starch 1/2
Meat 1/2; Fat 2 1/2

3 egg yolks
¾ cup sugar
1 15-ounce can evaporated milk
3 tablespoons baking cocoa
1 teaspoon vanilla extract
1 unbaked pie shell
3 egg whites
6 tablespoons sugar

Beat egg yolks in bowl. Add ¾ cup sugar, evaporated milk, cocoa and vanilla; mix well. Pour into pie shell. Bake at 350 degrees for 20 to 25 minutes or until set. Beat egg whites with 6 tablespoons sugar in mixer bowl until stiff peaks form. Spread on pie, sealing to edge. Bake just until meringue is brown.

Ramona P. Cheek, Graham

COCONUT PIE

1 1/2 cups sugar
3 eggs
6 tablespoons melted
  margarine
1 tablespoon lemon
  juice
1 cup coconut
1 teaspoon vanilla
  extract
Salt to taste
1 unbaked 9-inch pie
  shell

Combine sugar, eggs, margarine, lemon juice, coconut, vanilla and salt in bowl; mix well. Spoon into pie shell. Bake at 350 degrees on lower oven rack for 40 minutes or until set.

Connie Kelly, Mocksville

BUTTERMILK COCONUT PIES

1/2 cup margarine,
  softened
2 cups sugar
4 eggs
2/3 cup buttermilk
2 teaspoons vanilla
  extract
1 1/2 cups coconut
2 unbaked pie shells

Cream margarine and sugar in mixer bowl until light and fluffy. Beat in eggs 1 at a time. Add buttermilk and vanilla; mix well. Stir in coconut. Spoon into pie shells. Bake at 350 degrees for 45 minutes or until firm.

Lois W. Beck, Greensboro

FRENCH COCONUT PIE

Yield:
8 servings
Utensil:
pie plate
Approx Per
Serving:
Cal 375
Prot 5 g
Carbo 42 g
Fiber 2 g
T Fat 22 g
Chol 104 mg
Sod 331 mg

Dietary
Exchanges:
Milk 0
Vegetable 0
Fruit 0
Bread/Starch 1/2
Meat 1/2; Fat 41/2

3 eggs
6 tablespoons melted
    margarine
1¼ cups sugar
¾ cup buttermilk

1 teaspoon vanilla
    extract
1½ cups coconut
1 unbaked 9-inch pie
    shell

Beat eggs slightly in bowl. Add margarine, sugar, buttermilk, vanilla and coconut; mix well. Pour into pie shell. Bake at 350 degrees for 45 minutes.

Susie Pearson, Pfafftown

COCONUT CUSTARD PIE

Yield:
8 servings
Utensil:
pie plate
Approx Per
Serving:
Cal 289
Prot 5 g
Carbo 32 g
Fiber 1 g
T Fat 16 g
Chol 85 mg
Sod 244 mg

Dietary
Exchanges:
Milk 1/2
Vegetable 0
Fruit 0
Bread/Starch 1/2
Meat 1/2; Fat 31/2

1 tablespoon
    (heaping) flour
¾ cup sugar
2 eggs, slightly beaten
2 tablespoons melted
    butter

1 cup evaporated milk
1½ teaspoons vanilla
    extract
1 cup coconut
1 unbaked pie shell

Mix flour and sugar in bowl. Add eggs; mix well. Add butter, evaporated milk and vanilla; mix well. Stir in coconut. Pour into pie shell. Bake at 350 degrees for 45 minutes or until nearly set in center.

Ruby Hudspeth, Yadkinville

GOOD COCONUT PIES

<table>
<tr><td>Yield:
16 servings
Utensil:
2 pie plates
Approx Per Serving:
Cal 404
Prot 4 g
Carbo 40 g
Fiber 4 g
T Fat 27 g
Chol 70 mg
Sod 305 mg</td></tr>
</table>

<table>
<tr><td>Dietary Exchanges:
Milk 0
Vegetable 0
Fruit 0
Bread/Starch ½
Meat ½; Fat 6½</td></tr>
</table>

¾ cup margarine, softened
2 cups sugar
4 eggs
¼ cup flour
½ cup milk
1 teaspoon vanilla extract
2 9-ounce packages frozen coconut, thawed
2 unbaked deep-dish pie shells

Cream margarine and sugar in mixer bowl until light and fluffy. Add eggs, flour, milk and vanilla; mix well. Stir in coconut. Spoon into 2 deep-dish pie shells. Bake at 450 degrees for 10 minutes. Reduce oven temperature to 350 degrees. Bake for 20 to 25 minutes longer or until set.

Nancy Garner, Burlington

CHEESECAKE PIES

<table>
<tr><td>Yield:
8 servings
Utensil:
pie plate
Approx Per Serving:
Cal 588
Prot 10 g
Carbo 63 g
Fiber 1 g
T Fat 34 g
Chol 153 mg
Sod 504 mg</td></tr>
</table>

<table>
<tr><td>Dietary Exchanges:
Milk ½
Vegetable 0
Fruit 2½
Bread/Starch 2
Meat ½; Fat 7</td></tr>
</table>

1 cup fine graham cracker crumbs
¼ cup sugar
¼ cup melted butter
16 ounces cream cheese, softened
2 eggs
⅓ cup sugar
½ cup sweetened condensed milk
1 teaspoon vanilla extract
1 21-ounce can blueberry pie filling

Combine graham cracker crumbs, ¼ cup sugar and butter in bowl; mix well. Press over bottom and side of 9-inch pie plate. Beat cream cheese in mixer bowl until light. Add eggs and ⅓ cup sugar; beat until smooth. Beat in condensed milk and vanilla gradually. Spoon into prepared crust. Bake at 300 degrees for 45 minutes. Cool to room temperature. Top with pie filling. May substitute strawberry or cherry pie filling for blueberry.

Angela White, Greensboro

Hawaiian Pies

1 16-ounce can crushed pineapple
1 cup sugar
1/4 cup cornstarch
3 bananas, sliced
3/4 cup coconut
1 cup pecans
2 graham cracker pie shells
16 ounces whipped topping

Combine undrained pineapple, sugar and cornstarch in saucepan. Cook until thickened, stirring constantly. Cool to room temperature. Layer half the pineapple mixture, bananas, remaining pineapple mixture, coconut and pecans in pie shells. Spread with whipped topping. Chill until serving time. May omit pecans if preferred.

Pauline B. Hart, Clemmons

Simple Honey Pie

1 cup honey
3 eggs, beaten
3 tablespoons butter
1 cup chopped pecans
Nutmeg to taste
1 teaspoon vanilla extract
1 unbaked 9-inch pie shell

Bring honey to a boil in saucepan. Beat a small amount of hot honey into egg yolks; beat egg yolks into hot honey. Add butter, pecans, nutmeg and vanilla; mix well. Spoon into pie shell. Bake at 325 degrees for 25 minutes or until set.

M. M. Gregory

ICE CREAM PIES

¼ cup packed brown sugar
1⅓ cups flour
½ cup chopped pecans
½ cup melted margarine
½ gallon vanilla ice cream, softened
⅓ cup baking cocoa
1 cup sugar
¼ cup milk
½ cup margarine

Mix brown sugar, flour, pecans and margarine in bowl. Press into two 9-inch pie plates. Bake at 350 degrees for 10 to 15 minutes or until brown. Cool to room temperature. Spread ice cream in cooled crusts. Freeze until firm. Bring cocoa, sugar, milk and margarine to a boil in saucepan. Cook for 1 minute. Cut pie into wedges. Spoon chocolate over servings.

Wadeene Sharpe, Gibsonville

JAPANESE PIE

½ cup melted margarine
2 eggs
1 cup sugar
1 tablespoon vinegar
½ cup coconut
½ cup raisins
½ cup chopped pecans
1 unbaked 9-inch pie shell

Combine margarine and eggs in bowl; mix well. Add sugar, vinegar, coconut, raisins and pecans; mix well. Spoon into pie shell. Bake at 325 degrees for 40 to 50 minutes or until set and brown.

Ruth L. Brown, Hamptonville

LEMON PIE

1 14-ounce can sweetened condensed milk
3 egg yolks
½ cup lemon juice
1 graham cracker pie shell
3 egg whites
6 tablespoons sugar

Combine condensed milk, egg yolks and lemon juice in bowl; mix well. Pour into pie shell. Beat egg whites with sugar in mixer bowl until stiff peaks form. Spread over pie, sealing to edge. Bake at 350 degrees for 15 minutes or just until brown. Cool to room temperature. Store in refrigerator.

Zane G. Gerringer, Elon College

OLD-FASHIONED LEMON PIE

¼ cup melted butter
1 cup sugar
3 egg yolks
¼ cup cold water
1 tablespoon cornmeal
1 tablespoon flour
Juice of 1 lemon
Grated rind of 1 lemon
3 egg whites, stiffly beaten
1 unbaked 9-inch pie shell

Combine butter and sugar in mixer bowl; mix until smooth. Beat in egg yolks. Add water, cornmeal and flour; mix well. Stir in lemon juice and lemon rind. Fold in stiffly beaten egg whites gently. Spoon into pie shell. Bake at 350 degrees for 40 minutes or until set. Cool to room temperature. May serve with whipped topping if desired.

Bernice H. Motsinger, Winston-Salem

NUTTY BUDDY PIES

Yield:
24 servings
Utensil:
3 pie plates
Approx Per
Serving:
Cal 484
Prot 9 g
Carbo 53 g
Fiber 1 g
T Fat 28 g
Chol 13 mg
Sod 369 mg

Dietary
Exchanges:
Milk 0
Vegetable 0
Fruit 0
Bread/Starch 2
Meat 1/2; Fat 6

8 ounces cream cheese, softened
1 cup milk
2 cups confectioners' sugar
2/3 cup chunky peanut butter
16 ounces whipped topping
3 9-inch graham cracker pie shells
3/4 cup chocolate syrup
1 cup chopped salted peanuts

Combine cream cheese and milk in mixer bowl; beat until blended. Add confectioners' sugar, peanut butter and whipped topping; mix well. Spoon into pie shells. Drizzle with chocolate syrup; sprinkle with peanuts. Freeze until serving time.

Hilda B. Allen, Mebane

FRESH PEACH PIE

Yield:
8 servings
Utensil:
pie plate
Approx Per
Serving:
Cal 297
Prot 3 g
Carbo 45 g
Fiber 2 g
T Fat 13 g
Chol 34 mg
Sod 243 mg

Dietary
Exchanges:
Milk 0
Vegetable 0
Fruit 1/2
Bread/Starch 1/2
Meat 0; Fat 2 1/2

5 fresh peaches, peeled, thinly sliced
5 slices bread, cubed
Nutmeg to taste
1/2 cup melted margarine
1 1/4 cups sugar
2 tablespoons flour
1 egg
1/2 teaspoon vanilla extract

Layer peaches and bread cubes in pie plate. Sprinkle with nutmeg. Combine margarine, sugar, flour, egg and vanilla in bowl; mix well. Pour over layers. Bake at 350 degrees for 25 to 30 minutes or until brown.

Ruby Hicks

PEACH CREAM PIE

3 fresh peaches, peeled   **3 tablespoons flour**
1 unbaked pie shell,   **3/4 cup half and half**
   chilled   **1/2 teaspoon cinnamon**
3/4 cup sugar

Cut peaches into halves. Arrange cut side down in pie shell. Sprinkle with mixture of sugar and flour. Pour half and half into pie shell. Sprinkle with cinnamon. Bake at 450 degrees for 10 minutes. Reduce oven temperature to 350 degrees. Bake for 30 minutes longer.

Ann C. Deitrick, Seminole, Florida

PEACH CRUMBLE PIE

1 cup sugar   **1 unbaked 9 or 10-inch**
3 tablespoons   **deep-dish pie shell**
   cornstarch   **1/4 cup sugar**
1/8 teaspoon salt   **1/4 cup packed light**
1 egg, beaten   **brown sugar**
1/2 teaspoon almond   **1/2 cup flour**
   extract   **1/4 cup margarine**
6 cups sliced peaches

Mix 1 cup sugar, cornstarch and salt in bowl. Stir in egg and almond extract. Add peaches; mix gently. Spoon into pie shell. Combine 1/4 cup sugar, brown sugar and flour in bowl. Cut in margarine until crumbly. Sprinkle over peaches. Bake at 375 degrees for 25 to 30 minutes or until golden brown. May substitute strawberries or blueberries for peaches; reduce sugar to 3/4 cup and add 1 tablespoon lemon juice for blueberry pie.

Ruth Kent Eslinger, Winston-Salem

PECAN PIE

1/2 cup butter, softened
1 cup sugar
3 eggs, slightly beaten
3/4 cup dark corn syrup
11/2 cups chopped
  pecans
1 teaspoon vanilla
  extract
1/4 teaspoon salt
1 unbaked 9-inch pie
  shell, chilled

Cream butter in mixer bowl until light. Add sugar gradually, beating until fluffy. Add eggs, corn syrup, pecans, vanilla and salt; mix well. Pour into pie shell. Bake at 375 degrees for 40 to 45 minutes or until set. Serve garnished with whipped cream and whole pecans.

Frances S. Marion, Kernersville

MOTHER'S PECAN PIE

3/4 cup sugar
11/2 cups light corn
  syrup
4 eggs, beaten
11/2 cups broken
  pecans
6 tablespoons butter
1 teaspoon vanilla
  extract
1 unbaked 9-inch pie
  shell

Combine sugar, corn syrup, eggs, pecans and butter in saucepan. Cook until butter melts, stirring constantly; remove from heat. Add vanilla. Pour into pie shell. Bake at 350 degrees for 30 minutes. Cool to room temperature.

Judy B. Allen, Burlington

COMPANY PECAN PIES

Yield:
16 servings
Utensil:
2 pie plates
Approx Per
Serving:
Cal 334
Prot 3 g
Carbo 39 g
Fiber 1 g
T Fat 19 g
Chol 52 mg
Sod 263 mg

Dietary
Exchanges:
Milk 0
Vegetable 0
Fruit 0
Bread/Starch 1/2
Meat 0; Fat 4

1 1-pound package light brown sugar
3 tablespoons flour
6 tablespoons milk
3 eggs, beaten
1/2 cup melted margarine
2 teaspoons vinegar
1 1/2 teaspoons vanilla extract
1 1/3 cups chopped pecans
2 unbaked pie shells

Combine brown sugar, flour, milk and eggs in large mixer bowl; mix well. Add margarine, vinegar and vanilla; mix well. Stir in pecans. Pour into pie shells. Place in cold oven. Set oven temperature to 300 degrees. Bake for 1 hour.

Gaylene Fogleman, Graham

FAVORITE PECAN PIE

Yield:
8 servings
Utensil:
pie plate
Approx Per
Serving:
Cal 509
Prot 5 g
Carbo 67 g
Fiber 1 g
T Fat 26 g
Chol 103 mg
Sod 294 mg

Dietary
Exchanges:
Milk 0
Vegetable 0
Fruit 0
Bread/Starch 1/2
Meat 1/2; Fat 6

3 eggs
1 cup sugar
Salt to taste
1 cup dark corn syrup
1/3 cup melted margarine
1 cup pecans
1 unbaked 9-inch deep-dish pie shell

Beat eggs, sugar and salt in mixer bowl. Add corn syrup; mix well. Add margarine; mix well. Stir in pecans. Pour into pie shell. Bake at 350 degrees for 1 hour and 5 minutes to 1 hour and 10 minutes. Let stand until cool.

Peggy Cassada, Clemmons

PECAN CUSTARD PIE

1 cup light corn syrup
1/2 cup sugar
1/4 cup margarine
3 eggs
1 teaspoon vanilla
extract
1 unbaked pie shell
1 cup chopped pecans

Combine corn syrup, sugar and margarine in saucepan. Cook until sugar dissolves and margarine melts, stirring constantly. Beat eggs in mixer bowl until light. Add hot mixture to eggs very gradually, beating rapidly and constantly. Stir in vanilla. Pour into pie shell; sprinkle with pecans. Place in cold oven. Set oven temperature to 325 degrees. Bake for 45 minutes to 1 hour or until brown and set.

Alice N. Wells, Winston-Salem

HONEY PECAN PIE

1 cup honey
1/2 cup sugar
3 eggs
1/4 cup melted butter,
cooled
11/2 teaspoons vanilla
extract
2 cups pecan halves
1 unbaked 9-inch pie
shell

Combine honey, sugar and eggs in mixer bowl; beat until smooth. Add butter and vanilla; mix well. Stir in pecans. Pour into pie shell. Bake at 350 degrees for 50 to 55 minutes or until filling is set around edge and soft in center.

Mary Pickett, Winston-Salem

HIGH DAY PECAN PIE

1 cup sugar
¹/4 cup cornstarch
2 eggs, slightly beaten
¹/2 cup melted margarine
¹/4 cup (or less) Bourbon
1 cup finely chopped pecans
1 cup chocolate chips
1 unbaked 9-inch pie shell

Mix sugar and cornstarch in bowl. Add eggs; mix well. Add mixture of margarine and Bourbon; mix well. Stir in pecans and chocolate chips. Pour into pie shell. Bake at 350 degrees for 35 to 40 minutes or until set.

Patricia Radisch, Kernersville

CREAM CHEESE PECAN TARTS

3 ounces cream cheese, softened
¹/2 cup butter, softened
1 cup flour
³/4 cup packed brown sugar
1 tablespoon butter
1 egg
1 teaspoon vanilla extract
²/3 cup chopped pecans

Combine cream cheese, ¹/2 cup butter and flour in bowl; mix well. Chill for 1 hour. Roll on floured surface. Cut into circles; fit into muffin cups. Combine brown sugar, 1 tablespoon butter, egg and vanilla in bowl; mix well. Spoon into pastry-lined muffin cups. Sprinkle with pecans. Bake at 325 degrees for 25 minutes.

Ellman Grubb, Springdale, Arkansas

Pecan Tarts

Yield:
24 servings
Utensil:
tart pans
Approx Per
Serving:
Cal 341
Prot 4 g
Carbo 37 g
Fiber <1 g
T Fat 20 g
Chol 69 mg
Sod 399 mg

Dietary
Exchanges:
Milk 0
Vegetable 0
Fruit 0
Bread/Starch 1
Meat 1/2; Fat 4

1/2 cup melted margarine
1 1-pound package light brown sugar
6 eggs, beaten
2 teaspoons vanilla extract
1 cup chopped pecans
24 tart shells

Combine margarine, brown sugar, eggs and vanilla in bowl; mix well. Stir in pecans. Spoon into tart shells. Bake at 350 degrees until brown and set.

Jane Dalton, Winston-Salem

Plantation Pecan Pie

Yield:
8 servings
Utensil:
pie plate
Approx Per
Serving:
Cal 543
Prot 5 g
Carbo 69 g
Fiber 2 g
T Fat 27 g
Chol 119 mg
Sod 347 mg

Dietary
Exchanges:
Milk 0
Vegetable 0
Fruit 0
Bread/Starch 1/2
Meat 1/2; Fat 6 1/2

1/4 cup butter, softened
1 cup packed dark brown sugar
1 cup light corn syrup
1 tablespoon evaporated milk
3 eggs, at room temperature
1/4 teaspoon salt
1 1/2 cups broken pecans
2 tablespoons vanilla extract
1 unbaked 9-inch pie shell

Cream butter and brown sugar in mixer bowl until light and fluffy. Add corn syrup and evaporated milk; mix well. Beat eggs and salt in mixer bowl until light. Add to filling mixture. Stir in pecans and vanilla. Pour into pie shell. Bake in preheated 400-degree oven for 10 minutes. Reduce oven temperature to 350 degrees. Bake for 35 to 40 minutes longer or until knife inserted in center comes out clean.

A Pioneer

PIÑA COLADA PIE

Yield:
8 servings
Utensil:
pie plate
Approx Per
Serving:
Cal 309
Prot 4 g
Carbo 33 g
Fiber 2 g
T Fat 19 g
Chol 21 mg
Sod 290 mg

Dietary
Exchanges:
Milk 0
Vegetable 0
Fruit 1/2
Bread/Starch 11/2
Meat 0; Fat 41/2

1 4-ounce package vanilla instant pudding mix
11/2 cups sour cream
2 tablespoons sugar
1/2 cup milk
1 teaspoon grated lime rind
1/2 teaspoon rum extract
1 8-ounce can crushed pineapple, drained
1 cup coconut
1 baked 9-inch pie shell

Combine pudding mix, sour cream, sugar, milk, lime rind and rum extract in medium bowl. Beat at low speed for 1 minute or until smooth. Fold in pineapple and coconut. Spoon into cooled pie shell. Chill for 3 hours. Garnish with whipped topping, fruit and mint leaves.

Barbara Westmoreland, Pfafftown

PINEAPPLE PIES

Yield:
16 servings
Utensil:
2 pie plates
Approx Per
Serving:
Cal 207
Prot 2 g
Carbo 23 g
Fiber <1 g
T Fat 12 g
Chol 50 mg
Sod 229 mg

Dietary
Exchanges:
Milk 0
Vegetable 0
Fruit 0
Bread/Starch 1/2
Meat 0; Fat 21/2

1 cup sugar
1 tablespoon flour
1/2 cup butter, softened
2 egg yolks, beaten
1 8-ounce can crushed pineapple
2 egg whites, stiffly beaten
2 unbaked pie shells

Mix sugar and flour in mixer bowl. Add butter. Beat until smooth. Add egg yolks and pineapple, mixing well after each addition. Fold in stiffly beaten egg whites. Spoon into pie shells. Bake at 350 degrees until golden brown.

Juanita Harris, Winston-Salem

DEEP-DISH PUMPKIN PIE

1 16-ounce can pumpkin
1 15-ounce can sweetened condensed milk
1 egg
1 teaspoon vanilla extract
1¼ teaspoons nutmeg
1¼ teaspoons ginger
1 teaspoon (heaping) cinnamon
½ teaspoon salt
1 unbaked deep-dish pie shell

Combine pumpkin, condensed milk, egg, vanilla, nutmeg, ginger, cinnamon and salt in large mixer bowl; mix well. Spoon into pie shell. Bake at 375 degrees for 50 to 55 minutes or until knife inserted near center comes out clean. Cool to room temperature. Chill for 1 hour or longer. Serve topped with whipped cream or whipped topping if desired.

Nell J. Miller, Winston-Salem

IMPOSSIBLE PUMPKIN PIE

¾ cup sugar
½ cup baking mix
2 tablespoons margarine
1 12-ounce can evaporated milk
2 eggs
1 16-ounce can pumpkin
2 teaspoons vanilla extract
2½ teaspoons pumpkin pie spice

Combine sugar, baking mix, margarine, evaporated milk, eggs, pumpkin, vanilla and pumpkin pie spice in blender container. Process for 1 minute. Pour into greased 9 or 10-inch pie plate. Bake at 350 degrees for 50 to 55 minutes or until knife inserted in center comes out clean.

Louise Case

PUMPKIN PIES

2 cups sugar
1 tablespoon
  (heaping) flour
2 cups cooked
  pumpkin
2 eggs

1/2 cup margarine,
  softened
1 teaspoon cinnamon
1 teaspoon vanilla
  extract
2 unbaked pie shells

Mix sugar and flour in bowl. Add pumpkin; mix well. Add eggs, margarine, cinnamon and vanilla; mix well. Pour into pie shells. Bake at 400 degrees for 1 hour or until center is set.

Earline Goin, Hamptonville

RAISIN PIE

1/2 cup margarine,
  softened
1 cup sugar
2 eggs
1 tablespoon flour
1 tablespoon vinegar

1 teaspoon vanilla
  extract
1/2 cup raisins
1 unbaked 8-inch pie
  shell

Cream margarine and sugar in mixer bowl until light and fluffy. Beat in eggs 1 at a time. Add flour, vinegar, vanilla and raisins; mix well. Pour into pie shell. Bake at 325 degrees until set.

Bernice H. Motsinger, Winston-Salem

SHOOFLY PIE

Yield:
8 servings
Utensil:
pie plate
Approx Per
Serving:
Cal 357
Prot 4 g
Carbo 63 g
Fiber <1 g
T Fat 10 g
Chol 34 mg
Sod 316 mg

Dietary
Exchanges:
Milk 0
Vegetable 0
Fruit 0
Bread/Starch 1½
Meat 0; Fat 2

1 teaspoon soda
1 cup boiling water
1 egg, beaten
1 cup molasses
1 cup flour
¾ cup packed brown
  sugar
2 tablespoons oil
1 unbaked 9-inch pie
  shell

Dissolve soda in boiling water in bowl. Add egg and molasses; mix well. Combine flour, brown sugar and oil in bowl; mix until crumbly. Reserve ¾ cup mixture. Add remaining crumb mixture to molasses mixture; mix well. Spoon into pie shell; sprinkle with reserved crumbs. Bake at 400 degrees for 10 minutes. Reduce temperature to 350 degrees. Bake for 25 minutes or until set. May add ½ to 1 teaspoon cinnamon or a mixture of ¼ teaspoon each nutmeg, cloves, ginger and allspice.

Ruth Kent Eslinger, Winston-Salem

FRESH STRAWBERRY PIE

Yield:
8 servings
Utensil:
pie plate
Approx Per
Serving:
Cal 162
Prot 1 g
Carbo 26 g
Fiber 1 g
T Fat 6 g
Chol 0 mg
Sod 163 mg

Dietary
Exchanges:
Milk 0
Vegetable 0
Fruit 0
Bread/Starch ½
Meat 0; Fat 1

2 cups fresh
  strawberries
1 cup confectioners'
  sugar
1 baked 9-inch pie
  shell

Mix strawberries and confectioners' sugar in bowl; mix gently. Let stand for 2 to 3 hours, mixing frequently. Spoon into pie shell. Chill until serving time. Serve garnished with whipped topping.

Ruby Hudspeth, Yadkinville

STRAWBERRY ICEBOX PIES

¾ cup sugar
1½ cups pineapple juice
2 eggs, beaten
1 3-ounce package strawberry gelatin
1 12-ounce can evaporated milk, chilled
2 graham cracker pie shells

Combine sugar, pineapple juice and eggs in saucepan. Cook until bubbly and thickened, stirring constantly; remove from heat. Stir in gelatin until dissolved. Cool to room temperature. Beat evaporated milk in mixer bowl until soft peaks form. Fold in gelatin mixture. Spoon into pie shells. Chill for 8 hours or longer. May used other flavors of gelatin if preferred.

Dovie Smith, King

EASY STRAWBERRY PIES

1 14-ounce can sweetened condensed milk
9 ounces whipped topping
Juice of 1 lemon
½ cup chopped pecans
1½ cups strawberries
2 graham cracker pie shells

Combine condensed milk, whipped topping, lemon juice and pecans in bowl; mix well. Fold in strawberries. Spoon into pie shells. Chill until serving time.

Lillie B. Allison, Burlington

STRAWBERRY PIES

1½ cups sugar
1½ cups water
¼ cup cornstarch
1   3-ounce package
    strawberry gelatin

2 quarts strawberries
2 baked pie shells

Bring sugar, water and cornstarch to a boil in saucepan. Cook until thickened, stirring constantly. Stir in gelatin until dissolved. Cool to room temperature. Slice strawberries and pat dry with paper towel. Place in pie shells. Spoon gelatin mixture over strawberries. Chill until firm. Serve with whipped topping.

Doris Whitesell

FAMOUS STRAWBERRY PIE

1 cup water
¾ cup sugar
2 tablespoons
   cornstarch
¼ teaspoon salt
½ (or more) 3-ounce
   package strawberry
   gelatin

Red food coloring
1 quart strawberries
1 baked pie shell

Combine water, sugar, cornstarch and salt in saucepan. Cook until thickened, stirring constantly; remove from heat. Stir in gelatin until dissolved. Tint as desired with food coloring. Cool to room temperature. Place strawberries in pie shell. Pour gelatin mixture over strawberries. Chill until serving time. Serve with whipped topping.

Thelma Wilson, Winston-Salem

Index

Zepole (Italian Doughnuts), 295

Tuna Spread, 20

This cookbook is a perfect gift for Holidays, Weddings, Anniversaries and Birthdays.

You may order as many of our cookbooks as you wish for the price of $9.00 each plus $2.00 postage and handling per book ordered. Mail to:

Telephone Pioneers of America
Jewel Smith
2400 Reynold Road
Winston Salem, NC 27106

Number of books ordered _____

Amount enclosed _____

Please make checks payable to:
Telephone Pioneers Chapter 79

Please Print:

Name _____

Street Address _____

City, State, Zip _____

Your Telephone No. _____

(In Case We Have Questions)

79